UNDERSTANDING COMMUNICATION RESEARCH METHODS

Comprehensive, innovative, and focused on the undergraduate student, this textbook prepares students to read and conduct research. Using an engaging how-to approach that draws from scholarship, real-life, and popular culture, the book offers students practical reasons why they should care about research methods and a guide to actually conduct research themselves.

Examining quantitative, qualitative, and critical research methods, the textbook helps undergraduate students better grasp the theoretical and practical uses of method by clearly illustrating practical applications. The book defines all the main research traditions, illustrates key methods used in communication research, and provides level-appropriate applications of the methods through theoretical and practical examples and exercises, including sample student papers that demonstrate research methods in action.

Stephen M. Croucher (Ph.D., University of Oklahoma) is a Professor of Intercultural Communication at the University of Jyväskylä in Finland. He researches immigrant cultural adaptation, religion and communication, quantitative methods, and conflict management/conceptualization. He is the recipient of numerous conference top paper awards, has authored dozens of journal articles and book chapters, authored/co-edited four books, and given keynote addresses in more than 15 countries. He has explored communication traits and behaviors on five continents. He has served as the editor of the *Journal of Intercultural Communication Research* and *Speaker & Gavel*. He is active in the International Communication Association, National Communication Association, and the World Communication Association.

Daniel Cronn-Mills (Ph.D., University of Nebraska) is a Professor of Communication Studies at Minnesota State University, Mankato. He has broad and ranging research interests in religion and communication, intercollegiate forensics, and rhetoric. He has authored numerous journal articles, book chapters, and books. He is a former editor of *Speaker & Gavel* and served on the review board of more than a dozen scholarly journals. He is active in the National Communication Association, the American Forensic Association, and the Communication and Theater Association of Minnesota.

UNDERSTANDING COMMUNICATION RESEARCH METHODS

A Theoretical and Practical Approach

Stephen M. Croucher and Daniel Cronn-Mills

Routledge
Taylor & Francis Group

NEW YORK AND LONDON

First published 2015
by Routledge
711 Third Avenue, New York, NY 10017

and by Routledge
2 Park Square, Milton Park, Abingdon, Oxon, OX14 4RN

Routledge is an imprint of the Taylor & Francis Group, an informa business

Library of Congress Cataloging-in-Publication Data
An introduction to community development / edited by Rhonda Phillips,
    Robert H. Pittman. — 2 Edition.
        pages cm
    Includes bibliographical references and index.
    1. Community development.   2. Economic development.   I. Phillips,
Rhonda, editor of compilation.   II. Pittman, Robert H., editor of
compilation.
    HN49.C6I554 2014
    307.1'4—dc23
    2014015459

ISBN: 978-0-415-83310-3 (hbk)
ISBN: 978-0-415-83311-0 (pbk)
ISBN: 978-0-203-49573-5 (ebk)

Typeset in Classical Garamond
by Apex CoVantage, LLC.

Printed and bound in the United States of America
by Edwards Brothers Malloy

CONTENTS

ACKNOWLEDGMENTS

Stephen: I want to thank my family, friends, and students for their support while writing this book. I especially want to thank Shawn for all that you do. My life is complete with you in it.

Dan: First, I thank Kirstin and Shae for all their support through this amazing project. Second, thanks to Jim for joining us for a couple of chapters. Finally, thanks to Stephen for another great opportunity to write together. Always a treat.

PART I

INTRODUCTION TO RESEARCH AND THE RESEARCH PARADIGMS

1 INTRODUCTION

Chapter Outline

- Why Take Research Methods?
- Key Terms to Start Course
- Outline of the Textbook
- Key Steps & Questions to Consider
- Key Terms

Welcome to Communication Research Methods

Sir Edmund Hillary (1919–2008), a New Zealand-born explorer, mountain climber, and philanthropist, is best known for being the first confirmed person to reach the summit of Mt Everest in 1953. Hillary sought out new areas of exploration and challenges, and also devoted a great deal of his efforts to building schools, hospitals, and other facilities for the Sherpa people of Nepal. He was known for believing all people are capable of great things. In fact, he is known for saying, "I have discovered that even the mediocre can have adventures and even the fearful can achieve."

The authors of this textbook agree with this sentiment when thinking about research methods. All too often we see students who do not naturally take to research and, for a variety of reasons, show a great deal of fear. Fear is natural with anything. However, we have seen all kinds of students excel in a communication research course, including those who did not think they would ever "reach the summit." The key is to look at learning research methods, as corny as it may sound, as a journey. You will confront challenges, face frustrations, celebrate victories, and possibly experience some losses. Yet, in the end, we can all achieve and enjoy the journey. Look around the room next time your class meets and you will see other people just like you. You are not alone in this journey. Enjoy the trip—let this textbook serve as your roadmap and your teacher as your Sherpa guide. As you start your research journey, we should first establish a few good reasons to study communication research methods, second identify key terms to help you progress quickly as a communication scholar, and finally provide an overview for the rest of the chapters in the textbook.

Why Take Research Methods?

You may be studying communication research methods because the course is required for your major or degree program. However, one of the things Dan and Stephen do whenever they teach research methods, and we are sure is one of the things your instructor does as well, is discuss the academic and practical (they often overlap) importance of research methods. Let's first talk about the academic benefits. First, research methods will improve your ability to locate, critique, and use academic materials. In many research classes, students have to look up information on a subject. With the university library and the Internet at your disposal, you can find stacks of information. The key is to know what is "good" information. This kind of class will help.

Second, you will likely have to write one or more papers in the course. Stephen and Dan have their students conduct research papers of various lengths. The students are graded on content, ability to follow a research design, and on their writing abilities. Effective writing is important. If we have the best ideas but cannot communicate them properly, our ideas lose merit.

Third, as you progress through your research methods course and your program of study, you will be introduced to a variety of concepts. Critical analysis of new concepts is important. What _____ _____ by critical analysis: 1) know what it means, 2) evaluate it, and 3) make a judgment about it. In this type of class you will learn some of these skills, particularly when you learn about concepts such as reliability, validity, and claims. Critical thinking is a great skill to have and crosses into every aspect of life.

Learning research methods has practical reasons and benefits. All teachers of research methods have stories about students who have taken the skills into other avenues of their lives. Stephen recently spoke with a former student of his who is now a Coordinator of Human Resources for a group of 15 hospitals. This student told Stephen:

> Research skills are integral to my responsibilities. I would be lost without them. Every day I need to make our hospitals better places to work. To do this I regularly propose new programs to the Board. When I do this, I have to be perfect in my proposal . . . the numbers have to add up, and it must be well-written. I constantly ask questions such as: is this plan valid, are the measures reliable? My team and I regularly do reviews of current literature to see the state of our industry, we always are analyzing data, and constantly writing reports. I am grateful I took this course. Whenever I interview applicants, this is one thing I look for . . . research skills.

A former student of Dan's had plans to become a pharmaceutical sales representative. She conducted a research project while a student that focused on the communication interactions between sales reps and physicians. She conducted extensive communication-focused interviews with reps and doctors, and was able to identify the strengths and weaknesses of what occurred when the groups met. She was able to take her findings and effectively use the results to advance her professional career.

A second student of Dan's worked at a popular local restaurant during college. The restaurant had a high rate of employee turnover. The restaurant was constantly hiring new staff. The student conducted a study, with permission of the restaurant management, comparing communication expectations between staff and various levels of management. The student identified several levels of mismatched expectations. The findings helped the restaurant significantly improve communication and greatly reduce employee turnover. The student listed the research report on his résumé. During his first postgraduation interview, the potential employer was intrigued by the study and they spent more than an hour discussing the research project during the interview. It seemed that the potential employer was also frustrated with their rate of employee turnover!

With each of these students, and many others, research methods enabled them to better communicate (e.g., prepare presentations, reports), understand the professional world, and compete in the world after graduation. As you can see, taking this course has lots of practical benefits. With these benefits in mind, let's move forward on this journey. Before we begin learning about research methods there are a few key terms we should define.

A Few Key Terms to Start the Course

Many of you may have already taken a basic communication course of some kind, while some of you may not have taken such a course. Either way, it is always nice to review a few terms that will be used in this book that were introduced in the basic communication course. The first term we want to define is communication. There are so many definitions we could provide of communication. In this text we provide one definition. **Communication is a process of sharing meaning with others.** There are a few elements of this definition that should be explained. A process explains how in communication there is a sender, a message, and a receiver. When the receiver provides feedback (a response of some kind), a transaction occurs between the communicators. Think about a conversation: person A (the sender) says "Hi" (the message). Person B (the receiver) receives the messages and responds with "Hi." This is the classic sender–receiver model. However, not all communication involves a direct response like the example we just provided. In some cases person B may just nod (a non-verbal response), or in other cases person B may not respond at all. When there is no response, you have one-way communication or unilateral communication.

Another key element of this definition is the idea of sharing meaning. When we "communicate" we are sharing something with others, whether we intend to or not. You may have heard the saying, "you cannot not communicate." What this means is that we are always communicating, even when we do not mean to communicate. The sending of messages to others, either verbally or non-verbally is always happening. If you sit in the back of the room and you cross your arms and you look away from the instructor, what are you communicating? Well, to non-verbal researchers you might be communicating that you are uninterested. Maybe you are not, but our body language tells a lot about what we are thinking or feeling. Ultimately, the thoughts or feelings we intend to or do not intend to share with others is done through this sender–receiver process we call communication. We will not go further into defining communication, but we wanted to provide a preliminary definition of this process, particularly as this textbook focuses on *communication research methods*.

A second key term to define is communications. **Communications** is a technological system for the transmission of information. Examples of communications systems include telephone, cable, television, fiber optics, the Internet, etc. . . . There is a key difference between communication and communications. *Communication* is a human process of sharing meaning with others; *communications* is a technological system for the transmission of information. Stephen and Dan both know professors and industry professionals who are very particular about this difference, so make sure you know the difference.

The third term we want to define is theory. A **theory** is a formal statement of rules on which a subject is based or an explanation of the relationship between variables. In essence, a theory is a statement that is intended to explain facts in the social or scientific world. If we look to social sciences or humanities, where communication is located, you will find various ways to approach theory. Chapters 3–5 each discuss different ways that communication researchers define and approach the study and research of "theory."

The fourth term is research. **Research** is the detailed or in-depth study of a subject (often a theory) to reach a greater understanding or to obtain new information about the subject. This is what you will be doing in this class, in other classes, and in life, when asked to do research; you will be reaching a greater understanding or obtaining new information about a subject (like a theory).

The fifth term is method. A **method** is a systematic technique or procedure used to conduct research. In Chapters 10–20 of this textbook we describe various methods you can use in communication studies. Each of the methods is slightly different; however, each of the methods is systematic. Each has particular "rules" or guiding principles you need to follow. Hopefully, as you read through the textbook you will find one or more methods that "speak to you."

The final term is methodology. While method and methodology may sound similar, they are quite different. **Methodology** is the study of one or more methods. A method is how you conduct your research, for example, using interviews to collect data for your project. Methodology is the study of interviews as a method. In a methodology, you would explain what makes interviewing an appropriate choice for your research, what is the history of interviewing as a method, what was your data analysis technique, etc. . . . Essentially, in a methodology you discuss the theory behind the method. So remember, the method is the "how to," and the methodology is the theory behind the method.

Outline of the Book

Whenever we approach a textbook, we think it's a good idea to know what we are getting into. We like to know the format of the text and what we will be reading. This textbook is divided into three main parts: 1) Introduction to Research and the Research Paradigms, 2) Research Design, and 3) Research Methods. At the end of each chapter you will find a list of activities, discussion questions, and key terms to help clarify each chapter.

The first part, "Introduction to Research and the Research Paradigms," has six chapters. The chapters define the various approaches to research (paradigms) and discuss ethical practices in research. "Chapter 1—Introduction" (you are reading it right now) is a brief introduction to key terms, discusses reasons for taking research methods, and outlines the other chapters in the textbook. "Chapter 2—Research Ethics" presents ethics in research and defines ethics, outlines the development of ethics in the scientific community, discusses ethics and human subjects, and explains the importance of and how to follow ethical practices in schoolwork and scholarly research. "Chapter 3—The Social Scientific Paradigm" presents the first of the three research paradigms. The chapter defines the social scientific paradigm, discusses the development of the paradigm, and outlines key questions underlying this paradigm. "Chapter 4—The Interpretive Paradigm" presents the second of the three research paradigms. The chapter defines the interpretive paradigm, discusses the development of the paradigm, describes the three main approaches to theory and method within this paradigm, and outlines key questions supporting this paradigm. "Chapter 5—The Critical Paradigm" presents the third of the three research paradigms. This chapter defines the critical/cultural paradigm, discusses the development of the paradigm, describes approaches to theory and method within this paradigm, and outlines key questions for the paradigm. "Chapter 6—Literature Review" explains why studies need a review of literature and discusses the process of choosing literature for a review, and describes how to write a review.

The second part, "Research Design," has three chapters. These chapters address issues related to what is data, how we evaluate research, and what constitutes hypotheses and research questions. "Chapter 7—Data" explores research data. The chapter describes the various sources of data, defines data sampling, explains the various data collection settings, and discusses the different levels of measurement (types of variables) available. "Chapter 8—Evaluating Research: Warrants" discusses the various approaches to evaluating what is considered "good" research. The chapter describes warrants for social scientific research, interpretive research, and critical/cultural research. "Chapter 9— Hypothesis and Research Questions" describes hypotheses and research questions. The chapter describes the reasoning behind hypotheses and research questions, explains when to use what kind of hypothesis and/or research question, discusses how to test hypothesis and/or research questions, defines error, and provides a case study that applies the principles learned in the chapter.

The third section, "Research Methods," has 10 chapters. Each chapter introduces you to different methods you can use to explore, test, or analyze phenomena, theory, or questions you might have. At the end of most chapters (except Chapters 13, 15, and 18), you will find an example student paper of the method discussed. These are real student papers written in a class like the one you are taking now.

"Chapter 10—Ethnography" guides you in learning how to conduct ethnographic research. The chapter defines ethnography and the different approaches to ethnography, explains how to make claims with each approach, how to collect and analyze data, what makes "good" ethnographic research, and provides a student paper example of ethnographic research. "Chapter 11— Interviewing" helps in learning how to conduct studies using interviews. The chapter defines interviewing and the different approaches to interviewing, describes data collection and grounded theory as a form of data analysis, and provides a student paper example of interviewing. "Chapter 12—Focus Groups" helps develop skills to conduct focus groups. The chapter defines focus groups and explains why they are used, describes how to prepare and conduct a focus group, outlines the advantages and disadvantages of focus groups, and provides a student paper example of focus group research. "Chapter 13—Qualitative Data Analysis" focuses on the various ways you can analyze qualitative data. The chapter explains grounded theory and the alternative methods of qualitative analysis, discusses the strengths and weaknesses of grounded theory, and provides a grounded-theory exercise.

"Chapter 14—Content Analysis" guides you in learning how to conduct research using content analysis. The chapter defines content analysis, data, how to develop categories, and units of analysis. The chapter then explains coding, pilot testing, reliability, and data analysis, and concludes with a student paper example of content analysis research. "Chapter 15—Surveys" helps you better understand the function of surveys. The chapter describes surveys, why they are used, survey creation, survey delivery, and data analysis. Finally, the chapter explains the advantages and disadvantages of surveys.

"Chapter 16—Descriptive Statistics" breaks down the purpose of and the uses of statistics to organize and describe data. The chapter defines visual data, measures of central tendency, variability, distribution, and provides a student paper example that uses descriptive statistics and survey research.

"Chapter 17—Inferential Statistics" illustrates how statistics can be used to test for differences, relationships, and prediction. The chapter explains the foundations of inferential statistics, tests of mean differences, tests of relationships and prediction, and provides a student paper example that uses inferential statistics. "Chapter 18—Experimental Design" focuses on helping you better understand the purpose of experiments. The chapter defines experimental design, explains experiment preparation, variable selection, experimental design types, validity threats, and data analysis. Chapter 18 unfortunately does not have a student paper because neither Dan nor Stephen has had a student in an undergraduate class who has conducted an experiment for their undergraduate research methods class. Although we contacted various teachers for examples, we could not find an example that was well-written, was in communication, was written by an undergraduate, and was a "true" experiment. If you happen to write a paper that you think fits and should be published in the next edition of this book, let us know!

"Chapter 19—Rhetorical Criticism" guides you in learning how to conduct rhetorical criticism. The chapter defines rhetoric, rhetorical criticism, and the various approaches to rhetorical criticism, explains how to conduct a rhetorical criticism, and provides a student paper example of a rhetorical criticism. "Chapter 20—The Process of Critique" guides you in learning how to conduct a critical/cultural study. The chapter explains the critical/cultural method, discusses various approaches, explains how to conduct a critical/cultural study, and provides a student paper example of a critical/cultural critique.

Summary

In this chapter, we explored the terrain of this course. Every class should be an adventure. Communication research methods are a process where you will exchange ideas on how to study a variety of different subjects. You will leave this class more prepared for your academic and non-academic lives. In the next chapter we examine research ethics. As budding communication scholars, it is essential to start off on the right foot and understand the ethical principles of research.

 ## Key Steps & Questions to Consider

1. Communication is a process of sharing meaning with others.
2. Communications is a technological system for the transmission of information.
3. There is a difference between communication and communications. *Communication* is a human process of sharing meaning with others; *communications* is a technological system for the transmission of information.
4. A theory is a formal statement of rules on which a subject is based or an explanation of the relationship between variables.

5. Research is the detailed or in-depth study of a subject (often a theory) to reach a greater understanding or to obtain new information about the subject.
6. Method is the systematic technique or procedure used to conduct research.
7. Methodology is the study of a method, or of multiple methods.
8. The method is the how to, and the methodology is the theory behind the method.

Key Terms

Communication	Method	Research
Communications	Methodology	Theory

2 RESEARCH ETHICS

What Will I Learn About Ethics?

Whenever a character in fiction wrestles with temptation, you commonly see two mini-me's on each shoulder. On one shoulder is an angelic version instructing the person to act in appropriate ways. On the other shoulder is a devilish version encouraging the person to act in inappropriate ways. Countless examples occur in advertising, film, literature, and music. The contrasting figures wage a battle of ethics. This is a battle called Psychomachia that is for our minds, attitudes, and behaviors. As we determine right from wrong we must weigh up three things: the id, the superego, and the ego. The id (personified as the devilish one) is our basic unconscious instincts. The id has no moral judgments of anything, no sense of morality; the id just acts on pleasure. The superego (personified as the angelic one) is our unconscious critical thinking-conscience based on what is socially acceptable. The ego (the primary person the two figures stand on) is the closest thing to the human mind. The ego is driven by the id and confined by the superego. The ego tries to balance the two to make the most appropriate decision.

The Disney tale *Pinocchio* is a classic example of the balance or battle between the id and the superego. Honest John is Pinocchio's id, a swindler who encourages Pinocchio to become an actor and gets him shipped off to Pleasure Island (a place where boys are turned into donkeys). Jiminy Cricket serves as Pinocchio's superego, providing the young boy/puppet with sage wisdom, such as "go to school," "don't lie," and "always let your conscience be your guide." Pinocchio must negotiate for himself various perspectives of right and wrong in order to survive the challenges.

At the heart of decision-making is ethics: weighing the actions and values that are right and wrong. Ethics are basically the thought processes we go through to determine what are the appropriate actions to take in life. Ethics are all around us and they affect us every day. To understand the nature of ethics, particularly in research, we need to know: 1) what are ethics, 2) how do ethics relate to schoolwork, and 3) how do ethics affect academic research? We explore these questions and others in Chapter 2 in our discussion of ethics.

Ethics Defined and Cultural Differences

Ethics has many different definitions. Aristotle considered ethics as living well and doing good things. Quintilian, a Roman orator, identified a clear relationship between communication and ethics when he defined an ethical man as one who speaks well. English philosopher Thomas Hobbes in his 1651 book *Leviathan* described ethics as the actions one takes in order to maintain a social contract in society. In *Leviathan*, Hobbes praised ideas such as autonomy, preservation of relationships, justice, and fairness. All of these ideas are essential for maintenance of the social contract, which is an ethical aspect of life. The *Cambridge Dictionary of Philosophy* defined ethics as the "principles of right and wrong that govern our choices and pursuits" (Audi, 1999, p. 286). Arnett, Harden Fritz, and Bell (2009) defined ethics as "practices that enact or support a good, a central value or set of values associated with human life and conduct" (p. xii). We define **ethics** as the actions, thoughts, values, principles, and communicative practices one enacts in determining how to interact with and treat others.

If you were to write a paper on ethics, paying particular attention to how Western (European and North American for example) scholars conceptualize ethics, you would find many of the same attributes as outlined in *Leviathan*. An ethical person, from a Western perspective, is one who typically upholds justice, fairness, the preservation of relationships, and autonomy (Pojman, 2005). Let's take a closer look and compare the two largest religious populations in the world today—Christianity and Islam. The emphasis among Christians for such qualities in an ethical person stems from the Bible and the teachings of Jesus Christ (Croucher, 2011). The 39 books of the *Old*

Testament provide a litany of rules, or ways one should live one's life to be a "good" or "ethical" Christian. While many Christians do not follow everything in the *Old Testament*, the rules and laws set forth paint a picture of what was meant at the time of the *Testament*'s writing of what was needed to be "good" (Croucher, 2011). For many Fundamentalist Christians (strict followers), many aspects of the books hold true as roadmaps to ethical behavior and salvation. The 27 books of the *New Testament* describe, among many things, the importance of autonomy, preservation of relationships, justice, forgiveness, and fairness in order to be a "good" or "just" person. In the *New Testament*, readers are taught that these values and actions lead to salvation. These actions and values have served as the bedrock of classical and modern Western thought on ethics (Croucher, 2011).

Traditional ethics in Islam, the second largest religious group in the world, differs a bit from traditional Christian ethics. Traditional Islamic ethics is based on the Koran and the teaching of the Prophet Muhammad. Three principles are of keen importance—forgiveness, shame, and patience. The Koran states that Allah (God) is forgiving and merciful. Thus, forgiving an individual who wrongs you is more valued and ethical than to demand justice and or punishment (Croucher, 2011). The tenets are similar to the Christian philosophy, "To err is human, to forgive divine." Shame is a trait of an ethical person, particularly in conflict situations. Let's say you have been disrespected in some way; it is easy to remain upset instead of being a better person and trying to work out the problem. The ethical solution is to work through the conflict with the person, maybe using a third party to avoid shame for all parties involved. An escalation of conflict only brings more shame to all involved. Patience is an important part of the Islamic ethic. One should not rush to judgment. One should contemplate a situation, pray for God's guidance, and seek the help of a third party if needed in situations. A decision should be based on a logical, patiently thought out plan. The different approaches to ethics between these two religious groups reveal various ways to think about "What is ethical?" With a basic understanding of what is ethics and how religious beliefs have shaped views of ethics, the next section traces the relationship between ethics and the scientific community.

While not emphasized as much in the film, the original tale of Pinocchio written by Carlo Collodi in 1883 is filled with Christian ethical guidelines. One of the 10 commandments is to honor your father and mother. Pinocchio violates this when he does not obey his father/maker Geppetto. His unethical decision to disobey Geppetto leads Pinocchio down a spiral of chaos and trouble, where he starts smoking, is kidnapped, grows donkey ears, and so forth. Had Pinocchio been ethical and followed his father's requests; who knows what would have happened. The story of course would not have been the same.

Ethics and the Scientific Community

The place of ethics in philosophy, science, and medicine used to be a much more contentious issue than it is today. Philosophers like John Locke and John Stuart Mill argued that ethical concerns had no real place in science because ethical issues belonged more to *a priori* knowledge (or knowledge independent of experience and evidence). For philosophers like Locke and Mill, science should be amoral, detached, and separate from moral obligations to best ascertain truth. These scientists were responding to fears that gripped the scientific community in the days of Copernicus and Galileo. Science was silenced by the Catholic Church because scientific discoveries and knowledge questioned or challenged Catholic doctrine. A fear of scientific knowledge being hindered by religious dogma, or other such "moral" or "ethical" principles, led philosophers like Locke and Mill to call for scientists who were amoral. Mary Shelley's 1818 novel *Frankenstein; or the Modern Prometheus* can be interpreted as a challenge to what Locke, Mill, and Max Weber were calling for with amoral science. For Shelley, when science is amoral, we are left with a Frankenstein monster. Mill (1861/1957) disagreed with Shelley concerning the place of morals or ethics in science. His philosophy of utilitarianism proposed a very different view of science or research than Shelley's Frankenstein monster. He asserted that individuals should have full liberty except in harming others. The concept of utilitarian ethics, which stems from utilitarianism, means one should have full freedom to conduct research, as long as the benefits of the research outweigh the potential harms of the research (Christians, 2000).

While medical and scientific research blossomed in the 18th and 19th centuries, the utilitarian ethic was misconstrued quite a bit in the 20th century. During World War I, medical researchers working for the United States, Germany, France, the United Kingdom, and other European powers experimented on humans with various chemical and biological agents. Researchers and governments argued that such experiments were carried out to better advance science and to protect national security. In World War II, Nazi doctors and Japanese doctors both conducted numerous experiments on prisoners. Such experiments explored pain thresholds, responses to poisons and temperatures, injecting individuals with viruses, and many other experiments. Numerous doctors were tried for crimes against humanity at Nuremberg for unethical and inhumane treatment of humans during World War II. The doctors argued they were following orders or that the work was for the benefit of mankind.

Numerous instances exist in the history of the United States during the 20th century in which researchers and doctors violated numerous ethical principles in the "name of science." For example, from the 1930s to the 1970s, black men in Tuskegee, Alabama who had syphilis were told they did not have the disease and were refused counseling for the disease. Many of these individuals were airmen in the U.S. military. Many other men, and some women, were intentionally injected with the disease. The purpose of the experiments was to study the progression of syphilis. The experiments lasted until the 1970s (Kampmeier, 1972). Countless people died and generations of lives were affected by U.S. government-sponsored experiments. In 1963, Drs Southam and Mandel at the Jewish Chronic Disease Hospital in New York injected 22 debilitated patients with live cancer cells without their consent (Mulford, 1967). The physicians were interested in exploring the effects of cancer on the human body.

In the social sciences, researchers have also been questioned about their ethics. The 1961 Milgram experiments at Yale University explored individuals' obedience to authority figures. While the experiment offered valuable insights into people's behaviors under pressure from authority, the techniques used by Milgram and his colleagues have been deemed less than ethical (Baynard & Flanagan, 2005). The psychological stress suffered by many of the participants is something you do not want when conducting research. The 1971 Stanford Prison Experiment is another classic example of a psychological experiment run amuck, ethically speaking. The experiment conducted by Philip Zimbardo concluded that, given the right circumstances, just about anyone's personality could shift from follower to leader, and vice versa (Stolley, 2005). These results are of particular interest in contexts such as the military and prisons. The study, which examined conflict between superiors and subordinates, was wrought with problems, such as physical abuse between participants and poor debriefing of participants. (We will talk about debriefing later in the chapter.)

In response to many of these incidents (Tuskegee in particular), the National Commission for the Protection of Human Subjects of Biomedical and Behavioral Research, a federally funded Commission, was created in 1974. This Commission met and wrote the Belmont Report, in which they outlined ethical guidelines and principles for research with human subjects. Three key principles were identified in the report regarding human subjects: 1) respect for individuals, 2) beneficence, and 3) justice. Along with these three guiding principles, the Belmont Report and the federal government required all organizations receiving federal funds to have an **Institutional Review Board (IRB)**. IRBs monitor, direct, and are responsible for enacting codes of conduct. Every American university/college has an IRB. IRBs consist of faculty members from diverse backgrounds (sex, ethnic, race, or discipline). An IRB needs faculty with various methodological and theoretical specializations. An IRB needs to have at least one member on the board who is not affiliated with the university or college to help make sure rules are followed.

Now, any research involving human subjects should be sent to the college or university IRB for approval before any data collection is conducted. All research involving human subjects must meet at least three minimum requirements before an IRB will permit it to take place (the same three principles as outlined by the Belmont Report). First, the researchers must *respect* the rights of the participants who take part in the research. Second, the benefits of the research should outweigh the potential harms of the research for the participants (*beneficence*). Third, all participants should be treated fairly (*justice*).

Based partially on these three principles, as well as on the procedures used in a research project, IRBs make determinations about levels of risk. An **exempt** research project has minimal risk—typically similar to the risk a person faces in a normal day. Examples of these kinds of projects include research conducted on existing data, research in educational environments, and surveys and interviews without highly probing questions. These projects receive **expedited** review by an IRB. An expedited application is typically reviewed by the head or chair of IRB and not the full board. To qualify for exempt research with humans, you must also make sure you are working with individuals who are able to personally consent to the research. An in-depth discussion of consent follows later in this chapter.

If a project involves higher levels of risk for participants, or if individual participants are not able to consent for themselves (children, individuals with mental disabilities, prisoners, and other "protected" groups), a project will be **non-exempt**. Non-exempt projects are sent to the full board for review. Such projects need closer scrutiny to make sure the project fulfills the three principles established in the Belmont Report. We include at the end of this chapter an approved IRB Application written by Stephen Croucher to show you how the IRB application process works. Now that you know a bit more about the relationship between ethics and the scientific community, and how an IRB monitors ethics, the following section discusses ethical practices we should all follow when working with human subjects.

Ethics and Human Subjects

When conducting research among human subjects, various principles must be followed. Along with the principles outlined in the Belmont Report, one should adhere to three additional procedural and ethical guidelines. The three key elements are informed consent, level of participant privacy, and debriefing.

Informed Consent

When conducting research we must get informed consent from participants. **Informed consent** is where you tell your participants, in a written document, what they will be doing in the study, explain the risks and benefits of their participation, explain that individuals have a right to stop participation at any time, provide the researchers' contact information, and obtain participant permission to take part in the study. Important!—the consent document must be in language the participants can understand. Try to avoid jargon and other language that may confuse participants. Informed-consent documents should be signed by participants to show they have given their permission. In such cases, the researcher should keep names confidential (private). In some cases when a researcher is not looking to keep names of participants (anonymity), acceptance of the form may count as agreeing to participate. We will talk more about the difference between confidentiality and anonymity shortly. Figure 2.1

INFORMED CONSENT
TO PARTICIPATE IN A RESEARCH STUDY

You are being asked to volunteer for a research study. Please read this form and ask any questions that you may have before agreeing to take part in this study.

Project Title: "A comparative analysis between Muslim and non-Muslim conflict styles."
Principal Investigator: Stephen M. Croucher
Co-Investigators:
Contact Information: INSERT ADDRESS AND PHONE NUMBER HERE

Purpose of the Research Study
The purpose of this study is to measure the conflict styles of individuals who reside in France, the United Kingdom, Germany, Spain, Costa Rica, and the United States.

Procedures
If you agree to be in this study, you will be asked to do the following things: you will be asked to complete an 11-page survey that examines how you rationalize and manage conflict. This survey should take you approximately 35–50 minutes.

Risks and Benefits of Being in the Study
There are no foreseeable risks to participating in this study.
The benefits to participation are: that you will be able to voice your opinion(s) anonymously on a controversial issue, which can help relieve stress. Also, this study is important because it examines how individuals from different cultures rationalize and manage conflict.

Anonymity
Because you have not signed a sign-up sheet, or any other form that includes your name, your participation in this study is completely anonymous. Furthermore, because your survey will be combined with other surveys (approximately 3,000–4,000), your responses will be virtually impossible to separate from the other responses.

Voluntary Nature of the Study
Participation in this study is voluntary. Your decision whether or not to participate will not result in penalty or loss of benefits to which you are otherwise entitled. If you decide to participate, you are free to not answer any question or withdraw at any time.

Contacts and Questions
The researcher conducting this study can be contacted at (INSERT EMAIL HERE). You are encouraged to contact the researcher if you have any questions.

You may also contact the Chair, Human Subjects Review Board, Bowling Green State University, (419) 372-7716 (hsrb@bgsu.edu), if any problems or concerns arise during the course of the study.

You will be given a copy of this information to keep for your records. If you are not given a copy of this consent form, please request one.

Figure 2.1 Sample Informed-Consent Document

is a sample informed-consent document, approved by the IRB at Bowling Green State University, which Stephen used in a study on conflict styles.

An informed-consent form has many elements. Each college or university's IRB may have slightly different requirements. As a student, if you conduct research as part of a course assignment you may not be required to produce an informed-consent form. However, it is better to be safe than sorry and always ask your teacher if you need informed consent and if you need IRB approval before conducting your research. An informed-consent form has eight elements.

Required Elements of Informed Consent

1. Title of the Project. You need to have some title for your project. A title is a requirement for an IRB application.
2. Names of the Investigators. List your name and the names of anyone else in your research group. If you are a student researcher you will need to also list your teacher as a sponsor of your research.
3. Contact Information. First, you must provide participants with your contact information in case they have questions about the project during and/or after the project. You should give them your physical address, email address, and phone number(s). If you are a student researcher, you will need to provide your teacher's contact information. Second, IRBs will require that you provide participants with the contact information of the IRB just in case participants have questions for the IRB to answer.
4. Purpose of the Study. You need to provide a brief description of the study. The description needs to be just enough to inform the participants of what you are studying.
5. Procedures. This is where you inform the participants of exactly what they need to do in the study. You need to describe in basic language what you expect from them. You must let the participants know how much of their time you will use and other obligations you have for them.
6. Risks and Benefits. First, you must tell the participants about any risks or harms from participating in the study. Second, you need to let them know any benefits to them, society, or the academic disciplines from their participation.
7. Anonymity. You need to let the participants know if you are keeping track of their names. Some studies keep track of participants' names. If so, tell them what steps you will take to protect their identities.
8. Voluntary Nature of the Study. You need to make sure all participants know that their participation is voluntary. Voluntary participation means that they can enter and end their involvement in the study at any time.

If you focus on these key issues when writing up an informed-consent form, you are being ethical in assuring you have informed your potential participants of the information essential for their involvement. Participant privacy is the next issue you must consider when collecting research.

Participant Privacy

An important part of informed consent is letting participants know how you will handle privacy issues. When you conduct research, people may answer questions about themselves or issues that provide insight into their private lives. In many cases, participants may want their names shared with others. However, in most cases researchers do not name their participants in research. In qualitative research (e.g., interviews, ethnography), researchers often use pseudonyms for participants. In quantitative studies (e.g., surveys), research-ers generally report statistical results; participant names are never reported. It is important for participants to have the ability to speak freely and to answer questions without fear of being "outed" to the public. This is why participant privacy is so important.

You can take two approaches with participant privacy in a study. One approach is **confidentiality**. Confidentiality is where the researcher knows the names and personal information of the participants but does not share the information with anyone else. Having this information can be very helpful if you ever need to contact the participants again (e.g., follow-up interviews). **Anonymity** is when not even the researcher knows the participants' names or personal information. In Stephen's study on conflict styles anonymity was used. Stephen did not know the participants' personal information because the par-ticipants were filling out anonymous surveys and Stephen had no intention of contacting the participants again. As long as you are upfront with your partici-pants as to which kind of privacy you are using, you are being ethical concerning privacy. In some rare cases you may want to or some participants may ask that their real names be used.

Debriefing

In Milgram's studies at Yale University, he explored the power of control on individuals' actions. He showed that, with the right amount of influence exerted on an individual, most people will do just about anything to another person. In his experiments, he had two people in separate rooms who could not see one another. One person read a series of numbers and the other person had to read the series of numbers back. If they got the series wrong, they were given an electric shock. The voltage increased each time they got an answer wrong. Over time, the person receiving the shocks would scream in pain, complain of their heart, and ask to end the experiment. The person giving the shocks would ask a helper in the room if they could stop, and they were told they could not. The helper giving the order was a **confederate** (a person who is in on the project and assists with the data collection). A confederate secretly takes part in the project and guides it along the way. A confederate would guide the participants into continuing the electric shocks. Some participants stopped, but many continued to shock the other person until the screams ended. The person could have been dead from a heart attack. At the end of the experiment the confederate reunited the two individuals. The one giving shocks finally knew they did not kill the other person. They were told the other person was in on it all along.

Our recounting of the Milgram experiment is necessary to provide an example of a debriefing exercise. **Debriefing** is when a researcher explains all of the aspects and purpose(s) of the research process after the research is completed. The researcher provides participants during debriefing with a chance to ask questions and to remove their data from the study if they wish. The purposes of the study should be explained well in the informed-consent form. However, deceiving participants may be necessary in some cases. If you are trying to study how people respond to persuasive messages in the media, you do not want to predispose them to your persuasive tactics. You might tell participants in the informed-consent form you are studying individuals' preferences for media messages. The IRB will weigh up whether the benefits of your research outweigh deceiving your participants. Many IRBs will, in fact, ask you for a copy of your debriefing script, especially if your research includes any kind of deception.

> Granted, Honest John is not honest in Pinocchio. He just plain lies to get what he wants. An ethical Honest John needs to first get informed consent from all the young boys before sending them to Pleasure Island. He needs to tell the boys that going to the island means they will turn into donkeys; just try getting informed consent!

Now that you have a better grasp of ethics among human participants, the next section details the basics of being an ethical student researcher. Many of the issues we outline in this section apply to all researchers.

Ethical Practices in School and Scholarship

As a college or university student, you have ethical responsibilities in your everyday academic studies and in any research you conduct. If you are conducting research for a methods class, you must consider the ethical issues we have outlined. Now you may be asking yourself, "I don't plan on presenting or publishing this paper. It's just a class project, so why do I need to go through the entire IRB process?" However, you have an ethical responsibility to get approval for your project. Formal approval ensures your project follows appropriate ethical research guidelines. Your instructor will know if you are required to get official approval for a research project. Many instructors require their students to complete an IRB application even for in-class research projects.

Next, we must all work to avoid plagiarism. **Plagiarism** is using someone else's words or ideas without giving credit to that person or institution. Blatant examples of plagiarism include borrowing, buying, or stealing a paper and calling it your own. However, most examples of plagiarism are not this blatant. In the years Dan and Stephen have been teaching, the two have encountered borrowing, buying, or stealing someone else's paper fewer than five times (even five is too many). The most common form of plagiarism is when people (students and faculty/researchers alike) paraphrase too closely to a source and do not give adequate credit to the source. We may find a wonderful source that helps us make a great point in a paper, but sometimes we are either apprehensive to cite quotations from it too much, or we do not know how to synthesize our own ideas well enough. So what happens is people "paraphrase" almost word for word. Changing a word or two in a sentence does not make it your own.

Stephen asks if the student thinks their paraphrasing sounds too similar to the original statement from the author(s), then the section needs reworking into the student's own words. Stephen reminds them that even a paraphrase needs to be cited. Author(s) deserve credit for their ideas. Most students do not intend to plagiarize when trying to paraphrase. This is why many faculty members will ask students about their intent in these situations. If you are aware of the need to avoid this situation and make things your own you can avoid plagiarism.

Ultimately, thanks to some wild adventures, the Blue Fairy, and Jiminy Cricket, Pinocchio learns how to be a good puppet, and in the end he becomes a real boy (sorry if we ruined the story for you). A main moral of the story is that if you are a good person, such as if you tell the truth, good things will come of you. It is the same with research and academics. One should always be ethical and follow good principles to avoid being sucked up into the advice of Honest John, your id. Listen to your superego instead, Jiminy Cricket.

Summary

In this chapter we focused on ethics in research. The very idea of "ethics" differs culturally, which has affected the development of ethical standards and principles in the scientific community. When working with human subjects in particular, ethics are of the utmost importance. When conducting any kind of research, you should strive to follow the ethical principles laid out in this chapter, and others presented to you by your university or college. In the following three chapters we take on a slightly different subject, that of research paradigms. What you will find in Chapters 3–5 is that researchers approach research from vastly different ways. In Chapter 3, the next chapter, we discuss the social scientific paradigm.

 Key Steps & Questions to Consider

1. Ethics are the actions, thoughts, values, principles, and communicative practices one enacts in determining how to interact with/treat others.
2. Most research on ethics has come from a Western perspective, with a lot of this research coming from Judeo-Christian scholars.
3. Our ethical perspective on life is often shaped by our religious heritage.
4. Utilitarian ethics comes from utilitarianism, which means one should have full freedom to conduct research as long as the benefits of the research outweigh the potential harms of that research.
5. Institutional Review Boards were developed after the Belmont Report was published. This report outlined various abuses of researchers and described ways to protect research participants.
6. The main difference between exempt and non-exempt research projects is the level of risk to research participants.
7. Informed consent is where you tell participants, in a written document, what they will be doing in the study, explain the risks and benefits of their participation, explain that participants have a right to stop participation at any time, provide contact information for the researchers, get participant permission to participate in the study, and other things.
8. Two important elements of participant privacy are confidentiality and anonymity.
9. Debriefing is when a researcher explains all of the aspects and purpose(s) of the research process after the research is completed.

 Activities

1. Select one or more communication journal article(s) that collect data from human subjects and have the class "reverse engineer" the IRB documentation, including the consent form(s) and debriefing procedure.
2. Identify the members of your campus's IRB.
   a. What are the qualifications of the members?
   b. What different groups are represented (race, sex, ethnicity, discipline)?
   c. Who is the non-campus member of your IRB?
3. Invite the intercultural communication specialist in your program to visit the class and discuss how cultural factors can influence perceptions of ethics.

💬 Discussion Questions

1. What does your campus IRB identify as exempt research?
2. What is your department's and campus' policy on plagiarism?
   a. If a student (or faculty!) is accused of plagiarism, what are the procedures?
   b. What are the penalties for academic dishonesty?

Key Terms

Anonymity	Exempt	Non-exempt
Confederate	Expedited	Plagiarism
Confidentiality	Informed consent	Utilitarian ethics
Debriefing	Institutional Review	
Ethics	Board (IRB)	

SAMPLE IRB/HUMAN SUBJECTS REVIEW BOARD APPLICATION

HUMAN SUBJECTS REVIEW BOARD

Application for Approval of Research Involving Human Subjects—
as of February 2007

(The most current version of this application is available online at
www.bgsu.edu/offices/orc/hsrb.)

Please answer all applicable questions and provide the material identified.
Please complete electronically.

- *Applications judged to be illegible, incomplete, or vague will be returned to the Principal Investigator (PI) for revision.*
- <u>*All boxes are expandable*</u> *so be sure to include complete information, attaching continuation sheets as necessary.*
- <u>*Submit the original, signed, hard-copy*</u> *application and necessary supporting documentation to the Human Subjects Review Board (HSRB), 201 South Hall.*
- **SUBMISSION LEAD TIMES**—*For* <u>*Full Board projects*</u>—*submit* <u>*at least*</u> **2 months** *before your planned start of recruiting and data collection. For* <u>*Expedited Review projects*</u>—*submit* <u>*at least*</u> **2 weeks** *before your planned start of recruiting and data collection.*
- <u>*For projects reviewed via the expedited review process*</u>—*You should receive notification of the results of the initial review of this application* <u>**5–7 business days**</u> <u>**(7–9 during the summer and breaks)**</u> *from the date of receipt of the application by the Office of Research Compliance.*
- <u>**IMPORTANT NOTE**</u>: *This application* <u>**will not be reviewed**</u> *unless Human Subjects training has been completed by the PI (and the Advisor, if the PI is a student)—see the HSRB web page for scheduled training dates.*

Ia. General Information:

Name of applicant (Principal Investigator): <u>Stephen M. Croucher, Ph.D.</u>

The Principal Investigator is (check one):
☒ Faculty ☐ BGSU Staff ☐ Undergraduate Student ☐ Graduate Student
☐ Off-campus applicant (check this box if you are not affiliated with BGSU but propose to conduct research involving BGSU Faculty, Staff, or Students)

Department or Division: <u>Department of Communication</u>
Campus Phone: <u>XXX-XXXX</u>
E-mail: <u>XXXXXXXXXX</u>   Fax: _____
Have You Completed BGSU Human Subjects Training?
    ☒ Yes (Office of Research Compliance will confirm training date)
    ☐ No (Please see **IMPORTANT NOTE** above)
The HSRB will send all correspondence to your <u>**departmental**</u> *address unless otherwise indicated below:*

_____

Figure 2.2 Sample IRB/Human Subjects Review Board Application

Title of the Proposed Research Project:
<u>A comparative analysis between Muslim and non-Muslim conflict styles</u>

Names of Other Students or Staff Associated with the Project (Student PIs note—<u>Do not</u> include your advisor for this research project here): _____

Have you requested, or do you plan to request, external support for this project?
    ☐ Yes   ☒ No
    If yes, external Funding Agency or Source:_____
(Note: If the funding source requires certification of IRB approval or *if federal funding is requested*, this application will go to the full Board for review—in that case please submit the original plus 13 copies of the application and supporting materials.)

Ib. **If you are a BGSU student, please provide the following information:**
    This research is for: ☐ Thesis ☐ Dissertation ☐ Class Project ☐ Other__

    (**Note:** *If the class project box is checked and the PI is a student no continuing review form will be sent. The PI will receive an expiration notice at the end of the approval period. The Office of Research Compliance must be notified in writing, before the end of the approval period, of intent to continue the project.*)

    Advisor's Name (This is the advisor for this research project):   _____

    Department or Division: _____   Phone: _____   Fax: _____   E-mail:

    Has Advisor Completed BGSU Human Subjects Training?
    ☐ Yes (Office of Research Compliance will confirm training date)
    ☐ No (Please see **IMPORTANT NOTE**, page 1)

II. **Information on Projects Using Pre-existing Data (Skip to Section III if this project does NOT use pre-existing data. Existing data includes retrospective medical chart reviews, public data sets, etc. Sometimes it is referred to as secondary data or archival data.) Some projects involving the use of pre-existing data may not require review by the HSRB. However, it is the HSRB's responsibility to make that determination—not the researcher's.**

    NOTE: If you are obtaining medically related information from a "Covered Entity" (a health plan, health care clearinghouse or a health care provider who bills health insurers—e.g., hospitals, doctor's offices, dentists, the BGSU Student Health Service, the BGSU Speech and Hearing Clinic, the BGSU Psychological Services Center), the HIPAA Privacy Rule may apply.

Figure 2.2 (*Continued*)

a. Name(s) of existing data set(s) [Include any ancillary data sets you might be linking the main data set(s) to]:

b. Source(s) of existing data set(s):

c. Please provide a brief description of the content of the data set(s):

d. When you **obtain** the data, will the individual records be anonymous or will they have identifiers/codes attached?

☐ Anonymous *(i.e., no identifiers or codes attached to any records in any of the listed data sets)*

If your project also involves direct data collection, please go to section III and complete the rest of the application. Otherwise, please go to and complete sections VIIa, VIIb, and IX.

☐ Identifiers/codes attached *(examples would include, but not be limited to, record numbers, subject numbers, case numbers, etc.)*

d.1 If the records have identifiers or codes attached, can you readily ascertain the identity of individuals to whom the data pertain *(e.g., through use of a key that links identifiers with identities; linking to other files that allow individual identities to be discerned)*?

☐ Yes, I can ascertain the identity of the individuals.

Please explain in the box below how you will protect the confidentiality of subjects. The Human Subjects Review Board is concerned about 2 dimensions of confidentiality: (1) that the researcher has legitimate access to the records, i.e., the records are not protected by any special confidentiality conditions, and (2) that the researcher will not reveal individual identities unless permission has been granted to do so.

Please continue with section IIe

☐ No, I cannot readily ascertain the identity of the individuals.

Please describe in the box below, the provisions in place that will not allow you to ascertain identities (e.g., key to decipher the code/identifier has been destroyed, agreement between researcher and key holder prohibiting the release of the key).

Figure 2.2 *(Continued)*

(If your project also involves direct data collection, please go to section III and complete the rest of the application. Otherwise, please go to and complete sections IV (as appropriate), VIIa, VIIb, and IX.)

e. Are the data from a public data set? (A public data set is data available to any member of the public through a library, public archive, or the Freedom of Information Act. Data obtained from private companies, hospital records, agency membership lists, or similar sources are not usually public data.)

☐ Yes

Are you requesting permission to conduct multiple research projects with these data?

☐ Yes ☐ No

(If your project also involves direct data collection, please go to section III and complete the rest of the application. Otherwise, please go to and complete sections VIIa, VIIb and IX.)

☐ No (if no, please answer the following questions)

f. If you are obtaining access to non-public information, please explain in the box below how you will obtain access to the information (e.g., permission from the CEO, permission from the Board of Education). <u>Note</u>: a condition for approval will be written documentation of this permission—this can be hard copy or an email from the relevant authority.

┌───┐
│   │
│   │
└───┘

g. Before the data were collected, did respondents give their permission for the information to be used for research purposes?   ☐ Yes ☐ No

h. Are you **recording** the data in a manner that will allow you to identify subjects, either directly or through identifiers linked to the subjects?
☐ Yes   ☐ No

i. If your project also involves direct data collection, please continue completing the rest of the application. Otherwise, <u>please go to and complete sections IV (as appropriate), VIIa, VIIb, and IX</u>.

III. **General Project Characteristics:** Does the research involve any of the following? (If the response to any of the following is "yes," provide a justification and/or rationale in the box provided below.)

Yes   No

☐   ☒   a. Deception of subjects

(if "yes," please submit the original plus 13 copies of this application and supporting materials).

Figure 2.2 *(Continued)*

☐	☒	b.	Shock or other forms of punishment (if "yes", please submit the original plus 13 copies of this application and supporting materials).
☐	☒	c.	Sexually explicit materials or questions
☐	☒	d.	Handling of money or other valuable commodities
☐	☒	e.	Extraction of blood or other bodily fluids
☐	☒	f.	Questions about drug and/or alcohol use
☐	☒	g.	Questions about sexual orientation, sexual experience, or sexual abuse
☐	☒	h.	Purposeful creation of anxiety
☐	☒	i.	Any procedure that might be viewed as an invasion of privacy
☐	☒	j.	Physical exercise or stress
☐	☒	k.	Administration of substances (food, drugs, etc.) to subjects
☐	☒	l.	Any procedure that might place subjects at risk (e.g., disclosure of criminal activity)
☐	☒	m.	Systematic selection or exclusion of any group. This includes the selection or exclusion of any group based on age, gender, race, ethnicity, etc.

IV. **HIPAA:** If you answer "Yes" to any of the following questions, your project is subject to HIPAA and you must complete the HIPAA Supplement (available online at www.bgsu.edu/offices/orc/hsrb) and attach it to the application.

Yes No

☐ ☒ a. Will health information *(information relating to the past, present, or future physical or mental health or condition of an individual)* be obtained from a covered entity *(a health plan, health care clearinghouse, or a health care provider who bills health insurers—e.g., hospitals, doctor's offices, dentists, the BGSU Student Health Service, the BGSU Speech and Hearing Clinic, the BGSU Psychological Services Center)*?

☐ ☒ b. Will the study involve the provision of health care in a covered entity?

Yes No

☐ ☒ b.2 *(Complete this only if you answered "Yes" to IVb— otherwise, skip this item).* If the study involves the provision of health care, will a health insurer or billing agency be contacted for billing or eligibility?

Figure 2.2 *(Continued)*

V. **Subject Information:** (If the response to any of the following is "yes," the researcher should be sure to address any special needs of the potential subjects in the informed consent process. For example, if subjects are over the age of 65, then it may be appropriate to use a larger font in all correspondence with subjects to ensure readability.)

Yes	No	Does the research involve subjects from any of the following categories?
☐	☒	a. Under 18 years of age as the target population (If "yes" signed, active parental consent is required unless a waiver is granted by the HSRB. If you are requesting a waiver of parental consent, please submit the original plus 13 copies of this application and supporting materials.)
☐	☒	b. Over 65 years of age as the target population
☐	☒	c. Persons with a physical or mental disability as the target population (If "yes" please submit the original plus 13 copies of this application and supporting materials.)
☐	☒	d. Economically or educationally disadvantaged as the target population
☐	☒	e. Unable to provide their own legal informed consent (If "yes" and the subjects are not children, please submit the original plus 13 copies of this application and supporting materials.)
☐	☒	f. Pregnant females as the target population (If "yes" please submit the original plus 13 copies of this application and supporting materials.)
☐	☒	g. Victims of crimes or other traumatic experiences as the target population
☐	☒	h. Individuals in institutions (e.g., prisons, nursing homes, half-way houses) (If "yes" please submit the original plus 13 copies of this application and supporting materials.)

VI. **Risks and Benefits:** (Note: the HSRB retains final authority for determining risk status of a project)

Yes	No	Please answer the following questions about the research.
☐	☒	a. In your opinion, does the research involve more than minimal risk to subjects? ("Minimal risk" means that "the risks of harm anticipated in the proposed research are not greater, considering probability and magnitude, than those ordinarily encountered in daily life or during the performance of routine physical or psychological examinations or tests.") If the answer is "yes,"

Figure 2.2 (*Continued*)

explain in the box below and provide an explanation of the **benefits** of the research to the subjects and to society.)

☐ ☒   b. Are any **emergencies or adverse reactions** (physical, psychological, social, legal, or emotional) probable as a result of the research? (If "yes," then explain the measures to be taken in case of emergency in the box below.)

☐ ☒   c. Will participation in this research result in any appreciable negative change in the subject's emotional state? (If "yes," explain the nature of the change and the process for assisting subjects in the box provided.)

VII. **Project Description:** (Please provide as much information as you feel will adequately answer the following questions. Attach additional sheets if necessary.)
  a. What are you going to study? What is (are) the research question(s) to be answered/hypotheses to be tested?

> This project will measure the conflict styles of Muslims and non-Muslims who reside in France, the United Kingdom, Germany, Spain, Costa Rica, and the United States. When measuring the conflict styles of Muslims and non-Muslims, multiple dimensions of communication will be measured including: argumentativeness, verbal aggressiveness, self-construals, conflict styles, ethnic identification, and religiosity. The specific hypotheses and research questions being addressed are:
>
> H1: Muslims are less verbally aggressive than non-Muslims.
>
> H2: Muslims are less argumentative than non-Muslims.
>
> H3: Muslims have a more interdependent self-construal than non-Muslims.
>
> H4: An individual's religiosity influences their verbal aggressiveness, argumentativeness, and self-construal.
>
> H5: An individual's ethnic identification influences their verbal aggressiveness, argumentativeness, and self-construal.
>
> H6: Muslims in the United States will have a weaker religiosity than Muslims in Europe.
>
> H7: Christians in the United States will have a stronger religiosity than Christians in Europe.
>
> RQ1: Which conflict style(s) are Muslims in Europe and the United States more likely to have?
>
> RQ2: What are the differences in conflict management styles between Muslims and non-Muslims?

Figure 2.2 (*Continued*)

b. Discuss the benefit(s) of this study. Why is this study important? (Provide scholarly support.) Include a discussion of benefits to individual participants as well as to society as a whole.

> While the current research into conflict management, resolution, and styles is lengthy, there is no research addressing the growing global Muslim population and interpersonal conflict. This research hopes to fill that void by examining the Muslim population in the European Union, Costa Rica, and the United States (two political entities with the two largest growing Muslim minority populations in the world). Moreover, this research will benefit the participants involved in the study because if a better understanding can be garnered as to how Muslims handle interpersonal conflict better psychological and social programs can be developed for this population.

c. Are there any risks associated with this study? If so, explain how you will minimize the risks to subjects.

> There are no risks to this study aside from the risks associated with daily life.

d. Who will be your subjects?

> The subjects for this study will be Muslims and non-Muslims who live in France, the United Kingdom, Germany, Spain, Costa Rica, and the United States.

e. Approximately how many subjects do you plan to <u>enroll</u>? Please provide a realistic estimate. *(<u>Recruiting is not enrollment</u>—you will likely recruit more individuals than will be enrolled in the project. Also, don't forget to factor in the possibility of withdrawals, which may require enrolling of additional subjects in order to achieve your desired sample size. If, during the course of the project, you need to increase the number of subjects to be enrolled, you should request Board approval for the increase—in many cases the Office of Research Compliance can handle this administratively.)*

> We intend to recruit approximately 300–400 Muslims and 300–400 non-Muslims in each nation, for a total of 1,800–2,100 Muslims and 1,800–2,100 non-Muslims.

f. How will you recruit your subjects? Please describe the method(s) you will use to recruit (examples include via telephone, mailings, sign-up sheets, etc.). Please include recruitment letters, scripts, sign-up sheets as appropriate with the application.

Figure 2.2 *(Continued)*

Muslim Participants will be recruited primarily through posting flyers at Muslim community centers in each listed nation. The flyers will instruct the individuals in how and when to meet to complete a survey. The flyers will be translated into the dominant language(s) used in each nation (French, German, English, Spanish, Arabic, and Urdu). Moreover, Muslim subjects will be recruited through social networks already established in each nation at local mosques.

As for non-Muslim participants, they will be recruited through vast social networks established in each nation. Also, non-Muslim participants will also be recruited through posting flyers in public squares. These flyers, like those at the Muslim community centers, will instruct the individuals in how and when to meet to complete a survey. Surveys will be translated into the dominant language(s) used in each nation (French, German, English, Spanish, Arabic, and Urdu). Non-Muslim participants will also be recruited through using contacts among students in Interpersonal Communication 307, a class being held in fall 2007, taught by the Principal Investigator at BGSU. Students who volunteer to assist with the project will be able to approach individuals they know with surveys and informed consent forms and have them fill out surveys. The results of these surveys will be placed in sealed envelopes to protect the confidential results of the surveys.

g. Describe the process you will use to seek informed consent from the subjects (example—provide information sheet to potential participants, allow them to read over the information, ask them if they have any questions, answer questions to their satisfaction, then request them to sign the consent form). If you are using an information sheet please include that with the application. (See *www.bgsu.edu/offices/orc/hsrb/Informed_Consent_Check_List.doc for relevant elements of consent, sample wording, and a suggested outline of a consent form.*)

In order to seek informed consent, each individual will be provided with a sheet describing the study's protocol. They will be instructed to read it, ask questions, have any questions answered, and clarify any issues.

Yes No

☒ ☐ g.1. Are you seeking consent/assent from all relevant parties? (If "No," explain why not in the box provided below)

Figure 2.2 (*Continued*)

Yes	No
☐	☒

g.2. Are you having your participants <u>physically sign</u> consent/ assent form(s)?
(If "No," you are requesting a waiver of written consent. Provide justification in the box below.) [*For more information relative to requesting and justifying a waiver of written consent see HSRB Policy and Procedure Statement "Waiver of Written Consent—Request and Review" at www.bgsu. edu/offices/orc/hsrb/HSRB_Pol_Proc.htm.*]

h. If deception or emotional or physical stress is involved, subjects must be debriefed about the purposes, consequences, and benefits of the research and given information on procedures they can follow or resources that are available to them to help them handle the stress. Please attach a copy of all debriefing materials, if applicable.

Debriefing form attached: ☐ Yes   ☒ No

i. Explain in the box below the procedures you will follow to protect the confidentiality of your subjects. Include considerations associated with data and/or consent form collection and storage, and dissemination of results. Explain whether or not the study is anonymous. *(Note: It is not always necessary to protect the confidentiality of your subjects, but they must be informed if you plan to quote them directly or reveal their identities in any way.)*

> While the overwhelming majority of respondents are anonymous (those collected in all countries outside of the United States), we will be collecting signed informed consent forms from participants in the United States. After we confirm their participation in the research project, we will then shred their signed consent forms, thus guaranteeing their anonymity.

j. Describe what subjects will be asked to do or have done to them from the time they are first contacted about the study until their participation in the study ends. Note—a summary of this information should be included in information provided to the subjects as part of the consent process.

Figure 2.2 *(Continued)*

The participants will be asked to complete an 11-page survey. The average completion time of this survey should be approximately 35–50 minutes. The principal investigator, Stephen M. Croucher, will be doing the data collection. The surveys and consent documents will be translated into the dominant languages like the flyers will be. If a participant does not speak English or French (two languages spoken by the principal investigator), the principal investigator will ask a fellow participant who speaks one of the aforementioned languages and the participant's language to assist in explaining the project's protocol. I predict the overwhelming majority of the respondents due to historical demographic characteristics will have some fluency in English, Spanish, French, German, or Arabic.

VIII. **Supplemental Materials:**
Attach a copy of the following:
1. All materials (including scripts, advertisements, etc.) that will be used to recruit subjects.
2. The consent/assent form(s) or script(s), if applicable (see the Informed Consent Checklist, which can be found at www.bgsu.edu/offices/orc/hsrb, for guidance in developing consent documents).
3. Survey instrument(s), interview questions, observation protocols, etc.
4. If your project is subject to HIPAA, the HIPAA Supplement.

NOTE: You should receive notification of the results of the initial review of the application within **5 to 7 business days (7 to 9 during the summer and breaks) of the date of submission** of the application to the Office of Research Compliance.

IX. **Assurance by Principal Investigator (PI) and Advisor (if applicable):**
By signing below as the Principal Investigator, I:
1. Certify that the information provided in this application is accurate and complete.
2. Acknowledge ultimate responsibility for the protection of the rights and welfare of human subjects and adherence to any study-specific requirements imposed by the HSRB.
3. Will comply with all HSRB and BGSU policies and procedures, as well as with all applicable federal, state, and local laws and regulations regarding the protection of human subjects in research.
4. Also agree to the following:
   - I accept responsibility for the scientific and ethical conduct of this research study
   - I will obtain HSRB approval before amending or altering the research protocol or implementing changes in the approved consent documents or recruitment procedures

Figure 2.2 (*Continued*)

- I will immediately report to the HSRB any serious adverse events and/or unanticipated effects on subjects which may occur as a result of this study
- I will train study personnel in the proper conduct of human subjects research
- I will complete and return the Continuing Review form when requested to do so by the HSRB
- I will retain signed consent forms for at least 3 years following completion of the study

Signature _____

Date_____

Required for student applicants:

By signing below as Project Advisor, I certify that:

1. I have reviewed the information provided in this student's HSRB application and approve of the procedures (including subject recruiting, obtaining informed consent, provisions for protection of confidentiality, and data collection) described therein.
2. I will facilitate my student's compliance with all HSRB and BGSU policies and procedures, as well as with all applicable federal, state, and local laws and regulations regarding the protection of human subjects in research.

Advisor Signature _____ Date_____

Submit the application to the **Human Subjects Review Board, 201 South Hall.**

Steps in the Process of Review by the HSRB

1. A completed Application for Review (the original) should be submitted to the 201 South Hall. (When necessary, a letter to a prospective funding agency will be issued stating that the proposed research protocol is under review and that the HSRB will make a decision within 60 days.)
2. The Chair assigns the application to two reviewers. The reviewers may either make a recommendation regarding approval or call for review by the full HSRB at a regularly convened meeting.
3. If the reviewers decide that the research project is *exempt or expedited* and is eligible for *expedited* review and the Chair concurs, then approval can be granted either with or without conditions. If there are conditions, they will be specified in a letter to the Principal Investigator and must be addressed before the project can be fully approved and subject recruitment and data collection may begin. Research projects deemed expedited will be reviewed within 5–7 business days of submission.
4. If the reviewers or the Chair decide that the project should receive *full Board review*, the Chair places the application on the agenda of the next

Figure 2.2 (*Continued*)

regular meeting of the HSRB. The Board may approve the application as submitted, approve it with conditions, disapprove it, or defer a decision if sufficient information is not provided by the investigator. The action of the committee will be reported in writing to the investigator. Any conditions must be addressed before the project can be fully approved and subject recruitment and data collection may begin. The HSRB meets the first Wednesday of each month.

5. Either the Board or the investigator can request that the investigator be present at the part of the meeting of the HSRB when a specific project is being considered.

6. If required, a letter describing the decision of the HSRB will be addressed to the funding agency. Normally, this letter will be forwarded to the agency by the investigator.

POLICIES AND PROCEDURES FOR RESEARCH INVOLVING HUMAN SUBJECTS

All research involving human subjects must receive review and approval from the Human Subject Review Board (HSRB) prior to collecting data in accordance with Federal Regulations and University Policy. *THERE ARE NO EXCEPTIONS.* Failure to receive prior review can result in disciplinary action by the University and/or legal actions against the faculty members, student assistants, staff members, and the University; suspension or termination of a research project; and, in the case of graduate students, potential delays of graduation.

The legal authority for the Human Subjects Review Board (HSRB) comes from the Federal Policy for the Protection of Human Subjects (described in 45 CFR Part 46). In addition, Bowling Green State University has on file with the Public Health Service a statement of assurance committing the University to compliance with Federal Policy. No research involving humans may be undertaken without prior review and approval by the HSRB.

When in doubt about whether HSRB review is necessary or not, the appropriate course of action is to **seek review**. The role of the HSRB is to ensure compliance with federal regulations of research projects for faculty, staff, and student researchers, as well as to protect the rights of human subjects. The Office of Research Compliance (372-7716 or hsrb@bgnet.bgsu.edu) can assist researchers in making decisions about all aspects of the research process.

Any research project involving human subjects that is conducted by BGSU faculty, staff, or students must be reviewed. Research using BGSU faculty, staff, or students as research subjects must also be reviewed. Even if the researcher is from another institution, the Human Subjects Review Board has the authority to require review of a project if it involves the recruitment of BGSU faculty, staff, or students as subjects.

Figure 2.2 *(Continued)*

Class projects

Data to be collected in a *classroom* must be reviewed if it is part of a research project (as opposed to teaching). Also, *class projects* conducted by students must be reviewed if they:

- Would identify the interviewee or respondent either by name or by the responses to specific questions and/or recorded behaviors.
- Systematically select subjects from a potentially vulnerable or sensitive group (e.g., prisoners, pregnant women, children who are gifted and talented, alcoholics, sexual minorities, people with disabilities, people with cognitive impairment, people unable to give informed consent).
- Systematically collect private or protected information about individuals (e.g., school records, medical records, criminal records, membership or participation in self-help organizations).
- Propose to investigate opinions, behaviors, and/or experiences regarding sensitive topic areas (e.g., sexually explicit materials or questions, questions about drug use, questions about sexual orientation or sexual experience, illegal activities, purposeful creation of anxiety).
- Ask participants to engage in behavior that carries greater than minimal risk (see section V of the application above for a definition of minimal risk).
- Have the potential to become a thesis or dissertation project.
- Have a reasonable expectation of being externally funded (regardless of the source), published, and/or presented outside the course for which the project was originally conducted.

Any research project using *vulnerable individuals* as subjects requires extensive review (usually by the full HSRB). Vulnerable individuals include:

- Children involved in certain types of research
- Individuals in institutions (e.g., prisons, nursing homes, halfway houses)
- Physically or mentally impaired individuals
- Economically or educationally disadvantaged individuals; or
- Anyone unable to provide their own informed consent

If using members of vulnerable groups, the HSRB recommends you submit your application at least 2 months prior to the desired project start date.

Any research project must have extensive review if it involves *socially controversial stimuli* or *potentially questionable procedures or materials* such as (but not restricted to) the following:

- Shock or other forms of punishment
- Sexually explicit materials or questions
- Handling of money or other valuable commodities
- Extraction of blood or other bodily fluids
- Questions about drug use
- Administration of substances to subjects

Figure 2.2 (*Continued*)

- Questions about sexual orientation or sexual experience
- Purposeful creation of anxiety, or
- Any procedure which might be considered an invasion of privacy

If you are doing research for a thesis or dissertation and human subjects are involved, it must be reviewed. You must be sure to list the faculty advisor on the form and have them sign the application.

LEGAL REQUIREMENTS AND DEFINITIONS FOR RESEARCH INVOLVING HUMAN SUBJECTS

These following definitions are taken from the Federal Policy for Protection of Human Subjects (45 CFR Part 46)

"*Research* means a systematic investigation, including research development, testing, and evaluation, designed to develop or contribute to generalizable knowledge."

"*Human subject* means a living individual about whom an investigator (whether professional or student) conducting research obtains (1) data through intervention or interaction with the individual, or (2) identifiable private information."

"*Intervention* includes both physical procedures by which data are gathered and manipulations of the subject or the subject's environment that are performed for research purposes."

"*Interactions* include communication or interpersonal contact between investigator and subject."

"*Private information* includes information about behavior that occurs in a context in which an individual can reasonably expect that no observation or recording is taking place, . . . and which the individual can reasonably expect will not be made public."

"*HSRB approval* means the determination of the HSRB that the research has been reviewed and may be conducted at an institution within the constraints set forth by . . . institutional and federal requirements. . . . An IRB shall have the authority to suspend . . . research that is not being conducted in accordance with the IRB's requirements."

"No investigator may involve a human being as a subject in research unless the investigator has obtained the legally effective *informed consent* of the subject or the subject's legally authorized representative."

"An IRB shall require *documentation* of informed consent. . . . Informed consent will be sought from each prospective subject or the subject's legally authorized representative. Informed consent will be appropriately documented . . . by the use of a written form approved by the IRB."

Figure 2.2 (*Continued*)

"When some or all of the subjects are likely to be *vulnerable* . . ., such as children . . ., or economically or educationally disadvantaged persons, additional safeguards (should) be included . . . to protect the rights and welfare of these subjects."

Confidentiality means that the name or other identifying characteristics of the individual providing information to the researcher is known to the researcher but will not be revealed and will remain secret.

Anonymous means that the name or other identifying characteristics of participants will not be disclosed to the researcher.

Figure 2.2 (*Continued*)

3   THE SOCIAL SCIENTIFIC PARADIGM

What Will I Learn About the Social Scientific Paradigm?

This is a photo of Professor Michael Pfau, a former Department Chair at the University of Oklahoma. He passed away in 2009, but not before he taught or inspired generations of scholars, including Stephen. While he respected all paradigms of thought, he was at his heart a social scientist. On Stephen's first day of Introduction to Graduate Studies at the University of Oklahoma, Michael said, "You should be any kind of researcher you want, as long as you are good at it." When he said he was a social scientist, a student asked what that was. He said something to the effect of how his approach to research closely resembles the natural sciences, and that he looks for causal laws, to develop testable theories, gathers empirical data, and is value-free in his testing of theory. These four issues came up a lot in his discussions of social scientific theory and method. Michael made a prolific career out of being a social scientist; his work on inoculation has spawned countless studies (for reviews see Pfau & Burgoon, 1988; Pfau, Kenski, Nitz, & Sorenson, 1990; Szabo & Pfau, 2002). Stephen became a social scientist under Michael's mentorship.

The social scientific paradigm is one of the three main paradigms, or approaches to method, discussed in this book; the other two are the interpretive (Chapter 4), and the critical/cultural paradigm (Chapter 5). For social scientists (Michael and Stephen for example), their preference when doing research is to look for causal laws, describe and predict things, to gather empirical data, and to try to be as value-free as possible in research. This brings up a lot of broad questions. For example: 1) what is theory, 2) what are causal laws, 3) what is empirical data, and 4) what does it mean to be value-free in research? We explore in Chapter 3 these questions and other aspects of the social scientific paradigm to research.

Social Scientific Approach Defined

The social scientific paradigm is one of the three main paradigms of research, along with the interpretive (Chapter 4) and the critical/cultural (Chapter 5) paradigms. Social science research borrows heavily from the scientific method. **Social science** is an organized method of research combining empirical observations of behavior with inductive and deductive logic to confirm and test theories that are then used to describe and/or predict human activity. For social scientists, describing and/or predicting human behavior, particularly through the testing of theory, is of the utmost importance. The testing of theory is where the scientific method comes in to play.

The **scientific method** is a four-step systematic process in which a researcher conducts "research," which as we discussed in the introduction can be done in various ways. The ancient Egyptians, Greeks, and Romans all created systems for conducting research that closely resemble today's scientific method. These systems were modified by Muslim philosophers, Sir Francis Bacon, René Descartes, David Hume, Charles Peirce, and many others. The scientific method has four basic steps that form the backbone of social scientific research: theory should be proposed or present, predictions should be made (hypotheses), observations should be made, and empirical generalizations are generated.

The first step in the scientific method is proposing a theory. A **theory** is any conceptual representation or explanation of a phenomenon. Theories are attempts by scholars to represent processes. We all know Isaac Newton's (1642–1726) theory of gravity, *very simply* put "what goes up must come down." Countless scientists have made careers out of refining and expanding this theory into new horizons. Thanks to Newton's initial explanation of how gravity works, we have had breakthroughs in mathematics, architecture, and science. We identify eight important things to know about theories (Craig & Tracy, 1995; Littlejohn, 1999).

Important Things to Know About Theories

1. Theories organize and summarize knowledge. What we know about the world is organized into a collection of systematic theories created by researchers.

2. Theories focus attention on specific variables and the relationships between those specific variables. When you are thinking about a project and wondering what variables to look at, look to the body of theory for guidance on variable selection.

3. Theories clarify what is observed or studied and how to study it in our research. In essence, theories provide roadmaps for explaining and interpreting human behavior.

4. Theories allow for prediction of human behavior. As theories are systematic explanations of phenomena, we can make predictions based on certain kinds of data. (We talk more about that later in the chapter.)

5. A "good" theory should generate research; this is the heuristic function of a theory.

6. No theory can reveal the whole truth about a phenomenon. Some descriptive and/or explanatory aspects will always be left out, which leaves the theory abstract and partial.

7. People create theories. Therefore, theories represent how people see the world and not how some divine entity sees the world. Thus, it is important we recognize theories are not perfect and we continue to test theories with new research. The issue of continued testing is at the heart of being a social scientist and represents what Popper (1968) argued is a key aspect of a theory—a theory must be falsifiable (or testable through empirical research).

8. Some theories have a generative function, which means the theory's purpose is to challenge existing cultural life and generate new ways of living.

The second step in the scientific method is developing predictions about the relationships between phenomena. Predictions usually come in the form of hypotheses. A **hypothesis** is a prediction about what a researcher expects to find in a study. Hypotheses are educated guesses (predictions) about relationships between variables. When conducting research, the purpose of hypotheses is to help researchers make predictions based on theories. We will come back to hypotheses in much more detail in Chapters 7–9.

The third step in the scientific method is testing hypotheses, or the observations step. A researcher can test hypotheses in multiple ways; one purpose of this book is to provide new researchers with numerous ways to observe (test) hypotheses. One important criterion for a social scientist when it comes to observation is the method must be empirical, objective, and controlled. **Empiricism** is the notion a researcher can only research what they can observe. Something you can't observe is generally outside of the realm of science. For example, most empirical scholars will not conduct research on the existence of God. Why you ask? The existence of God is a matter of faith, and something one cannot empirically observe. **Objectivity** refers to the need for a researcher to be sure their emotions and personal feelings do not interfere with their research and/or predictions. For a social scientist objectivity is an important thing; many social scientists strive for it in research. For an interpretive or critical/cultural scholar, objectivity is not as much of a concern. All researchers should recognize that the choice of method they make is a subjective choice. An interpretive/critical/cultural scholar relies more on subjectivity. For example, Dan is a rhetorical scholar while Stephen is a quantitative scholar (statistics). The fact that they use these methods represents a choice (subjectivity) on their part. Stephen discusses in his work his role as an objective observer of Muslim behavior. Stephen is taking a scientific approach to his analysis.

Control is where the researcher prevents (or at least tries to prevent) personal biases and other influencing variables from interfering with a research study. As much as social scientists attempt to make research value-free, we are all human, and so our personalities and pre-determined preferences will influence our research methods (and our findings) to some extent (Condit, 1990). Those working in the natural sciences, in pharmaceuticals for example, take many steps to make research value-free. In medical experiments, researchers work to prove the medicine is affecting the body and not some other random variable like researcher personality, or the weather. This is why prescriptions go through massive and long clinical trials including control groups and often the use of things like placebos.

Once you have chosen a theory, generated a hypothesis/hypotheses, and tested the hypothesis/hypotheses, you move to the fourth step of the scientific method, making empirical generalizations. An **empirical generalization** is where you describe a phenomenon based on what you know about it from your research. Your generalizations should build on and/or refine the theory in some way, and if at all possible provide some practical (real-world) implications from the research you conducted.

Michael Pfau's primary area of research was on inoculation theory. Basically, the theory asserts an individual can be inoculated against negative messages by giving them a small dose of the message before they encounter the full message. In essence, this is a persuasive form of a flu shot. Michael and his research teams developed countless hypotheses over the years. They tested the hypotheses using surveys and experiments. Their research was empirical, they were objective, and they took numerous steps to control for interfering variables. In all, this body of research has provided countless refinements to inoculation theory and numerous practical implications for media, politics, economics, and other walks of life. For example, Pfau argued that if a message had the right level of persuasive elements it could affect viewers enough so that they would not be impacted by future negative messages. Think about this in terms of political campaigns. If a candidate knows bad news is coming out about them, it serves them well to craft a pre-emptive message to counter the bad news before it hits the airwaves. While this tactic may seem counter-intuitive, it actually works.

Now that we have gone over the basic definition of social science and the scientific method, the next section of Chapter 3 offers a brief historical review of the development of the social scientific paradigm.

Development of the Social Scientific Paradigm

The process of social science dates back to ancient Greeks, Romans, and Egyptians. During these times, ancient thinkers combined empirical observations of behavior with deductive logic when confirming and discovering theories used to describe or predict human activity. Scholars such as Hippocrates (the father of the Hippocratic Oath) would typically gather massive amounts of empirical (scientific) data on specific issues and write about their observations. As the centuries progressed, and data collection/scientific methods advanced, researchers continued to develop the social scientific paradigm.

Great leaps forward were made in the social scientific paradigm in Europe in the 1700s, 1800s, and 1900s. Two British philosophers furthered a concept known as positivism, a highly social scientific paradigm. David Hume in his *A Treatise of Human Nature* (1739–1740) outlined how human nature affects scientific research, and outlined his experimental method. John Stuart Mill (you might remember him from a certain "Social Contract"), in his *A System of Logic* (1840), discussed the relationships between logic and scientific research; specifically he outlined five principles to inductive reasoning known as Mill's method. Émile Durkheim, a noted French researcher, argued that science should be value-free in *Rules of the Sociological Method* (1895). Durkheim argued that sociology must study social facts and researchers must use a scientific method. Auguste Comte in *Cours de Philosophie Positive* (The Course of Positive Philosophy) (1830–1842) outlined the key principles of social science. He argued that the natural sciences were already being studied/ conducted properly and that the social sciences would soon be conducted properly as well. Popper, an Anglo-Austrian (1934), argued that a key aspect of social scientific research—theories and knowledge—"can never be proven or fully justified, they can only be refuted" (Phillips, 1987, p. 3). This is the falsification aspect of a theory again. Collectively, the researchers paved the way for a wave of researchers who have continued to strive for value-free, logical, empirical, and predictive social scientific research.

With a basic understanding of the social scientific paradigm, and some of its early researchers, the following section outlines nine key questions guiding the social scientific paradigm.

Key Questions that Underlie the Social Scientific Paradigm

1. How do the Social Sciences Differ from the Natural Sciences?

Social scientists are concerned with describing and predicting human behavior. But the "social" part of social science can be very unpredictable. While a biologist might be able to predict the exact composition or behavior of a single-cell organism, social scientists are more concerned with predicting patterns based on general human behaviors. For example, a social scientist could be interested in the relationship between levels of violence and how much someone plays video games, such as *World of Warcraft* or *Resident Evil*. This relationship will differ quite a bit depending on countless variables: what kind of video games does the person play, how long do people play the games per day, the person's psychological state before and during play, their relational status, their age, their sex/gender, and the list goes on and on. The following studies have all looked at this phenomenon using the social scientific paradigm (Ivory & Kalyanaraman, 2009; Lachlan & Maloney, 2008; Williams, 2011). We will discuss more in Chapters 14–18 how social scientists measure these behaviors and make claims based on human behavior.

2. What is the Purpose of Research?

As with every research paradigm, an important question to ask is, "What is the ultimate purpose of the research?" For the social scientist, the purpose of research is the discovery of theories to explain and predict human behavior and traits (Lindlof & Taylor, 2002). In this quest, social scientists collect data and test the data with systematically developed theories of human behavior and traits. The process of testing theories is endless for a social scientist, just as knowledge is endless (Neuman, 2011). It is important to note, though, that one of the reasons why the process is never ending is because theories are never perfect. Theories are constantly being refined as testing methods improve and as our understanding of phenomena changes.

3. What is Reality?

For social scientists, reality can be observed by the researcher because reality is "out there" waiting to be observed, identified, and explained. Social scientists adopt a realist ontology. If we can see and/or touch something through our research, then it really is not complex at its basic root. For example, we can see or measure someone's sex, gender, race, and age. When variables relate to other variables, we work to explain why. For example, scholars have found males are more likely to express argumentativeness than females (Schullery, 1998). Perhaps males express more argumentativeness because they are males? Research has shown sex/gender is related to heightened expression of argumentativeness, along with numerous other variables. Second, social scientists view reality as generally stable. Our traits and behaviors do not change dramatically over time; this is why if we conduct sound research today we can make predictions about human behavior that can be viable for many years.

4. What is Human Nature?

Social scientists recognize human beings are still essentially animals (mammals). While we sometimes forget this fact, humans are, unlike other mammals (as far as we know), consciously self-interested, rational, take steps to avoid pain, and seek out pleasure (Neuman, 2011). A social scientist typically tries to observe the stimuli occurring outside of the animal (humans). These researchers understand the difficulty (if not impossibility) in isolating everything (phenomena) happening in the brain of an animal (human). As Durkheim (1938) argued, "social phenomena are things and ought to be studied as things" (p. 27).

5. Do Humans Have Free Will?

It is important to know that social scientists are deterministic in their thinking. **Determinism** means social scientists believe humans and their actions are mainly caused by identifiable external forces as well as internal attributes. This means a lot of the decisions we make in life are determined by not only our internal makeup, but also our surroundings (culture, people, politics, economics, etc. . . .). Social scientists, therefore, study how external behaviors affect humans: in essence, how these factors lead us to do certain things or act in certain ways. We are not saying humans are robots who bend to the will of external commands (though some social scientists do operate under this philosophy). However, with determinism backing social scientific thought, we are able to make our predictions about human behavior because we can estimate how specific stimuli may lead to a change in some behavior.

For example: Michael Pfau's research on inoculation showed that, if you give an audience the right amount of a persuasive message, you could inoculate them against a future persuasive message. This is powerful information if you consider how political candidates and corporations are constantly trying to persuade us to do things . . . and they are doing it quite well as we are regularly inoculated against messages without even knowing it.

6. What is Theory?

Theory is one of the most important factors for a social scientist. Stephen fondly remembers Michael Pfau talking about how one of the goals of a social scientist is theory testing *and* theory building. In Stephen's early theoretical training, he was told social scientific theory involves the following. First, a theory can be descriptive, predictive, or causal in its explanation. If a theory is causal: X causes Y because Y and X are related in some way. If a theory is descriptive or predictive: X is related to Y because of the following reasons. Second, a theory should clearly outline the situations under which it operates/ applies. The situations are typically stated as boundary conditions (Dubin, 1978). One should not use a theory meant to study the immigrant cultural adaptation process when studying a potential spiral of silence around a political issue. Third, for social scientists, a theory should typically have axioms, postulates, and theorems. These statements add to the testability of theories. Fourth, a theory should, if at all possible, be applicable in various cultures.

7. How do You Determine if an Explanation is Good or Bad?

Social scientists use two criteria to determine whether an explanation or results are good or bad. First, you must ask yourself if the results are logical. Are contradictions evident in what you are presenting? If your results contradict previous research, can you offer a logical response as to why this might be the case? Croucher (2011) found Muslims in Western Europe prefer to oblige and compromise in conflicts than to dominate in conflicts. The stereotype was that Muslims would want to dominate a conflict and be an aggressor. Croucher had to provide an argument as to why Muslims would logically not be more dominating in a conflict. He argued that Muslims were not dominating because they were minorities in Western Europe, and so they had less power in the cultures. Second, social scientists are big fans of replication, more replication, and even more replication. A standard scientific practice is to repeat experiments to make sure they work the same way for every researcher every time. The same holds true for social scientific research. If you look at the method section of a statistics article in any communication journal, you will find the author(s) provides detailed information about how they conducted their research. The details are provided so other scholars can replicate the study.

8. How do You Determine Good or Bad Claims?

Claims are weighed based on our knowledge of empirical facts and theory. Popper argued knowledge claims cannot be proven or entirely justified: "they can only be refuted" (Phillips, 1987, p. 3). In this sense, refuting claims to knowledge is the never-ending quest that social scientists consider the testing of theory.

> Michael Pfau once told Stephen being a social scientist is forever looking for the outlier . . . or the one odd ball that makes us question our outlook on reality as we know it.

9. What is the Place of Values in Social Scientific Research?

Social scientific researchers try to be devoid of values (objective). When conducting research from a social scientific paradigm, values and morals should not influence research decisions or outcome. Social scientists strongly believe that research should be free of interference from religious, political, and other personal influences that may alter the objectivity of a researcher's process and/or findings. A researcher should be a disinterested scholar, one who observes and reports on phenomena without allowing values or morals to interfere. Value-free research is the ideal for social science. However, this is not always the case, as humans are by nature value-laden creatures. The job then of the social scientist is to recognize the place and impact of values on their research (Condit, 1990).

Michael Pfau told Stephen when he was a student that to be a social scientist he should do his best to be an observer and not allow his personal feelings and/or other values to interfere with his research. Pfau told his students that scientists like Copernicus and Kepler were persecuted because others around them allowed their religious values to interfere with how they interpreted research. For social scientists, research should be separate from values, but this is not always 100 percent possible.

Summary

This chapter explored the first of the three paradigms, the social scientific paradigm. As stated earlier in the chapter, these researchers emphasize research combining empirical observations of behavior with inductive and deductive logic to confirm and test theories that are used to describe and/or predict human activity. For social scientists, describing and/or predicting human behavior, particularly through the testing of theory, is of the utmost importance. In the following chapter, Chapter 4, we delve into a different research paradigm, the interpretivist paradigm.

 ## Key Steps & Questions to Consider

1. Social science is a method of research combining empirical observations of behavior with inductive and deductive logic to confirm and test theories used to describe and/or predict human activity.
2. A theory is an explanation of a phenomenon. Theories are not perfect. Theories should be continually refined.
3. Social science research is often based on hypotheses, which are educated guesses (predictions) about relationships between variables.
4. Social scientists differ in their preferred level of objectivity than do interpretive and/or critical/cultural scholars.
5. While we try to describe, predict, and show causal relationships, human beings are not 100% predictable. Social science is the study of human nature, not natural science.
6. Social scientists strive for value-free research. However, 100% value-free research is virtually impossible.

 ## Activities

1. Look up a definition of the scientific paradigm and compare the standards, assumptions, and expectations with the social scientific paradigm. Where do the two approaches agree and diverge?
2. You have significant experience with classroom communication. (After all, you have been attending classes for more than a decade—stretching back to

kindergarten!) Reflect on your years and write down a list of classroom communication behaviors you can recall. Apply the standards of empiricism to your list. What communication behaviors were observable and could count as data for a social scientific study?

3. Using the lists from the second activity, create a master list of classroom communication behaviors. Are any of the behaviors more tied to a specific grade (first, second, third, etc.) or to a specific stage of school (elementary, middle school, college, etc.)? Can you draw any basic theories from the observations?

 ## Discussion Questions

1. What is the purpose of communication research for social scientists?
2. How do the requirements for a social scientific study change how we approach the study of communication? What aspects of communication do you see as worthwhile for study? What aspects of communication might be difficult to study from the social science paradigm?

Key Terms

Control	Empiricism	Scientific method
Determinism	Hypothesis	Social science
Empirical generalization	Objectivity	Theory

4 THE INTERPRETIVE PARADIGM

What Will I Learn About the Interpretive Paradigm?

This is a cubistic face. We have always found abstract art to be fascinating because every picture can tell numerous stories. Anyone who looks at this picture will focus on different points of the face, which is one of the purposes of abstract art, particularly cubist art. The goal of the artist is to produce a work that makes us think and to create a piece that demonstrates their feelings. The use of color, shapes, shading, and a myriad of other techniques bring us into the picture and helps the artist achieve these goals. What do you see in this face? What do you think the artist is trying to convey? There will be multiple interpretations of this face, as the people reading this book all come from different walks of life, have different lived experiences, and will thus focus on different aspects of the face.

The concept of varied interpretations is at the heart of the interpretive paradigm. The interpretive paradigm is the second of the three paradigms discussed in this book; the other two are the social scientific (Chapter 3), and the critical/

cultural (Chapter 5). For interpretivists, the preference when doing research is to look for the varied interpretations or different meanings. The multitude of interpretations and meanings in phenomena provide a wealth of information about said phenomena. As with the social scientists, the interpretivists are interested in theory, relationships, data, and value, but approach such things differently. Thus, some key questions for interpretivsts, like all researchers, are: 1) what is theory, 2) what is meaning, 3) what are data, and 4) what is the place of value in the research process? We explore in Chapter 4 these questions and other aspects of the interpretive paradigm to research.

Interpretive Approach Defined

The interpretive paradigm is one of the three main paradigms of research. The **interpretive paradigm** focuses on the belief that reality is constructed through subjective perceptions and interpretations of reality. Such researchers, unlike the social scientists, believe the study of human beings should not/cannot be held to the same standards or methods as the natural sciences. Researchers in this paradigm study the social construction of meaning through the analysis of individualized purposes, goals, and intentions in social sciences, humanities, and/or communication.

Unlike the social scientists, who strictly follow the scientific method, you will find that interpretivists differ in their approach to the scientific method. This is not to say the interpretive paradigm lacks scientific rigor. On the contrary, interpretive research can answer many of the same questions as social scientific and critical research, just in different ways. As with the other research paradigms, interpretivists will often generate or test theories. However, an interpretivist has their view of "theory." We will discuss this in depth in the "Key Questions that Underlie the Interpretive Paradigm" section of this chapter. Interpretivists rarely use hypotheses, instead using research questions to guide their work. Research questions are another form of educated guesses about the relationships between constructs (variables).

Interpretivists reject the social scientific notion of empiricism (the notion that scholars can only research what they can observe). Instead, interpretivists generally embrace rationalism. **Rationalism** is the notion that we gain knowledge through the use of logic. In this sense, we learn and describe the world around us through a variety of means. For example, most empirical researchers (social scientists mainly) would not conduct research on the existence of God. However, a rationalist could conduct this research because individuals can describe in a variety of ways how they experience the existence of a God(s).

Subjectivity is the condition for a researcher to be involved or inseparable from the research context. A common practice for interpretive researchers is active participation in the research process, which means their personal feelings and identity can often be observed in the writing.

A researcher would have a hard time trying to explain from an empirical and objectivist (social scientific) point of view the varied interpretations of what the cubist face means to each one of you. All of us come to the picture with different lived experiences or backgrounds. The subjective nature of art makes it interesting and brings to the table the broad diversity of opinions.

Now that we have gone over a basic definition of the interpretive paradigm, the next section of Chapter 4 offers a historical review of this paradigm. The review serves to help further define the interpretive paradigm.

Development of the Interpretive Paradigm

Interpretivism developed as a response to the growth of social scientific inquiry in the 1800s and the 1900s. As the social scientific calls from scholars such as Émile Durkheim (1858–1917) and Auguste Comte (1798–1857) began to grow, many researchers, mostly German, questioned such calls to study human behavior from a more natural science perspective. Scholars like Georg Wilhelm Hegel (1770–1831), Edmund Husserl (1859–1938), Ferdinand Tönnies (1855–1936), Max Weber (1864–1920), and Georg Simmel (1858–1918) pioneered ideas such as *Verstehen* (the interpretive approach to social science). These researchers claimed that the natural sciences were inappropriate for studying human behavior, as such methods did not consider cultural norms, symbols, values, and individual social processes (Weber, 1991). Tönnies, in fact, asserted the major flaws of social science was that it did not consider the influences of the community (*Gemeinschaft*) or the society (*Gesellschaft*) on human behavior (Cahnman, Maier, Tarr, & Marcus, 1995). Through the work of these scholars, the interpretivist paradigm developed into various research fields still widely used today including hermeneutics, phenomenology, and symbolic interactionism.

Three Key Interpretive Approaches

Hermeneutics

Hermeneutics scholars were at first interested in interpreting or studying sacred texts, such as the Bible, the Talmud, or the Vedas. In the late 19th and early 20th centuries, this philosophy expanded into the examination of various kinds of texts. Wilhelm Dilthey (1833–1911) in his classic work "The Understanding of other persons and their manifestations of life" (1910) emphasized the importance of hermeneutics in understanding the individual spiritual experiences of others. Scholars such as Martin Heidegger (1889–1976), Hans-Georg Gadamer (1900–2002), Jürgen Habermas (1929–) have all expanded hermeneutics to focus on how interpreting a text will reveal something about the author(s), the social context, and provide a shared experience between the author(s) and the reader(s) (Gadamer, 2003).

Hermeneutic researchers in communication studies identify three key points to remember. First, when exploring social activity, subjective understanding is paramount (not prediction, explanation, or control, which are key to the social scientific paradigm). For example, Waisanen (2013) in his analysis of the Los Angeles County seal controversy discussed how different groups formed around the controversy. Each group had a different stake, different opinions, and a different way of experiencing the removal of a cross from the Los Angeles County seal. Second, a variety of objects, concepts (things), can be considered "texts" for analysis. In the case of Waisanen's study, the texts were the seal, the cross, and the hearing between the Board of Supervisors and the public. Third, hermeneutic scholars assert it is impossible to separate the observer from what they are observing and where subjectivity comes into play. For Gadamer (2003), the observer is an intrinsic part of the research process.

Phenomenology

Phenomenology is the systematic explanation and study of consciousness and subjective human experience (Husserl, 1970). Simply, the study of phenomena is how we experience things in life and the meanings things have for us. The key thinkers in this philosophy are Edmund Husserl (1859–1938), Martin Heidegger (1889–1976), Alfred Schütz (1899–1959), Jean-Paul Sartre (1905–1980), and Maurice Merleau-Ponty (1908–1961). Husserl, in his concept of transcendental phenomenology, was keenly interested in the experiences we take for granted. All of our activities or experiences have a structure to them and we often overlook these structures. Thus, the process is to step back—transcend the phenomenon—in order to better understand what is or has happened.

For example, every time you have class you may have a verbal exchange with your teacher. How does this exchange happen? What do you say, and what does the teacher say? How do the two of you verbally and non-verbally interact? This experience has probably become second nature to you both. However, if you investigate the interaction or experience, you are trying to transcend the taken-for-granted aspects. Why do we interact the way we do? The process of transcending is what Husserl called epoché, or trying to set aside taken-for-granted aspects of an experience to gain a deeper grasp of the experience. In Leonard's (2013) phenomenological analysis of a Polar-Eskimo language in northern Greenland, he explains his experiences of engaging with language and culture. In this analysis, Leonard dissects the experience of speaking and knowing a language, which are often things people take for granted.

Symbolic Interactionism

Symbolic interactionism is an area of research emphasizing the relationships between symbols, the social world, and social interaction. Charles Horton Cooley (1864–1929), George Herbert Mead (1863–1931), and Herbert George Blumer (1900–1987) are primarily credited with founding and furthering this approach to research. Even though Mead never used the phrase "symbolic interactionism," he is still credited with founding the approach. The interpretive symbolic interactionists were primarily associated with what became known as the "Chicago School" (most were located in or near Chicago). In 1934, Mead outlined three connected ideas that have become essential for symbolic interaction studies. Human thought (the mind) and social interaction (self and others) help us make sense of the world in which we live (our society). When you consider these three essential ideas, it is possible to see how researchers today conduct studies from this perspective.

MacLean (2008) explored framing organizational misconduct through deceptive sales practices. Using archival data, interviews, and a published report, MacLean found the notion of misconduct is shaped by organizational members acting on behaviors socially constructed by the organization and society. These three interpretive philosophies, approaches to research, can all be conducted using a variety of research methods. You will find that all three approaches can use ethnography (Chapter 10), interviewing (Chapter 11), focus groups (Chapter 12), content analysis (Chapter 14), and other methods.

With a basic understanding of the interpretive paradigm, its development, and three approaches to interpretive research, the following section outlines the same nine questions posed in Chapter 3 for the social scientific approach. This comparison will help you understand the interpretive approach and the differences between the paradigms.

Key Questions Underlying the Interpretive Paradigm

1. How does the Interpretive Approach to Science Differ from the Natural Sciences?

In Chapter 3 we talked about how biologists and other natural scientists may be able to predict the exact composition of an organism, but social scientists are not able to make similar predictions of human behavior. Interpretivists are not interested in *predicting* human behavior. These researchers are interested in *understanding* human experiences. For example, while a social scientist might try to predict a relationship between how much someone plays *World of Warcraft* and their violent behavior(s), an interpretivist is more likely to try to understand how a player understands and/or experiences the violence in the game. Klimmt *et al.* (2006) conducted interviews with players of violent video games. Their analysis focused on trying to understand why people play the games through the moral justification given for enjoying violent games. Such an analysis would be difficult to achieve through a social scientific approach.

2. What is the Purpose of Research?

The main goal of research for interpretivists is to understand how people construct meaning in life and understand experiences. If you look back at the definitions of hermeneutics, phenomenology, or symbolic interactionism, you will see all have one thing in common: they each study some aspect of meaningful social action or interaction. Geertz (1973) asserted that human actions are meaningless unless they are considered in the context of their social and cultural contexts. This exploration of meaning is at the heart of the interpretive paradigm.

3. What is Reality?

For interpretivists, reality is created through social interaction. The social interaction, and thus reality, are primarily what people perceive them to be (experiences and meaning). Our subjective experiences create our individual realities. As opposed to the social scientists, who see the world in a very objective, realist ontological point of view, interpretivists take a constructionist perspective (Neuman, 2011). This means people construct reality out of their own experiences. For example, "snow." When you see snow falling to the ground we all experience this reality differently. In October and November in Finland, Stephen and his friends look forward to snow because October and November are rainy, dark months where we get very little sunlight. When the snow comes, we all feel a little bit better because the snow reflects the stars, we know holiday lights are coming, and things will get a bit brighter, literally. Stephen's parents, on the other hand, in the United States see snow as a sign of slushy roads and shoveling, not happy things. The constructions of "snow" differ, which lead to different realities.

4. What is Human Nature?

While social scientists look for patterns in behaviors that can lead to prediction, control, and explanation, interpretive researchers understand patterns differently. Interpretive researchers believe patterns exist in human nature, but the patterns are a result of ever-evolving meaning systems, norms, and conventions people learn through interactions. The study on video game moral concerns (Klimmt *et al.*, 2006) is a prime example of how researchers are interested in exploring how human nature evolves around a particular issue in a given context. A paramount idea is that the morality of the players is socially constructed (Klimmt *et al.*, 2006).

5. Do Humans Have Free Will?

Many social scientists support the idea of determinism—the belief that humans and their actions are mainly caused by identifiable external forces and internal attributes. Interpretive researchers generally advocate for voluntarism—the idea people are able to make conscious choices based on reason. Researchers in this kind of work must be considerate of their subjects' individual feelings, and decision-making processes. Such processes and feeling can often reveal how participants understand phenomena (phenomenology), or interact with society (symbolic interactionism).

6. What is Theory?

Social scientific research strives to be descriptive, predictive, or causal in its explanations. Interpretive theories try to describe or understand the lives of people in their social environment. Interpretive theorizing may make limited generalizations. However, interpretive theories focus on the social and lived experiences of individuals. Collier and Thomas's (1988) cultural identity theory was designed as an interpretive theory (Collier, 1998). This theory explains how identities are negotiated in discourse.

7. How do You Determine if an Explanation is Good or Bad?

While social scientists are big fans of replication, interpretive researchers do not see replication as a major necessity. For interpretive researchers, two closely connected issues are key. First, the explanation must make sense to those the researcher is studying. As a researcher, you are studying a group of people and trying to convey their experiences. Your interpretation of their experiences should make sense if they read it. Second, the explanation should make enough sense so others can also understand the experiences of the group(s) you studied. When someone tells you a story and then you try to retell the story to someone else, you should try to be as true to the original story as possible. If you are not true to the original story, you may lose important information and the original intent of the storyteller.

8. How do You Determine Good or Bad Claims?

For social scientists, claims are weighed based on empirical facts and theory. For interpretive researchers, explanations or research should provide in-depth description of phenomena, and offer coherent interpretation of experiences. For interpretive research, a goal is to provide what Geertz (1973) calls "thick description." Interpretive researchers detail the experiences of others by providing a "thick" or rich description to substantiate the analysis.

9. What is the Place of Values in Social Scientific Research?

Interpretive researchers embrace and analyze their position in the research process. For these scholars, separating values and morals from research decisions or outcomes is impossible. An interpretive researcher should not be a disinterested, objective scholar who reports on phenomena. Instead, an interpretive researcher is a subjective participant who is actively involved in the research process.

Returning back to the cubist face. An interpretive researcher could conduct in-depth interviews (Chapter 11) with individuals on their understanding of the painting. The researcher will more than likely get numerous responses. How have the social interactions, upbringing, and culture shaped how participants perceive the face? How does the background of the researcher influence how they see the face? The extent to which the researcher is involved in the process is an important factor to consider. The level of research involvement in interpretive methods will be discussed in Chapters 5, 10, 13, and 14.

Summary

In this chapter we examined the interpretivist paradigm. Unlike the social scientific paradigm, which we discussed in Chapter 3, the interpretivists believe reality is constructed through subjective perceptions and interpretations of reality. Such researchers, unlike the social scientists, believe the study of human beings should not/cannot be held to the same standards or methods as the natural sciences. Researchers in this paradigm study the social construction of meaning through the analysis of individualized purposes, goals, and intentions in social sciences, humanities, and/or communication. In the next chapter, Chapter 5, we present the critical/cultural paradigm.

 ## Key Steps & Questions to Consider

1. The interpretive paradigm focuses on the belief that reality is constructed through subjective perceptions and interpretations of reality.
2. Rationalism is the notion we gain knowledge through the use of logic. In this sense, we learn and describe the world around us through a variety of means.
3. Subjectivity is the need and desire for a researcher to be involved or inseparable from the research context.
4. Hermeneutics scholars were first interested in interpreting or studying sacred texts, such as the Bible, the Talmud, or the Vedas. This expanded into the examination of various kinds of texts.
5. Phenomenology is the study of phenomena, how we experience things in life, and the meanings things have for us.
6. Symbolic interactionism is an area of research that emphasizes the relationships between symbols, the social world, and social interaction.
7. Interpretivists are interested in understanding human experiences.
8. Interpretive researchers generally advocate for voluntarism, or the idea that people are able to make conscious choices based on reason.

Activity

1. Develop a "cheat sheet" for comparing the different research paradigms.

   a. Prepare a chart with four columns and 10 rows.
   b. Label the four columns (in the first row): 1. Key Questions; 2. Social Science; 3. Interp Paradigm; 4. Critical/Cultural.
   c. Fill in the rows of column 1 under your Key Questions heading with abbreviated versions of the Key Questions listed earlier in the chapter (e.g., "interpretive approach vs. natural sciences").
   d. Fill in your Social Science and Interp Paradigm columns with significant components to help you remember how to distinguish between the different approaches. You can add to the Critical/Cultural column after reading Chapter 5.

 Discussion Questions

1. How will following the interpretive paradigm alter approaches that you might take for different communication research projects?
2. Researchers, while familiar with all the research approaches, tend to gravitate toward one of the paradigms. What aspects of the interpretive paradigm do you find compelling? What aspects do you find disquieting?

Key Terms

Hermeneutics	Rationalism	Voluntarism
Interpretive paradigm	Subjectivity	
Phenomenology	Symbolic interactionism	

5 THE CRITICAL PARADIGM

James P. Dimock

Chapter Outline

- Traditional Approaches to the Study of Power
- Rise of Marxism and Critical Theory
- Postmodern Turn
- Postmodernism
- Key Steps & Questions to Consider
- Activities
- Discussion Questions
- Key Terms

What Will I Learn About Critical Theory in This Chapter?

In the Disney-Pixar film *A Bug's Life*, an ant named Flik stands up to Hopper, the leader of a gang of grasshoppers who tyrannize the ant colony. As winter approaches, however, many of Hopper's gang are not interested in going back to Ant Island to deal with one rebellious ant. Hopper demonstrates the importance of dealing with Flik through a brilliant, if violent, metaphor:

> "Let's pretend this grain is a puny little ant," Hopper says, throwing a few seeds at a couple of reluctant gang members. He asks, "Did that hurt?"
>
> "Nope," says one gang member.
>
> "Are you kidding?" laughs another.
>
> "How about this?" Hopper asks, opening a chute and burying them under thousands of seeds. Hopper explains the way the world works to the rest of his gang. "You let one ant stand up to us then they all might stand up. Those 'puny little ants' outnumber us a hundred to one and if they ever figure that out, there goes our way of life. It's not about food. It's about keeping those ants in line. That's why we're going back!"

Hopper's monologue is about power. The grasshoppers' power over the ants isn't physical. One grasshopper is stronger than one ant or even several ants put together, but if the ants collectively stand up to the grasshoppers, they are physically stronger. The grasshoppers' power is what critical theorists call **ideological**; that is to say, ideological power functions at the level of the ants' thinking about the world, about what they are—and are *not*—capable of doing. Hopper's power is over the ants and his fellow grasshoppers. His companions would have been satisfied living out the winter without going back to Ant Island. Hopper uses both the threat of violence and the use of language to interpolate the ideology of power and control in the minds of the grasshoppers. After all, their entire "way of life" is at stake. If the grasshoppers are reluctant to use their power, they will lose everything.

Critical theorists are primarily concerned with power and especially with **oppression**, or the exercise of power, by one entity (e.g., a person, group, organization) for its own benefit over another entity. Critical theory is different from other approaches to communication research since it looks for ways to change the relationships of power and overcome oppression. In this chapter you will learn about critical methods of research. You may notice this chapter is longer than the other two paradigm chapters (Chapters 3 and 4). By its nature, the critical paradigm is complex and convoluted. A number of brief history lessons are needed to understand how the critical paradigm came about. Take your time as you move through the chapter. Let the concepts "percolate" for a while until they reach a nice strong brew. Then you will be ready to take a good long drink and enjoy the critical approach to research methods.

Traditional Approaches to the Study of Power

Power, sometimes called influence, has been a subject of interest for social theorists, political scientists, and communication researchers for a long time. In fact, the earliest communication theorists and scholars, the Greek Sophists, were interested in how to use language to influence large groups of people, such as juries and legislative assemblies. Traditionally, **power** has been understood by communication scholars as the ability to perform an act that will result in a change in someone else (Cartwright & Zander, 1968). For example, Olivia could tell Peter she will beat him up if he does not give her his lunch money. If Peter gives Olivia his lunch money, an act he would not otherwise have done, then we can say Olivia has power over Peter. This type of power is called **coercive power** because it threatens some harm. Olivia also could have convinced Peter to give up his lunch money by promising to do his homework for him (**reward power**) or by reminding Peter he had borrowed money from her earlier and promised to pay it back (**legitimate power**). Olivia could have used **persuasive power** by making a compelling argument to turn over the lunch money. Persuasive power is the form of most interest to communication scholars.

A traditional understanding sees power as both a thing (an object people have and use) and a performance (an action people carry out). This locates power in the consciousness of the person with power (Olivia) and in the consciousness of the person over whom power is exercised (Peter). One of the most influential philosophers of the early 19th century was Georg Wilhelm Friedrich Hegel. Hegel came to believe that all history was "the history of thought" and the way people think determined material and historical conditions under which they lived.

Hegel's approach was a philosophy of change. The rationalism of the Enlightenment was founded on mechanical physics. The universe and everything in it, including human beings and societies, functioned much like a pocket watch. The universe is a closed-system in which matter in motion causes other matter to move. But rationalism could not explain how things changed. In mechanical physics, change only comes from the outside. As the pocket watch winds down and runs out of energy, a force outside the system—a key and a hand to turn it—makes the watch go again. However, for mechanical physics, there is nothing outside of the universe to compel the change.

So what produces change? Hegel believed in dialectic—a tension—between an idea and its contradiction. We tend to think of a contradiction as something's opposite. Black is the contradiction of white; yes is the contradiction of no. However, this is not precisely what Hegel meant. Gasper (2010) explained contradiction with an example: Within every caterpillar lies the potential to become a butterfly. At the point when a butterfly exists, the caterpillar ceases to exist. And a butterfly does not have the potential to become a caterpillar. Thus, within every caterpillar lies its own negation (the butterfly negates the existence of the caterpillar). If you negate the caterpillar, though, you also negate the butterfly. The important part of the story for Hegel is the movement from one to the other—the process of becoming. This Hegel called the **dialectic** or the contradiction between an idea and its negation.

Hegelian thought is extremely dense and complicated, and we provide only a brief glimpse of his ideas. Suffice to say for Hegel, a person's place in the universe is determined by thought (the world of ideas). For Hegel, "the sole method by which those who have the good of society at heart can improve society, is to develop in themselves and in others the power of analyzing themselves and their environment" (Berlin, 1963, p. 49). An analysis of self and others is now called **critique** (or spelled in the German form as "*Kritik*"). Systems of human interaction are systems of the mind; they are ideas and they resist change. However, the ideas contain the elements of their own negation in the same way that a butterfly may negate the caterpillar. True change comes from changing ideas or what Hegel called the Spirit.

Hegel's philosophy came to dominate the thinking of Europeans, especially Continental philosophers, during the 19th century. In the wake of the French Revolution and the Napoleonic Wars, the thinking took on a decidedly anti-revolutionary, or reactionary, form. Ideas were understood to be the driving force of history. A nation was the manifestation of a particular idea that simply cannot vanish through revolutionary action or through the efforts of reformers. Only through the nation and the state could a person be what they were supposed to be and the desire to radically transform the state was self-destructive. Hegel's philosophy elevated intellectuals and idea-shapers such as artists, writers, scientists, and philosophers as the true agents of change.

> Let's return to the example of Olivia and Peter. The change is not in the action of Peter giving Olivia his lunch money but rather in the ideas that permitted Olivia to believe she had a right to demand Peter's lunch money and Peter believing in the ideas he must do so.

Rise of Marxism and Critical Theory

Many philosophers embraced the earlier works of Hegel, which stressed the importance of change and freedom, while rejecting his later works about the importance of the nation and state even when the state was authoritarian. These philosophers were called the Young Hegelians and believed ideas are the driving force in history. Others agreed with Hegel's philosophy of change but rejected his idealism. One of the most influential of these philosophers was Karl Marx.

Karl Marx was born in 1818 in the town of Trier in the German Rhineland. In the years following the French Revolution and the Napoleonic Wars, many Germans hoped the hotchpotch of independent feudal states would be united to form a single nation-state like France and Britain. When Napoleon subjugated the Germans, he imposed a set of laws called **the Napoleonic Code** that, among other things, lifted many of the prohibitions on Jews entering civil life. Marx's father, Herschel Mordechai (Heinrich Marx), who came from a long line of rabbis in the Rhineland, took advantage of this and became a lawyer. The hopes for a liberal Germany were lost following Napoleon's disastrous invasion of Russia in 1812 and his final defeat at Waterloo in 1815. The aristocracy in Germany was restored and promptly reasserted its authority. In 1816, anti-Jewish laws effectively cut off Levi's livelihood. The year before Karl Marx was born, his father converted to Lutheranism and changed his name from Herschel to the more German-sounding Heinrich. Isaiah Berlin (1963) recounts a story of Heinrich giving a speech at a public dinner. Heinrich suggested that a wise and benevolent ruler ought to support moderate political and social reform. This mild criticism attracted the attention of the Prussian police and Marx's father was quick to recant his statements. In Berlin's words,

> It is not improbable this slight but humiliating contretemps, and in particular his father's craven and submissive attitude, made a definite

impression on his oldest son Karl Heinrich, then sixteen years old, and left behind it a smoldering sense of resentment, which later events fanned into flames.

(p. 23)

In his adult life, Karl Marx went on to become one of the most insightful and outspoken critics of the new social and political order called capitalism.

Human history has been a struggle for survival. Humans need clothing and shelter for protection from the elements and other animals. Humans need food in a never-ending quest to stay alive. Human beings are, however, different from other animals. Much of philosophy is the effort to determine what makes humans different from other animals. Aristotle, for example, said human beings were logical and political animals. Others have said it was the ability to produce and use tools that made humans unique. For Marx, the central and defining aspect of human beings is **labor**. Many creatures transform their environments—birds build nests and beavers build dams. Human labor is fundamentally different. Through labor, humans transform their environments and themselves.

Our early pre-human ancestors were primarily vegetarian and needed wide, flat teeth to grind plant material and a long digestive tract to turn plant material into calories. When humans started eating meat, this changed. Our digestive tract became shorter and the energy it took to digest plant matter was re-routed to our brains. In order to become meat-eaters we needed tools. Cutting tools do for us what teeth do for other predators. Hunting tools were used to catch fast-running prey. Tools made our gathering, processing, and eventually storage of grains, fruits, and other nutritious plants more efficient. Together, all this meant we could have leisure time: time to think, to plan, and to create. We did not become just better versions, but were fundamentally and physically transformed beings.

From the Marxist point of view, it wasn't changes in our consciousness that transformed us physically, but our physical transformation that made thought possible. Labor power, which for Marx consists of the "aggregate of those mental and physical capabilities existing in a human being, which he exercises whenever he produces a use-value of any description" (1978, p. 336), transformed and continues to transform the human being. This eventually leads to the formation of **classes**. The concept of the division of labor appears in social thought as far back as Plato in the 4th century bce and was central to the work of economic philosopher Adam Smith writing in the late 17th century ce. Writing a generation after Marx, Durkheim (1955) argued that the division of labor defined civilization. This division regulates our interactions lest conflicts "incessantly crop out anew" and "mutual obligations had to be fought over entirely anew in each particular instance" (pp. 5–6).

A society without division of labor has each person equally trained and responsible for every task. In such a society, every person is his or her own farmer, blacksmith, police officer, etc. Division of labor maximizes efficiency and permits specialization and innovation. One person specializes in farming, another in breeding oxen for plowing, a third in making plows and farm implements. Given time to specialize and engage in a craft, each person gets better, recognizes opportunities to improve, and become more efficient. Over time, people identify with the work they perform and take pride and find meaning in their work. The division of labor depends upon fixing social and economic roles. As Marxists understand it, the division of labor is part of a system of **relationships of production** based on social and political classes.

Understanding Class

Many people have trouble understanding class, particularly in places like the United States where class is not something we talk about very often. The United States does not have a history of formal nobility so we don't have many historical, material indicators of class and those we do have are indicators not of *class* but *wealth* (e.g., lower class, middle class, and upper class). What Marx understood by the relations of production was that there are two classes, the bourgeoisie (the ruling class) and the proletariat (the working class).

The definition of class has little to do with how much money a person has or makes but, rather, with their relationship to the **means of production**. Every society has means of producing wealth. In an agricultural society, production is the land, which is necessary to produce food for humans and animals. In an industrial society it might be the factories, which produce consumer goods. The ruling class owns the factories; the working class works in the factory. The working class has nothing to sell but their labor. Remember, for Marx, labor is what defines the human being so to sell one's labor is to sell one's self. The worker does not really have any choice in what is made, or the conditions under which it is made, or how it is disposed of, or to whom it is sold. Of course, as capitalist economists point out, the worker can choose to work or to work somewhere else, yet the worker is never in control of those conditions. The factory owner, on the other hand, has all kinds of options. He can choose not to hire anyone, close the factory, move to another city, or make a different product.

In a world in which a person owns their own labor, they decide what they will make and when and how it will be used. Let us say a cobbler makes shoes and comes up with a way to improve his efficiency and make more shoes in less time. He benefits from his innovation by having extra time to do something else or by making even more shoes and thus more profit. But if a worker in a shoe factory comes up with the same innovation, the rewards of this creativity go to the factory owner.

In mass production, the worker typically only produces a small part of the final product. This **de-skilling** of labor alienates the worker, reducing him or her to a tool. The alienation extends to the social system as a whole. Workers see others as competitors with whom they must compete to keep their jobs. Alienation is helped by racial and cultural myths that may further divide workers, preventing them from realizing the power of unification. Alienation **dehumanizes** us. Separating workers from their labor makes them less human in how they relate to one another and how they understand themselves. The ruling class (the bourgeoisie for Marx) is also caught up in the cycle of dehumanization. They are separated from themselves because, while they do not labor the same as workers, they purchase, which furthers an insatiable need to find meaning through consumption.

In order to understand the distinction between classes, it might help to think of a professional football team. The players—even while many of them make significant amounts of money—are the working class. Their bodies are put on the line, suffering damage from being hit over and over again. Their labor produces the game. While we may think of the players as rich and part of the ruling class, they are workers alienated from their labor in many respects. Most have little say in who they play for, and no control over the line-up, the game schedule, or the rules. A player cannot decide he does not want to play in Detroit's Ford Stadium. Perhaps the player is Jewish and is troubled playing in a stadium named for a renowned anti-Semite. The rules are set by, and set up to benefit, the owners in the league. It isn't about money but where one is positioned in the relationships of production that determines one's class.

Understanding Ideology

Next, we need to understand Marx's distinction between the **base** (also called the **substructure**) and the **superstructure**. Our social world begins with real, material, productive forces and resources. Some communities are built along rivers that provide transportation or fishing, while others are on salt flats or grazing lands. The available resources are real material forces, which determine the range and scope of economic relationships. In order to live, individuals enter into economic relationships with each other. These material resources and the necessary economic relationships are the base (substructure) of society. Upon this base, the superstructure of the society is built. The superstructure consists of the visible forms of society such as art and culture, and institutions like the courts, police, and religion. If the function of the base is production, the function of the superstructure is to reproduce the conditions of production.

In order for the means of production to keep on producing, labor power requires "the material means with which to reproduce itself" (Althusser, 1989, p. 63). These means are wages, the money paid to the worker to ensure he or she has housing, food, clothing, and other necessities necessary to "to present himself at the factory gate" (Althusser, p. 64) each morning, ready to offer his labor power.

But what of the relations of production? At the beginning of this chapter, we looked at an important scene from the movie *A Bug's Life*. The ants, if they gathered together and stood up to the grasshoppers, would surely win. They outnumber the grasshoppers at least a hundred to one. This, Althusser argued, is ideology.

Ideology is a difficult word to understand because many people use the word and they use it—even pronounce it—in many different ways. We are going to use the term the way Marx and his co-writer Fredrick Engels (1978) used it in their work *The German Ideology* and how Althusser (1989) used the term in his article "Ideology and Ideological State Apparatuses." The term means a type of false consciousness: an illusion that makes the real world difficult, but not impossible, to see and understand.

Power, from a Marxist perspective, is maintained in two ways. The first is through what Althusser called the **Repressive State Apparatus**. For Althusser, like Marx and Engels, the **state** does not refer to a political subdivision (e.g., the State of Illinois, the State of Kansas) but to an independent political entity (e.g., the United States, Great Britain). The state has sovereign power since not subject to any other power. Althusser (1989) described the state as "a 'machine' of repression, which enables the ruling classes to endure their domination over the working class" (p. 68). The state maintains law and order by protecting the established relationships of production. The state makes capitalist exploitation of the working class possible.

In his 1919 essay "Politics as a Vocation," German sociologist and economist Max Weber (n.d.) defined the state as "a human community that (successfully) claims the *monopoly of the legitimate use of physical force* within a given territory" and while "the right to use physical force is ascribed to other institutions or to individuals only to the extent to which the state permits it" (p. 1). Any other use of violence or force is considered criminal. The state is allowed to do things that are illegal for others. The state can declare that a portion of the money you earn belongs to them. The state can tell you what you can, cannot, and must do. If you refuse to accept its rules, the state can fine you or lock you up or even, in extreme circumstances, kill you. The state reserves for itself the exclusive right to the legitimate use of violence. For Althusser (1989), "the Government, the Administration, the Army, the Police, the Courts, the Prisons, etc." are entities, which "function by violence" (p. 73).

In order to understand this, we need to understand the second way that power is maintained, which is through what Althusser called the **Ideological State Apparatus**. Ideological apparatuses serve the interests of the state and work hand-in-hand with repressive state apparatuses, yet function in different ways. First, repressive state apparatuses are singular and under public control while ideological state apparatuses are plural (many coming from different directions). Ideological state apparatuses may be held in state hands but more likely under the control of private powers outside the state. Finally, repressive apparatuses work through violence while ideological state apparatuses operate through **interpellation**; that is to say, they impact the way we see and understand the world around us. They shape our consciousness in particular ways. Ideological apparatuses include things like:

Religious institutions help to explain why some people have power and others don't, and provide for an ultimate justice in an afterlife for those who suffer in this one. Religious institutions often teach respect for and obedience to authority as part of a divine and unquestionable plan.

Educational institutions provide for the training of the next generation of workers, making sure we have the right workers in the right proportions to meet our economic needs. Educational institutions provide us with our knowledge of history, science, politics, and other important ideas.

Communication networks, such as radio, television, news, and the Internet, give us the information we need to make decisions about our lives. They have considerable control over how we understand issues. Audiences rarely get to see news that challenges corporate, economic powers. The institutions that control the media are themselves corporations who are dependent on still other corporations for advertising revenue.

Cultural institutions are an important means of shaping our understanding of the world. Painters and sculptors have long painted religious scenes, portraits of nobility and the wealthy. Operas and theatre glorify the achievements of great men to whom we should look for our salvation. In our time, the artistic community often appears to be liberal, even radical in their politics. Like the media, television and movies have been advocates of social change including civil rights, women's rights, and rights for lesbian, gay, bisexual, and transgendered persons. Marxists, however, would be skeptical of this support. Media corporations, radio, television, movies, and publishers are part of the corporate power structure.

Althusser (1989) included institutions like legal theory and scholarship, electoral politics, and even political parties and trade unions as ideological state apparatuses. These structures help to create the impression that the state is balanced, fair, and responsive to everyone's needs. This is a false consciousness: a vision of the world that does not line up with reality and which obscures reality, making it hard to see and harder to reform.

We need to keep in mind no hard dividing line exists between repressive state apparatuses and ideological apparatuses. Courts, for example, rely on legal scholarship and precedent to shape the law giving courts both ideological power and repressive power. The military fights wars and may suppress an insurrection, yet also trains millions of young men and women, indoctrinating certain values and beliefs about the nation and world.

The Postmodern Turn in Criticism

Marxist criticism is both rationalist and modernist in its outlook and scope. In this sense, criticism may be seen as part of the social scientific paradigm described in Chapter 3. Postmodernism is an important movement that some say breaks from Marxism, turning back to a Hegelian idealism, while others argue it is a logical and necessary extension of radical thought going beyond the narrow limitations of Marx's economic determinism. Postmodernism much more closely resembles the interpretive paradigm we talked about in Chapter 4.

What Happened?

The world has changed dramatically since the 19th century when Marx was writing. Marx's proletariat consisted of German men working in factories or on farms. Since the end of World War II, world-wide movements against colonialism and domestic struggles for civil rights by women, racial minorities, and by lesbian, gay, bisexual, and transgendered persons have radically changed the way we see and think about the world.

Marxism has declined in public acceptance. The rise of reformist movements and the post-war economic boom raised the standard of living for much of the working class in Europe, North America, and parts of Asia while at the same time the outsourcing of production has pushed many of the problems faced by the 19th century proletariat to the developing world. Because the inequities of capitalism may be harder to see, they are harder to challenge.

Finally, the rise of the world's first communist state, the Soviet Union, beginning with the Russian Revolution in 1917 had an important impact on the development of socialist thought. Led by Vladimir Lenin, the brand of communism pursued by Russians was called Bolshevism and favored a top-down approach to implementing socialism. Once in power, there was a strong impulse among radical movements around the world to support the Soviet Union and to model themselves on the Russian model. The Soviets furthered the **Russianization** of leftist movements by supporting Bolshevist movements at the expense of other leftist groups such as Trotskyists and anarchists.

After World War II, revelations about the crimes of the Soviet leader Stalin and repression of Marxist thought during the Cold War led many leftists to distance themselves from revolutionary politics. Marxists became just another political party, joining coalitions with other leftist parties in an effort to legitimize themselves. In the academic world, Marxists retreated to the realm of ideas rather than political reforms.

What is Postmodernism?

Postmodernism is notoriously difficult to understand, often marked by complex and sometimes mind-numbing language. Jean-François Lyotard (1993) defined postmodernism as "an incredulity towards metanarratives" (p. xxiv). Lyotard's definition, while a simplification of postmodern thought, highlights a primary assumption of postmodernity and what makes it different from traditional Marxist thought. Marxists understood ideology as a "false consciousness" or a screen between us and reality. For postmodernists, there is no definitive Reality or singular Truth, known as the **metanarrative**. Cloud (1994), a communication scholar, argued postmodernism is both idealist (treats ideas as the primary foundation for realities) and relativistic (with rejection of Truth in favor of a plurality of truths and perspectives). Eagleton (2003), a Marxist critic, defined postmodernism as a "movement of thought which rejects totalities, universal values, grand historical narratives, solid foundations to human existence and the possibility of objective knowledge" (p. 13). So if they don't believe and study reality, what *do* postmodernists believe and study?

Materiality of Discourse

Like Marxists, postmodernists are concerned with the material world but, unlike Marxists, they define it differently. For postmodernists, **discourse** (the totality of our language use) *is* material in three senses. First, discourse affects the material world. The way we talk about the world shapes our understanding of it and thus how people act in the world. When President George W. Bush spoke of an "axis of evil" during his 2002 State of the Union Address, it helped to convince many Americans that it was imperative we go to war in Iraq. Second, discourse is material because it serves the material interests of those in power. For example, as when advertisers use images and slogans to influence our purchasing or political practices. Finally, in its most radical form, discourse doesn't just influence the material world, it *is* material. Reality isn't just socially constructed but discursively constructed. All of our relationships, "economic, political, or ideological are symbolic in nature" (Cloud, 1994, p. 142).

Discourse as Performance

In rationalist thought, power has a center. For Marxists this center is the means of production. Postmodernists attempt, however, to **de-center** power. Power is not something one *has* but rather something one *does*. Power is discourse performed over and over again making it possible to do some things and not others. For Michel Foucault, arguably the most important postmodernist, knowledge as a product of discourse is always "controlled, selected, organised and redistributed according to a certain number of procedures, whose role is to avert its powers and its dangers, to cope with chance events, to evade its ponderous and awesome materiality" (1972, p. 216). Separating knowledge and power is impossible. The two are not the same—knowledge is not power and power is not knowledge—yet we always find them together. So to change the discourse, or what Foucault called the discursive formations, changes the structure of power.

Polysemy

Because there is no metanarrative, no truth that exists independently of a person's perspective, there is no singular truth for which we should be searching. Representations of discourse such as a conversation, movie, book, or speech are both **fragmentary** (always part of a larger whole) and **intertextual** (comprised of fragments of other texts). The implication is we cannot find just one truth but are surrounded by many truths and meanings, or what postmodernists call **polysemy**. The idea that communication scholars should look at the multiplicity of perspectives has had a significant impact on the field.

Identity

Unlike Marxists, who operate with a simple definition of identity based on class, postmodernists take a much broader view of identity. Like power, identity is not something we have or are born with but something we perform. Because power has no center, postmodernists view the **binary** (a two-part opposition) of bourgeoisie and proletariat or oppressor and oppressed as too simplistic. Because power has many formulations, oppression takes many forms and postmodernists have looked beyond the class struggle to consider questions of gender, sexuality, and race. Postmodern approaches to criticism thus recognize that the oppression faced by working-class white men is not the same as faced by Chicano laborers or African American lesbians. If the nature of their oppression is fundamentally different, it only makes sense to assume that the mode of their liberation must also be different.

Conclusion

In the introduction to their work on critical theory, Ingram and Simon-Ingram (1992) wrote:

> Unlike most contemporary theories of society, whose primary aim is to provide the best description and explanation of social phenomena, critical theories are chiefly concerned with evaluating the freedom, justice, and happiness of societies. In their concern with values, they show themselves more akin to moral philosophy than to predictive science.

(p. xx)

Marxism and postmodernism, while opposed on several key points, are best understood not as competing paradigms but as two different perspectives within the same overall paradigm. A whole range of thinkers fills the space between Marxism on one end of the spectrum and postmodernism on the other. What unites them is the commitment to using theory and research to bring an end to oppression in whatever form it takes and to maximize human freedom and happiness.

Summary

In this chapter we explained the critical/cultural paradigm, the third of the three research paradigms. This paradigm focuses on various issues, such as the place of power and ideology in society. While each of the three paradigms discussed in Part I of this textbook approach research differently, each shares very similar qualities. We will discuss some of those shared qualities in Part II of this textbook, "Research Design." The following chapter, Chapter 6, continues the introduction to research with a description of literature reviews.

Key Steps & Questions to Consider

1. Critical theorists are primarily concerned with power and especially with oppression, or the exercise of power.
2. A traditional understanding of power includes influence, coercive power, legitimate power, reward power, and persuasive power.
3. Hegel was concerned with the dialectic—the contradiction between an idea and its negation.
4. An analysis of self and others is now called critique (or spelled in the German form as "*Kritik*").
5. For Marx, labor is the central defining condition of being human.
6. A Marxist critique focuses on the system of relationships of production based on social and political classes.
7. The substructure, the superstructure, and influences by Repressive State Apparatus and Ideological State Apparatus are key components in the Marxist approach.
8. Postmodernism questions the role and function of a societal metanarrative.
9. Discourse is material within the postmodern perspective.
10. Discourse as performance focuses on power as something one does.
11. Polysemy means discourse is both fragmented and intertextual allowing for multiple truths, meanings, and realities.

 Activities

1. Divide the class into groups. Each group is given a different issue. The issues are slavery, prohibition, women's suffrage, same-sex marriage, and child sex abuse by priests.
   a. How would a Marxist understand the issue?
   b. How would a postmodernist understand the issue?
2. Bring the groups back together and share their insights.
   a. What commonalities emerged from the discussions?
   b. How were the situations different in both a Marxist and postmodern perspective?
   c. Hang on to your notes from this activity. The notes may come in handy in Chapter 20.

 Discussion Questions

1. What types of research questions do critical theorists ask?
2. How do critical methods of research differ from other methods you have studied in this book?
3. How does Marxist criticism differ from postmodern criticism? In what ways are they the same?

Key Terms

Base
Binary
Coercive power
Critique
De-center
Dehumanizes
De-skilling
Dialectic
Discourse
Fragmentary
Ideological
Ideological State
  Apparatus

Interpellation
Intertextual
Labor
Legitimate power
Means of production
Metanarrative
The Napoleonic Code
Oppression
Persuasive power
Polysemy
Postmodernism
Power

Relationships of
  production
Repressive State
  Apparatus
Reward power
Russianization
State
Substructure
Superstructure

6   LITERATURE REVIEW

Chapter Outline

- Reasons for a Literature Review
- Selecting Articles for a Literature Review
- Steps of Writing a Literature Review
- Writing Tips and APA Basics
- Key Steps & Questions to Consider
- Activities
- Discussion Questions
- Key Terms

What Will I Learn About Writing a Literature Review?

The picture shows a stack of journals and books next to a laptop computer. The image identifies the critical pieces of writing a literature review—the stacks of literature you will read and a computer for writing up your review (well, we suppose you could use a typewriter if you're "old school"). In this chapter you will learn about the process of writing a literature review. A literature review is a critical part of any research paper or article. The literature review provides the intellectual foundation for the communication phenomenon you are studying. You will want to spend time and energy preparing a strong and compelling review. The literature review is one of the first sections of a paper or article. The strength of the review can help set the tone for the scholarly potential for your entire study.

Why Your Study Needs a Literature Review

As you prepare for your research project, one of the first steps is conducting a literature review. The literature review lets you (and others when they read your paper or article) know what work has already been conducted in your area of interest. The literature review is where you demonstrate you've done your background reading and that you understand the issues, theories, connections, and results from related studies. The review identifies points of similarities and conflict between researchers.

Bourner (1996) provides a number of reasons why a literature review is an important part of your research project:

1. To identify gaps in the current research. Your study can help to fill the gaps.
2. To avoid repeating research already done by others (unless you're conducting a replication study).
3. To take the next step and extend research conducted by others.
4. To identify scholars researching in similar areas of interest. Knowing the "big names" can help you to develop a network of scholars as you continue to grow in the discipline.
5. To increase your breadth and depth of communication research. The more scholarship you read, the more research ideas will come to mind.
6. To recognize seminal/germinal studies in your areas of interest. Knowing the foundation article(s) is important to understand how the subject has developed and matured over time.
7. To provide context for your own research so you can see how your own ideas interrelate with the work of others.
8. To find methods helpful to your own research agenda.

Next, you will read about the process for selecting articles for your literature review.

Selecting Articles for Your Literature Review

One major conundrum facing students new to digging into the journals is selecting their key terms. Students are often tripped up when they key into too many terms or too specific terms. Searching for articles related to your communication issue of interest is a process of working back and forth between breadth and depth. **Breadth is** the expanse of issues; while **depth** is how far into the details you dig for your literature review. Think of finding material for your literature review as a standard dartboard. Each "pie" in the board is a potential subject, theory, or concept related to your study. Each ring is how close you can "strike" to the center of your study.

You should always start by trying to strike the center of the target. However, a relatively new area of scholarly interest will produce few articles for your literature review. Then you need to back-expand your search terms and move out a "ring" on your dartboard. For example, a student a few years ago was interested in investigating the persuasive strategies used by dating websites to attract and retain customers (e.g., eHarmony, match.com, Zoosk, ChristianMingle.com). The student could not find any articles that specifically focused on dating websites. The subject was too new or she had found an area that no one else had yet researched (very cool if you find a new area others have not yet explored!). She had to expand out a ring on her dartboard. The student found a number of studies about online dating. The studies provided one angle for her literature review. However, none of the online-dating studies intersected with persuasion. The online-dating studies were more interpersonal and relational than focusing on persuasion. She had to shift to a new "wedge of pie" on her target and find those articles that identified online persuasion strategies. She found articles related to textual, visual, and design elements that she included in her literature review. Since the student could not "dig deep" into articles and provide depth, she was compelled to broaden her scope and provide breadth in literature review.

Other times, depth is required. The more a communication issue has already been studied by others, the more articles you will find directly linked to the issue. For example, communication apprehension (CA) has been a hot topic for research for decades. James McCroskey has published extensively on CA starting with his seminal study in 1970. A search of the EBSCO database Communication and Mass Media Complete returned more than 4,000 peer-reviewed journal articles related to CA. Now, obviously you cannot discuss 4,000+ articles in a literature review (the paper would be hundreds—maybe thousands—of pages long). In such a situation, you need to dig deep and refine your search to better focus on the specific articles that best fit with your specific CA interests. For example, a student working on his senior thesis was interested in levels of CA among aviation majors. Pilots must converse with co-pilots, aircrew, ground crew and, most importantly, air traffic control. A pilot with moderate to high levels of CA could be problematic. However, trying to write a literature review with thousands of sources was well beyond the student's abilities (and the time constraints of the course). He talked over the issue with the student's instructor and focused his literature review on CA in professional settings, removing personal and educational studies from the mix. The student decided on a progressive-level study and administered the CA measurement instrument to all majors and minors in the aviation program. He found levels of CA increased as grade level increased. In other words, freshmen had the lowest overall CA score while seniors ranked the highest. He surmised the increased communication demands placed on student-pilots as they progressed through the program heightened their CA. He presented the study to the aviation program and encouraged the faculty to implement coursework specifically designed to enhance communication skills for student-pilots.

Keeping your dartboard in mind will help when the time comes to organize and write up your literature review. Each slice of the pie is a major section of your literature review. Each ring on the dartboard may help provide guidance for sub-sections in your review.

As you start to stack up possible sources for inclusion in your literature review, you will need some guidelines to make sure you are using quality sources. You will read various standards for making such decisions.

Different Types of Sources

A key lesson for all new communication scholars to learn is the difference between different types of sources. Learning how to distinguish between sources is critical; not all sources are created equal. Some sources have more credibility than others. **Scholarly sources** are the "gold standard" for a research article. The best scholarly sources have undergone a double-blind peer review process. Here's a quick explanation of how a **double-blind peer review** works. First, a researcher conducts a study and writes up the results. The researcher submits the paper to a journal. The editor of the journal receives the manuscript and removes the name of the researcher and any reference to the researcher (e.g., institutional affiliation). The editor will then send out the paper to members of the journal's editorial review board. The review board is composed of highly respected scholars in the specialized area of the journal. The review process is double-blind since the researcher does not know which members of the board will review the article and the board members do not know the name or school of the researcher. Only the journal editor knows all the information, and professional standards of conduct prohibit the editor from revealing information either way. Stephen and Dan are familiar with the double-blind review process from all angles. Both have submitted numerous manuscripts to journals for consideration, both are members of multiple review boards, and both have served as editors of national peer-reviewed journals.

The members of the board selected to read the manuscript write up their opinions about the strengths or weaknesses of the research. The members usually tag the article with one of four labels:

- **Accept As Is.** The highest mark indicating the article needs no changes and is ready for publication "as is."
- **Minor Revisions.** Indicates the article needs some revisions, but is a fairly strong piece of research.
- **Major Revisions.** Indicates the article has potential but needs significant overhaul before being ready for publication.
- **Rejected.** You can figure out what this indicates!

The editor will collect the opinions from the review board, appraise the reviewers' comments and labels, and make a final decision on what to do with the submission. A paper tagged with Minor Revisions or Major Revisions is considered a "**revise and resubmit**" and will be returned to the researcher. The researcher can then read the comments from the editor and review board and decide if they want to undertake the expected revisions. A resubmitted paper with Major Revisions may be returned to a researcher for a second time (and sometimes a third time) with additional requested revisions. The editor has final say when a paper is ready (if ever) for publication in the journal. The double-blind review process is designed to guarantee quality research is published in state, regional, national, and international journals.

Popular Press vs. Scholarly Sources

Chuck Dintrone (1991, March), a coordinator of bibliographic instruction (now retired) at San Diego State University, developed a convenient chart for determining if a source you find is intended for scholars or a general audience. The chart is very popular. You will find copies and references to Dintrone and the chart all over the Internet. While the chart was developed in 1991 at the beginning of the Internet age, the standards are still appropriate for differentiating between sources. We've adapted the chart for the 21st century.

	Popular Press	*Scholarly Sources*
Authors	Journalist; layperson. Sometimes author unknown. May be scholar but not in field covered	Expert; scholar. Author is a professor, professional, specialist, etc. in a field covered by the article
Notes	Few or no references or notes	Includes notes and/or references

Style	Journalistic, written for average reader	Written for experts, shows research
Editing	Reviewed by one or more persons employed by the magazine	Editorial board of outside scholars review articles before publishing
Audience	General public	Scholars or researchers in the field
Advertisements	Many, often in color	Few or none; if any, look for books, graduate programs, and other scholarly items
Look	Glossy, many pictures often in color	More sedate look, mostly print
Published	Usually weekly or monthly	Usually quarterly or yearly
Contents	Current events; general interest	More specialized; research topics
Indexes	Found in general periodical indexes (e.g., *Readers Guide*)	Found in subject-specialized indexes

Run an article, book, or online source you find through the chart. A scholarly source will not be determined by just meeting one or two criteria; nor do all standards have to be present. A source that meets a majority of the characteristics will likely qualify as a scholarly source worthy of inclusion in your literature review.

Your library will have access to journals and books in the communication discipline. The process of collecting materials for a literature review has changed considerably with the advent of the Internet. A significant amount of preparation for writing a literature review can now be done online using specialized journal databases. Most of the **databases** require a subscription or fee to access. Fortunately, most college and university libraries subscribe to many of the more popular research databases. The libraries have found they can provide more materials for students and faculty and can save space (since they don't need stacks of shelves to hold current and back issues of journals). For example, both Stephen's and Dan's home institutions subscribe to dozens of different databases spanning a wide range of disciplinary interests. A key component for a communication scholar is selecting the best databases to find articles related to your area of interest.

Popular Communication Databases

Subscription Online Databases and Resources

1. Communication & Mass Media Complete (EBSCO).
2. Sage Premier.
3. Academic Search Premier.

4. Dissertations & Theses (ProQuest).
5. ERIC (Education Resources Information Center) (limited access is free at www.eric.ed.gov).
6. Lexis/Nexis Academic Universe.

Free Online Databases and Resources

1. Online Index of Forensic Research (http://fmp.mnsu.edu/forensicindex/online_index.htm).
2. American Rhetoric (including Online Speech Bank) (www.american rhetoric.com).
3. Famous Speeches & Audio (History Channel) (www.history.com/speeches).
4. Silva Rhetoricae (http://humanities.byu.edu/rhetoric/silva.htm).
5. Voices of Democracy: The U.S. Oratory Project (http://voicesof democracy.umd.edu).
6. GoogleScholar.com.

Resources to Avoid

1. Wikipedia.com.
2. Google, Bing, Yahoo, Ask.com, duckduckgo (and other general search engines).

You can find a lot of interesting stuff online using a general search engine, including some worthwhile communication research resources. However, the amount of sifting you must do to find good stuff and the amount of time to determine which ones are worthwhile may prove more time consuming than beneficial. Instructors regularly see students cite web pages of questionable content and dubious quality. Check out www.malepregnancy.com and www.dhmo.org for two sites that exemplify why we must be careful about citing information from any web page. *Wikipedia* is, for example, a good background resource to learn about a subject. But we must be careful about citing *Wikipedia* since anyone can edit *Wikipedia* content. The *Colbert Report* has a classic episode highlighting the weaknesses of *Wikipedia*. Just do a Google search for "Colbert Report wikiality" and enjoy the show. Remember, you are developing your skills as communication scholars, so drawing on scholarly resources is a critical step in the process.

The final steps for preparing a literature review are the actual process of writing up the review. You will read about the options, basic scholarly writing standards, and the most common mistakes made in APA style.

Writing Your Literature Review

Literature reviews have two basic types—exhaustive and exemplary. An exhaustive literature review attempts to find and include *all* relevant material connected to the research. An exhaustive literature review is comprehensive and tends to be quite long, complicated, and complex. You will not see exhaustive literature reviews in most published scholarship. The length alone would cost too much to publish in journals. You will see exhaustive literature reviews (or at least attempts to be exhaustive) most frequently in master's theses and doctoral dissertations. A graduate student writing a thesis or dissertation must prove their mastery of published research through the development of exhaustive literature reviews. A review in a thesis or dissertation can frequently run for dozens of pages. The more common literature review for conference papers and published articles is an exemplary literature review. An **exemplary literature review** is a representative sample of the strongest and/or key studies related to your research. You draw from the articles that best represent and link to your study. An exemplary review, while shorter than an exhaustive review, still takes time and attention to develop.

You have a number of different choices for organizing your literature review. Each has different strengths and weaknesses. You should be sure to talk with your instructor about the organization of your literature review. Your instructor may prefer one approach over others.

Article-by-Article Approach

The **article-by-article approach** is basically a series of extended abstracts strung together one after the other. The approach is a good start for beginning scholars. The write-up for each article contains both descriptive and evaluative paragraphs on the source. Your purpose is to inform the reader of the relevance, accuracy, and quality of the source. You will want to provide an overview or summary of the source, the usefulness or relevance of the source to your selected research focus, and any conclusions, observations, and insights you reached. The approach is relatively quick and easy to write. However, your readers may struggle to see how the articles work together to support your research. Most of the burden of seeing the connections between the concepts and issues is left to the readers to piece together. While the approach is a good start for beginners or for a first draft of a literature review, the approach is rarely used by accomplished communication scholars.

Thematic Approach

A second approach is to identify key themes and concepts and let the themes guide the development of the literature review. A **thematic approach** is more complex and takes more time to develop. The thematic approach requires 1) finding stacks of articles related to your research; 2) reading the articles; 3) identifying the themes (key issues, concepts, and patterns) that permeate through the articles; and 4) organizing the themes into a coherent whole. You read earlier in this chapter about finding scholarly articles. Identifying the themes is a process that you will become better at over time as your scholarly skills develop. One of the best ways to develop your skills at thematic identification is by noting how the authors of the articles you read for your literature review identified and organized their own reviews. In other words, pay attention to how skilled researchers write up their literature reviews and mimic their approaches. After all, as the common expression notes, "imitation is the sincerest form of flattery." Your themes may be organized using many of the same patterns you learned in Public Speaking. You can arrange your themes topically, chronologically (useful for demonstrating the growth of a research issue over time), problem-solution, general-to-specific, specific-to-general, cause/effect (only useful if addressing causal factors), and comparison/contrast. Rather than go into detail here on how all these approaches work, just pull your Public Speaking textbook from your bookshelf for a quick review (because, of course, you keep your textbooks to develop your personal communication library).

A literature review has other factors connected to what you learned in Public Speaking. In fact, much of what you learned in Public Speaking has application in writing your literature review. Your review must have 1) an introduction that includes a thesis statement, significance about the research topic, and a primary preview; 2) a body organized around a recognizable pattern with main points and sub-points; 3) a conclusion that includes a restatement of the thesis, a primary summary, and a kicker to cap off the literature review. And just as you learned in Public Speaking, tie it all together with strong transitions.

Writing Tips

1. Be frugal with the use of quotations. Quotations only demonstrate the ability to retype what you read in an article or book. Quotations do not demonstrate comprehension. Quotations should be used when the original language is critical or so beautifully worded that paraphrasing would be "research sin."
2. Paraphrase, summarize, and synthesize. Putting the research you've read into your own words establishes that you understand the scholarship.
3. Organize, organize, organize your literature review. Nothing is more frustrating than not having an idea why you're reading what is on the page. So guide your reader through the literature review with clear and precise organization.
4. Edit and proofread. Then edit and proofread again. Good writing rarely occurs on the first draft. A good literature review that is well written requires editing and proofreading. Remember, you are putting your scholarship *bona fides* on display when you write a research paper so grammar, spelling, and punctuation *always* count.

Basics of APA Style

Writing a literature review requires familiarity with a research writing style. Many different research styles have been developed over the years including Chicago Style, Turabian, MLA (Modern Language Association), APA (American Psychological Association), APSA (American Political Science Association), and CSE (Council of Scientific Editors). This is just a small list of all the available scholarly writing styles available. The most common styles in communication studies are APA, MLA, and Chicago. However, the most dominant and the one we focus on here is APA. Your instructor or department may, however, require use of one of the other styles. Make sure to ask your teacher which style is preferred for your class.

Use of a style is critical to help everyone, author and readers, make the process of identifying resources easier for everyone. The entire *Publication Manual of the American Psychological Association* is hundreds of pages long so we take an exemplary approach and identify common issues we see in our own students' papers.

Tips for Using APA Style

1. Buy a copy of the APA manual and keep it for your entire time as a communication scholar. Having the resource available will save you significant time and frustration.
2. Keep your copy of the APA manual handy. Dan and Stephen have been researching for many years and they still keep their manuals in easy reach. Like we said, the manual is hundreds of pages long. You will, over time, memorize certain formatting requirements but other style and formatting issues arise that must be looked up on a regular basis.
3. Write your literature review in past tense ("Cronn-Mills (2012) argued . . .") or present perfect tense (Croucher (2012) has established . . .).
4. APA prefers active voice instead of passive voice in sentence construction.
5. People are always "who," never "that". "That" is for inanimate objects; "who" is for people.
6. APA requires you use the same typeface and font size for the entire paper, including the cover page. Do not demonstrate your inexperience with APA by filling your paper with different font styles and sizes. The most common font is 12-point Times New Roman.
7. Quotations (which you will use infrequently!) must include a source citation, date, and a page number (and look up in your APA manual what to do if you are citing an online source without page numbers). Make sure the period is *after* a closing citation.
8. A quotation longer than 40 words (which you will use infrequently!) is placed in a block format. The entire quotation is a new paragraph, indented 1/2", and no quotation marks start or end the quotation. End

with the source citation. The period in a block quotation comes *before* the citation.

9. Confusion when to use "e.g.," and "*et al.*"

    a. Use "e.g.," inside parentheses in place of "for example". The term is an abbreviation for the Latin phrase "*exempli gratia.*" If providing parts of an incomplete list then "e.g.," is appropriate. Using both "e.g." and "etc." in the same sentence is redundant. You can use "e.g.," at the beginning of a sentence or "etc." at the end of a sentence, but should not use both in the same sentence.

    b. Use "*et al.*" to indicate parts of a complete list. The term is a Latin abbreviation for "*et alia.*" You will see "*et al.*" used for in-text citations when a source has more than six authors or with the second in-text reference for 3–5 authors. The term implies the rest of the complete list.

10. Properly format numbers in the body of the paper. The general rule is numbers one through nine are spelled out, while numbers 10 and higher use digits.

11. APA only uses authors' last names with in-text citations and in the References.

12. When to use "and" or "&" with an in-text citation. If the citation is outside parentheses, use "and". For example, "Cronn-Mills and Croucher (2012) contended . . . ". If the citation is inside parentheses use "&." For example, "the study demonstrated strong CA tendencies (Croucher & Cronn-Mills, 2012)."

13. An online citation is more than just the Internet address. Make sure you have complete information and that the information is formatted accurately according to APA requirements.

14. APA has References; APA does *not* have Works Cited or a Bibliography.

15. References must have a 1/2" hanging indent with the citations arranged in alphabetical order.

Summary

In this chapter we discussed literature reviews. You may be asked to write a few literature reviews during your undergraduate career; so, it is always a good thing to have some basic knowledge of: what they are, how to select materials for one, and how to design one. This chapter also went over a few writing and APA tips. The next chapter begins the second section of the textbook. Chapter 7 explores various aspects of data.

 ## Key Steps & Questions to Consider

1. Have you used the "dartboard" metaphor to help guide the development of your literature review?

2. Are you selecting scholarly sources (e.g., journals, books, conference papers, websites)?

3. Are you avoiding sources that are part of the popular press?
4. Did you run your sources through the Dintrone chart?
5. Are you selecting appropriate databases, which specialize in or focus on communication studies?
6. Does your study (or class) need an exhaustive or exemplary literature review?
7. Are you challenging yourself to write a review with a thematic approach?
8. Did you edit and proofread your paper?
9. Now edit and proofread your paper again!
10. Double-check your paper for compliance with APA style.

 ## Activities

1. Select your favorite communication term (e.g., ethos, groupthink, message, feedback, argument, debate, interpersonal, nonverbal). Search the term in a search engine and in a scholarly database. Compare your results.
    a. How many "hits" meet Dintrone's requirements as a scholarly source?
    b. How much filtering and screening did you have to do before finding a quality source?

2. Take one of the scholarly articles from Activity 1 and check out the literature review.
    a. Does the review appear to be exhaustive or exemplary?
    b. Did the author(s) use an article-by-article or thematic approach?
    c. Did the article use APA or a different writing style?
    d. Challenge Task: Can you find any APA mistakes in the literature review?

3. Use a search engine to find the homepage for the *Journal of International and Intercultural Communication*. Dig around on the site until you find the manuscript submission guidelines.
    a. Does the journal use a double-blind peer review process?
    b. What style(s) does the journal accept for manuscript submissions?

 ## Discussion Questions

1. To which subscription databases does your school subscribe? Which of those databases are communication-specific or have communication-specific sections? (Hint: interviewing a reference librarian may prove helpful.)
2. What are the strengths or weaknesses between the article-by-article approach vs. the thematic approach?
3. What are the different ways you can organize the body of a literature review? What are the strengths or weaknesses of each approach? (Hint: use your Public Speaking text as a resource!)
4. Why is following a writing style (e.g., APA, MLA, Chicago) important when preparing a literature review?

Key Terms

Accept as is
Article-by-article
  approach
Breadth
Databases
Depth
Double-blind peer
  review

Exemplary literature
  review
Exhaustive literature
  review
Literature review
Major revisions
Minor revisions
Popular press

*Publication Manual of
  the American
  Psychological
  Association*
Rejected
Revise and resubmit
Scholarly sources
Thematic approach

PART II
RESEARCH DESIGN

7   DATA

What Will I Learn About Data in This Chapter?

Data are all around us. Data impact everything we do. In *The Matrix* trilogy, Neo and his compatriots battle evil machines and "agents" in a fight to protect and liberate humanity from the Matrix. We learn in the films that the Matrix is really nothing more than a simulated reality, a computer program created to control humanity. Neo, the one who has been pre-chosen to free humanity and end the Matrix, is one of the few people who can see the truth of the Matrix. The Matrix is a string of numbers, like the one above. It is a collection of numeric data, that when taken together tell us something about what they describe. In the case of the Matrix, the numbers Neo and his fellow freedom fighters saw were the Matrix formula. They saw the Matrix "talking." Data in Neo's world were all around him. Most technological things we do in life function with such matrices behind them: bank transactions, the Internet, phone calls, etc. . . . However, data do not have to just be numeric. Data can also include interview transcripts, observations, paintings, and song lyrics, just to name a few.

Data are an integral aspect of the research process. Without some kind of data, how can research take place? This question brings up other important questions. For example: 1) what are data, 2) how are data collected, 3) where do data take place, 4) and what are the different levels of data? We explore these questions, and others, in Chapter 7 in our discussion of data.

Sources of Data

When you conduct research you are going to collect and/or analyze some kind of data. **Data** are information that have been collected in a systematic manner. The information can be numeric (quantitative) or non-numeric (qualitative, critical, rhetorical). Most communication scholarship comes from one of four kinds of data: 1) texts, 2) observations and/or interviews, 3) self-reports, and/or 4) other-reports.

Texts are written, spoken, performed, or symbolic messages. The texts can be intentional or unintentional (like non-verbals we don't even know we do). If your interest is written texts, you can choose from a wide range of forms to use in your research project. We discuss in the method chapters later in the book how to analyze such texts. Written texts can be drawn from newspapers, magazines, books, diaries or journals, obituaries, emails, maps, photographs, poems, policy statements, chat room logs, bank account records, and the list goes on. Spoken texts include inaugural addresses, wedding toasts, concession speeches, acceptance speeches, and so forth. Performed texts can include music, stand-up comedy routines, performance art, a circus routine, mime, etc. Finally, symbolic messages are wide open and can include paintings and other kinds of art, architecture, fashion, jewelry, hair designs, landscaping, tattoo art, etc. If a "text" communicates a message, the "text" can be analyzed from a communicative perspective. The key is to find an effective theoretical and methodological perspective. Many texts are analyzed using methods such as content analysis, rhetorical criticism, or critical/cultural analysis, but other ways exist. For example, Lengel (2004) conducted a critical-ethnographic study of women in Tunisia. The study showed how women perform their femininity using music and dance as a way to empower themselves. We will talk more about critical research (Chapter 20) and ethnography (Chapter 10), as well as ways you can analyze texts in Part III of the book. Social scientific, interpretive, and critical scholars all analyze texts.

Observations represent data when you watch human behavior in action. Anthropology has a rich history of this kind of research. Anthropologists such as Margaret Mead (1901–1978) and Franz Boas (1858–1942) spent long periods of time observing groups of individuals. Occasionally, these researchers would break away from the observation of their participants and interact (conduct interviews) with them. Most of Mead's research involved studying the Samoan people, while Boas primarily researched Eskimos of the Canadian Artic and Native Americans in the Pacific. The primary purpose of their research was to watch human behavior in action. This is the main goal: to observe behavior (communication) in action. The data in an observational method are your field notes as you write down what you see occurring. What kind of communicative behavior do you see? What is happening? Why do you think such behaviors are happening? These kinds of questions, and many more discussed in Chapter 10 on ethnography, comprise observations as data.

Observing can be taken a step further when a researcher decides to interact with the participants by observing and interviewing. In this case, the interview questions become a second form of data that works in conjunction with the observation field notes. With developed interview questions related to the context, a researcher can delve deeper into the behaviors they are interested in studying. We talk more about interviewing in research in Chapter 11. A classic example of observation and interview used by *many* communication instructors is Philipsen's (1976) analysis of "Teamsterville," which is a certain area of Chicago. In the analysis, Philipsen discussed how he observed and interviewed participants in "Teamsterville" to understand the various places for certain kinds of talk. You will find many social scientists do not use observation and interview data due to their subjective nature. This type of data is generally preferred by interpretive and critical scholars.

A third type of data is self-report data. A **self-report** is when you ask individuals to report about their own behaviors. Typically, this kind of data is quantitative in nature, but may be qualitative. Quantitative self-reports are usually closed-ended surveys, such as "on a scale of 1–7, with 1 being *strongly agree,* and 7 being *strongly disagree,* please rate how much you agree with the following statements." You have all seen such questions on a survey before. Qualitative self-reports can include open-ended questions on a survey. For example, you may be asked to "Describe how you felt about Candidate X after watching the debate." The question is asking you to self-report on your feelings about Candidate X. Self-reports are often used in communication research (Oetzel, 1998). Self-report data collected in a survey form is a preferred approach for many social scientists. Some statistical problems can emerge, of course, when analyzing self-report data. For example, some scholars argue that people taking surveys tend to over- or under-estimate their behaviors. For example, Nicotera (1996) stated individuals are likely to under-estimate their true level of argumentativeness, and instead score themselves lower to be more socially desirable. Croucher, Kassing, and Diers-Lawson (2013) found a minor statistical difference between our self-reporting and how others report our level of dissent in organizations (less than people had thought). Thus, aside from a handful of studies suggesting people tend to over- and/or under-estimate their own behaviors, self-reports appear to be a reliable and valid form of measurement.

An other-report can be used in conjunction with self-reports to uncover how a communicative act affects a person, or to compare the results of a self-versus-other perception. **Other-reports** are when you ask individuals to report on the communicative behavior of another person. In conjunction with self-reports, other-reports can help verify a result. Imagine you are a marriage counselor working with a couple who have problems with jealousy.

You may decide to measure each person's self-report of jealousy and to get an other-report of jealousy. You can then combine the results to get a mean (average) score of jealousy for each partner in the relationship. A second option is to design a questionnaire asking each partner how the other person's behavior affects them. In this case you are measuring how the other person's behavior affects the receiver of the behavior. Third, you could give the wife a self-report of jealous behaviors, the husband (sexual intimate of the wife) an other-report of jealous behaviors the wife enacts, and a friend (non-sexual) of theirs an other-report of the wife's behaviors. Then compare the results to see if the wife over/under-estimates her behaviors compared with the other two. The third approach can be useful to see if people really do know their own behaviors, or how others perceive them (Croucher, Kassing, & Diers-Lawson, 2013; Spitzberg & Hecht, 1984).

Going back to *The Matrix*, you can analyze this film in many ways. Maiorani (2007), for example, analyzed the grammar and visual design of the promotional posters and showed how the posters promoted different kinds of messages based on the social impact of each film. Milford (2010) discussed how evangelical Christian audiences in the United States responded to the films. Milford described the allegory (rhetoric) surrounding the films. Frentz and Rushing (2002) critiqued the film as having a diluted narrative because of its use of special effects, which negate the influence of the feminine. In each example of published research, a different aspect of the film or materials surrounding it was analyzed.

Now that we have gone through the four basic kinds of data, the next section of Chapter 7 describes data sampling.

Data Sampling

Collecting and analyzing all the available evidence when conducting research is not always possible. Let's imagine, for example, you are interested in the relationship between the amount of self-disclosure and length of dating among college students in the United States. However, surveying every college student in the United States is *impossible*. U.S. college students are your **population,** or the group of cases or units from which you want to collect data. What you need to do is survey a **sample** of college students in the United States. Essentially, when we sample, we are analyzing a smaller group (sample) we have taken out of a larger group (population) in order to make claims about the larger group (the population). Remember that your sample population can provide a wide range of data: textual data, observations or interview data, self-report data, or other-report data. Many descriptions of samples and populations focus on self-report data, but other forms of data are available.

For social scientific (mainly quantitative) researchers, the purpose of sampling is to create an objective sample that best represents the population so one can make **generalizations** about the population from the sample. The generalizations are inferences about the behavior of the population one makes from studying the sample (usually statistical for a social scientist). For interpretive, critical, and rhetorical researchers, generalization is not an important issue to consider, as these scholars focus more on subjectivity (think back to Chapters 4 and 5).

Inferences (generalizations) are possible from a sample to a population because of the Central Limit Theorem. The **Central Limit Theorem** states the following. First, under normal conditions, data taken from larger samples will tend to be more normally distributed. Second, as more and more samples are taken from a population, you have a greater chance of having your sample represent the population. Third, random selection is the best way for a sample to represent the population. Fourth, if you are unable to get a random and/or a large sample you must ascertain the amount of error present in your sample. We will talk more about the Central Limit Theorem and it tenets in Chapter 9 on hypotheses and research questions. For now, it is important to note that the tenets behind the Central Limit Theorem provide mathematical laws for generalizing from a sample to a population.

We see a classic example of population and sampling every four years in election night polling. Many Americans are glued to their televisions and computers watching election results come in and waiting for states to be called for their local, state, and national candidates. Many students have asked how a network can call a state for a candidate before all of the votes are counted. The answer is simple—sampling. None of the networks has the entire voting population counted, but they have large enough samples counted to make a generalization (in this case a prediction) about who will win. These samples include the number of votes already counted, exit polls, and other forms of polling. Election night sampling is an intricate process, and does not always work. Think back to the 2000 election when Florida was called for Gore and then in the end went for Bush. Social scientists work hard to avoid the problems that occurred in the 2000 election in Florida.

Data sampling should be a systematic process, whether you are doing a quantitative or qualitative study. After you have chosen your topic of study and defined your data population, you need to consider whether better to use a random or non-random sampling procedure. **Random sampling** is when you choose data in a way that ensures everyone or everything that is part of your data has an equal chance of participation in your study. Random sampling increases your ability to generalize to the overall population. **Non-random sampling,** on the other hand, is when not everyone or everything that is part of your data has an equal chance of participation. Therefore, your ability to generalize to the population decreases. We argue random sampling (specifically simple random sampling) is virtually impossible in most cases. Here is an example of how one could do a random sample though.

> Let's say your university wants to find out if students on campus prefer Coke or Pepsi products. The university has access to the names and contact information of every registered student. A person from the university, let's say Institutional Research, could email every student's official email account with a survey. With this research project, every registered student has an equal chance of participating in this study of soda preference. It is extremely difficult to get access to such a list; such lists often do not exist for many populations, and some populations are just too large for a list. So, in many ways, simple random sampling is impractical, but still theoretically possible.

Researchers commonly use four kinds of non-random sampling procedures: convenience, snowball, purposive, and quota sampling. You may use non-random sampling for a number of reasons. A **convenience sample** is when your data is easily accessible. For example, many quantitative studies published in communication studies journals have been conducted using surveys of undergraduate communication majors. You may have, in fact, participated in such a research project for a professor on your campus. Data from convenience samples are easy to collect and generally fairly cheap. Unlike trying to collect random data, which we will talk about shortly, one generally does not need to pay for access to population databases. However, convenience samples have some disadvantages. First, convenience sampling is not random and tends to produce *relatively* non-generalizable results. Second, some researchers may pick specific people or data samples to further their research agenda. That is to say, they "cherry-pick" their data. Focusing only on college students as representative of the American population for example has received quite a bit of criticism, but college students are rather convenient research participants.

Snowball sampling is particularly relevant to interview data and is similar to convenience sampling. Snowballing can occur when the researcher meets with the first interviewee and the interviewee suggests a second participant. The second interviewee then recommends a third person, and so forth. The sample builds based on participant recommendations. Smith, Coffelt, Rives, and Sollitto (2012) used snowball sampling to interview 29 people in Western Kentucky regarding their sense-making (response) to a natural disaster, in this case a massive ice storm. Snowball samples generally start out of convenience, so the same advantages and disadvantages of convenience samples hold for snowball samples. An additional disadvantage can be lack of diversity in the final sample set. For instance, the group of recommended individuals may share common characteristics and lack diversity, thus not resembling the overall population (after all, each interviewee generally knows the person they are recommending as a participant).

Purposive sampling is when the focus of the study is specific groups at the exclusion of other groups. Let's say you are interested in studying the verbal aggressiveness of hockey players. You would only sample hockey players, and not other athletes, thus you exclude other kinds of athletes from your sampling. For example, Kluever Romo and Donovan-Kicken (2012) interviewed 20 vegetarians to uncover communicative dilemmas faced by vegetarians and ways these individuals discuss their lifestyle with others. By focusing solely on vegetarians as their target group, they purposefully excluded individuals who were not vegetarians. The authors located their interviewees using "an online posting on the listservs of two local vegetarian networking groups and through snowball sampling" (Kluever Romo & Donovan-Kicken, 2012, p. 409).

The final kind of non-random sampling is quota sampling. **Quota sampling** is where you, as the researcher, pre-determine categories and how much data you want in each category. You then collect just enough data to fill each category. In this kind of sampling you may decide that you only want to interview or survey 50 smokers about how self-disclosure takes place while smoking in a group. With this kind of study design you have already determined your group, smokers, and determined the number of smokers to survey, 50. McMahon, McAlaney, and Edgar (2007) used a quota sample to interview a set number of individuals in different age categories about their feelings on binge drinking.

Three kinds of random sampling methods are available: simple, systematic, and stratified. **Simple random sampling** is a procedure in which every case in a population has an equal chance of being included in the sample. For instance, say you are interested in securing a random sample of all registered voters in Miami-Dade County (you want to study how political opinions may influence the next election). The board has registered voter information on file, but they may be hesitant to provide the list to just anyone (we will talk about this practical aspect shortly). If you had the list, you could generate a representative sample population of registered voters in Miami-Dade County. You could then survey a sample of the voters about their presidential choice. Since you are working from the official list of registered voters, you have a simple random sample.

A systematic sample takes a simple random sample a step further. In **systematic sampling** you randomly choose a starting point in your data and then carefully include every nth data point. For example, imagine you are working with the voter list for Miami-Dade County. You start with the fifth name on the list and then mail a survey to every fourth person on the list. All research method texts say the same thing (including the method textbook you are reading right now): a systematic sample and a simple random sample are more than likely going to produce similar results.

In a **stratified sampling** strategy, you first identify mutually exclusive categories or groups. Mutually exclusive means an item can appear in only one category or group. Most professional athletes play in only one pro sport—they are mutually exclusive to the one sport (in fact, contracts for most pro athletes prohibit them from playing in multiple sports, professionally or recreationally).

However, many high school athletes play in multiple sports—they are *not* mutually exclusive.

Once you have identified your categories/groups, you divide your sample into the categories or groups, and then use random selection to select cases or units from each category or group. For voters in Miami-Dade County, you may want to compare men and women and how they will vote in the next presidential election (men and women are mutually exclusive since someone cannot be both a man and a woman at the same time). So, you divide the population into men and women and then randomly select men and women to receive your survey (you will need to decide if your selection process is simple random sampling or systematic sampling). The act of dividing between men and women stratifies your sample.

While random sampling is statistically preferred for generalizability (we talk more about generalizability later in this chapter and in Chapter 8), in many cases you may find it difficult to get a random sample. Getting a random sample may be problematic for the following reasons. First, random samples are expensive, which we have already talked about a little bit. Depending on the population or type of data you are interested in, the cost may be prohibitive for buying a list of individuals or other types of data. Second, negotiating with individuals or groups who may hold access to lists of populations can be time consuming, particularly when working with humans as your population. Third, sometimes a random sample may be theoretically and/or methodologically impossible. In much of Stephen's work he is interested in researching how Muslim immigrants adapt to a new culture, like France or Germany. The French and German governments do not have lists of *every* Muslim immigrant within their borders. Thus, a complete list for generating a random sample of Muslim immigrants in France or Germany is impossible. Fourth, for the interpretive and critical paradigms, generalizability is not of paramount concern. Thus, random sampling is not really an issue. Fifth, your research may adapt based on your findings. If you are conducting an interpretive or critical study, your findings may emerge as you conduct your work. In these cases random sampling may not work, as you need to be able to identify sources of data and be flexible to change. See Figure 7.1 for a description of the strengths and weaknesses of each of the random and non-random sampling methods.

In Maiorani's (2007) analysis of *The Matrix* movie posters, the author did not do a systematic analysis of all movie posters produced to advertise the film. Instead, Maiorani chose posters she thought were the most "important." In this case, her sample is a purposive sample of *The Matrix* movie posters. Hamming (2008) similarly conducted a purposive sample when she considered similarities between *The Matrix* and other films that were released in the 1990s on their depictions of masculinity, femininity, post-industrial society, and a reconnection with the natural world.

Sampling Method	Advantages	Disadvantages
Simple random	Most generalizeable of all methods.	Hard to do without full list of population. Can be expensive and time consuming.
Systematic random	Also generalizeable. Can be less time consuming and less expensive than simple random.	What starting point do you choose? Still need a list of the population. More expensive and time consuming than non-random methods.
Stratified random	Can be sure specific groups are included by selecting them from the population list. Don't forget, since it's random you have more generalizeability.	More complex random method. You must carefully define the groups. Still more expensive and time consuming than non-random methods.
Convenience	Inexpensive and easiest way to collect data in general.	Can often be very unrepresentative; not generalizeable to the population.
Snowball	Can more easily include members of groups not on lists or people who would not be easily accessible.	How do you know if the sample represents the population? This goes back to a lack of generalizeability.
Purposive	Can ensure balance of group sizes when many groups are included.	How do you know if the sample represents the population? This goes back to a lack of generalizeability. Research bias and subjectivity can also be issues.
Quota	Can ensure the selection of appropriate numbers of subjects with appropriate characteristics.	How do you know if the sample represents the population? Again, a lack of generalizeability.

Figure 7.1 Advantages and Disadvantages of Sampling Techniques

You now have an understanding of the different kinds of data you can collect, and the importance of considering the kinds of samples you can collect. The next section of this chapter briefly discusses the three main places where data collection can take place.

Data Collection Locations

Data collection will usually take place in one of three locations: an archive, the field, or the lab. Where data collection takes place depends on the type of data you are gathering. **Archival research** refers to conducting research in a variety of places including the Internet, a library, a physical archive (many historical archives are available around the world on a variety of subjects), a local town hall of records—basically any place records and documents are stored. The key with archival research is the action of going to a location where you can search for the texts you are interested in analyzing. In the Internet age, archival research has become easier in many ways, as much of our data (texts) are now online. However, Dan and Stephen encourage you, if you are interested in texts, to go to physical archives and dig into the physical documents. Such an endeavor can be a rewarding experience.

The **field** is where communication takes place. Field research means you go out and interview or observe people in their natural habitats. Lengel (2004) went out into the field and met with participants in their natural habitats to better learn about their communicative behaviors. In her study she met with various men and women to understand the construction of female and Muslim identity through music and dance. In doing such research, you take risks. Often, you will be out of your comfort zone as you are not in your own habitat. You will have to adapt to the environment you are in while conducting your research. Participants, particularly in interpretive and critical studies, are generally more comfortable participating in research when they are in the field, as they are on their own "turf." In much of the research conducted today, researchers conduct online surveys using programs like SurveyMonkey. Thus, researchers are able to send surveys and interview questions out to people via the web and social media. This is a kind of fieldwork that could be considered the "field." We will come back to research in the field in Chapter 10 (Ethnography) and 11 (Interviewing).

The **lab,** on the other hand, is when you, as the researcher, control the setting (environment) in which the study takes place. The lab in this case does not mean a place with science equipment. In lab situations, the research is typically conducted on a college campus, or in a room at a business or organization where the researcher can control access to the research room (lab), the physical set-up of the room, and any other elements they want. A lab setting is a chance for you as the researcher to control many aspects of the data collection setting, unlike the field, where you are at the whim of the environment. If any of you have participated in a study sponsored by your communication department that has taken place in your building, this is a lab setting. Such a setting is often used by social scientists collecting surveys (Chapters 15–17), and/or running experiments (Chapter 18), or conducting focus groups (Chapter 12).

> Most researchers studying *The Matrix* can easily find their data online (archival research). If a researcher wanted to expand their understanding of *The Matrix* and possibly look at how the film's depictions of violence relate to teens, the scholar could conduct a study using human subjects. Such a study would be best conducted in the lab with participants watching the films and then filling out surveys. A lot of research in media studies explores the relationship (or lack thereof) between violence in film and enacting violence in real life. Such a study could further that line of research.

Definitions and Levels of Measurement

So now that you have a grasp of the kinds of data you can use, how to sample data, and where to get your data, the next important question to consider is how to define some key terms in your study. The terms we use in our study are important. We need to make sure we are clear in how we define our terms to the reader. Specifically, one should take great care to ensure they have offered concise conceptual and operational definitions of what you want to study before analyzing the data. When you are doing a study you will need to provide a conceptual definition of the key terms you are studying or testing. **Conceptual definitions** are similar to dictionary definitions of a term. These definitions are based on previous research and used to create an agreed-upon definition for a concept that the author(s) uses in their study. For example, Zarrinabadi's (2012) study explored self-perceived communication competence (SPCC) in Iran. In the study, Zarrinabadi provided a review of literature that defined self-perceived communication competence with a variety of references. This conceptual definition of SPCC makes it clear to the reader exactly what Zarrinabadi is studying. Second, one must define to readers how one plans to measure or observe the concept. The purpose of collecting data is to observe, describe, evaluate, or critique a concept. Therefore, you must be clear in your operationalization—how you link your concepts to your method. **Operational definitions** are explanations of the methods, procedures, variables, and instruments you use to measure your concepts. These definitions are in essence the "rules" researchers give themselves for identifying, analyzing, or measuring concepts. Zarrinabadi (2012) conducted a quantitative analysis of SPCC using McCroskey and McCroskey's (1988) SPCC instrument. The instrument is a 12-item survey for measuring SPCC, with each item ranging from 0 (*completely incompetent*) to 100 (*competent*). The key is to be clear in your description of your procedures: What method did you use? Why did you use the chosen method? And, if it comes from another source, cite it. We talk more about how to select from various methods in Part III of this book.

The next few pages focus primarily on operationalization in the social sciences. Knowing these terms is important since they can be used in all research paradigms, appear in many journal articles and books, and are fundamental to your basic understanding of the research process. Variables can be measured on four levels: nominal, ordinal, interval, and ratio. Nominal and ordinal level measurements produce categorical-level data, which is something that social scientists, interpretivists, and critical scholars all use. Interval and ratio level measurements produce continuous data, which is *typically* only used by social scientists. We will now dig a little deeper into each type of measurement.

Nominal variables (or data) are the least precise, and the lowest level of measurement. Data are placed into separate mutually exclusive categories. A classic example of a nominal variable is biological sex (male or female). When an individual on a survey is asked to choose their biological sex, they are often given the choice of male or female. Nominal variables are mutually exclusive categories (categories that do not overlap). Basic demographic questions are nominal data.

Ordinal variables (or data) are rank ordered. Ordinal variables share the same characteristics as nominal variables plus the categories can be ranked in some way: highest/lowest, least/most, best/worse, etc. An example of ordinal data is giving movies stars. A movie can generally get 1 to 5 stars. What is the difference though between a movie that gets 3 and 4 stars and its overall quality? The problem with ordinal data is that we can't really measure the difference between the stars; we just know that a movie with 4 stars was ranked better by the critics than a movie that got 3 stars, but how much more did the critics really like it?

Interval variables (or data) identify a measureable difference between categories and ranks. While an ordinal scale of measurement (like a grading scale) dictates a difference between levels, the difference between 3 and 4 stars is not 100% clear. Critics set different standards for what is required to earn stars. Interval-level measurements allow us to tell the exact distance between data points. Social scientific research (including communication research) uses two main kinds of interval-level scales: Likert scales and semantic differential scales. Most of you have seen a Likert scale before. A **Likert scale** is a form of questioning where individuals are provided with a list of statements that range from "strongly disagree" to "strongly agree." See Figure 7.2 for a typical Likert scale. The example is part of the shortened Organizational Dissent Scale (ODS) (Kassing, 2000). The ODS is an interval scale measuring an individual's tendency to express dissent in an organization. Scales that have similar items such as "almost never true" to "almost always true" are technically considered Likert-like scales.

Instructions: this is a series of statements about how people express their concerns about work. There are no right or wrong answers. Some of the items may sound similar, but they pertain to slightly different issues. Please respond to all items. Considering how you express your concerns at work, indicate your degree of agreement with each statement by placing the appropriate number in the blank to the left of each item.

1 = strongly disagree

2 = disagree

3 = agree some and disagree some

4 = agree

5 = strongly agree

1. _____ I am hesitant to raise questions or contradictory opinions in my organization.

2. _____ I complain about things in my organization with other employees.

3. _____ I criticize inefficiency in this organization in front of everyone.

4. _____ I do not question management.

5. _____ I'm hesitant to question workplace policies.

6. _____ I join in when other employees complain about organizational changes.

Figure 7.2 Organizational Dissent Scale (Kassing, 2000), 18-Item Version
Note: we are only including the first six items as an example of a Likert scale.

A **semantic differential** indirectly measures thoughts, feelings, or perceptions people have about things using a list of polar opposite adjectives or adverbs. Research participants are asked to indicate their feelings by marking a space between one of the opposing adjectives or adverbs. See Figure 7.3 for a semantic differential scale. We will talk more about how to design and use these kinds of surveys in Chapter 15 on surveys. Palmgreen, Stephenson, Everett, Baseheart, and Francies (2002) provide an example of a semantic differential scale. The scale measures an individual's message sensation and response to messages (advertisements, etc.).

For now, there are two key things to understand. First, the scales tap distinct differences between the values. For example, when an individual circles 4 on a scale of 1–5, the researcher has a measureable difference between 1 to 2, 2 to 3, 3 to 4, and 4 to 5. We can do more advanced statistical analyses based on how participants respond to these kinds of scales. Second, interval

Instructions: we would like you to rate the PSA (ad, message) you just saw on the following scales. For example, on the first pair of adjectives if you thought the ad was very *unique*, give a "1." If you thought it was very *common*, give it a "7." If you thought it was somewhere in between, give it a 2, 3, 4, 5, 6.

1. Unique	1	2	3	4	5	6	7	Common
2. Powerful impact	1	2	3	4	5	6	7	Weak impact
3. Didn't give me goose bumps	1	2	3	4	5	6	7	Gave me goose bumps
4. Novel	1	2	3	4	5	6	7	Ordinary
5. Emotional	1	2	3	4	5	6	7	Unemotional
6. Boring	1	2	3	4	5	6	7	Exciting

Figure 7.3 Perceived Message Sensation Value (PMSV) Scale (Palmgreen et al., 2002), 17-Item Scale

Note: we have included the first six items of the scale only.

scales do not have an absolute zero or a complete absence of something. For example, a participant could not score a zero on an IQ test.

A **ratio** variable (data) does the same as an interval variable, except it has a zero point. The presence of a zero point makes it possible to declare relationships in terms of ratios or proportions. For example, you can have $0 in your bank account, you can have zero sexual partners, you may have visited zero overseas nations, or spent zero days in jail. A variable ratio must include a zero for participants to respond.

Researchers from various paradigms prefer to use different kinds of variables. Social scientists will use all the levels of variables. Interpretive and critical scholars will rarely use interval- and/or ratio-level variables, as these variables lend themselves to higher-level statistical analysis and thus to things like generalization. We will talk much more about this in Chapters 14–17.

Let's go back to our research question linking media violence and real violence. You could approach this study in lots of ways. First, you need to conceptualize your terms. How do you define "media"? What counts as "violence"? The questions may sound simple, but you need to make sure the reader is on the same page as you. Second, in order to operationalize the study, you must ask, "How are you going to measure the relationship between media violence and real violence?" Basically, what is your data? What variables are you going to use? Someone like Stephen, who is a social scientist, is inclined to use a survey measuring self-reports about the media and how people perceive its effects. In this kind of survey, Stephen would have demographic questions (nominal and maybe ordinal data), and then include a collection of interval and/or ratio scales to measure people's perceptions or beliefs about the relationship between media and real violence. Stephen would operationalize the constructs through a combination of levels of measurement.

Summary

In Chapter 7 we discussed the various aspects of "data." Data are information collected in a systematic manner. We described various sampling techniques. We also identified the different places from where you can collect data. The chapter also defined the different levels of measurement. It is imperative to know what "counts" as data, how they can be measured, and what is "good" data. This dialogue continues in Chapter 8 on "Evaluating Research."

 ## Key Steps & Questions to Consider

1. Data are information collected in a systematic manner.
2. Data can include texts, observations, interviews, self-reports, and other-reports.
3. Texts are written, spoken, performed, or symbolic messages.
4. Observations are when you watch human behavior in action.
5. A self-report is when you ask people to report about their own behaviors, while an other-report is when you ask someone to report about another person.
6. Data sampling is analyzing a sample we have taken out of a population to make claims about the population.
7. Generalizations are inferences about the behavior of the population one makes from studying the sample.
8. The four kinds of non-random sampling procedures commonly used by researchers are: convenience, snowball, purposive, and quota sampling.
9. The three kinds of random sampling methods are: simple, systematic, and stratified.
10. The three data collection locations are: an archive, the field, or the lab.
11. A conceptual definition is when we define our term as in a dictionary or scholarly way, while an operational definition is when we define how we are measuring our terms methodologically.
12. The four levels of measurement are: nominal, ordinal, interval, and ratio. Remember that nominal and ordinal focus on categories, while interval and ratio focus on continuous data.
13. Likert scales and semantic differential scales are commonly used to collect interval-level data.

Activities

1. One example we discussed in the chapter was grades (A, B, C, etc.). Develop a survey you can distribute to collect data to answer the research question, "How do students talk about grades?" or "How do faculty talk about grades?" Remember to determine the type of data, population samples, the data collection methods, levels of measurements, and scales you will use.

2. A number of free online survey tools are available. Try prepping your survey from Activity 1 into an online tool, such as SurveyMonkey, kwiksurveys.com, and Google Forms (just go to Google Docs and create a new form). Your instructor may know other survey tools or have a favorite!

3. Distribute your survey. Remember, you will need to follow the research protocols you set for population sampling! What insights can you infer from the data you collected?

 Discussion Questions

1. Visit the U.S. Census Bureau at www.census.gov/aboutus/surveys.html. The Bureau conducts demographic and economic surveys (you will find dozens of surveys across a wide variety of interest areas). Explore a number of the surveys and identify the type of data, population samples, the data collection methods, levels of measurements, and scales used.

2. The American Association of Retired Persons (AARP) also conducts extensive data collection. You can find the AARP surveys at www.aarp.org/research/surveys. Pick a few surveys and explore the same issues—the type of data, population samples, the data collection methods, levels of measurements, and scales. Can you identify any differences between the U.S. Census Bureau and AARP approaches to data collection and analysis?

Key Terms

Archival research	Nominal	Ratio
Central Limit Theorem	Non-random sampling	Sample
Conceptual definitions	Observations	Self-report
Convenience sample	Operational definitions	Semantic differential
Data	Ordinal	Simple random
Field	Other-reports	sampling
Generalizations	Population	Snowball sampling
Interval	Purposive sampling	Stratified sampling
Lab	Quota sampling	Systematic sampling
Likert scales	Random sampling	Texts

8 EVALUATING RESEARCH
Warrants

What Will I Learn About Evaluating Research?

We evaluate almost everything. On a trip back to the United States in 2013, Stephen was reading in an airline magazine that a nose trimmer was the most reliable and best ranked for your money by *Consumer Reports*. The claim may sound silly, but somebody evaluates almost every product, or at least we are told it is. Products sell better when the consumer thinks they are buying a reliable product. Advertisers are interested in getting stamps of approval for products, including airlines, companies, hospitals, universities or colleges, and other for-profits. Even entities like towns and cities like it when they get "stamps of approval" saying they are reliable and/or good at certain things.

What does it mean to be reliable? We address this question and many others in this chapter. Researchers strive for reliable methods and results; however, the definition of "reliable" differs considerably depending on a researcher's paradigm (social scientific, interpretive, and/or critical/cultural). Along with having reliable method and results, issues of validity enter the discussion for many researchers. You may be pondering the following questions: 1) what is reliability, 2) what is validity, 3) how do the two concepts relate to one another, and 4) how do the different paradigms approach these concepts? Some of the concepts we discuss in this chapter may sound familiar from previous chapters, but a little repetition can help solidify your understanding. We explore in Chapter 8 these questions and other aspects of evaluating research. We approach the questions under the umbrella of research warrants. Warrants are assurances of results. In the case of research, warrants allow scholars to state how their data or evidence reliably support their arguments or claims. In Chapter 8 you will learn about the different ways in which researchers evaluate or determine what is "good" research.

Warrants for Evaluating Social Scientific Research

You may remember from Chapter 3 on the social scientific paradigm that social scientists approach research from a rationalist approach, emphasizing things like empiricism and rationalism. When evaluating "good research," social scientists focus on the warrants of precision, power, parsimony, reliability, and validity. Some social scientists focus heavily on cause and effect, the idea being that X causes a change in Y. We will talk more about this relationship in Chapter 18 on experimental design.

Precision is how accurate you are at measuring your variables. When a measurement is precise, we know exactly what it is, and what it is not. People can agree on a precise measurement. For example, during the writing of this book Stephen and his spouse were taking a flight from Amsterdam to Hong Kong. The two discussed how long the flight was going to be. They measured the flight in number of hours (the flight was eleven hours long). Both understand how long an hour is mathematically. While both passengers were able to agree on how to measure the length of the flight, they disagreed as to the evaluation of how eleven hours would feel. One passenger is 5-foot 9-inches and the other is 6-foot 5-inches and is much more uncomfortable in an airplane. Thus, even though they can agree on a precise measurement of the length of the flight (hours), there was room for disagreement on how those eleven hours feel.

Power is a multi-faceted concept. Conceptual power is the notion that definitions are powerful when they provide broad or detailed insight about a concept instead of niche or specific detail about small concepts. Methodological power refers to how it is better for data selection procedures to be as representative of the population as possible, as such samples allow for more powerful generalizations.

Parsimony is the combination of power and precision. A goal of research for social scientists is to be as detailed as possible (cover a broad range of issues), in a succinct way. Researchers strive to use the most powerful and appropriate method(s) for a study. Often researchers may use a variety of advanced statistical analyses to answer research questions.

Reliability, particularly measurement reliability, is an essential warrant to claiming social scientific research is "good." Your instrument should perform the same way over time and is the essence of reliability; a measurement used in 2009 should perform the same way in 2012. Think of reliability like the clock on your cell phone (since many of you do not use watches any more). A reliable clock will tell you the precise time, while an unreliable one will tell you it's 4:02 p.m. when it's really 4:05 p.m. Which one do you want? We want the one that correctly tells time.

Unfortunately, our measurements are never 100% reliable in research. A little bit of error is always involved in our measuring of human behavior. We talk more about error in Chapter 9 on hypothesis testing. For now, we want to point out some important points about error. Measurement errors are called noise or threats to reliability. Three main causes are linked to measurement errors: 1) errors in data entry, 2) instrument confusion, and 3) random human differences. First, humans can make mistakes when entering surveys into a computer program. Stephen often has his research teams enter thousands of surveys into a computer program every year and a survey may be multiple pages long. After data entry, the team goes through and double checks to make sure they did not key in any incorrect numbers. If you consider they have entered more than a million numbers, it is likely they have entered some incorrect data. For example, instead of entering a 3, they may have keyed in a 4. The hope is they have limited the number of mistakes.

Second, as hard as researchers try, some surveys are not effective. Instructions may not be clear or questions are worded in ways that confuse or even irritate people. In these cases, the instrument itself can cause a threat to reliability.

Third, humans complete surveys. Human beings are not perfect; as such, their completion of surveys is not perfect. Stephen and his team have seen participants skip pages, resulting in incomplete surveys. People's moods can affect how they answer questions. Finally, some people will agree to answer questions yet when they do the survey they do not take it seriously, randomly answer questions, or put 3 (on a scale of 1 out of 5) for every response.

With a basic understanding of error and reliability, the next section defines four ways to determine measurement reliability: 1) intercoder reliability, 2) alternate forms, 3) test-retest, and 4) internal consistency. **Intercoder reliability** is a statistical analysis of how similar or different coders are in coding data. Neuendorf (2002) stated that intercoder reliability is a "necessary criterion for valid and useful research when human coding is employed" (p. 142). Various statistical measures are available to evaluate intercoder reliability: percent agreement (a basic measure), Cohen's kappa (κ), Spearman's *rho,* Pearson's correlation (*r*), and Krippendorf's *alpha.* For more information on these measures see Neuendorf (2002) or Popping (1988). In most cases, your reliabilities should be above .75.

Alternate forms is when you use two or more instruments to measure the same construct or trait. The objective is to determine the equivalence or similarity of the scores for the participants. For example, instead of giving a participant one measure of introversion (shyness), give them two measures of introversion. With two measures we can: 1) better understand the introversion of the participants, and 2) assert that the measures are reliable measures of the same construct if the results are similar on both tests.

The **test-retest** method for measuring reliability is where you give the same measure(s) to participants at multiple points in time. You are measuring the similarity and stability of results at different points in time. Significant changes in people's scores on a measure may indicate something has happened since the last time they answered the questions. Often communication traits like communication apprehension do not change much in our lives. While we may become more comfortable communicating, our basic level of apprehension does not decrease all that much. Thus, if you develop your own measure of apprehension and the scores change dramatically for participants from point 1 to point 2, you may have a problem with the scale. Think back to the basic definition of measurement reliability—an instrument should perform the same way over time. The test-retest method is a good way to establish measurement reliability.

The final way to establish reliability is through measuring internal consistency (sometimes called homogeneity). **Internal consistency** means the items in the measure have generally consistent responses from participants. If you look to Infante and Rancer's Argumentativeness Scale (1982) in Figure 8.1 you see 20 items. Ten of these items measure how likely someone is to approach arguments, while the other 10 measure likelihood to avoid an argument. The 10 approach items and the 10 avoid items are each answered similarly. Answering the questions in similar ways shows internal consistency.

Validity is the final key warrant for social scientists in evaluating what is "good" research. When using measures, such as surveys, social scientists are interested in the extent to which the test measures what is it supposed to measure (Mason & Bramble, 1989). This is **validity**. There are three kinds of validity: content, construct, and criterion-related validity.

Content validity is the degree to which a scale, measure, and/or instrument measures *all* aspects of a behavior, trait, or state (Schilling, Dixon, Knafl, Grey, Ives, & Lynn, 2007). For example, a researcher claims to have developed a measure of communication apprehension. However, the scale does not include any items regarding communication in interpersonal settings. The scale only includes communication in group, public, and meeting settings. While the scale will measure apprehension in a variety of settings, it will not adequately assess apprehension because it lacks measures of apprehension in interpersonal contexts. Thus, this particular scale is limited and has low content validity. To determine the level of content validity, a group of experts in the field (communication apprehension) should analyze the scale and determine whether its content is appropriate based on the communication apprehension body of literature.

The questions listed below are when you argue about controversial issues. Indicate how often each statement is true for you personally by placing the appropriate number in the blank to the left of each item based on the 5-point scale. Remember, consider each item in terms of arguing controversial issues.

Almost never true	Rarely true	Occasionally true	Often true	Almost always true
1	2	3	4	5

1. While in an argument, I worry the person I am arguing with will form a negative impression of me.
2. Arguing over controversial issues improves my intelligence.
3. I enjoy avoiding arguments.
4. I am energetic and enthusiastic when I argue.
5. Once I finish an argument I promise myself I will not get into another.
6. Arguing with a person creates more problems for me than it solves.
7. I have a pleasant, good feeling when I win a point in an argument.
8. When I finish arguing with someone I feel nervous and upset.
9. I enjoy a good argument over a controversial issue.
10. I get an unpleasant feeling when I realize I am about to get into an argument.
11. I enjoy defending my point of view on an issue.
12. I am happy when I keep an argument from happening.
13. I do not like to miss the opportunity to argue a controversial issue.
14. I prefer being with people who rarely disagree with me.
15. I consider an argument an exciting intellectual challenge.
16. I find myself unable to think of effective points during an argument.
17. I feel refreshed and satisfied after an argument on a controversial issue.
18. I have the ability to do well in an argument.
19. I try to avoid getting into arguments.
20. I feel excitement when I expect a conversation I am in is leading to an argument.

Figure 8.1 Infante and Rancer's (1982) Argumentativeness Scale

Construct validity is the second type of validity. Construct validity has two important parts. First, the construct (a trait, behavior, or communicative state) must be clearly understood and defined. Second, the usefulness in measuring the construct must be established. **Construct validity** focuses on the extent to which the scale, measure, and/or instrument measures the theoretical construct. Let's return to our example—does the scale "really" assess communication apprehension, or does it assess willingness to communicate? The two are similar yet very different concepts. As before, bringing in a group of experts in the field is helpful to help assess construct validity.

The third kind of validity is criterion-related validity. A measure, scale, or instrument has **criterion-related validity** when it demonstrates effectiveness in predicting indicators or criterion of a construct (trait, behavior, or trait). Concurrent and predictive are the two kinds of criterion-related validity. **Concurrent validity** is when test scores are obtained at the same time as the criterion measures. This kind of testing demonstrates that the test scores accurately measure an individual's state with regards to the criterion. For example, a self-report of communication apprehension (the test) would have concurrent validity if it could accurately measure the person's levels of apprehension (physical response and emotional response). **Predictive validity** is when the criterion is measured after the test. Career, aptitude tests, and even the SAT/ACT are helpful in determining how successful people will do in specific occupations or how well they will do in college or university. We can analyze the results people get on these tests and their "success" in their jobs or in college or university to see how valid these career, aptitude, SAT, or ACT tests were.

Warrants for Evaluating Interpretive Research

While social scientists focus on things like objectivity, parsimony, precision, reliability, and validity to determine whether research is "good" or not, interpretivists use very different warrants to evaluate what is "good" research. A fundamental difference between social scientific and interpretive research-ers is that social scientists strive for reliable samples that are generalizeable. Interpretive researchers do not; instead they study smaller samples that are, for a better word, in-depth analyses of how groups or case studies understand the world. For a simple and thorough set of evaluative criteria we recom-mend Tracy (2010). Tracy provided eight "big-tent" criteria for excellent qualitative research. We believe these criteria (warrants) are appropriate and provide a clear understanding of how interpretive researchers evaluate research. The eight warrants for interpretive research are 1) worthy topic, 2) rich rigor, 3) sincerity, 4) credibility, 5) resonance, 6) significant contribu-tion, 7) ethical, and 8) meaningful coherence.

First, the topic under investigation should be a **worthy topic.** The topic should be interesting, significant, timely, and relevant to the discipline or society. Some topics get their relevance and interest factors because they may reveal something new or show something that researchers have overlooked about a theory or society. Stephen had a student do her MA thesis on the portrayal of Asian musicians in European music magazines. The research showed how communication and music research has generally overlooked the portrayal of artists in the media and how the media shapes artist identity (Leppänen, 2013).

Second, steps must be taken to make sure the research is done appropriately. This is **rigor.** To determine rigor, ask yourself some of the following questions (Tracy, 2010): 1) am I using the most appropriate theory or theories? 2) did

I spend enough time in the field (if you collected data in the field)? 3) is my sample the right size, the right data? and 4) are my data collection and analysis techniques the correct ones for what I am doing? We talk about methodological rigor in our qualitative method chapters (Chapters 10–13).

The third warrant is sincerity. **Sincerity** is how genuine and vulnerable you are as a researcher. We all make mistakes when we do research, and we should share these mistakes when we do our write-up. Discussion of a study's limitations is imperative to being an open and transparent researcher. Tracy (2010) encourages researchers to openly share their own experiences with their research subjects. The back and forth dialogue between researcher and participant will create a more open research environment.

Fourth, you should take steps to establish credibility. **Credibility** is how dependable and trusting you are at conveying the realities expressed to you. You can establish credibility in various ways. We will discuss two ways: thick description and triangulation. When you spend time in the field, particularly if you are doing ethnography, you will learn things about people, groups, and cultures. Your job as the researcher is to convey the details of what you have seen to your readers in the most detailed manner possible. Geertz (1973) said that one way of explaining contextual meanings unique to a cultural group is by providing in-depth descriptions of members, activities, and symbols of the culture. An in-depth explanation is called a **thick description**. The richness of your description is important. A thick (rich) description will provide details to the readers of what you as the researcher experienced, which the readers were unable to experience first hand. **Triangulation** is another way to show credibility. Triangulation is where you use multiple data sets, various methods, various theories, or various researchers all to explore the same phenomenon. The basic idea is that results of a study using triangulation are more credible because the study approaches data collection from various points. Holmes and Watson use triangulation when working together to solve mysteries. They are more successful when combining their different approaches than when they work alone.

The fifth warrant is resonance. **Resonance** is where interpretive researchers use impactful cases or quotations to impact an audience. Tracy (2010) provided various ways in which resonance could be done, two of which we discuss here: transferability and aesthetic merit. **Transferability** is where readers are able to transfer the results of one study to another context in their life. Stephen has done research on Muslim immigrants in Europe and the United States (Croucher, 2008, 2009, 2009a; Croucher, Oommen, & Steele, 2009). One way to evaluate research is to see whether or not these findings resonate with readers' own experiences, particularly if they are immigrants themselves. If another immigrant, Muslim or not, can read the results and relate them to their own life, then the study has resonance. **Aesthetic merit** is where a piece of research is artistically and imaginatively written to the point of affecting the reader(s) (Tracy, 2010). Stephen had a professor at the University of Oklahoma, Sandra Ragan, who told him a good piece of research is one that reads like a short story. Research should tell an interesting story, one the reader wants to keep reading. This is the essence of aesthetic merit.

As with all research (social scientific, interpretive, critical), the work needs to be some kind of contribution to scholarship. Tracy (2010) outlined four kinds of contributions for an interpretive study: theoretical, heuristic, methodological, and/or practical. A study does not need to make each contribution, but needs to make at least one. Research makes a theoretical contribution when the study develops, builds on, critiques, or further explains theory. A study could develop a new theoretical line of thinking. For example, Philipsen's (1975) seminal piece on Teamsterville developed codes (theories) of talk based on in-depth ethnographic work. With heuristic contribution, a study piques the interest of readers and calls for further investigations into the same subject. Goffman's work on the presentation of self and interaction (1959, 1961) had significant heuristic merit as these works and others have inspired countless researchers to explore human encounters. Third, a study can make a methodological contribution. The study could propose a new method of inquiry, like an entirely new way of analyzing qualitative data (Hymes, 1962a), or it could merge various interpretive methods not used before (Conquergood, 1992). A methodological contribution can be made in various ways. The final kind of contribution a study can make is to have a practical or applied contribution. A lot of research in health communication, aside from being theoretical, has a very practical or applied side. Such research offers advice to medical practitioners on best practices for better health outcomes.

Seventh, the study should be conducted in an ethical manner. Look back to Chapter 2 on ethics and review the basic ethical procedures present in all research projects. No matter the paradigm, informed consent, doing no harm, avoiding deception, and guaranteeing privacy or confidentiality are essential to a "good" project. In the method section of many studies, you will likely read how the researchers worked to ensure such issues.

Eighth, the study should demonstrate coherence. Tracy (2010) defined **coherence** as how studies should "(a) achieve their stated purpose; (b) accomplish what they espouse to be about; (c) use methods and representation practices that partner well with espoused theories and paradigms; and (d) attentively interconnect literature reviewed with research foci, methods, and findings" (p. 848). Essentially, does a study do what it sets out to do and does it make sense? For example, if you are interested in exploring jealousy between sexual partners; you should make sure you are asking about "jealousy" and not about "lust," "love," or "passion." These are all very different concepts and you should be careful to be sure you are actually measuring or exploring what you say you are. Ultimately, a coherent study for interpretive scholars shows coherency for the audience through linking their methods with literature and argumentation.

All in all, interpretive researchers strive for high-quality research that can be understood by scholars. By following these eight "big tent" criteria offered by Tracy (2010), your interpretive findings can be better understood and evaluated by your readers.

Warrants for Evaluating Critical and Cultural Research

One of the key issues discussed in Chapter 5 on the critical and cultural paradigm is how the approach to research emphasizes subjectivity, ideology, critique, and power. Thus, when evaluating research written from this paradigm, some of the same warrants apply as the interpretive paradigm. Critical researchers are concerned with worthy topics, rich rigor, sincerity, credibility, resonance, significant contributions, ethics, and coherence. Some important differences exist, however, between the interpretive and the critical paradigms. As we pointed out earlier, critical research is more like a moral philosophy than a research paradigm in that its principal aim is not "to provide the best description and explanation of social phenomena" but "with evaluating the freedom, justice, and happiness of societies" (Ingram & Simon-Ingram, 1992, p. xx). Thus, unlike interpretivists who are not concerned about generalizability, critical theorists attempt to draw broader conclusions about their research.

Critical theorists are often skeptical of social scientific methods of research for a number of reasons. First, critical theorists contend that social science incorrectly believes that facts exist independently of one's perspective. For a Marxist, the issue is class while a postmodern theorist will include other aspects of a person such as race, gender, and sexuality. A critical theorist believes positivistic social scientists, because they attempt to detach research from the material conditions of both the researcher and the subjects of the research, contribute to the alienation of society. Second, because positivistic social science tends to look for regularities (e.g., cause and effect), they may produce a sense of fatalism in readers who believe these things are beyond control and thus not subject to change. Third, scientific approaches to research disempower people who come to believe their conditions are the result of immutable social laws. Finally, as critical theories have argued, social scientific research has been used to support "forms of social engineering that enhance the power of those at the top—industrialists, government bureaucrats, and managers—who seek more efficient methods of controlling those at the bottom" (Ingram & Simon-Ingram, 1992, p. xxviii).

At the same time, critical theorists are not satisfied with traditional interpretive approaches to research. While interpretivists acknowledge the perspective of the research and emphasize ethical treatment of research subjects, the interpretivists' emphasis on deep understanding rather than praxis is problematic, particularly for critical theorists influenced by Marx's materialism. An over-emphasis on subjectivity means that the interpretivist is not able to evaluate communication practices. This form of moral relativism, or the belief that all moral judgments are subjective, makes it impossible to engage in the call for change that is the essence of critical theory. If everyone has their own moral code, we have no basis from which we can call one person oppressed and the other an oppressor. The oppressor and the oppressed are moral equals; each acting on their own moral code.

Critical theorists are concerned with the emancipation of their research subjects and their readers. Accomplishing the task requires combining the objective, explanatory methods of social science in order to describe conditions with an "empathic understanding of the subjective attitudes and experiences of actual historical agents" (Ingram & Simon-Ingram, 1992, p. xxix).

The difficulty is knowing when to think like a social scientist, when to think like an interpretivist, and when to think like a critical theorist. The Ancient Greek poet Homer told the story of Odysseus, who at one point on his epic quest was forced to pilot his ship through a narrow strait with the sea monsters Scylla and Charybdis on either side. The strait was narrow and, in trying to avoid one monster, the ship and its crew would certainly end up in the clutches of the other. Thus, the expression "between Scylla and Charybdis" means you are caught between two almost impossible dangers. Critical theorists often feel they are between Scylla and Charybdis, always running the risk of being overly objective or being too subjective in their research. So how do we deal with this dilemma?

Reflexivity is the solution for critical theorists. Reflexivity begins with the idea that research must be accountable for itself. For example, a researcher could not conclude that no conclusions are valid. If no conclusion is valid, the conclusion "no conclusions are valid" is not valid. So some conclusions must be valid. This kind of self-contradiction is important to critical theorists who seek to reveal contradictions within systems of thought as a way of destabilizing oppressive ideologies.

Reflexivity goes further, however. Reflexivity is the practice of turning criticism back on itself. The critical research invites others to critique their own work. Critical theorists, while they hope the results of their work contribute to emancipation of oppressed persons, do not claim to have produced a final or definitive statement but rather a statement that is itself subject to criticism. Only by turning criticism back on itself, by critiquing the critic, can we be sure we have not been paralyzed by subjectivism or been trapped in an illusion of objectivity.

Historically, reflexivity has been productive in furthering the critical theorists' hopes for liberation. Women made lasting contributions to the feminist movement by critiquing Marxism. They identified Marxism's failure to recognize their unique place within the relations of production. Likewise, oppressed people of color critiqued Marx's colorblindness. While traditional research paradigms attempt to advance our understanding, critical theorists hope to emancipate themselves, their subjects, and their readers by treating emancipation as an ongoing process and not a finished work. Finally, in a peculiar paradox, critical theorists are mindful that their own work may obscure or contribute to other forms of oppression, which other researchers should strive to illuminate.

Summary

In this chapter, we discussed how each of the three research paradigms evaluate and determine what is "good" research. Evaluating research is a critical skill as it is important for us in our everyday lives to be able to determine "good" from "poor" research. In the next chapter, Chapter 9, we continue this discussion as we explore hypotheses and research questions.

 Key Steps & Questions to Consider

1. Precision is how accurate you are at measuring your variables.
2. Powerful conceptual definitions should provide broader or more detail about a concept. Methodological power refers to how it is better for data selection procedures to be as representative of the population as possible.
3. Parsimony is the combination of power and precision.
4. A key difference between social scientists and interpretivists is that social scientists want generalizeable samples. Interpretive researchers instead use smaller samples that are in-depth analyses of how groups or case studies understand the world.
5. Reliability is the requirement that a measurement perform the same way over time.
6. There are three main threats to reliability: 1) errors in data entry, 2) instrument confusion, and 3) random human differences.
7. There are four ways to determine measurement reliability: 1) intercoder reliability, 2) alternate forms, 3) test-retest, and 4) internal consistency.
8. The extent to which the test (measure, survey, or instrument for example) measures what it is supposed to measure is validity.
9. There are three kinds of validity: content, construct, and criterion-related validity.
10. The eight criteria for "good" interpretive research are: worthy topic, rich rigor, sincerity, credibility, resonance, significant contribution, ethical, and meaningful coherence.
11. Sincerity is how genuine and vulnerable you are as a researcher.
12. Credibility is how dependable and trusting you are at expressing the words or realities expressed to you. Two ways you can establish credibility are through thick description and triangulation.
13. Resonance is where interpretive researchers use impactful cases or quotations to impact an audience. Two ways to do this are with transferability and aesthetic merit.
14. A study must make a contribution. The four kinds of contributions are: theoretical, heuristic, methodological, and/or practical.

15. Critical theorists emphasize subjectivity, ideology, critique, power, and emancipation.

16. Critical theorists position themselves in opposition to many of the standards of social science including independent facts, regularities, and causality.

17. The solution for critical theorists is reflexivity in research.

 ## Activity

1. Divide the class into four groups. Each group will find popular-press articles on a different pop-culture event (e.g., a Heisman winner, an Academy Award Best Movie, the Healthiest City in America, a top-ranked university). Each group will read the articles and identify the warrants that support the reasoning for each decision.

 ## Discussion Question

Communication scholars need to be versed in the entire range of research paradigms and methods at their disposal. Yet scholars tend to gravitate and focus within one paradigm. List the warrants that "speak to you." Share your list with classmates and explain, as best as possible, what you hear as the warrants speak. Based on your list of warrants, what type of communication scholar might you become?

Key Terms

Aesthetic merit	Intercoder reliability	Sincerity
Alternate forms	Internal consistency	Test-retest
Coherence	Parsimony	Thick description
Concurrent validity	Power	Transferability
Construct validity	Precision	Triangulation
Content validity	Predictive validity	Validity
Credibility	Reliability	Worthy topic
Criterion-related validity	Resonance	
	Rigor	

9 HYPOTHESIS AND RESEARCH QUESTIONS

Chapter Outline

- Reasoning Behind Hypotheses and Research Questions
- When to Use What Kind of Hypothesis and/or Research Question
- How to Test Hypotheses and Research Questions
- Error in Testing
- Case Study Applying Principles from the Chapter
- Key Steps & Questions to Consider
- Activities
- Discussion Questions
- Key Terms

What Will I Learn About Hypothesis and Research Questions in This Chapter?

In the 2004 film *The Day After Tomorrow,* scientist Jack Hall (Dennis Quaid) discovers an ice sheet has broken off of Antarctica. After further investigation he hypothesizes the event, and others, are leading to a massive and catastrophic global climate shift. Essentially, he claims that based on the evidence he has the earth's climate is going to shift because of global warming. Hall and other scientists around the world collect various kinds of data to test this hypothesis, and prove it to be true. Unfortunately, they can do nothing about it. The earth's climate shifts and a new ice age begins, killing billions of people in the process. This film is one pop-culture example of how hypotheses are created and then tested, at least in the natural sciences. The process is virtually the same in the social sciences.

The development of and the testing of hypotheses and research questions is an important part of the research process. Hypotheses are basically statements about the relationships between variables, while research questions are questions about proposed relationships between variables. Data are then used to test hypotheses and research questions. To understand the nature of both, we need to know: 1) what are hypotheses and research questions, 2) what do they do, and 3) when do we know if our hypothesis or research question is "right" or not. We explore these questions and others in Chapter 9 in our discussion of hypotheses and research questions.

Types of Hypotheses and Research Questions

A research question is similar to a hypothesis in some ways. A **research question** is the focus of your study. It is what you are trying to answer when you do research on a topic of your interest. A research question is based in research, which shows some kind of relationship or difference between variables. Research questions can be written to explore processes, understand behavior, discover meaning, describe experiences, and report stories (Creswell, 2009). We will provide examples, don't worry.

A **hypothesis** is a testable statement that two or more concepts or ideas are related or differ in some way. We derive our hypotheses from theoretical propositions, which are statements based in research asserting the concepts or ideas are related. Hypotheses take these propositions a step further through empirical testing. The focus of the researcher is to test hypotheses through empirical testing. After empirically testing a hypothesis repeatedly, our confidence in our propositions increases. You will typically only see hypotheses in quantitative studies; rarely will you ever see them in qualitative or critical studies. Hypotheses can be divided into two separate kinds: null and research.

It is important for many social scientists to focus on confirming and disconfirming what we know. This means some researchers are interested in exploring the existence of no relationship or existence between variables. The **null hypothesis** states there is no relationship between variables, or there is no significant effect of an independent variable on a dependent variable. The null hypothesis exists for researchers so we can examine how different our findings are from the null. The null is what we compare our results to, so we can understand how "important" or significant our results are. For example, we may be interested in exploring the relationship between biological sex and college GPA. Thus, we propose a relationship between sex and college GPA. The null hypothesis in this case is:

H_0: There is no relationship between a student's sex (male or female) and college GPA.

Your null hypothesis is essentially saying there is no difference between male and female students' college GPA. A **research hypothesis** on the other hand is a hypothesis that proposes an independent variable has a significant effect on a dependent variable. A research hypothesis states that difference or relationship exists. Research hypotheses come in three main forms. The first form is a non-directional research hypothesis. A **non-directional hypothesis** states there is a difference or relationship, but does not state in which direction or magnitude. With this kind of hypothesis your job is to test the significance of the relationship/difference. Non-directional research questions work in the same way as non-directional hypotheses. For example you could propose:

H_1: There is a difference between the college GPAs of men and women.

An example of a non-directional research question could be:

RQ_1: Is there a difference between the college GPAs of men and women?

The main difference between the hypothesis and the research question is that if you were to pose the hypothesis you would have enough literature/research behind you to put forth the hypothesis so you are trying to *confirm* the difference present in previous research. With the research question you have read some research that *leads* you to think there may be a difference or relationship, but you are not sure. Therefore, you are exploring to see if there is a difference or relationship.

Craig and Wright (2012) in their study of relational development and Facebook hypothesized that: "attitude similarity will be predictive of social attraction for Facebook partners" (p. 122). With this hypothesis, the authors did not hypothesize "how" predictive attitude similarity would be for social attraction of people on Facebook, just that being more similar in attitude will predict social attraction to others on Facebook.

Craig and Wright (2012) also provided directional hypotheses in their research on relational development and Facebook. A **directional hypothesis** states there is a difference or relationship and does state the direction or magnitude (directional research questions work in the same way). Examples of directional hypotheses or research questions could be:

H_2: Female college students have higher college GPAs than male college students.

RQ_2: Will female college students have higher college GPAs than male college students?

Unlike non-directional hypotheses/research questions, directional hypotheses/research question posit the direction of difference. This is because there is more evidence for the researcher to put forth a statement of direction or magnitude of difference or relationship.

In the Craig and Wright (2012) study, the authors state, "Individuals who report high levels of social attraction should also report having greater breadth and depth of self-disclosure with their Facebook friends" (p. 122). In this hypothesis, high levels of social attraction are related to greater breadth and depth of social disclosure with Facebook friends; a direct relationship is posited, and it is one where all variables increase with one another. We will talk more shortly about why you would choose a directional or a non-directional hypothesis over the other, after we discuss the third kind of research hypothesis, causal.

A **causal hypothesis** is a research hypothesis that proposes a relationship between variables in which a cause–effect relationship is expressed. We will talk a lot more about cause and effect hypotheses and how it is *very* difficult to show a true cause and effect relationship without conducting a true experiment in Chapter 17. For the time being, one might propose:

H_3: The more education one has, the more money one will make in one's life.

RQ_3: Does educational level lead to increased monetary stability in life?

The purpose behind this hypothesis and research question is that increased education leads (causes) one to have increased economic stability, more money, when one gets older (the effect).

Chang (2012) hypothesized in a study of ambivalence (or the state of having simultaneous conflicting feelings about a thing or person) toward the mass media that: "strong arguments generate more favorable (a) ad attitudes and (b) brand attitudes than weak arguments only when individuals feel ambivalent toward the endorser" (p. 337). In this hypothesis, strong persuasive arguments (the cause) lead to more favorable attitudes toward ads and brands (the effect). A nice way to think about causal hypotheses is from a medical perspective. If you have ever taken a pill and received relief from it, think cause and effect. The effect is relief, which is caused by the medication entering your body and influencing various vital organs and internal processes.

> In Jack Hall's case, he hypothesized that a dramatic global climate shift would cause the world's temperatures to decrease, massive storms, rising ocean surfaces, and various other natural disasters. His research consisted of various cause–effect hypotheses.

What Kind of Hypothesis or Research Question to Use?

You may be asking yourself, when should I use a directional, non-directional, or causal hypothesis or research question? In research there are various kinds of hypotheses and research questions you can use. If you want to test if a difference or relationship exists between variables, you use a research hypothesis. When you want to test or explore for differences or a relationship, a research hypothesis or research question may be appropriate. These can be directional, non-directional, or causal. When you use a directional hypothesis based on previous research you already know, or at least you think you know, the direction of the relationship or difference between the variables. Thus, you are confirming the relationship or difference. With a directional research question you have almost enough evidence to pose a hypothesis but are being safe and posing a research question.

With a non-directional hypothesis, your hypothesis is still based on previous research, but your hypothesis is generally broader as you do not have enough information to make a specific prediction of the direction of the relationship/difference, or your purpose is to just confirm a difference or relationship between variables (Neuman, 2011; Ragin, 1994). Similarly, a non-directional research question is more exploratory in nature.

When you use a causal hypothesis or research question you have a significant amount of evidence to facilitate an argument for a cause and effect relationship between variables. With these kinds of statements you must take great care to make sure you have ruled out other variables that can influence your proposed relationship. For example, with H_3 and RQ_3, there are a significant number of other variables that could in fact *cause* the effect we are predicting. Think about it. We will come back to this in Chapter 17. Now that we have defined hypotheses and research questions, another important question to consider at this point is what makes a "good" hypothesis or research question. The next section discusses this important point.

Hypothesis and Research Question Characteristics

So, you may be asking yourself, "What makes a good hypothesis?" There are five essential elements to a "well-written" hypothesis.

Elements of a "Good" Hypothesis

1. Be a declarative sentence. This means a hypothesis should be a statement and not a question. For example, a hypothesis: "Is there a relationship between self-disclosure levels and shyness?" is not an effective hypothesis because it is a question and not a declarative statement. This is in fact a research question.
2. Posit an expected relationship between variables. The hypothesis: "There is a relationship between self-disclosure levels and shyness" posits an expected relationship.
3. A hypothesis is based on literature. This means that a hypothesis furthers previous research. In the research by Chang (2012) and

Craig and Wright (2012), both articles include in-depth reviews of literature that demonstrate relationships between various variables. The hypotheses were put forth to test these relationships.

4. Should not be too long; it should be succinct and to the point. You will find that most hypotheses are only one sentence in length. The Craig and Wright hypotheses are a great example of direct and to the point hypotheses.

5. Must be testable. An example of an un-testable hypothesis is: "God exists." Now our point with this statement is not to criticize faith, but to point out that this statement is not testable; one must accept belief in God on faith; you cannot test the existence of a supreme being. Therefore, this hypothesis just does not work. A testable hypothesis related to religion could be: "Individuals with higher self-professed faith are more likely to attend religious services more regularly." This is a declarative sentence, posits a relationship between variables, is based in literature, is not too long, and is testable.

So what about a good research question? There are five important elements to a "good" research question.

Elements to a "Good" Research Question

1. In the form of a question. This may seem obvious, yes, but sometimes it is nice to point out the obvious.

2. Tells the focus of your study. While many research questions include asking about some relationships or differences between variables, this is not always the case. Exploring relationships between variables and differences between variables is a very social scientific way to look at research questions. Interpretivists and critical scholars use research! For an interpretive scholar like Toyosaki (2004) exploring Japanese accounts of American culture, a research question may be something like: "How do Japanese international students understand US American communication?" (p. 161). A more social scientific take on a research question comes from Nan and Zhao (2012) in their study of self-affirmation and anti-smoking messages: "will the effect of self-affirmation on reducing negative responses to anti-smoking messages be more pronounced among low-reactant smokers compared to nonsmokers and high-reactant smokers?" (p. 487).

3. Is based on literature. The Toyosaki (2004) and the Nan and Zhao (2012) pieces both included extensive reviews of literature that led them to pose their research questions.

4. Not too long. The Toyosaki research question is a great example of a succinct question. Two other examples are provided by Eguchi and Starosta (2012): *"RQ1:* Are we the model minority? *RQ2:* Should we perform as if we are the model minority?" (p. 92). Based on their review of literature related to the model minority image among Asian American professional men, the authors present two direct and simple questions that guide them to an in-depth analysis.

5. Must be something you can research. A bad research question would be: "What is the true meaning of life?" How do you plan on researching that? You could ask: "What do college students believe to be the meaning of life?" Focusing your research on a group and uncovering their meanings of life has made the focus of the study on this group and their interpretations of life, instead of some abstract idea that is impossible to uncover. We will discuss in Chapters 10–20 various methods you can use to answer this question and many others in your research.

Testing

Developing a research idea is the first step in the research process. This idea will lead you to collecting research, which will help you write your literature review (step two). The culmination of your literature review will be one, multiple, or a combination of hypotheses or research questions (step three). Next, you will need to conduct your research project (step four). In Chapters 10–20 we describe various methods you can use to collect data, analyze data, and report data. Each of these methods offers a way for you to test hypotheses or explore research questions and we offer in-depth discussions of how each of these methods will help you in your research. The fifth and sixth steps (which we will talk about shortly) apply only to the social scientific paradigm: you must consider the amount of error involved in your study and decide whether your results are significant or not, which determines whether you accept or reject your hypothesis. We will now talk about error and significance. The seventh step is to write up your results and conclusions; a discussion of how to do this is included in each of the method chapters (10–20).

Error

Two assumptions underlying hypothesis testing and the social scientific paradigm are the Central Limit Theorem and the bell curve. As discussed in Chapter 7 on data, the Central Limit Theorem asserts: 1) that under normal situations data taken from larger samples will tend to be more normally distributed, 2) as more and more samples are taken from a population you have a greater chance that your sample represents the population, 3) random selection is the most preferred selection procedure, and 4) if you can't get a random sample you must estimate the amount of error present in your sample. There are two very important elements to the Central Limit Theorem that we need to discuss at this point. The first is the normal distribution principle.

Statistical distributions can be symmetrical or asymmetrical. An asymmetrical distribution is one that is skewed in some way, meaning the majority of scores are shifted either to the right or the left of the distribution's center. A symmetrical distribution is one in which there is a single peak in the distribution at the mean, called a **bell curve.** In a bell curve, the dispersion of scores is relatively stable. Figure 9.1 depicts how scores are distributed within a normal distribution. Under such a distribution, 68 percent of all scores will fall within +/– 1 standard deviation of the mean, 95 percent will fall within +/– 2 standard deviations of the mean, and 99 percent will fall within +/– 3 standard deviations of the mean. Based on this distribution rule we can test hypotheses and determine scores that are inside or outside of the normal distribution. Such tests of normality will prove to be an important part of inferential statistics, which we will talk about later in the book.

Based on the Central Limit Theorem, the larger your sample and/or the more samples you collect, the more likely you are to have a normal distribution. Normal distributions are likely to occur when a fundamentally random process is at work, but most real-life variables are not random. For example, measures of marital satisfaction are not only non-random but generally have

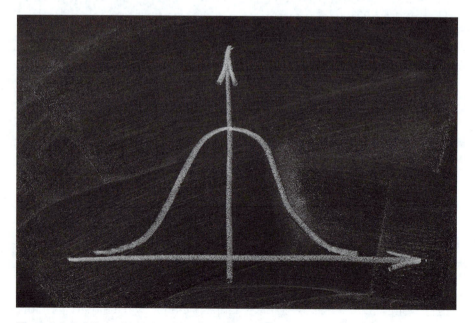

Figure 9.1 Bell Curve Depicting Scores Distributed Within a Normal Distribution

negative skew, because most married couples report very high satisfaction. It is because real-life distributions are not normal in theory that we need to test hypotheses and research questions. In every distribution you will also have an amount of **error,** or the degree to which a sample differs from the population. It is important to consider error as it helps us determine the outcome of our hypothesis or research question testing. Let's examine the following case study to better understand error and probability level.

Case Study

Stephen is mainly a cross-cultural researcher. This means most of his research compares phenomena in different cultures. One of the regions he is paying particular interest to is Finland. Not only does he live there, but also little research has examined Finnish communication traits. In 2012 he and his research team collected data on how Finns approach conflict situations in organizational situations, specifically on the conflict styles (avoiding, compromising, dominating, integrating, and obliging) they take in conflict situations. The surveys were distributed online; a total of 244 people completed the surveys. The average age of the participants was 31.99 years old (SD = 10.46 years). The research team based their definition of conflict styles on work by Oetzel (1998), who defined conflict style as "the general pattern or behavioral orientation an individual takes toward conflict" (p. 133). They used a survey in English and then translated it into Finnish. The survey included demographic questions and various scales to measure conflict styles and other communication traits.

SD = standard deviation. The standard deviation is the average distance between a score (measurement) and the mean. The standard deviation can be negative and or positive. Larger standard deviations (ignoring the sign) represent more variability in the distribution, while smaller standard deviations represent less variability. We discuss standard deviations at greater length in Chapter 16. At this point in time it is interesting to note that this study had a relatively large SD for age, 10.46 years.

Based on previous research (Cai, Wilson, & Drake, 2000; Carbaugh, 1995; Croucher, 2011; Lehtonen & Sajavaara, 1985; Sallinen-Kuparinen, Asikainen, Gerlander, Kukkola, & Sihto, 1987; Siira, Rogan, & Hall, 2004), the authors found that researchers classified Finland as a collectivistic society. Some of the research argued that Finns would more prefer the avoiding conflict style, while some of the research said Finns would in fact prefer to control conflict situations (dominating). Moreover, all previous research on Finnish conflict style preference was conducted on college students. A null hypothesis to help frame this research on conflict styles in Finland could have been:

H_0: There is no difference in conflict style preference among Finns.

The research team believed there was difference based on the research evidence and on their lived experiences in Finland. Thus, as there was division as to whether Finns prefer the avoiding or the dominating conflict style in organizations, the group decided it was best to develop research questions, which formed the purpose of the project:

RQ_4: What is the overall conflict style orientation of Finns?

RQ_5: To what extent do an individual's age and sex predict his or her conflict style orientation?

The only hypothesis the researchers proposed was one based on the relationship between conflict styles and educational level. The research team knew from reading previous research that there is a relationship between conflict style preference and level of education. Previous research has shown that educational level predicts each of the five conflict styles differently (Croucher, 2011; Schaubhut, 2007). So they posed the following non-directional hypothesis:

H_4: Educational level will predict conflict style preference.

If we look to this research, 244 people are nowhere near the population of Finland! The research team took a sample of the Finnish population. Stephen and his team have to be careful of two key things when interpreting their results: error and significance interpretation. To answer just one of the questions in this study for now (RQ_4), we will come back to the other ones later. The research team found Finns prefer the avoiding ($M = 6.22$; $SD = 1.74$) conflict style the most, and least prefer the dominating conflict style ($M = 4.04$; $SD = 1.09$), $F (2.23, 540.15) = 181.75$, $p < .0001$. These results represent the means for these samples. You may notice a few statistical terms you are not familiar with yet. That is alright; we'll explain one to you now. After the standard deviations we have included p, which signifies the alpha significance level. When the research team examined conflict styles among Finns, they ran their results in SPSS, a statistical program we will talk much more about in Chapters 15–17, and got their results. However, how do we know if the results are statistically significant? We just said that: Finns prefer the avoiding ($M = 6.22$; $SD = 1.74$) conflict style the most, and least prefer the dominating conflict style ($M = 4.04$; $SD = 1.09$), $F (2.23, 540.15) = 181.75$, $p < .0001$. While the avoiding style ($M = 6.22$) has a higher mean than the dominating style ($M = 4.04$), this does not mean Finns prefer dominating more, statistically speaking. That tells the researchers there is a statistical difference, $p < .0001$, or probability level (p).

When conducting statistical research you must be certain your results are statistically significant before claiming you have found something. Most researchers in the natural sciences and the social sciences rely on the 95 percent rule, or **confidence interval** as a minimum standard. This means researchers expect their results to be accurate 95 percent of the time, and allow at the most 5 percent inaccuracy. Inaccuracy in results can be attributed to various things (which we talk more about in Chapters 15–18) such as sampling errors, how people answer questions on a survey, researcher bias, alternative variables, etc. . . . Ultimately, you as the researcher want to be as sure as possible that the results you get are not by chance, and the data in your sample actually represent the relationship or difference between the variables in the population.

Think of it this way: a pharmaceutical company is conducting a clinical trial of a new drug (let's call it Pain Drug X). They are conducting this clinical trial on a sample of volunteers, which is how most clinical trials take place. They set a 95 percent confidence rate ($p < .05$), and find the drug has adverse effects on 5 in 100 people. This is not a very good rate if you consider that 1 million people could take the drug, meaning 50,000 people could be hurt by it. So, what many companies do is raise the confidence interval/rate to 99.9 percent ($p < .001$). In this case, the company will keep working on the drug until only 1 in every 10,000 could possibly be hurt by the drug.

The probability level simply helps us determine if our results are statistically significant or not. As statistics are related to a sample, the significance of our results tells us how confident we can be that those results really do represent the population. Figure 9.2 includes some tips to help you determine if a statistical finding is statistically significant.

In the case of the conflict styles study in Finland, the research team's p was rather significant, $p \leq .0001$, and the errors for both conflict styles were

---

$p \geq .05$, there is more than a 5 percent chance that the null hypothesis is true; there is not a significant statistical finding. We are *not* sure there is something going on.

$p \leq .05$, there is less than a 5 percent chance that the null hypothesis is true; there is a significant statistical finding. We are 95 percent sure there is something going on.

$p \leq .01$, there is less than a 1 percent chance that the null hypothesis is true; there is a significant statistical finding. We are 99 percent sure there is something going on.

$p \leq .001$, there is a less than .1 percent chance that the null hypothesis is true; there is a significant statistical finding. We are 99.9 percent sure that there is something going on.

Figure 9.2 Alpha Significance Levels

very low. The probability level represents the research group being 99.99 percent sure the results found in their sample would be found in the population. In fact, due to this high confidence interval the researchers could confidently say there is a statistical difference between Finns' preference of the dominating and the avoiding conflict styles.

With this statistical result in mind, the research team *rejects* their null hypothesis, which they used to guide their research but did not include in their research project. The null hypothesis H_0 for this project was: "There is no difference in conflict style difference among Finns." The statistical finding clearly reveals a difference, so "There is a difference in conflict style preference among Finns." If you conduct research and the results are not significant, $p \geq .05$, then you must *accept* the null because your results are not significant and you have not shown a statistically significant difference or relationship.

To summarize, here are a few key points about hypothesis testing. Data from a sample will never perfectly reflect what is really the case in the population from which it comes. For that reason, we cannot be sure whether what appears to be a hypothesized difference or relationship in one's sample truly reflects a difference or relationship in the real world. But statistical analysis allows us to estimate the odds that this is the case. Here is how it all works. First, we start by assuming the null hypothesis, that there is no difference or relationship. Second, we use statistics that allow us to estimate the likelihood of any difference or relationship in the sample data. Third, if the odds that there is really no difference or relationship in the real world are high, we cannot trust that our research hypothesis is supported; it is too likely that there is no difference or relationship in the real world despite what our data look like, so the null hypothesis is supported. If the odds are low, then we do not trust that a difference or relationship exists in the real world, so we support the research hypothesis, by rejecting the null.

In *The Day After Tomorrow*, Jack Hall hypothesized the world would end because of a dramatic climate shift. Through meticulous data collection and analysis he was able to confirm his hypotheses, which unfortunately in this case meant the world as we knew it was going to end. Thankfully for us the film was not based on real events. Yet the art of hypothesis creation and testing is something natural that social scientists do every day to expand our understanding of the world around us.

Summary

This chapter was devoted to hypotheses and research questions: what they are, when to use them, what makes a "good" hypothesis and/or research question, and what is the role of error in testing. We see and use hypotheses and research questions all the time, so it's important to know how to use them properly. The following chapters, Chapters 10–20, provide how-to-guides for various research methods. Chapter 10 is a how-to-guide for ethnographic research.

Key Steps & Questions to Consider

1. A hypothesis or research question is the focus of your study; it is what you are trying to answer or explore.
2. Hypotheses are testable statements that two or more concepts or ideas are related or differ.
3. The null hypothesis states that there is no difference or relationship between variables.
4. A non-directional hypothesis states that there is a difference or relationship, but it does not state the direction or magnitude of the difference or relationship.
5. A directional hypothesis states that there is a difference or relationship, and it states the direction or magnitude of the difference/relationship.
6. A causal hypothesis identifies how at least one variable causes a change in at least one other variable. It is extremely difficult to show cause and effect as you must make sure the effect is caused by your variable of interest and not other variables. We talk more about this in the experiments chapter.
7. Hypotheses should: be declarative statements, state expected relationships, be based on research, succinct, and testable.
8. Research questions should: be questions, tell the focus on your research, be based on research, succinct, and testable.
9. The Central Limit Theorem is essential to testing hypotheses and exploring research questions because it helps us understand the normal distributions (bell curve) and standard error, which aid us in understanding how similar our similar sample is to the population.
10. The minimum threshold for statistical significance is $p \leq .05$. This means we are 95 percent sure our results are not by chance.

Activities

Scan through a recent copy of a newspaper. Select an article dealing with communication in some form. Articles dealing with politics or sports are good options. Break the class into groups and have each group:

1. Develop a research question, which helps to shape a potential research project.
2. Turn the research question into a null hypothesis.
3. Turn your null hypothesis into a non-directional hypothesis. (Assume you have sufficient evidence to support the hypothesis.)
4. Turn the non-directional hypothesis into a directional hypothesis. (Assume you have compelling evidence to support the hypothesis.)

5. Turn the directional hypothesis into a causal hypothesis.
6. Use the standards in the chapter for a "good research question" and a "good hypothesis," and critique the research questions and hypotheses from the different groups. Notice how the same article (communication issue) can generate multiple different research directions!

 Discussion Questions

1. How does the decision to use a research question or one of the hypothesis forms change the nature of a communication research project?
2. How will the selection of a specific confidence interval change what you can say about your results?
3. What steps can we take to control for error in a communication research project?

Key Terms

Bell curve

Causal hypothesis

Confidence interval

Directional hypothesis
  error

Hypothesis

Non-directional
  hypothesis

Null hypothesis

Research hypothesis

Research question

PART III

RESEARCH METHODS

10 ETHNOGRAPHY

What Will I Learn About Ethnography?

This is a photo of the outside of a typical Finnish sauna.[1] The sauna is located in Jyväskylä, Finland. Saunas are an integral part of Finnish culture, and a place to socialize as a family, do business, and relax. Saunas date back hundreds of years in Finland. In a nation with roughly 5 million people, there are more than 2 million saunas, going to show just how significant the sauna is to the Finnish people. When Stephen first moved to Finland, he had to learn very quickly about Finnish sauna culture. He had to culturally adapt to this one element of Finnish life. Other scholars have commented on the need to understand and adapt to Finnish sauna life. Edelsward (1991) described how the sauna is an important part of becoming Finnish, learning about Finnish culture, and being accepted by many Finns. Scholars of cultural adaptation (Croucher, 2008; Kim, 2001; Kramer, 2003) have asserted some important elements of adapting to a new culture include learning about the culture and being accepted by the host culture. When considering the relationship between the Finnish sauna and adapting to Finnish culture, a researcher could ask various questions: 1) how does one learn culturally appropriate communication behaviors related to the Finnish sauna? 2) how does one truly experience a Finnish sauna? (a performance of communication question), and 3) how does one experience Finnish culture through a Finnish sauna? Among the methods one could use to approach this research are: interviews, statistics, and content analysis. The method explored in Chapter 10 is ethnography.

Ethnography Defined

Ethnography originally comes from cultural anthropology (Malinowski, 1922). Ethnography is the study of, writing about, and or a description of (*graphy*), people or folk (*ethno*) (Berg, 1998; Spradley, 1979). At its very essence, **ethnography** is attempting to describe a culture from the viewpoint of a cultural insider (Denzin & Lincoln, 2003). By using ethnography, the researcher describes individuals' behaviors while inferring meaning from those behaviors. The researcher draws inferences from cultural knowledge they have. **Cultural knowledge** includes the explicit and implicit cultural knowledge we have about life. Explicit knowledge includes things we know and can easily talk about.

> For example, Stephen recently moved to Finland, and saunas are very popular; in fact saunas are a national pastime. Before moving to Finland he knew what a sauna was, and he could describe saunas (explicit knowledge). After spending more time in Finland he learned cultural norms about Finnish saunas (implicit knowledge): such as the use of boughs of birch to beat oneself for massage and stimulation, and that it is rude to swear in the sauna. He also learned it is an honor to be invited into someone's sauna. The job of the ethnographer observing Finnish sauna behavior is to draw upon your explicit and implicit knowledge about Finnish sauna life to provide a thick description of sauna life.

Edelsward (1991) conducted such an ethnographic analysis on Finnish saunas. In her ethnographic book, she described how the sauna is a place for people to come together with nature and culture. What Edelsward (1991) provided in her analysis was a thick description of sauna life and its relationship to Finnish culture. Geertz (1973) defined **thick description** as a detailed explanation of a social setting and of the lives of the people. Thick description is integral to ethnography. The descriptive essence is the meat of an ethnography. The description we provide our readers of what we are studying shows them culture in action. We will discuss thick description and how to write an ethnography more in this chapter as we go through the different types of ethnography. One can take various ethnographic approaches; we outline three approaches in this chapter: ethnography of speaking, ethnography of communication, and autoethnography.

Approaches to Ethnography

Ethnography of Speaking

Hymes's (1962) **ethnography of speaking** (EOS) is a method for studying culturally specific communication practices and patterns. EOS is the analysis of factors relevant to understanding how a communication event accomplishes its goals. Philipsen (1992) stated that EOS consists of "hearing and representing distinctive ways of speaking in particular speech communities" (p. 9). Two assumptions are key to the EOS approach. First, speaking differs cross-culturally. Second, speaking represents social life, and thus tells us something distinct about the group. Therefore, observing and describing the speech behaviors of a group can tell us a lot about a group. Numerous scholars, following an EOS approach, have found that speech differs cross-culturally and that our speaking tells something about our culture (Basso, 1970; Croucher, 2008; Engstrom, 2012; Leitner, 1983; Philipsen, 1975; Pratt & Weider, 1993; Zenk, 1988). The acronym **SPEAKING** was developed by Hymes (1962, 1974) to explain how to conduct an EOS analysis within a speech community. A **speech community** is a group of individuals who share a common set of norms or rules for interpreting and using speech (Carbaugh, 1988; Philipsen, 1992). The SPEAKING framework is a list of key questions one should ask when conducting an EOS analysis. See Figure 10.1 for a description of the SPEAKING framework.

S—Setting and scene. What is the setting, or the time and place, of a speech act? What is the scene, or the psychological situation or cultural meaning of a scene?

P—Participants. Who are the people involved (particularly the speaker and the audience)?

E—Ends. What is the purpose or goal of the speech event?

A—Act sequence. What is the order of the event? How does the event progress?

K—Key. What are some hints to help understand the tone or spirit of the speech event?

I—Instrumentalities. What are the forms and styles of speech used by the speaker in the speech event?

N—Norms. What are the social norms that regulate the speech event?

G—Genre. What kind of speech event is taking place? What genre of speech is it?

Figure 10.1 Hymes's (1974) SPEAKING Framework

Ethnography of Communication

Closely linked to Hymes's (1962, 1964, 1974) ethnography of speaking is ethnography of communication. Scholars who conduct **ethnography of communication** (EOC) research also focus on the speech acts/events of speech communities, but are more interested in learning and comparing the shared and varied codes of communication among and between groups (Cameron, 2001; Lindlof & Taylor, 2002). These ethnographers recognize that there is not one way to communicate in every social group, and thus they are specifically interested in how "shared meaning and coordinated action vary across social groups" (Philipsen, 1989, p. 258). EOC scholars combine linguistic and anthropological approaches to research. Various scholars have approached ethnography from the EOC method, and/or combined the EOC with the EOS approach (Carbaugh, 2005; Croucher, 2006; Croucher & Cronn-Mills, 2011; Katriel, 1990; Katriel & Philipsen, 1981; Ojha & Holmes, 2010; Philipsen, 1975; Sherzer, 1983).

Here is an example of how Stephen's encounters with Finnish sauna life is analyzed using Hymes's SPEAKING framework (EOS) and the EOC approach to ethnography:

S—While visiting Oulu, a city 300 miles north of Helsinki, the capital of Finland, Stephen stayed at a hotel in the city center. The event took place in the late summer of 2012. He was still learning about Finland. He decided one night to go to the sauna.

P—Stephen sat in the sauna for about 5 minutes and was joined by a man (mid-30s, like Stephen) and the man's two sons who were 8 and 10 years old. Nobody else was in the sauna.

E—The father began to speak to Stephen in Finnish (Stephen knew very little Finnish at the time). When Stephen told him in Finnish that he spoke English or French, the man spoke English to him and asked why there was no steam in the sauna. Stephen did not know why. The man explained and showed Stephen how to properly use the empty metal bucket and ladle by their feet to throw water on the hot stones in the corner.

A—He went out of the sauna, filled the bucket with water, and tossed multiple ladles full of water on the hot stones, and, with each ladle, steam arose and filled the sauna. Every few minutes more water was thrown on the stones by different individuals (the children included). The sauna participants began to sweat profusely. After 10 minutes the father instructed Stephen and his children to get out and take a cold shower, then return to the sauna; the shower, he said, helped cleanse and refresh the skin. So they did, and they returned to the sauna.

K—During the whole process, the children chuckled at how Stephen did not know about Finnish saunas. The father smiled and was happy to help and asked a lot about American culture.

I—The interaction took place in English and some broken Suomi (Finnish) was thrown in by Stephen to practice the Suomi he learned at school.

N—The four males were nude; in the United States public saunas generally require bathing suits. You will rarely if ever find a situation in the United States where children are brought along with a parent to a sauna. Furthermore, if they are brought to a sauna, we doubt you will find them enjoying it to the same level as these 8- and 10-year-olds. To them, the sauna is a way of life. Stephen also learned norms about throwing water on the stones. There are saunas in the United States that require water in the same way, but here all four people took turns, and there was an unwritten rule as to when water was thrown, something that the father said you just learn as you become one with the Finnish sauna.

G—This was a lesson on Finnish sauna protocol. Moreover, this experience demonstrated differences between saunas in Finland and the United States.

The job of the EOS and EOC scholar is to provide such thick description (Geertz, 1973) of the community they are studying. Whether you are using the SPEAKING framework (EOS) or focusing less specifically on language use (EOC), your study should provide for your readers a clear understanding of the phenomena you set out to explore. You need to provide and analyze specific examples to back up your claims (we talk more about this in the claims section). Examples, or your data, can come from a variety of places (interviews, observation, media, documents, artifacts, etc.), which we outline in greater detail later. Ethnographies from the EOS and EOC approaches are typically written in the first person, but can also be written in the third person. The writing choice is up to you (or as required by your instructor), as this form of research is from the interpretive or critical paradigm.

Autoethnography

When a researcher describes or analyzes personal experiences to better understand a cultural event, the researcher is conducting autoethnography (Bruner, 1993; Denzin, 1989; Ellis, 2004; Holman Jones, 2005; Spry, 2001). **Autoethnography** is a combination of ethnography and autobiography. In this sense, while analyzing cultural events, the researcher, along with describing events or happenings in the cultural setting, reflects on their own past experiences, includes those experiences in their text, writes about any epiphanies they have had during the research process that might influence their lives and the research, and discusses how past experiences and epiphanies come from and/or are made possible by being a part of the culture they are studying (Couser, 1997; Denzin, 1989; Goodall, 2006). The key is to integrate or weave theory and method with descriptions of past and current experiences, epiphanies, and cultural descriptions. Autoethnography is almost always written in first person (Ellis & Bochner, 2000), and your writing may come in different forms than the EOS or EOC approaches. Many autoethnographies are written as journals, short stories, poems, personal essays, prose, and in any other form fitting the needs of the authors.

After moving to Finland, Stephen decided to keep a journal of his experiences of adjusting to Finnish life. The following excerpt refers to the same night in the sauna in which Stephen met the father and his two sons.

> September 7, 2012—I (Stephen) will be the first one to say that sitting in a sauna with a man and his two sons completely naked is not something I would normally say is normal for me. I have always been a relatively shy person when it comes to my body. However, I must say I found it very liberating, relaxing, and interesting to sit in the sauna tonight. For someone who studies cultures, or tries to at least because I don't think I can ever truly understand a culture 100 percent, this was an interesting event. I really did not feel out of place or embarrassed, as the others were in the same position I was in. I mean, the father was nude, and so were his sons. It is perfectly normal in Finnish sauna culture to be nude . . . in fact one cannot wear a bathing suit and one should not cover themselves with a towel or they look like a weirdo tourist. For me, this was one of the first times I really felt like I was learning some insider information about Finland from a stranger.

With the knowledge of the different approaches to ethnography, the following section discusses the types of claims used in ethnographic research.

Ethnographic Claims

Now that we have basic definitions of the three main kinds of ethnography used in communication, the next section describes how claims are substantiated. Ethnography affords the researcher a chance to make descriptive, interpretive, evaluative, and reformist claims.

Descriptive Claims

Lofland and Lofland (1995) stated that ethnographers typically set out to describe the norms and practices of a group of individuals in a culture. While descriptive claims tend to be the most typical from an EOS or EOC approach, interpretive, evaluative, and reformist claims are possible. Those using an EOS approach are particularly interested in how individuals or groups name and describe their speech events, the parts of those speech events, and the functions of those speech events. Hymes (1962) described how naming and parts of speech events include things like the senders, receivers, and channels. The functions of the speech events are essentially what speech events achieve within a speech community.

Interpretive Claims

Ethnographic methods can aid in furthering interpretive claims about the relationships between communication and culture. An interpretive claim can enhance our understanding of how, for example, communication creates culture and how culture creates communication. In Philipsen's (1975) analysis of Teamsterville, he found the various ways that participants in the community spoke like men created a shared sense of identity. This speech community's language created a shared sense of identity that shaped interactions among members and with non-members. His EOC approach to this study revealed various elements of life in Teamsterville. An analysis of just some of Philipsen's work (1975, 1992) shows how he used an EOC and an EOS approach to describe and interpret cultural events or meanings.

Evaluative and Reformist Claims

For example, scholars who use autoethnography may use this type of ethnography to make descriptive claims, and may also use autoethnography to make evaluative and reformist claims. Often, ethnographies containing evaluative and reformist claims are considered critical ethnographies (Ang, 1990; Conquergood, 1991). Evaluation claims are used when you judge the worth of or value of a communication message you are analyzing or studying (Denzin & Lincoln, 2003; Lofland & Lofland, 1995). Evaluative claims are often used to advocate for a change in some behavior or practice in a culture. Reformist claims take evaluation a step further and describe negative consequences of a current economic, political, or social system. Therefore, you can approach an ethnography with the intent of describing some behavior or communicative practice and calling for possible change. Patton (2004) described how sexism and racism are often accepted forms of discrimination in higher education; however, this situation does not have to be the case.

Two descriptive/interpretive claims can be made about Finnish sauna culture. First, many Finns are happy to help someone learn about saunas. Stephen has found himself in many situations where a Finn has taught him something new about the sauna. Second, the sauna is a comfortable place for communication. At first, Stephen did not think the sauna would be a comfortable place to talk to other people, because you are naked. However, after numerous experiences, it is clear the sauna is a relaxing environment in which to have a conversation. As for an evaluative or reformist claim, Stephen believes the saunas best represent the inclusiveness of the Finnish people. Thus, from an evaluative standpoint, he evaluates the saunas as a positive representation of Finnish society.

Now that you have a grasp of the different approaches to ethnography, and ethnographic claims, the following section describes the various kinds of data used in ethnographic research.

Ethnographic Data

Whenever you are collecting data for a research project, an important question to consider is what your data will be. When conducting ethnography research, you will typically conduct participant observation or conduct interviews.

Participant Observation

The backbone of ethnographic research is participant observation. **Participant observation** entails learning about and watching a cultural setting by participating in the cultural setting (Briggs, 1986; Warren & Karner, 2005). Your level of participation or membership in the setting can vary from extensive (become a part of the culture) to minimal (simply observing and not participating). Here are some standards for deciding, as a researcher, a level of participation: your comfort level with the setting/participants, the comfort level of the participants with you, how competent you are with the communication of the setting or participants, your purpose in doing the research, and how long you can be in the setting (just to name a few) (Spradley & McCurdy, 1972).

In Croucher's (2005, 2006, 2008) ethnographic analysis of North African immigrants to France, he has participant observation. In this line of work, he has observed this community as a "field researcher" and has not been extensively integrated with the community. Thus, his participation has been minimal. Other scholars, such as Angrosino, have taken a more active role in their ethnographic studies. In this line of work, Angrosino (1992, 1997, 1998) took on the role of a "volunteer" with a community-based mental illness agency to better understand the lives of children and adults with "mental retardation." Both scholars spent a considerable amount of time with their participants, but in two different kinds of roles, one as only a "researcher," and the other as a "researcher-volunteer."

If you look at Stephen's analysis of saunas, he is a participant/researcher. He has not volunteered to work at the saunas.

Interviews

Interviews are an integral part of the ethnographic research process (Babbie, 2002; Briggs, 1986). Interviewing is when you ask questions and get answers from the participants involved in your study. Lofland and Lofland (1995) explained how interviewing in an ethnographic research project involves conversations and storytelling between researchers and participants. In ethnographic research, interviews are often used in conjunction with participant observation to better understand cultural phenomena. Ethnographic interviews have various forms, but generally take one of the following: (1) oral history, (2) personal narrative, or (3) topical interview (Babbie, 2002; Bernard, 1999; Creswell, 1998). An **oral history** is when participants retell historical moments in their lives. A **personal narrative** is a participant's personal opinion or perspective on an event or experience. A **topical interview** is where the participant gives their opinion or perspective on a particular subject or topic. Often the three types of interviews will overlap, and these interviews can be structured, unstructured, and/or semi-structured. The choice is yours as the researcher as to what kind of interview you may use in your project, depending on the purpose of your project. After you have collected the interviews you will need to transcribe the interviews to make analysis easier (we will talk about analysis shortly). In Croucher's (2006) work with Muslim and Chinese immigrants, he used semi-structured interviews that were topical in nature to ascertain how the immigrants felt about external pressures to assimilate to France and Canada. In both contexts (France and Canada), the conversations were very open, but focused on the topic of pressures to assimilate.

Individuals Stephen met in the saunas gave personal narratives about saunas. He conducted very informal conversations with individuals in this setting, so as to not intrude on individuals enjoying their relaxation in the saunas.

When you are conducting participant observation and interviews, you must keep a few things in mind. First, before you are able to interact with the community, you must gain access to the community. Will the community allow you to observe or participate with them? Gaining access is one of the hardest steps in ethnography (Patton, 1990). You will normally find it easier to gain access to a community of which you are already a member. For example, if you are in a fraternity or sorority, it may be easier for you to gain access to this group for an ethnographic study, as you are already a part of this group. However, researchers not part of a group often rely on **gate-keepers** or insiders in a community who are willing to facilitate the researcher's entry into the community (Babbie, 2002; Briggs, 1986). In Croucher's (2005, 2006, 2008) research, his gatekeeper was a Muslim imam in Paris who introduced him to numerous Muslim immigrants in France. The importance of gatekeepers cannot be understated, because, without them, many researchers would not be able to gain access to a community.

> Fortunately, Stephen does not need a gatekeeper to go into a Finnish sauna, as the ones he goes into are in hotels, where paying guests are allowed to go.

Second, you must strive to establish **rapport** (defined in more depth in Chapter 11) with your participants (Babbie, 2002; Briggs, 1986). If participants do not trust you, they are not likely to allow you to observe their lives and learn about their culture. So, listen to the participants, do not cut them off in conversation, show some empathy for what they are saying, reciprocate in the conversation, and try to show commonalities when possible (Bernard, 1999; Patton, 1990).

> Stephen spends a great deal of his time listening to the individuals in the saunas talk about sauna culture. Listening is often underrated in rapport building.

Third, you need to be open to change. When you are out in the field, you will find that things do not always go as planned. You may go into a setting expecting one thing, and find something else. Unexpected findings and surprises frequently teach us the most about a culture (Babbie, 2002; Croucher, 2008).

> It is expected that only men will enter a men's sauna in Finland. In Turku a nude Russian woman walked into the men's sauna and surprised all of the men. She said she did not understand the written signs. However, stick figures of men are on the wall designating the sauna for men only.

Fourth, you need to take detailed notes while in the field. When you are conducting an ethnography, you will be in the field for an extended period of time, and the length of time depends on your project. You, therefore, need to write down or log what you see, hear, smell, taste, etc. in a journal of some sort. A journal is an essential tool to help you, as the researcher, not to forget what you saw, heard, learned, etc. Take notes about things such as key actors in the field, conversations you hear, actions you see, etc. . . . These types of things will be vital later in your analysis. Your journal will be essential when you write up your final report (Berg, 1998; Creswell,

1998). Date all the entries in your journal—any and every observation could be important in the end. Take notes in a way comfortable for you, and take notes often.

> Stephen will put notes on his computer every night after visiting a sauna. Often, the notes are a few pages long and will detail any conversation he had.

Fifth, when you are done collecting data in the field, you will depart the community/setting. As with interviewing, you will reach a data saturation point: a point where you do not feel as though you are learning anything new. We will talk more about this in Chapter 11 on interviewing. The task of leaving the field is not as easy as simply picking up your suitcase at the airport luggage carousel and walking out to your car. When you leave the field, you should do the following. First, you may want to think about whether or not you want to stay in contact with your participants. Staying in contact is a personal choice you need to make based on your research and personal situation. Second, you need to decide whether to share your results with your participants. In some situations, sharing is impossible as you may not be able to contact participants again. However, if you have access to participants, will you share your results with them? Various scholars have shared results with their participants (Angrosino, 1997, 1998; Croucher, 2006, 2008; Spencer, 2011). Sharing is a personal choice.

> Stephen is still in the field. He will not be able to directly share his results with his participants because he does not keep their names on file.

Sixth, if you are doing ethnographic work, you will need to work on reflexivity. **Reflexivity** is the ability to reflect on your own experiences to understand how they are both product and producer of a given cultural experience (Ellis, 2004). Look back at experiences in your own life, be retrospective, and see how your experiences are created by and create other cultural experiences. Your experiences in life will influence how you interpret what you encounter in the field. It is important that you recognize this and reflect on it in your writing (Alvesson & Skoldberg, 2000).

Now you have a grasp of the types of data collected for an ethnographic research project, the following section briefly discusses how to analyze ethnographic data.

> Stephen's work will be mainly from an EOC perspective.

Ethnographic Data Analysis

Grounded theory (Glaser & Strauss, 1967; Strauss & Corbin, 1991) is often used to analyze ethnographic data (see Chapter 13 for a more in-depth discussion of grounded theory). The process can be used to look for themes in your interview transcripts, and to induce categories from your observation field notes (Bernard, 1999). Scholars also take a symbolic interactionist approach to analyzing ethnographic data. **Symbolic interactionism** is associated with Mead (1934) and Blumer (1969). In essence, shared meanings are created through interactions and these meanings become reality. Patton (1990) outlined three premises essential to symbolic interactionism: (1) humans act towards things on the basis of pre-determined meanings; (2) meanings come from social interactions; and (3) meanings are modified as individuals encounter new experiences and individuals.

Here are a few hints about ethnographic data analysis. First, keep in mind the approach to ethnography you are using, which will help determine your analytic approach. If you are using the EOS approach SPEAKING, you will enter the analysis with pre-determined categories to guide you. A SPEAKING analysis is different than an EOC analysis, in which you will allow more of your categories to emerge from the ground up (a form of deductive analysis). Second, always be on the lookout for categories or themes in your data. Third, before you enter the setting you will have done a lot of research on the topic. The key is to not allow your previous knowledge of the setting, as opposed to the observations and interview data in front of you, to override your interpretations of the data. Your interpretations must come from what you experienced in the field.

> Stephen will want to make sure he allows his observations and interview data to drive his analysis of Finnish sauna culture, and not his book knowledge.

If you look to the work of scholars who have used the EOS and EOC approaches (Carbaugh, 2005; Croucher, 2008; Katriel, 1990; Ojha & Holmes, 2010; Philipsen, 1975; Sherzer, 1983), you will find some have used the SPEAKING framework to analyze their data, and some have used grounded theory. Autoethnographic scholars have used: metaphors as a form of analysis (Fox, 2010), grounded theory (McKemmish, Burstein, Manaszewicz, Fisher, & Evans, 2012), and symbolic interactionism (Olson, 2004). So you have your data, and you have some options of how to analyze your data. The next section of the chapter reviews warrants for ethnographic research.

Ethnographic Warrants

As with evaluating whether data support your claims in interview-based research, warrants for ethnographic-based research follow a very similar path.

Researcher credibility, adequacy, coherence, and thick description are key issues to consider.

There are three components to determine researcher credibility: level of training or experience, degree of membership in the social context, and faithfulness. First, how trained is the researcher at conducting interviews and/or observations? For new researchers, the art of observation and interviews can be somewhat daunting. Ethnography, like all forms of research, is a process one will never truly master. However, you must prepare yourself before you enter the setting by studying the culture in question to the best of your ability. Even for those who are conducting an autoethnography, this is not an easy task. Many individuals find it very difficult to link theory to their ethnographies, to write about their own experiences, and to then link these experiences to other cultural experiences or phenomena. Second, you need to determine how involved you are going to be with the community if you are conducting EOS or EOC research. One of the first elements of participant observation is determining how involved you are. Your degree of membership must be made clear to the readers. Are you an emic or etic researcher? Third, you must be detailed in your note taking and transcriptions. Ask yourself if you have spent enough time in the field, if you have enough interviews, etc. . . .

Adequacy and coherence relate to two key issues. First, have you collected and/or covered enough of the available data to make an adequate argument (Patton, 1990)? Have you kept a detailed enough journal of your thoughts or epiphanies on a particular issue to make up your autoethnography? When Stephen did his work among Chinese immigrants in Canada, he not only spoke with them, but he also observed their shops, their interactions with clients, family members, their entire surroundings. Observing and recording their entire surroundings helped him better understand their daily lives. Second, you need to consider whether the results you are presenting lay out a coherent argument for the descriptive, interpretive, evaluative, or reformist claims you are making. Look at your examples (observations or interviews) and make sure they back up your claims. Provide more than one example to back up a claim and show the reader evidence. As you are providing the examples, you should also strive to vividly describe the examples. The use of thick description (Geertz, 1973) is essential to supporting ethnographic (EOS, EOC, and autoethnographic) claims.

Stephen will want to make sure his observations and notes from sauna culture illustrate the various aspects of how Finnish saunas represent Finnish culture. He could also discuss how he has begun to acculturate (Kim, 2001) into Finnish culture through his use of these saunas.

Summary

This chapter, the first of the how-to guides, was a how-to guide to ethnographic research. Ethnographic research is generally approached from the interpretive or critical/cultural paradigm. Hopefully, after reading the chapter, and the accompanying student paper, you feel comfortable enough to go out there and conduct your own ethnographic study. The next chapter, Chapter 11, is a how-to guide to interviewing.

Key Steps & Questions to Consider

1. Choose your topic and research it.
2. Choose your population.
3. How will you access this population?
4. Are you doing a random or non-random sampling?
5. Is your project going to be an observation, interview, a mixture of the two, or an autoethnography? Why?
6. If you do an interview-based ethnography project, are your questions structured, semi-structured, or unstructured? How many questions are you going to ask? How many people are you going to interview?
7. If your project is an observation, how long will it be/its duration?
8. Before you enter the field did you write, submit, and get approval from your Human Subject Review Board or Institutional Review Board?
9. Remember rapport!
10. Will you tape or video-record the interviews and the observations or not?
11. Remember you will need to transcribe the interviews (or have someone else do it for you). This takes a lot of time but it makes analysis of the interviews so much better as you will have a better understanding of what you have in your data!
12. Take good field notes!
13. Be open to change in the setting.
14. Self-reflect on your position as the researcher. Are you a part of the group you are studying or an outsider? This self-reflection is always helpful as it aids in uncovering meaning.
15. Reflexivity!
16. Look through your transcripts and field notes for either pre-determined themes or emergent themes.
17. Support your themes with coherent examples.
18. Throughout this whole process you may have already been writing some of your research paper (analysis of literature for example); if not, start.

Activities

1. Pick a location on campus or in your community and conduct a non-participant mini-ethnography. Spend enough time in the location to develop some insight and gather some thick description. Focus on one aspect of a communication theory and see what critical or interpretative observations emerge.

2. Visit the same location and switch to a participant observation ethnographic approach. Focus on the same communication theory as the first activity. Again, see what insights emerge from your ethnography.

3. Compare your observations from the non-participant and participant observations. How did your thick description change? How did your critical or interpretive insights change?

 Discussion Questions

As you read the student paper provided at the end of this chapter, consider the following questions.

1. Using the ethnographic descriptions the student provides, interpret the data in light of different communication theories.

2. Again, using the student descriptions, re-analyze the data using Hymes's SPEAKING framework described in this chapter.

Key Terms

Autoethnography
Cultural knowledge
Ethnography
Ethnography of
  communication
Ethnography of
  speaking

Gatekeepers
Oral history
Participant observation
Personal narrative
Rapport
Reflexivity
SPEAKING

Speech community
Symbolic
  interactionism
Thick description
Topical interview

Notes

1 This photo is included courtesy of Janiika Vilkuna.

Undergraduate Student Paper

How does self-disclosure differ in dyadic relationships?

An authoethnography

Gina Sirico

Communication is a part of our daily lives, and we self-disclose, or voluntarily reveal information, to others in order to create and maintain relationships. Self-disclosure is crucial to maintaining dyadic or interpersonal relationships. Self-disclosure is a way to gain information about another person and learn how they think and feel. Once one person engages in self-disclosure, we expect the other person will self-disclose back in return, which is the act of reciprocity (Borchers, 1999). Mutual self-disclosure helps relationships become stronger by building trust and understanding for each other.

Depending on the type of relationship and what stage of Knapp's coming together we are in, the amount of self-disclosure varies. Knapp's stages of disclosure are as follows: the initiation stage, experimenting, intensifying, integrating, and bonding (Borchers, 1999). Initiation is your first impression of the other person, usually within a few seconds of meeting them. In the experimenting stage, questions are asked to each other to determine if you want to continue the relationship. In the intensifying stage, self-disclosure is exchanged and each person is committed to starting a relationship with the other person. In the integrating stage, the individuals become a pair by doing things together and starting to share an identity. The final, or bonding, stage is when a couple makes their relationship official (Borchers, 1999).

Studies on self-disclosure are sometimes done by observing other people's relationships. A study can be conducted where the researcher collected surveys from people in different stages of their relationships to analyze their amount of self-disclosure. The participants could be asked by the

Gina has a strong opening by setting up a theory for understanding the focus of her paper. Our one suggestion is to rely on primary sources instead of secondary sources (e.g., read and cite from the original Knapp article instead of relying on Borchers's (1999) explanation of Knapp.

researcher to do a self-report and disclose their own behaviors of communication to show how they think and feel about their self-disclosure (Merrigan & Huston, 2009). Or an autoethnography can be done by the researcher about their own self-disclosure.

An autoethnography is a self-narrative that critiques the position of self with others in social contexts (Merrigan & Huston, 2009). Autoethnography is the interpretive or critical analysis of a social setting or situation that connects the "personal to the cultural" (Porter, 2004). Autoethnography relies on systematic gathering and analysis of field data from people involved in genuine life experiences. Written in the first person, autoethnography is based on the interpretive paradigm values of rich description to include one person's multiple realities (Merrigan & Huston, 2009). The writer's focus is on the degree of membership in describing and interpreting one's own sense-making in a cultural situation or setting. In this type of research, the key informant is the researcher himself or herself (Merrigan & Huston, 2009).

I chose to do an autoethnography for my research about my level of self-disclosure with my boyfriend compared with my roommate. The amount of self-disclosure I engage in is different in each relationship. I looked at how I self-disclose with each person as well as the reasons for my self-disclosure. I discuss why I do and why I do not disclose with each person. I reflect back on my disclosure with each individual during a two-year period (my freshman to sophomore year of college).

My relationship with my boyfriend of three years is an integrated relationship. We have passed through all of the stages of coming together that Knapp described. In the initiating stage, we knew we wanted to continue this relationship based on the visual and auditory cues we gave each other. When I first approached him, his response to my greeting was warm and positive. We exchanged eye contact and smiled, and offered some self-disclosure. I told him our fathers worked together, and it

Gina has an effective "big picture" explanation of autoethnography, but could use more details of the "nuts and bolts" about the steps involved in the process of conducting an autoethnography.

Gina has a good opening for her descriptive section of the research paper.

was all a continuous spiral from there. We continued to talk and flirt in our SAT class we had together. We moved on to the experimenting stage, where we continued to share more information with each other, realizing we had similar values and interests. For example, we are both Catholics, and we both previously had our hearts broken. We were each other's sounding boards, and we helped each other cope with the heartbreak, and began to develop a new, better relationship with each other. The experimenting stage lasted a few months, where we dated and went different places together that allowed us to develop our trust, and self-disclose to each other. We began going everywhere together as a couple. In this stage, he was able to self-disclose to me about his parents and their divorce, and I was able to help him deal with this still sensitive situation. In the intensifying stage, we made the commitment to be each other's one and only partner. In this stage, we also began to self-disclose more deeply, and used "we" and "us" instead of "you" and "I". We are currently still in this stage, talking about our future plans together as a couple. We also have more physical interaction, and touch (like holding hands, always being close) is comfortable to us. The integrating stage overlaps with the intensifying stage, where we are starting to take on characteristics of our partner. We smile the same big smile, laugh the same laugh, and have already merged our social circles. Self-disclosure is no longer an issue, and we self-disclose to each other every day. Family and friends are now "ours" and not just "mine". Activities that we care about separately, we now do together. An example is his love of football and my love of dance. We watch football games together, and we took salsa classes together. We are starting to become "one". Our final stage of coming together would be the bonding stage, where we would get married to make our commitment to each other permanent.

The ways in which I self-disclose to my boyfriend are as a means to vent my feelings, clarify

Gina walks us through Knapp's stages, but could use more thick description to provide the reader with a commanding picture of the relationship with her boyfriend. More specifics and details will help build a thick description.

my beliefs and opinions, and to get advice and support. I cannot wait to call my boyfriend by the end of the day to self-disclose to him about my day; tell him how I felt about my classes, or if I am stressed. It feels so good to have someone like him to always be there for me, and tell me everything will be okay. He offers me advice on how to help me de-stress. He cares about my opinions and beliefs, and is always there to support me. He listens, which is the most important thing when I feel the need to have someone to talk to. I also self-disclose to him to encourage him to disclose to me.

My boyfriend sometimes has a hard time expressing to me how he feels, so I am sure to encourage him to tell me. He knows I won't tell anyone else; our conversations are between us two only. I have to work on getting him to open up to me more often, because I can tell when something is bothering him, I just have to get him to talk about it with me. Second, I self-disclose because we trust, care, and support one another. The most important reason I self-disclose to him is to get his support. I need him to tell me everything will be fine, and know that he believes in me. We are at a point in our relationship where I can self-disclose to him about anything, because we have that trust.

The ways in which I may avoid self-disclosing to my boyfriend are only if I cannot find the opportunity (not the right time or place), or if I cannot think of a way to self-disclose. There are some times when I want to self-disclose, but we will be in a public place, or with other people. I only want to self-disclose to him; I do not want others to hear. A reason for not disclosing is if I can't think of a way to self-disclose; sometimes, I cannot think of the right way to say what I am trying to say. I may also avoid self-disclosing if I feel I do not want to hurt him by saying something wrong that will make him upset with me. If I say something in the wrong way, I may be misunderstood. This has happened before, when I mentioned something that I felt

Here is an opportunity for Gina to add to a thick description by providing specific instances of venting feelings, sharing opinions, or helping her to de-stress. The reader needs stories and examples to see her explanation in action and how the actions support her interpretation of the theory.

was no big deal, but he took it more seriously, and got mad over it. I try my best to avoid these types of situations, so I am careful as to when and how I self-disclose.

Self-disclosure is necessary, and important in order to sustain a healthy, loving, romantic relationship. I self-disclose to my boyfriend as a way to get to know each other better, and as a way to learn about ourselves. We self-disclose to gain each other's trust, the most important aspect in a loving relationship. We gained, and continue to gain, trust with one another through self-disclosing often. I self-disclose to my boyfriend as a means of catharsis (get something off my chest), self-clarification, and self-validation. There would be many problems in our relationship if we had problems self-disclosing, because we need to meta-communicate, or communicate back and forth to each other. We must talk to each other, and never run out of things to say in order to maintain our relationship through marriage. The more self-disclosure and meta-communication we have as a couple, the better our marriage will be.

My relationship with my roommate is in the initiating/experimenting stages of coming together. We were still getting to know each other in the freshman year, so our self-disclosure was limited. After two years of knowing each other, we are more comfortable with each other, and self-disclose more often.

The most important reason for me to self-disclose to my roommate is to get advice, support, or assistance from her. We both have boyfriends, and that connection makes it easier for me to self-disclose. I can self-disclose with her easily about him and my relationship problems. We both have the same little arguments with our significant others. We are able to give each other advice about how to deal with those problems. We are learning to support each other. I also self-disclose to her as a way to vent my feelings, especially about school. I am able to self-disclose about my course work, as well as my relationship with my boyfriend.

Gina may have inadvertently provided a level of thick description when she shifted from describing a girlfriend/boyfriend relationship to a married-couple relationship.

Gina could be clearer with her description of her roommate relationship. We can infer, but not be sure, if they have been roommates for two years since being freshmen.

Since we are roommates, we share our food and living space.

As a part of the experimenting stage, we go places together, such as for meals, and for activities, such as yoga. She is fluent in Spanish, so she is able to help me with my Spanish homework, and is always willing to offer assistance. I am able to help her with her English homework, since I am good at editing papers. Slowly, through self-disclosure, my roommate and I are learning to care about, support, and trust one another.

My main reason for not self-disclosing to my roommate is because I do not want what I self-disclose to be told to others. I may not self-disclose because I feel I may not get the support I need after I self-disclose to her. I am still afraid of being misunderstood, or hurting her if she herself is in a difficult situation. I do not want to impose on her too much information, where she feels that she can't self-disclose back to me. Sometimes, I cannot find the opportunity to self-disclose because I do not want to "bother" her, or distract her. I want to self-disclose, but feel like I can't when she is preoccupied with homework, her phone, or watching TV.

My relationship with my roommate is still growing, but self-disclosure is important for me to express my feelings, and for us to become trusting of one another. We need to learn to find the right times to continue to self-disclose and become closer friends. I self-disclose to my roommate as a means of impression formation, catharsis, and reciprocity.

In conclusion, self-disclosure is important in building and maintaining relationships. I see this importance through my romantic relationship with my boyfriend and through my friendship with my roommate. I have to self-disclose, and we have to self-disclose with each other to get to know one another and grow together. The reasons I self-disclose in each relationship differ. Self-disclosure brings two people closer together and creates trust, which is important in a dyadic relationship.

The yoga, Spanish homework, and English homework help to build thick description and provide insight on their relationship.

Gina could better integrate how impression formation, catharsis, and reciprocity are defined and evident with her autoethnography. She included the concepts but could provide more guidance to the reader how they are apparent within her analysis.

References

Anderson, L. (2006). Analytic autoethonography. *Journal of Contemporary Ethnography, 35,* 373–395. doi: 10.1177/0891241605280449.

Borchers, T. (1999). *Interpersonal communication, self-disclosure.* Retrieved from: www.abacon.com/commstudies/interpersonal/indisclosure.html.

Borchers, T. (1999). *Interpersonal communication, relationship development.* Retrieved from: www.abacon.com/commstudies/interpersonal/indevelop.html.

Merrigan, G., & Hutson, C. L. (2009). *Communication research methods.* New York: Oxford University Press.

Porter, N. (2004). *CMA methodology, autoethnography.* Retrieved from: http://anthropology.usf.edu/cma/CMAmethodology-ae.htm.

11 INTERVIEWING

What Will I Learn About Interviewing?

This is a photo of Stephen Croucher taken in October 2008 in Kolkota, India. Stephen was attending Durga Puja festivities. Durga Puja is an annual Hindu festival that celebrates the Hindu Goddess Durga. For many Hindus, particularly those in West Bengal, this is the biggest festival and cultural event of the year. There are Durga Puja celebrations around the world because Indians have migrated from India to multiple corners of the world. The festival takes place during a 6-day period, during which large pandals, or temporary structures made of bamboo and cloth, are made. Some of these pandals are very simple, but some are extremely elaborate. The purpose of the pandals is to house the stage where the Durga idol stands; the idols are almost entirely made of clay and paint. During the festival worshipers enter the pandals and worship the idols. At the end of the festival, the idols are taken to a local river and "given" back to the river. As a communication researcher and as someone who greatly admires Indian cultures, the celebration of Durga Puja has always fascinated Stephen. One thing he learned during this particular Durga Puja was that for some Indians celebrating Durga (the Goddess) enhances their sense of "Indianness" (a chance to celebrate culture, history, and/or being Indian), while for others the celebration is just a chance to drink and be merry with friends. The communication scholar might approach Durga Puja and look at how this celebration relates to an individual's identity (Collier & Thomas, 1988; Cupach & Imahori, 1993; Ting-Toomey, 1993, 1999). The scholar could ask if the celebration of holidays and identity are possibly related to one another (in fact, Noth, 1995, argued that the two are related). Such a relationship could be explored through a variety of research methods (e.g., ethnography, focus groups, and statistics). The method we explore in Chapter 11 is in-depth interviewing.

Approaches to Interviewing

Interviews are widely used in communication, the social sciences, the humanities, business, and other fields of inquiry to gain an understanding of cultural, sociological, psychological, linguistic, and consumer behavior (Briggs, 1986; Giles, Bourhis, & Taylor, 1977; Hall, 1989; Neuman, 2011). The purpose of **interviewing** is to ask questions and get answers from the participants involved in your study in order to discover knowledge. Interviewing has three traditional approaches: structured, semi-structured, and unstructured. No matter which approach a researcher may use, using the interview as a data collection method should be guided in some way by theoretical inquiry (see Chapters 3–6 if you need a refresher on the relationship between theory and method).

Structured Interviews

A **structured** interview is *very structured*, hence the name structured. With this type of interview protocol, the interviewer: 1) prepares all the questions ahead of time (called an **interview guide**); 2) asks each participant the exact same questions in the exact same order; 3) has few if any open-ended questions in the interview guide (such questions allow the participant too much room for variation from an interviewer's script); and, 4) does not insert personal opinion into the interview (e.g., by agreeing or disagreeing with a response).

"How do I prepare questions?" This is a common question for many students conducting interview projects. We recommend the following. First, you should have some understanding of a theory or context you are interested in studying. Second, from that understanding think of some key issues you are interested in studying. Third, ask yourself what questions you think you need to ask to better understand your area of interest. Fourth, write down these questions and see if they help you better understand what you are interested in. Fifth, if your list looks so long that you would not interested in answering it, then most other people probably would not be either. So, you might want to cut it down some. Sixth, revise the questions to make them conversational in tone; we will talk more about how an interview is a conversation shortly. In the case of Stephen's Durga Puja project, he did extensive reading on identity, religious holidays, and India. He then determined he was interested in the relationship between Durga Puja and religious identity in India. Third, he asked questions such as: 1) how is Durga Puja part of being Bengali? and 2) is it important to celebrate Durga Puja? These easy to understand and very open-ended questions helped him better understand the holiday, identity, and India.

Often, self-administered questionnaires (self-reports where people write down their answers) are a type of structured interview (Kvale, 1996). Other typical types of structured interviews include telephone interviews where the interviewer fills in the participants' responses and Internet-based interviews with closed-ended options (a popular one is SurveyMonkey). Another type of structured interview many of us have experienced is an initial medical interview. In these kinds of interviews, the health professionals have a set list of questions they want to ask, and in a set order. The benefits of structured interviews are: 1) the individuals conducting these kinds of interviews only need to be trained to follow basic data collection instructions; 2) less of a relationship is generally developed between the interviewer and participants; and 3) data collected are considered by many who conduct this type of research to be more reliable (see Chapter 8 for a refresher on reliability) (Patton, 1990; Warren & Karner, 2005).

Semi-structured and Unstructured Interviews

Semi-structured and **unstructured** interviews are, in some ways, fairly similar to one another. First, the interviewer and participant have a formal interview where they meet with one another and chat about a specific topic or topics. In these types of interviews, the interview is more of a conversation than a one-way process like a structured interview. Types of semi-structured and unstructured interviews include narrative interviews or interviews where someone is collecting a person's life history. The selection of where to conduct an interview is often, but not always, agreed upon by both the interviewer and the interviewee. While many structured interviews are conducted in predetermined locations, over the phone, and/or over the Internet, many semi-structured and unstructured interviews are conducted in mutually agreed upon locations. Agreeing upon a location for an interview makes participants feel more comfortable about the entire interview process (Patton, 1990).

Second, semi-structured and unstructured interviews are similar since the interviewer has developed an understanding of the setting or context to allow the majority of the questions to be open-ended in nature. The questions are written to allow participants to answer in a variety of ways. An interviewer will, for example, ask few questions requiring a "yes" or a "no" response. This is where the similarities end.

Researchers who conduct semi-structured interviews combine techniques of structured and unstructured interviews. The interviewers typically prepare a flexible interview guide to help guide the conversation with their participants. The guide (or list of questions) is flexible to allow the interviewer to follow the flow of the conversation (e.g., if something is important to the participant, the interviewer can spend more time on the subject than something else on the guide).

Individuals who prefer to use unstructured interviews generally do not have an interview guide (a prepared series of questions). The researcher will instead spend time building rapport and allowing each participant to shape how they want to talk about the subject of the study (Briggs, 1986).

Patton (1990) said building **rapport** during the interview process is important. He defined rapport as showing "respect [for] the people being interviewed, so that what they say is important because of who is saying it" (p. 317). The building of rapport can be done in many ways. When Stephen was conducting research in Montreal among Chinese shopkeepers, he would spend a great deal of time browsing the participants' shops before he began the interviews (Croucher, 2003, 2008b). Stephen used the information he gained from browsing the shops, what they sell, prices, etc. . . . to establish rapport at the beginning of the interviews. Asking the interviewees about their business showed them he was interested in their stories as immigrants and shopkeepers, and their business. Stephen also tried (and continues to try to this day) to appear professional but not too formal, because the latter may intimidate his interviewees.

This could be tricky in India. Even if you are from India and conducting emic research, it can be hard to establish rapport with individuals. Most researchers start conducting (or only conduct) their research among people they know, such as family and friends, or rely on student samples. If you are conducting your research among family and friends, you should already have rapport. If you are conducting your research among students, you will need to take some steps to establish rapport; however, students often are given an incentive to be involved in the interview and so establishment of rapport should be relatively easy. If your interview involves individuals you do not have previous contact with, you must take steps to show them you are interested in their stories . . . or else why should they share the stories with you?

Semi-structured interviews are typically used when 1) interviewers only have one chance to meet with a particular participant and/or are meeting with many participants in the field, and 2) ethnographic observation can precede the interviews (Bernard, 1999). Unstructured interviews, on the other hand, are often employed when researchers: 1) plan to revisit the same participants on multiple occasions, and 2) are open to having the participants influence their understanding or approach to the subject or context (Briggs, 1986). Generally, researchers will ask participants if they can audio-record or video-record semi-structured and unstructured interviews. In-depth note-taking is always a good idea during interviews, even when permission to record is granted. A researcher can jot down observations and insights, which may not be as apparent on a recording. Notes are also your back-up in case the recording files are damaged.

Both semi-structured and unstructured interviews offer participants a chance to openly express their opinions on the issue at hand. This open expression of views can provide what Geertz (1973) called **thick description.** Thick description is an in-depth understanding of a culture or setting provided by the members of the culture and captured by others (researchers and journalists). Semi-structured interviews offer interviewers the opportunity to prepare a flexible interview guide before the interview, which can make the interview process a lot easier.

> Thinking back to the relationship between identity and Durga Puja, we should think about what structure of interview we want to do: 1) since we have a fairly strong grasp of identity theories, 2) we may only be able to talk to people once, maybe twice, and 3) we are open to revising or altering our theoretical ideas of the relationship between Durga Puja and identity. So, we might go for semi-structured interviews. Our next step is to look at our data, claims, and warrants for the interview.

Now that you have an understanding of the different approaches to interviewing, the next section of the chapter discusses the types of data that are typically used in interview projects.

Data in Interviews

When you are collecting interviews, whether structured, semi-structured, or unstructured, you must ask yourself what are your data? Your data—what you are analyzing—will likely be spoken or written words. If you are conducting semi-structured and unstructured interviews, the data are almost always the spoken word. Structured interviews might use the written word if the participants completed a questionnaire or survey. You will need permission from your participants to audio-record or video-record the interviews.

Your data consist of the transcripts of the interviews and any notes you take during the interviews.

Transcription of interviews is a very individualized process—meaning everyone does it differently. There are some tips that help make this process easier for you. First, if you are audio-recording your interviews there are various software programs you can buy that can make transcribing a lot easier (e.g., Interact-AS, NCH Software, Nuance, Vocapia, VoiceBase, etc. . . .). These programs often work in conjunction with a foot pedal, where you can stop-start conversation while you transcribe. If you don't want to or can't buy one of these programs you can still transcribe while listening to an audio file. You will need to do a lot of stopping and starting to make sure you get all of what your participants say on file. Second, we have both found that it is beneficial to transcribe interviews shortly after they are conducted. Some researchers will not do this, but in our opinion it is best to transcribe them while the interview is fresh in your mind. Third, once you have the interview transcribed, it is helpful to insert notes in the margins of what you remember happening during certain parts of the interview. Trust us; you will forget a lot about the interviews in the future. Transcribing is a time-consuming process, but in the end you must get your interview data into some visual form to fully understand them.

Sampling is very important in interviewing (so you may want to review Chapter 7 on random and non-random sampling). Depending on the population you are working with, a random sample may prove difficult (if not impossible to get), thus necessitating a non-random sample. In fact, in most cases non-random sampling is necessary and useful in interviewing. Stephen regularly interviews Muslim immigrants in France (Croucher, 2006, 2008, 2008a). Stephen has found that a random sample is nearly impossible in any nation that does not keep records based on religious affiliation (including France). Even when governments track religious affiliation, many individuals are undocumented and other variables make a random sample impossible. Stephen has found convenience and/or snowball sampling appropriate for his research. Often he has conducted work in cultures where he is not an insider, and a snowball sample has been the only way for him to locate participants.

Another important question often asked in interview projects is "How many interviews do I need?" This is not an easy question to answer. **Data saturation,** or the point at which no new data emerge, is a matter of judgment. As you conduct more and more qualitative research, such as interviewing and ethnography, you will develop the skills to evaluate what you have collected and tell yourself the following: "I have enough information because my participants keep repeating themselves."

As we prepare to conduct our semi-structured interviews, we ask if the participants will let us video-record the interviews. The recordings, our interview notes, and a transcription of the interviews are our data.

With the knowledge of the approaches to interviews, and the types of data used in interviews, the following section discusses the types of claims used in interview research.

Claims in Interviews

Researchers who use interviews as a method are generally more likely to identify as interpretive (Chapter 4) or critical (Chapter 5) scholars; some will identify with the social scientific paradigm (Chapter 3), and some will identify with more than one research paradigm. The key for researchers using interviews (and any other method for that matter) is the claims they are trying to make. Two different claims are primarily associated with interviewing as a method, descriptive and interpretive. Granted, other claims can be associated with interviews (evaluative and reformist). You will remember that Chapters 3 and 4 describe how claims can define what is occurring and reveal individual meaning structures within society.

Journalists, for example, continuously ask questions to find out what is happening about daily events. These descriptive tales or accounts of what is happening are the backbone of journalism. From local to national to international events, personal accounts told to journalists in the field, via telegraph to telephone to Skype, add thick description to what is occurring. Along with simply describing the events, journalists often add what we call the "human element" to the story. Interviewing individuals on the street and getting their point of view on an issue, and how a particular issue affects them personally, helps the reader better understand how those affected by the issue understand it.

During the writing of this chapter, journalists from around the world were sneaking into Syria to report on events in the city of Homs and other Syrian cities (outside journalists were banned from entry by the Syrian government). Along with reporting the facts about troop movement, the death toll, the political responses, and human rights issues (defining what is occurring), reporters for CNN, the BBC, and other news agencies were quick to report on how the violence in Syria was affecting individuals on the ground (revealing individual meanings). The individual stories reinforced the reporters' descriptions and showed stories from individual participants.

Communication researchers use interviews to define what is occurring in a setting and to reveal individual meanings. Philipsen (1992, 1997) in an in-depth analysis explored being a member of Teamsterville, a neighborhood just outside of Chicago. Through in-depth semi-structured and unstructured interviews, Philipsen was able to define specific characteristics of masculinity/femininity in Teamsterville. For example, the front porch is for women, the bar is for men, and conflicts were not settled through talking but fighting (defining what is occurring). He learned by interviewing various individuals why certain rules existed for specific behaviors in Teamsterville. The collective reason for these behaviors came down to what the participants understood to be a "code of honor" (revealing individual meanings).

Well, the purpose of our interviews with Indians is to describe how Durga Puja relates to Indian identity. So, we hope during our interviews that participants will discuss Durga Puja, their identity, and how the festival and/or Goddess affect them in some way or another. We recognize our participants will be just a small sample of Indians; many others think like them and others think nothing like them. This is part of the interpretivist paradigm.

As with all research, warrants are necessary; therefore, the following section describes the warrants used to evaluate research using interviews.

Warrants in Interviews

The standards used to judge whether the data support your claims in an interview-based project or study are subjective, especially since most researchers using interviews subscribe to the interpretivist approach. As the purpose of interviews is generally to define what is occurring and/or reveal individual meanings, warrants for interviews address the ability of the researcher to describe multiple realities. Therefore, issues of researcher credibility, adequacy, and coherence are key issues to consider (Lindlof, 1995; Miles & Huberman, 1994; Strauss & Corbin, 1998). The credibility of the researcher is an important standard by which interpretive research is judged because the researcher is the instrument through which interpretations and meanings are made (Merrigan & Huston, 2009; Patton, 1990). Components used to determine researcher credibility are: level of researcher training or experience, the researcher's degree of membership in the social context, faithfulness or coherence, and reflexivity.

Training and Experience

Unlike research conducted through a discovery approach, where issues of reliability and validity are paramount to determine the effectiveness of an instrument and/or experiment, the researcher is the instrument in the interpretive approach. Therefore, one's level of experience in interviewing is paramount. Researchers conducting and analyzing interviews will develop their techniques and optimize their ability to observe and analyze the experience of their participants with experience. As long as one is methodologically aware of what should happen, there are some things we all learn while in the field. For example, when Stephen first went into the field as a master's student to interview shopkeepers in Montreal, he did not have much experience. However, he was aware of what he should be doing. He had taken various method courses as an undergraduate and graduate student. Such courses prepared him in theory for this work. Stephen learned quickly that some things he was taught (in books like this) were spot-on accurate. Unfortunately, some things were not as quite as clear. Stephen realized quickly the difficulty of taking notes while conducting interviews. His participants found his note-taking rude, and the textbooks did not prepare him for the reaction. So, Stephen combined what he learned in the field with what he learned from research method books and courses. Stephen is now theory-aware *and* field-aware . . . his training and experience developed in tandem. To this day, he is continually expanding his training and experience.

Degree of Membership

When conducting an interview-based project, an integral warrant is your degree of membership. Fitch (1994) stated that researchers should be, "deeply involved and closely connected to the scene, activity, or group being studied," while at the same time "achieve enough distance from the phenomenon to allow for recording of action and interactions relatively uncolored by what [you] might have had at stake" (p. 36). The two statements may seem like a difficult balancing act. Interpretive researchers who are involved and connected with the social context are better equipped to interpret participants' statements and look for individual meanings in their statements, as the researchers who are involved and connected with the social context better understand the participants' lives. However, when a researcher is *too* involved and is unable to achieve distance from the phenomenon they are studying, the lack of distance may affect the interpretation of the study. An individual *too* close to a phenomenon (an insider, for example) could be more likely to tilt their interpretation to a critical perspective (which is perfectly fine, but not interpretive), and/or a researcher could be *too* subjective and therefore less faithful to the results and participants.

In his study of the *Tico Times,* an English-language newspaper in Costa Rica, Spencer (2011) argued that, "English-language media outlets could and should be viewed as minority-language media outlets as they are cultural negotiators for tourists, sojourners and other transnational migrants" (p. 31). Spencer spent months observing and interviewing staff members at the newspaper for the project, he is fluent in Spanish, and has spent years traveling and living in Latin and South America. In this study, as in his other work, Spencer makes every effort to be deeply involved with his participants and/ or the phenomenon, while at the same time not becoming too involved to potentially alter his perceptions.

Faithfulness

Morse (1998) described faithful researchers as being "meticulous about their documentation," and making sure to "file methodically, and keep notes up-to-date" (p. 67). Simply put, faithfulness means being detailed. When a researcher is in the field conducting interviews, they should consider the following: have

I spent enough time in the field, have I interviewed enough people, have I gone over my notes and transcripts enough, and have I conducted enough research to support my findings (Lofland & Lofland, 1995; Patton, 1990)? Answering such questions will help ensure research is thorough and faithful.

Coherence

Other ways to look at coherence are logic and internal validity. When conducting an interpretive study using interviews, a researcher must ask if the results logically support the claims they are making. When our examples are coherent, we are more able to relate our findings to other social situations that share similarities (Fitch, 1994). In a classic example, Philipsen's (1976, 1992) analysis of Teamsterville discussed among many things the importance of place and what it meant to be a man. Philipsen provided a plethora of interview examples to illustrate each of his arguments. The arguments emerged from his analysis of the interview transcripts and ethnographic observations. Each of the examples supported the points Philipsen was illustrating. For example, when Philipsen (1976) discussed the issues of inclusion in Teamsterville, he described how:

> Once a stranger is located, talk might be relatively free, depending on the kind of person he is. "The hillbillies" and "the Mexicans" live within the neighborhood boundaries but do not, in the eyes of the long-term white residents really "belong" there.
>
> (p. 17)

The example of "Hillbillies" and "Mexicans" not belonging in Teamsterville clearly illustrates the point Phillipsen was making about who is and who is not a member of this community, thus adding coherence to his arguments.

Reflexivity

When we reflect on the research process, we are considering the research process and our place within it. Different theoretical approaches, values, and interests all can potentially affect the research process. As a researcher you should consider your position in relation to what you are studying. For example, how can your religious beliefs, age, gender/sex, sexual orientation, political views, and personal experiences affect what you pay attention to the most during an interview? How do these aspects of you impact what questions you are interested in asking? These are questions you should personally reflect on and be cognizant of while conducting your interviews and then while analyzing them.

While Stephen has a strong grasp of Indian culture, he is not Indian. Thus, any of his attempts to understand Indian culture, identity and Durga Puja are those of an outsider (etic research). We want to be meticulous in our research, so we will make sure we take a lot of notes, and spend plenty of time trying to understand our participants to make sure our representation is faithful. Finally, we will use clear and concise examples to support our claims to make sure our analysis is coherent.

The following section describes how to analyze your interview data.

Analysis of Interview Transcripts

A researcher can use various methods to analyze interview transcripts from an interpretive approach. Researchers can conduct a content analysis of their interview transcripts (see Chapters 13 and 14), they could perform a rhetorical analysis (see Chapter 19), they could approach the project and the analysis from a critical/cultural perspective (see Chapter 20), and/or the researcher could do a grounded-theory analysis (see Chapter 13). Grounded theory is one of the more popular forms of qualitative data analysis. Glaser and Strauss (1967) defined **grounded theory** as "the process of breaking down, examining, comparing, conceptualizing, and categorizing data" (p. 61). Through the process of inductive coding, themes or "salient categories of information supported by the text" (p. 22) "emerge" from the analysis of texts, instead of being pre-chosen by the researcher. Glaser and Strauss (1967) claimed researchers conducting a grounded-theory analysis should follow four steps:

1. Collect data from participants (conduct interviews).
2. Take detailed notes during each interaction (the interviews).
3. Code (write) in the margins of transcripts of interviews the central theme or purpose of each line or passage of an interview. Bernard (1999) recommended using a highlighter to differentiate ideas (themes) that are similar within transcripts and from one interviewee to another. The coding stage allows themes to naturally "emerge."
4. Memo—or write down generalized links between what is coded and established theory. The researcher will pull out quotations they have identified from their coding (step 3) to support specific theoretical arguments in the literature.

After the four stages are finished, researchers sort their memos into broad theoretical categories, which Strauss and Corbin (1991) claimed facilitate making theoretical arguments and conclusions. A more in-depth description of how to conduct a grounded-theory analysis is provided in Chapter 13.

Stephen will want to make sure he uses clear examples from his interviews to illustrate the different ways Durga Puja relates to identity. After sifting through the transcripts, some themes may emerge that relate to Collier and Thomas's (1988) or Ting-Toomey's (1993, 1999) conceptions of identity. Stephen's job is to use examples that coherently relate to theory.

Summary

This chapter was a how-to guide to interviewing as a research method. As seen in the chapter, interviewing is generally approached from the interpretive or critical/cultural paradigm. We hope after reading the chapter, and the accompanying student paper, you have enough know-how to conduct your own study using interviews. The next chapter, Chapter 12, is a how-to guide to focus groups.

 ## Key Steps & Questions to Consider

1. Choose your topic and research it.
2. Choose your population.
3. How will you access this population?
4. Are you doing a random or non-random sampling?
5. Is your questioning going to be structured, semi-structured, or unstructured?
6. How many questions are you going to ask?
7. How many people are you going to interview? This is a hard question to answer. There is no magic number of interviews you need to do to reach data saturation.
8. Before you enter the field did you write, submit, and get approval from your Human Subject Review Board or Institutional Review Board?
9. Remember rapport!
10. To tape/video-record the interviews or not?
11. Remember you will need to transcribe the interviews (or have someone else do it for you). This takes a lot of time but it makes analysis of the interviews so much better as you will have a greater understanding of what you have in your data!
12. Self-reflect on your position as the researcher. Are you a part of the group you are studying or an outsider. This self-reflection is always helpful as it aids in uncovering meaning.
13. Look through your transcripts for either pre-determined themes or emergent themes. Your grounded-theory analysis.
14. Support these themes with coherent examples. Continuation of your grounded-theory analysis.

15. Throughout this whole process you may have already been writing some of your research paper (analysis of literature, for example); if not, start.

Activities

1. *Identifying interview questions.* Type "interview questions" into an Internet search. You will get millions of results. Pick a "top 10" or "top 100" list of interview questions. Work through the list and identify which questions work best with a structured, semi-structured, or unstructured interview. You can divide the class into groups with each group working through different lists (and with millions of hits, you will have no shortage of lists available!).

2. *Practice interviewing.* Divide the class into pairs. Have the students interview each other using a few of the interview questions from activity 1. The students can conduct brief interviews, rotating to a new partner every 5–10 minutes (and switching between being interviewee and interviewer). How did the students establish rapport in each interview? What do the results from the interviews reveal?

3. *Analyzing interview data.* Pick a "riveting talk" from TED.com. Select a communication theory that relates to the TED talk. Treat the TED talk as interview data. Conduct a grounded-theory analysis. See what themes and patterns "emerge" from the talk. For a challenge, try transcribing the TED talk! Try dividing the class into groups with each group analyzing a different TED talk.

Discussion Questions

1. How will the student's data and analysis change if switched from Likert-scale questions to open-ended questions?
2. Discuss how different sampling approaches will affect the student's data and results.
3. Discuss possible communication theories, which may tie in with the student's paper. How will the inclusion of theory/theories into the study make the research stronger?

Key Terms

Data saturation
Grounded theory
Interview guide
Interviewing

Rapport
Sampling
Semi-structured
Structured

Thick description
Unstructured

Undergraduate Student Paper

No matter the letter, we're all Greek together

Heather Kerr

Freshman year of college is an exhilarating, one of a kind experience for students. Most freshmen are 17 or 18 years old living on their own for the first time. This major life change usually leads to students reevaluating and reworking their social identity. Some students may rely on behavior that has worked for them in the past. Others may emulate behavior they have seen work for others in high school. Still more seek social acceptance and validation from their peers by joining clubs and organizations. Perhaps the organizations with the worst reputation in many colleges are the fraternities and sororities. Despite years of negative media portrayal and assorted hazing scandals across the country, thousands of students continue to pledge their lifelong loyalty and define their social identity with them every year.

> Heather has started with a strong introduction, which sets the context for her study.

I am on my journey to understand the broad correlation between Greek life and social identity and how wearing letters (clothing, usually T-shirts, with the Greek letters of an organization) affect one's sense of social identity. I decided the best way to understand this would be to go directly to the source. My study consisted of eight willing participants from three different organizations. Four participants were boys and four were girls. They ranged in age from 18 to 21. Every grade was represented with one freshman, four sophomores, two juniors, and one senior. I met with each participant at their convenience for an interview. Each interview lasted between 10 and 15 minutes. I had a list of approximately eight questions but went in with an open mind and asked follow-up questions whenever I deemed necessary depending on participants' answers. Instead of recording the interviews, I went with a pen and paper to take notes. After my final interview was completed, I had nearly six pages front and back of notes. Each participant chose an alias and all information pertaining to this study were kept in a private location accessible only to myself.

The theory I was interested in testing was Social Identity Theory. Social Identity Theory was developed in the late 1970s by Tajfel and Turner (Mcleod, 2008). Tajfel and Turner proposed a system of three mental processes involved in determining whether a person is part of the "in" group or "out" group (Mcleod, 2008). These groups are extremely important because they give the people who belong to them a sense of pride and self-esteem. They also provide a sense of belonging and contribute greatly to social identity. People divide the world into groups of "us" vs. "them" because it helps us understand things better. By enhancing the status of our own group and diminishing the status of opposing groups, we increase our own sense of self-worth (Mcleod, 2008). This division into groups of "us" vs. "them" is the first step in Social Identity Theory, also known as categorization.

The second stage is social identification. In this stage, people adopt the traits and behaviors they attribute to their selected group (Mcleod, 2008). For example, a new member or pledge of a Greek organization who knows nothing of Greek life aside from what he or she has seen in *Animal House* or *Van Wilder* movies would most likely drink heavily and engage in risky behavior at parties or other social events. This type of behavior may not be the norm for all Greek organizations but, because the new member may not know otherwise, they choose to act this way in an attempt to fit in. If this is not the way the rest of the group behaves, the individual will usually catch on quickly and adapt his or her behavior again to better match the rest of the members.

The third and final stage of Social Identity Theory is social comparison. Now that the member has identified and begun to act similarly to the rest of the organization, he or she starts

Heather is not clear if she belongs to a Greek organization. The reader does not know her *degree of membership* within the organizations she is studying. Heather provides good demographic information on the people she interviewed, but is less clear how the participants were selected for the study. Standards for selecting interviewees are best if set before the interview process begins. Sometimes the selection process needs to be adjusted as the selection process proceeds, in which case the researcher acknowledges the variations that occurred and why they were implemented. It appears from her description that Heather is using a semi-structured approach. She can strengthen her paper by stating the approach she is using instead of leaving it up to a reader to infer the interview protocols. Finally, Heather clearly states her method of data collection (pen and paper).

comparing his or her group to other groups (Mcleod, 2008). Since people's measure of self-worth relies so heavily on how their group compares with other groups, competition and prejudices arise (Mcleod, 2008). It is extremely important to be aware that once groups have been labeled rivals their standing is critical for its members' self-esteem (Mcleod, 2008). These rivalries tend to become exacerbated during the spring semester when many colleges including Marist hold their annual Greek Week challenges. Greek Week at Marist College is a week of events such as a belly flop contest, relay races, pop tab collection, a talent show performance promoting Greek unity, as well as other events that organizations can use for winning points. At the end of the week, the fraternity and sorority with the most points are dubbed Greek Week Champions and the prize is bragging rights for the next year.

When asked to describe their respective organization in three adjectives, members of the same organization had similar results. The brothers of Alpha Phi Delta, the Delta Theta chapter I interviewed, all thought their organization was hardworking, welcoming, and motivated, or used close variations of those adjectives (Chaz, Chunk, Fink, personal communications, 2011). The sisters of Kappa Kappa Gamma, Zeta Chi chapter, generally thought their organization was intelligent, classy, and supportive (Cookie, Forge, Luce, Procs, personal communications, 2011).

Six out of eight participants reported major positive changes in their self-image and self-worth since joining their respective organizations. Girls were more likely to admit to deeper emotional connections and reported feeling "lost," "having trouble finding people [they] clicked with," and unsure of "having a group of friends that would be with [them] forever" without their organizations (Cookie, Procs, personal communications, 2011). Boys, on the other hand, were more likely to feel "like any other kid" (Fink, personal communication, 2011) and be less emotional about Greek life giving them "more of a sense of purpose and belonging" (Chunk, personal communication, 2011). Only one participant reported Greek life "has not had any impact on [her] self-image" (Forge, personal communication, 2011).

Every participant reported wearing their letters at least once a week (Chaz, Chunk, Cookie, Fink, Forge, Luce, Procs, Turtle, personal communications, 2011). One participant reported wearing letters "as often as possible" (Chaz, personal communication, 2011) and another reported carrying a tote bag with the letters of her sorority on it every day (Luce, personal communication, 2011).

Despite the obvious pride in one's organization, there was no evidence of blatant dislike for members of other Greek organizations or non-Greek students. One participant claimed to not have an opinion because she did not feel everyone had to be involved in Greek life (Forge, personal communication, 2011) but the general consensus was pity when non-Greeks miss out on opportunities Greeks may experience:

> I certainly don't think anything negative about people outside of Greek life. I think they're missing out on some absolutely wonderful aspects and everybody could benefit [from it] but I also understand why people are hesitant to join after the way [Greek life] is portrayed in the media . . . it looks like drinking, hazing, and being [sexually promiscuous] but it's really so much more than that.
>
> (Procs, personal communication, 2011)

Even the rivalries between organizations seem relaxed. "I feel connected [to members of other Greek organizations] because they are part of a sisterhood as well" (Cookie, personal communication, 2011). I believe the attitudes come from the idea of Greeks wearing their letters 24/7. "I'm still a brother and as long as I am I will represent [my organization] as best I can" (Fink, personal communication, 2011). The negative stigma against Greek life, especially fraternities, makes

Heather is effectively using *thick description* to support her analysis of the interview data.

students even more conscientious of their behavior and determined to turn opponents into advocates:

> Not all Greeks are the same. We are as diverse as the population, so one bad experience does not represent all of us. That would be like saying that all lacrosse players are rapists because a few Duke lacrosse players were accused of it.
>
> (Chaz, personal communication, 2011)

My research concludes little correlation between physically wearing the letters KKΓ, ΑΦΔ, or TDX across one's chest and social identity. The members of these organizations all seem to realize, especially at a school as small as Marist College, that they must be conscientious and responsible for their words and actions at all times. They work hard to maintain and protect their own reputation and to build up Greeks collectively.

Heather has a brief, yet effective, interpretation of what her analysis means for social identify—at least on the Marist College campus. Interview data/analysis can be limited to the context in which the interviews occurred. Extrapolating to other campuses is problematic. However, exploring the issue on other campuses opens up opportunities to engage in additional communication research!

References

Chaz, Personal Communication, 5 December 2011.

Chunk, Personal Communication, 5 December 2011.

Cookie, Personal Communication, 4 December 2011.

Fink, Personal Communication, 5 December 2011.

Forge, Personal Communication, 8 December 2011.

Luce, Personal Communication, 8 December 2011.

Mcleod, S. (2008). Social identity theory. *Simply psychology*. Retrieved December 9, 2011, from: www.simplypsychology.org/social-identity-theory.html.

Procs, Personal Communication, 7 December 2011.

Turtle, Personal Communication, 7 December 2011.

12 FOCUS GROUPS

What Will I Learn About Focus Groups?

During the 2012 elections, many of the news channels (e.g., CNN, Fox, MSNBC) used focus groups of voters to discuss the candidates before, during, and after the presidential debates. A moderator was in the room while the participants watched the debate. The moderator asked questions about the issues and the candidates. The questions helped the news channels make claims about the candidates, including who "won" the debate, and what issues Americans care about.

While the news channels were running their focus groups, the candidates were running their own focus groups. Modern candidates have agencies or consultants working for them who help develop campaign materials (e.g., slogans, advertisements, even campaign colors). The materials are generally pre-tested on focus groups. The campaign materials are tested so the agencies or consultants can get preliminary feedback from a group, make alterations, and then release the materials to the general public. Focus groups are standard practice in advertising and filmmaking (Morrison, 1998). Researchers interested in political communication could easily employ focus groups to study a variety of communication theories and/or communication situations. For example, a researcher could use focus groups to look at different ways candidates try to persuade voters using theory of planned action (Ajzen, 1985), social judgment theory (Sherif, Sherif, & Nebergall, 1965), elaboration likelihood model (Petty & Cacioppo, 1983), or inoculation theory (McGuire, 1964; Pfau, 1992). In Chapter 12 you will learn how to conduct research in communication studies using focus groups.

What is a Focus Group and Why Use One?

A **focus group** is a research method where people are interviewed about a specific topic. Focus groups can range from formal group interviews, to informal group interviews, to brainstorming sessions, to group interviews in the field (Lindlof & Taylor, 2002). Like interviews and ethnography, focus groups typically fall under the interpretive and/or the critical/cultural paradigms. As with the previously discussed qualitative methods, two claims are generally associated with focus groups as a method: descriptive and interpretive. However, social scientists are also known to use focus groups. Focus groups are led by a **moderator** (sometimes called a facilitator). The moderator leads the discussion among the participants in the group. We will talk more about the role of the moderator or facilitator shortly.

Focus groups have been used extensively in mass communication and advertising (Lindlof & Taylor, 2002), and have recently gained prominence in the social sciences (Berg, 2009). By broadly exploring the thoughts of a group of people on a specific subject of interest, focus groups are able to identify "general background information about a topic of interest" (Stewart, Shamdasani, & Rook, 2006, p. 15). Today, researchers use focus groups for a variety of research projects.

Peterson, Anthony, and Thomas (2012) explored "successfully home stable individuals" and the various factors that challenge their home life stability. Their study brought forth numerous thoughts about what individuals think causes homelessness.

Sanders and Anderson (2010) analyzed the conflicts that arise between faculty and students over disappointing college or university grades. The results revealed the discussions could be uncomfortable, yet also positive and constructive.

Focus groups explore general information about topics for a variety of reasons. First, moderators in focus groups generally have a list of discussion questions that guide the group. These questions are intended to help the moderator elicit information from the participants about the topic of interest. Since numerous participants are in the group, numerous points of view should emerge from the discussion. Second, the moderator's questions are a starting point. Focus groups generally take on a life of their own (if run well by the moderator).

Sometimes focus groups can be used to help "generate important insights into topics that [are] not well understood" (Berg, 2009, p. 165). Often with qualitative methods like interviews and ethnography, researchers are trying to learn more about constructs and how they occur in real life. Researchers are able to tap what Carey (1994) called the **group effect.** When group members interact, new data and insight emerge that previously, on individual levels, may have been less accessible. Group interaction can lead to more in-depth understandings of communication phenomena.

The following is an example of how using focus groups can tap a variety of opinions. Shyles and Hocking (1990) found that U.S. Army troops were not all that fond of the U.S. Army's "Be All You Can Be" campaign. Through the use of 12 focus groups, the authors showed how active members of the Army saw the campaign in a negative light and this may lower troop morale. Shortly after Shyles and Hocking completed their data analysis, the advertising firm that developed the ads contacted the authors and were not pleased with their results. Shyles and Hocking discussed the data with the firm and "went so far as to offer to conduct one of these replications at the ad agency's expense. The conversation ended abruptly, and not only were Shyles and Hocking not sued, neither researcher ever again received a communication from the advertising agency" (Hocking, Stacks, & McDermott, 2003, p. 402). A few years later, after new ads were aired with "Be All You Can Be," the ads were modified; the modifications fit some of the issues noted by Shyles and Hocking.

How to Prepare for a Focus Group

In order to generate insights, a researcher must prepare a well-designed focus group. One must consider seven important components when preparing to conduct a focus group. First, as with all of the other forms of research discussed in this text, you need to be sure you have a research focus for your study; both research questions and hypotheses can be explored with focus groups. Second, you can determine if a focus group design is the most appropriate for your study. For example, while a focus group could be used to collect data on people's public behaviors, ask individuals about their self-disclosures, or study how conflict styles differ across age groups, other methods could produce more fruitful findings.

Let's say you want to explore the effectiveness of a new campaign slogan developed for a political candidate. A survey could work, but will only take a snapshot of people's feelings at one point in time. An ethnographic approach could work, but observing people watching the slogan or reading it really will not provide you with much information about how potential voters feel about the slogan. Individual interviews could work, but will lack interaction between potential voters; a focus group really is the best method for this study. A focus group has the voters talk to each other and you—as the researcher—can use their interactions with your questions as data.

Third, once you have decided on the focus group approach, you need to determine how many focus groups you will conduct and how many people you will have in each group. Debates happen over both of these questions. Here's the rule on the minimum number of focus groups: never settle on just one focus group. You need more than one focus group so you can compare the results from each group to the other. You are able to see emerging trends in your data when you conduct multiple focus groups. Let's return to our political communication scenario. You may see members of groups to consistently point out strengths and/or weaknesses in a political slogan, regardless of who is in a group. Lindlof and Taylor (2002) argued you should have a minimum of two to three focus groups for a sound study.

You want between 6 to 12 people in each focus group. When you have three people in a group, you have less chance of really seeing the group effect (Carey, 1984), because fewer group members are interacting. However, a group that is too big can become hard to handle. We talk more about this later. Many researchers who use focus groups typically want six to 12 people (Lindlof & Taylor, 2002). Just like interviewing and ethnography, you next need to find your participants. Do you post flyers in significant places, work your gatekeepers, use e-mail lists . . .? Use the best means available to locate your participants. One of the things we talked about in Chapters 10 and 11 was that often your participant selection method for this kind of research is non-random, such as a convenience or purposive sample. In a study using a focus group you should try to include people with a variety of opinions to generate the true group effect, as groups generally have a variety of opinions.

So, set up two or more groups with six to 12 potential voters and ask them to look over the new slogan for the candidate. One common technique in focus groups is to show some sort of stimulus material and ask participants to respond to it. In the case of the slogan, you could show the group the statement and record their opinions. In each group, try to have voters who are from a broad range of the political continuum; this way you can get opinions from multiple sides of the political spectrum. Having both males and females is good for seeing how both sexes respond to the slogan. You might want to have people from different ethnic/racial backgrounds; the more diversity you have in the group the better chance you have of learning more about how the general public may respond to the slogan.

Fourth, you should also ask yourself if you are going to pay your participants. In ethnography, you as the researcher are observing human behavior. The level of participant involvement in the research process can range from very passive to active. In an individual interview project, the participant is actively engaging with the researcher. Thus, in some cases researchers may offer participants compensation for their time, either financial or other (e.g., food, extra credit). To set up a successful focus group, you may need to offer incentives for participation. **Incentives for participation** are paid or unpaid ways of encouraging people to participate in a study. The type of incentive will depend on your population. Some focus groups can range from 30 to 90 minutes (and sometimes longer); a researcher is taking time from the participants. At the University of Jyväskylä, where Stephen teaches, some departments offer movie tickets to research participants. Some university departments offer students extra credit for participation. In advertising research, firms may pay or provide free products for participation. The issue of incentives is something you need to determine and be upfront about with your participants in the informed-consent form.

Since you are occupying the time of each of your participants, you might want to consider offering them some kind of incentive for participation. Since these individuals are not undergraduate students, extra credit in a class is not an appropriate incentive. Maybe you provide them with lunch, movie tickets, a gift certificate for coffee, or something similar in value. If your incentive for participation does not draw in enough participants, you may need to increase it. . . .

Fifth, you need to determine where the focus group will take place. Unlike ethnographies, which take place in the natural setting of the participants, and interviews which can take place in the natural setting or a "lab," focus groups almost always take place in a controlled environment (the lab).

You, as the researcher, determine the place and time for the group to meet. Hocking et al. (2003) listed a few pre-conditions that explain why focus group locations are pre-determined by the researcher:

> Most focus groups are run at night, with one group following a second by 10 to 15 minutes. Because of the interaction required, most groups run between one and two hours, with at least one refreshment and bathroom break included. Some research companies have two-way mirrored and electronically monitored rooms that you can rent. You need a room that is conducive to communication and not too formal. Preferably you want your participants to face each other, perhaps in a circle around a table.   (p. 205)

These conditions make clear why a researcher wants a focus group to meet in a pre-determined, controlled location—too many variables cannot be controlled in a natural environment.

So, choose a location that best suits your needs. Some university departments have focus group or laboratory rooms you can use. Many advertising firms and other corporations have specially designed rooms for focus groups. The key is to have a plan for where you will do the focus group, keeping in mind: 1) how many people will be in each group, 2) how long each group will run, 3) if you are recording the groups (we will talk about that shortly), 4) how the room is set up, 5) if there are bathroom facilities nearby, and 6) if the location is easy to find for the participants.

Sixth, as discussed in Chapter 11 on interviewing, recording interviews can make data analysis a whole lot easier. With focus groups, your data may involve more than what people say, but also *how* they say it. So, you will need to decide if you are going to audio- or video-record the groups. You will, of course, need to get permission from the participants to record. Once you have permission to record, your data will be recordings and the transcripts (if you decide to transcribe). We recommend you record the focus groups and then transcribe the data as soon as possible after conducting each group. Numerous software programs can make transcribing easier (Interact-AS, NCH Software, Nuance, Vocapia, VoiceBase, etc. . . .). Remember, you should still take notes during a focus group even if you are recording. Taking notes will add to your understanding later when you analyze the transcripts of the data because you can jot down notes about what is happening while you are in the group at those very moments.

You decide that you are only interested in what the participants say about the slogan. In this case, it is only necessary you audio-record the focus group. So, you get permission from all of the participants to audio-record the focus groups.

The seventh element you need before you conduct a focus group, and one of the most important ones, is the moderator. The moderator is the one who leads the focus group and makes sure that the discussion guide is followed. A **discussion guide** is the program for the focus group. The guide includes your opening and closing statements, and the questions for the group. The moderator of the group uses the discussion guide as a roadmap on how to lead the group. The questions in the discussion guide are based on the main purposes of the study. Figure 12.1 is an example discussion

---

PARTICIPANT INTRODUCTION

Hello my name is [name here] and I have been asked to lead a discussion today about a new slogan Candidate X is developing for his/her election campaign. What we are going to do today is watch his/her new advertisement, which includes the new slogan, and then I am going to ask you some questions. There are no right or wrong answers. I am just interested in what you think about the slogan and the advertisement.

Everything you say here will be kept completely confidential. We will be audio-recording the focus group today, and then transcribing the session. The transcripts from the group will be summarized and presented in such a way that no individual could be identified in the future.

What I am passing out to each of you now is an informed-consent form. This form outlines everything that you will be doing today, all of your duties and responsibilities. This form also explains the benefits of this study, how to contact the researchers in case you have any questions or concerns about the study. The form also notes that for participating in this study, which should take about 60 minutes, you will receive a $10 Starbucks gift card. However, if you stop your participation before completion of the study, which is your right, you will not receive the gift card.

One last thing before we get started. I would like each of you to take a nametag and put your first name on it. It can be your real first name or a fictitious one; it is up to you, whatever you feel comfortable with. Can everyone now take a couple of minutes and read over the informed

---

Figure 12.1 Sample Discussion Guide for Study on Political Slogan Effectiveness

nt, ask any questions you might have, and if it is okay, sign it. Let now when you have signed it and I will collect it.

is everyone signed the forms? Okay, let's get started. I am going to on the audio-recorder now. Can I have each of you say your name he group and introduce yourself [THIS IS A GREAT WAY TO GET EVERYONE'S NAMES ON THE RECORDER.]

[FROM THIS POINT, THERE IS A LOT OF VARIABILITY IN WHAT YOU CAN DO.] I would like you all to watch the following new advertisement that was just developed by Candidate X's team—play advertisement.

FOCUS GROUP QUESTIONS

Okay, now that you have seen the new ad, I have some questions for us to think about. [HERE THE QUESTIONS ARE GUIDED BY THE FOCUS OF THE STUDY; WE WILL LIST TWO SAMPLE QUESTIONS. DEPENDING ON HOW LONG THE GROUP IS, REMEMBER TO BREAK FOR BATHROOM.]

1. What did you like and what did you dislike about the advertisement?
2. Candidate X in this advertisement is trying to persuade you that he/she is the best candidate for President. How does he/she do that?

[THE GROUP COULD CONTINUE WITH MORE QUESTIONS ABOUT THE ADVERTISEMENT UNTIL THE MODERATOR IS READY TO WRAP UP THE GROUP.]

Well I would like to thank you for your participation in this discussion today. I think we have really uncovered some interesting insight into (name the advertisement). As I said at the start, if you have any questions about the study, feel free to contact us via the information provided on the forms. Now, I think it's time to pass out some coffee gift cards. Thanks again.

Figure 12.1 (Continued)

guide. The questions in the discussion guide are only as successful as the moderator. Morgan (1988) described how a moderator should be a good interviewer and especially a good listener. A moderator should be prepared to adapt questions if participants do not respond to some questions. "Moderators try to achieve a fine balance between enfranchising individuals to speak out and promoting good group feelings" (Lindlof & Taylor, 2002, p. 183). A good moderator is someone who has a knack for bringing in quiet participants and politely silencing aggressive or overly anxious participants. Many advertising firms hire moderators with strong communication skills to lead focus groups. Hocking et al. (2003) strongly urge the researchers of projects *not* to serve as the moderators of their own focus groups. The authors urge researchers to try to hire professional moderators if possible. Of course, few student-researchers can afford to hire a professional moderator, so you need to be prepared to moderate your own focus groups.

How to Conduct a Focus Group

If you have taken the proper steps to prepare, then conducting the group should be rather systematic. You should already have your questions designed, your number of groups and participants set, incentive for participation determined, the location set, be prepared to record (assuming permission is received), and have a moderator chosen. When you conduct a focus group you need to: 1) make sure the location is functional, 2) double check the recording device(s), 3) conduct the discussion using the guide, and 4) analyze the results. First, while you may have a location set for the group, always make sure the location is ready before the participants arrive. This may sound silly, but Stephen and Dan have been involved in research projects (as researchers and participants) where we have arrived and things are not ready.

Second, as you will more than likely be recording (audio or video), it is a good idea to do a check of the equipment before the group begins. What a shame if your participants are ready and the technology fails you.

Third, use the discussion guide to conduct the focus groups. The purpose of the discussion guide is to help the moderator(s) facilitate the focus group. If you look at Figure 12.1, this kind of guide can be modified in many ways to help a well-trained moderator lead a discussion. The moderator is looking for the participants to answer specific questions about issues pertinent to the research subject. However, the moderator does not give the participants answers. Thus, the moderator needs to be open to the participants providing a variety of expected and unexpected answers. This is one reason why the discussion guide needs to be somewhat flexible in its format. Like open-ended interviews, these guides should be open for change, to a point, meaning the moderator (and the discussion guide) try to remain on the same research theme but allow the participants to talk about issues important to them and relevant to the group's subject.

Fourth, once a focus group is complete and you have transcripts of what was said during the group, you need to analyze the transcripts (your data). You can analyze qualitative data in numerous ways. You can approach your data analysis from a variety of different approaches. For example, you could conduct a grounded-theory analysis (Glaser & Strauss, 1967; Strauss & Corbin, 1991), a metaphoric analysis (Gill, 1994), a conversation or discourse analysis, or a content analysis. We will talk more in depth about some of these methods in Chapter 13 on qualitative data analysis and in other chapters in this text. You should also consider the notes and observations of the moderator as an important part of your analysis. A well-trained moderator should be versed in taking good notes and understanding human behavior. Talk to the moderator(s) and find out what they thought about the groups and use their insight as one kind of data to help your analysis.

With our advertisement for Candidate X, we decide on our day for the first focus group. We have recruited our participants, we have our discussion guide and moderator, we have our coffee gift cards, and we have the recording device all ready. So, we (the advertising firm) show up an hour beforehand with the moderator to make sure the location is all set up and ready for the session. We then do a test run of the audio-recorder (it works great!). Then the participants arrive. The moderator reads the introduction and goes through the script on the guide. After the session, which was a lively discussion about the advertisement by the way, we go back to our firm and get a debriefing from the moderator on their thoughts about the participants and the session. We add their notes and thoughts (as data) to our transcripts. We are still debating whether we will analyze our data using a content analytic approach (Chapter 14) or a grounded-theory approach (Chapter 13), but we will decide that soon. Tomorrow, we have another session, our second of six focus groups.

Advantages and Limitations of Focus Groups

Focus groups have numerous advantages and a few limitations. The five main advantages to focus groups are: 1) cost, 2) speed, 3) quantity of participants, 4) ability to reach sensitive populations, and 5) the group effect. The first three advantages of a focus group are closely linked to one another: cost, speed, and quantity of participants (Berg, 2009; Lindlof & Taylor, 2002). Focus groups often provide an inexpensive and quick way to gather data from a lot of participants. If one conducts three focus groups with seven people in each group, this means that the person has collected responses from 21 people at three separate points in time. If one wants to conduct individual open-ended interviews with 21 people, these interviews will often take place over 21 separate occasions. The data for the three focus groups likely take less time to collect. The cost of data collection (e.g., transportation, recording, incentives for participation) may end up being less for three focus groups than for 21 individual interviews. The fourth advantage of focus groups is the ability of these groups to reach sensitive populations. In many situations you may want to investigate a sensitive topic, such as sexual abuse. In such studies, participants may not feel as comfortable discussing the issue one-on-one. However, people are more likely to open up about sensitive topics when in the presence of other individuals who have similar experiences (Morgan, 1988). This is one reason why you may want to employ a focus group to explore sensitive topics with hard-to-reach populations. Finally, as previously mentioned, focus groups allow us to tap the group effect (Carey, 1994). When people are together with others discussing an issue, they are likely to bounce ideas off one another and feed off each other. These group interactions will produce more insights into the communication phenomena under investigation.

Focus groups have two limitations you should to keep in mind: 1) the moderator(s) and 2) the participants. While the moderator(s) is necessary to facilitate a successful focus group, you must make sure the moderator(s) is well trained. If the moderator(s) is not well trained and able to successfully manage the group, then the focus group could be a failure. The discussion could stagnate and interaction between the participants may stagnate, or some participants may monopolize the conversation, or (worst-case scenario) the moderator(s) could monopolize the conversation and be the only one talking. The role of the moderator(s) really is integral to the success of the focus group. Second, the participants themselves can make or break a focus group. Participants are volunteers. Like Forrest Gump said, "Life is like a box of chocolates, you never know what you're gonna get." Well, participants are like that: you never know what you're gonna get.

> Based on the participants in our focus groups to discuss Candidate X's advertisement, we should learn some things about how average voters think about the advertisement. If we have been careful in our development of the discussion guide, particularly in the questions, and chosen a good moderator or moderators, our job should be a success. Focus groups are increasingly used by advertisers, and also by researchers in communication. This qualitative method, if executed properly, can be an effective tool to analyze how groups perceive messages and how groups interact.

Summary

This chapter was a how-to guide for focus groups. As discussed in the chapter, focus groups are generally approached from the interpretive or critical/cultural paradigms. Hopefully after reading this chapter, and the accompanying student paper using focus groups, you will feel comfortable enough to use focus groups for your own research project. Considering that Chapters 10–12 focused on different qualitative methods, the next chapter, Chapter 13, is a description of various qualitative data analysis techniques.

Key Steps & Questions to Consider

1. A focus group is a research method where a group of people are interviewed about a specific topic.
2. The types of focus groups range from formal group interviews, to informal group interviews, to brainstorming sessions, to group interviews in the field.
3. Focus groups are led by a moderator (sometimes called a facilitator), an individual who leads the discussion that takes place among the participants in the group. Typically the moderator(s) is not the researcher in charge of the project.
4. The group effect is when a researcher is able to tap a multitude of opinions because a group is responding to one another's ideas and opinions in a group setting.

5. You should try to conduct at least two or three focus groups, if not more.
6. A focus group generally has between six to 12 people.
7. Some researchers will provide incentives to participate in focus groups.
8. Focus groups typically take place in a "lab" setting and not in the natural environment.
9. Audio- or video-recording of focus groups is a best practice.
10. The discussion guide is a tool used by the moderator(s) to lead the focus group through a series of questions.
11. Like most qualitative research methods, researchers have many options for analyzing focus group data.
12. Two different claims are associated with focus groups as a method: descriptive and interpretive.
13. Researcher credibility, adequacy, and coherence are key issues to consider regarding warrants in focus group research.

 ## Activities

1. Try a series of practice focus group sessions. Divide the class into groups of 6 to 12 students. Each group will select a communication issue and develop a short discussion guide of three to five questions. Once the guide is ready, each group exchanges their discussion guide with another group. Each group selects a moderator and, using the discussion guide from the other group, holds a focus group. The process continues with groups exchanging discussion guides until every group has held a focus group with each guide.
2. The class as a whole can use the data from the practice group sessions and try a practice analysis of the data. What themes emerged from the data collected from each discussion guide?
3. Run a web search for "focus group advertising." Compare how the websites explain focus groups with what you've learned in this chapter. What differences emerge between academic research focus groups and corporate focus groups?

 ## Discussion Questions

1. What types of research questions can be answered with data collection through focus groups?
2. When should a researcher avoid using a focus group for data collection?
3. What limitations should be taken into consideration with focus group data?
4. What approaches can you take for analyzing data from focus groups?

Key Terms

Discussion guide   Incentives for participation   Moderator
Focus group
Group effect

Undergraduate Student Paper

Communicating emotions through visual framing and influence

Rebecca Rachel Engels

Each individual expresses, processes, and interprets emotions differently. My research is constructed around the notion that we each interpret artwork differently, mainly shocking photographic images, by the use of visual framing. I am also interested in the message that the photographer is attempting to communicate through their artwork, as well as how our personal interpretations may be influenced by others, especially those who tend to dominate the conversation. According to Rodriguez and Dimitrova (2011), "Many consider audience frames as mental maps people form to cope with the flood of information to which they are subjected everyday. Audiences actively classify and organize their life experiences to make sense of them. These 'schemata of interpretation' or 'frames' that enable individuals to 'locate, perceive, identify, and label' the world around them" (p. 49). This statement reaffirms my thesis: each individual has their own unique framework for interpretation. Although individuals may possess their own opinions and emotions regarding a specific text, photograph, or work, their initial response may fluctuate due to the strong opinions of others. I've found dominant individuals or people in a position of power have a profound impact on the views of others. The influential factor possessed by some individuals makes them capable of manipulating the perception of other viewers, possibly because of advanced knowledge, intimidation, or ulterior motives.

My research consisted of six photographs, each photograph aiming towards a specific basic human emotion. I had two photographs for death, one for happiness, loneliness, fear, and love. I set up two focus groups from 11 beginner and advanced photography students. I posed two questions regarding each image: what emotions does this image evoke and what emotions do you feel the photographer was trying to induce? Participants were asked to provide answers to said questions by writing down an immediate response, I was able to get the participants' initial response to the image, without manipulation by others during the conversation regarding the image. After participants gave their initial written response, I conducted an engaging and open discussion regarding each image shown. By doing so, I was able to observe if the conversation was being steered in a certain direction or potentially opinions changing due to the power structure of the discussion. By taking detailed notes throughout the discussion, returning back to them later and comparing them with the participants' written answers, I was capable of obtaining honest results from the students both verbally and non-verbally.

Rebecca sets up an intriguing question in her introduction. She has merged multiple areas of communication—textual, visual, and verbal into her study. Her use of focus groups to explore the question should produce interesting results.

Literature Review

While initially researching prior work similar to my study, I found minimal research that was like mine. According to Rodriguez and Dimitrova (2011), "One of the main reasons why there are relatively few studies that employ visual framing compared to textual framing is that there is a great deal of confusion as to how visual frames are supposed to be identified in the first place. To this day, identifying visual frames remains a challenge; the methods of doing so cover the gamut" (pp. 50–51). Because of our high-functioning society and advancing technology, the general population has grown accustomed to images that have been manipulated and stray away from reality. This makes it difficult for viewers to see an image and question whether the image is depicting reality or fantasy. According to Brantner, Lobinger and Wetzstein (2009), "frames can be described as interpretation patterns which serve to classify information for handling it efficiently" (p. 524). Each individual establishes meaning for a certain image; how we organize information stems from life experience and general knowledge.

Brantner, Lobinger and Wetzstein (2009) high-lighted the importance and significance of powerful imagery in association with our perception and interpretation of the image at hand. I agree with the notion that emotions are easily portrayed through visual stimuli rather than words, although words are arbitrary.

Another interpretation is from Rodriguez and Dimitrova (2011) regarding visual framing. Although images may show reality, certain horrific aspects of reality are not seen by everyone, and are even attempted to be hidden from society, a dead body for example. A portrait of nightmarish qualities is not something an ordinary photographer would try to capture, unless they were attempting to expose a hidden reality.

Methods/Procedures

My method for collecting data is two focus groups. I expect to find each subject's written reaction to each photograph will be similar to his or her verbal reaction to the image. I am curious to determine whether subjects whom are knowledgeable about photography will produce significantly dif-ferent opinions regarding each image compared with those whom are not as knowledgeable. I will have a threefold analysis of my observations: First, what the subjects' initial written reactions were in both groups. Second, the subjects' verbal and non-verbal communication styles when discussing each image. Finally, initial reactions compared to verbal reactions with both groups.

The participants were aged roughly 18 to 24 years old, upper-level digital photography students, and basic photography students. The first focus group included the advanced photography students, with three white/Caucasian females and one Hispanic male. Students participated of their own will; it was remarkable how much effort the advanced students

> The literature review provides sufficient background to understand the nature of research conducted in her area of interest. However, be careful of using an article-by-article approach. Look for themes, which permeate across the journal articles, and then organize the review around the themes. Otherwise, you are counting on your readers to figure out how the articles interact.

put forth towards the research. Each student involved provided detailed responses and actively participated in the group discussion; they gave honest opinions and were incredibly respectful towards one another.

The participants in the second focus group, the beginner students aged 18 to 21, had little to no knowledge regarding photography. Most if not all were freshmen varying in educational backgrounds, majors, and belief systems. I decided to incorporate the beginner photography students to obtain a variety of results pertaining to each image. Also, this was done to establish if more influence during the discussion occurred in the beginner students versus advanced students. I anticipated the beginner students would produce original, potentially vague ideas and bring new emotions to the table.

Results

The results I obtained were slightly skewed, but helped me comprehend the significance of an educational background on such a subject versus having none whatsoever. During the first focus group, throughout our discussion each participant derived their own set of unique meanings from each photograph. My method for collecting data consisted of observing the conversation and its progression by taking detailed notes, as well as analyzing the written answers provided by participants.

The first photograph portrayed happiness. Female participants brought up the idea of skin cancer. The male participant thought the girl in the photograph was shy. He noted the light and colors portrayed sunshine, or happiness.

The second photograph was the first of two images portraying death. The photograph was taken in the Japanese wilderness of a dead body found, possibly a suicide. The male student was already aware of the phenomenon of Japanese suicide in the woods, something I had not anticipated. He pointed out the sadness of dying alone, a melancholy aspect of this image, an emotion many attempt to repress.

The female participants expressed an extreme depression while viewing this saddening illustration of a human who died alone in the woods.

The third photograph is of a bearded man who sits alone naked on a chair in front of a small audience. A female participant verbally expressed the emotion of feeling awkward; she also found the image to be humorous.

The fourth photograph portrayed love. It did not communicate the emotion of love very clearly, I realized. During the discussion, a female participant voiced her opinion that there was a feeling of betrayal or possibly adultery. The male participant thought the man in the photograph was a customer and the woman was a prostitute because of a half-hearted embrace. Another female participant brought up the notion of despair or potentially false love or mental illness.

The second photograph depicting death was a Vietnamese man about to be shot in the head. The discussion proved to be interesting because many of the students did not initially respond to the photograph with the idea of death. The male student voiced his opinion of possible fear, power, or even control. He had been exposed to the video of the same man getting shot in the head, although did not bring up the notion of death. The female participants felt the photograph was attempting to communicate the idea of war, potentially anger. After allowing participants to express themselves, I quoted the photographer of this image, Eddie Adams: "two people died in that photograph: the recipient of the bullet and General Nguyen Ngoc Loan." After using the word *death* many of the students agreed this image was trying to portray death in its most obvious form, a photograph of a man moments before his death.

The final photograph portrayed loneliness. Not one student voiced an opinion on loneliness throughout the discussion. The female participant brought up the idea of the old woman being desperate. Another female participant found herself coming to the conclusion that the woman was suffering, possibly because of a mental illness or a brain disorder.

The beginner students were different from the advanced students in a few ways. There were two males and three females; all students were ages 18 to 21. The beginner students were profoundly more shocked and/or confused when viewing the images in comparison to the advanced students. The written answers proved very useful for the beginner group because answers differed from the group discussion, many words were misspelled, and the responses were much more naive than the advanced participants' written responses.

The first photograph was happiness. All of the participants wrote down happy/happiness, three out of five wrote down sunshine or warmth, and one male wrote down that perhaps the woman in the photograph was sending or receiving a text message. The text message notion was surprising, but after thinking critically for a moment, perhaps this emotion is a reflection of the dominance that technology has on our modern society. All of the participants verbally expressed sunshine and/or happiness and agreed the photographer was attempting to communicate the allure of happiness, warmth, and sunshine.

The second photograph was the dead body in the Japanese woods, portraying death. Four out of five participants wrote down death or tragedy. One participant wrote down war and murder. All the students were silent at the beginning. None of the participants quite knew what exactly the image was or how they should feel about it. At first, one of the female students began giggling nervously when this particular image was presented. Perhaps the photograph was slightly too intense for the demographic.

The third photograph depicted fear. Most if not all of the students could not contain their laughter at this image. I understand the fact the man was nude and slightly uncomfortable looking. All of the participants' written answers differed, as well as their verbal discussion. One male participant wrote down "sad because he is frail" for his response to the image. Perhaps the controversy surrounding this shocking image was too much for young minds to bear.

The fourth photograph depicting love did not generate such a response from the beginner group. Only one male student wrote down love, but did not express such an emotion verbally. Each participant wrote down "awkward" or "disgusting." One female student wrote down that she believed the photographer was attempting to communicate the vulnerability of love.

The fifth photograph attempting to communicate death was the image of the man getting shot in the head. All of the students wrote down sadness/oppression/suffering. Two of the female students had a similar idea, which was that the photographer was attempting to communicate the notion of the things happening in other areas of the world. None of the students saw death in the image. Each student seemed unable to associate the idea of death because the man was still alive in the photograph. Since he was Vietnamese it was difficult for the younger minds to find a common ground with the image. To them it seemed he was just a man in a country, which they did not have any prior knowledge of, therefore could not come to terms with a set emotion other than war and oppression.

The sixth photograph was the old woman clutching the doll in the hospital or nursing home showing loneliness. Each participant expressed on paper the emotion of being lonely, feeling bad for the woman, the aspect of old age, etc. The male students wrote down for the image "confusion" and "bliss." Perhaps participants wrote these emotions down because the image is very haunting, a true reality of what lies ahead for every human being. All participants agreed the old woman was clearly depicting loneliness in the most obvious form. The discussion continued to a deeper level; one female student expressed seeing her grandmother in the nursing home suffering from memory loss. She disclosed to me how this image reminded her of her grandmother, making her feel sad and empathetic towards the matter.

The results are interesting, but the picture-by-picture approach through each focus group may make tracking the results awkward. Rebecca can strengthen the results by identifying themes in the results and then writing up the themes. Some of the results may be better laid out in one or more tables. Tables make comparing the results quick and efficient, especially when multiple data sets are involved (e.g., two focus groups).

Interpretation

Through the research, many aspects I did not antici-
pate surfaced through the discussion portion; the
written answers disclosed significantly more personal
emotions. While I was initially constructing my
project, I was quite convinced that the advanced
photography students would produce a specific set
of results because of their knowledge regarding
photography. I assumed some, if not all, would
have already been exposed to at least one of the
images. I was correct in such a sense because the
male participant in the advanced focus group recognized two of the images but derived different
meanings than the ones I had established for each
one. The emotional responses provided by the advanced
students proved very intriguing. Participants
brought up specific emotions I had not recognized,
adding weight to the notion of visual framing differing in each individual.

The results I did find were fairly accurate to
the information I anticipated to gain. I understood not all students, especially the beginner
ones, would be able to grasp the concept I had
assigned to each photograph. Often at times, the
answers provided by the beginner students differed
tremendously from the verbal answers, also something I had expected. Younger minds are more sus-
ceptible to influence and peer pressure; maturity
only comes with age, knowledge, and cohesiveness.
I gathered, through my research, the idea that we
each construct our own meanings for images based
on a general knowledge and the aspects of life
to which we have been exposed.

Rebecca provides good interpretation of her results. She draws some insights from the results of her study.

Implications and Conclusions

The participants may have kept certain emotions to
themselves for a variety of reasons, perhaps embar-
rassment or uncertainty of how to process such
strong emotions with each image. The scope for my
focus groups could have been larger, involving more

participants to produce more results and emotions. I feel as though if the groups had been larger, the discussions would have been longer and perhaps a bit more in depth because more opinions would have surfaced. If I were to involve more participants in focus groups, instead of simply gathering more photography or art students, I would involve students who had absolutely no background in the field of art or communication. I feel this additional aspect to my research could have added more weight to my thesis, involving a variety of students rather than such a narrow scope for my research.

It would have been interesting to merge the two focus groups into one large group, to gather more data regarding the influence factor of the research. Perhaps the advanced students would have a profound impact on the views of the beginner students because of their knowledge and age difference. Reasoning for not merging the groups came from potentially anticipated discomfort derived from both parties; if the group became one not all the participants would be acquainted with one another and would potentially hold back from expressing themselves to their full potential.

I expected to find a substantial distinction between the beginner and advanced students. Although the two groups produced entirely different results, there were some similarities such as overall confusion for the image depicting fear, and uncertainty regarding the image portraying death, particularity the man getting shot in the head. Perhaps the confusion circulating around these two images in particular stems from discomfort while viewing the photographs. I believe my research is additional to the field of communication because, although prior research exists involving the analysis of visual framing, the research does not include the aspect of shocking images, or influence. My research may be similar to certain studies but is unique in its own field.

Larger focus groups or combining the focus groups may not provide the additional insight Rebecca believes. Larger groups tend to fragment into mini-groups and the researcher can lose track of the multiple discussions going on. Expanding beyond photography to other students' interpretations of the images might add an interesting dimension. Finally, Rebecca found that initial selection of the images was a critical component of her study.

References

Adams, E. (Photographer). (1968). *General Nguyen Ngoc Loan killing Viet Cong operative Nguyen Van Lem.* [Print Photo]. Retrieved from: www.famouspictures.org/mag/index.php?title=Vietnam_Execution.

Arbus, D. (Photographer). (1970). *Dominatrix Embracing Her Client.* [Print Photo]. Retrieved from: http://diane-arbus-photography.com/

Brantner, C., Lobinger, K., & Wetzstein, I. (2009). Effects of visual framing on emotional responses and evaluations of news stories about the Gaza conflict 2009. *Journalism & Mass Communication Quarterly, 88*(3), 523–540.

Haggblom, K. (Photographer). (2012). Retrieved from: www.kristianhaggblom.com/public/jukai.html.

Hill, S. (Photographer). (n.d.). *Ron Mueck Exhibition at the NGV.* [Print Photo]. Retrieved from: http://xtremeprints.com/stock/.

Macdonald, I. (Photographer). (2011). *The Greatest.* [Print Photo]. Retrieved from: http://noneedforalarm.wordpress.com/page/5.

Rodriguez, L., & Dimitrova, D. (2011). The levels of visual framing. *Journal of Visual Literacy, 30*(1), 48–65.

Stevens, C. (Photographer). (2008). *Victoria, Nursing Home Resident.* [Print Photo]. Retrieved from: http://vervephoto.wordpress.com/category/ohio-university/page/2/.

13 QUALITATIVE DATA ANALYSIS

Chapter Outline

- Grounded Theory
- Strengths and Weaknesses of Grounded Theory
- Alternative Methods of Qualitative Analysis
- Grounded-Theory Exercise
- Key Steps & Questions to Consider
- Activities
- Discussion Questions
- Key Terms

What Will I Learn About Qualitative Data Analysis?

Growing up, Stephen was a big fan of the television cartoon *Inspector Gadget* and the *Pink Panther* films. In both, we see bumbling detectives (Gadget and Clouseau) try to solve mysteries, only being successful with the help of others. When faced with a crime or mystery, detectives must solve them based on the available evidence. The process of gathering, analyzing, grouping, and making conclusions based on evidence is essential to solving crimes. Whether it's a cartoon, film, or a show (think *CSI* or *Law and Order*), collecting information to solve crimes is commonplace. Such a process is also necessary when analyzing data collected for research purposes, particularly qualitative data.

The analysis of qualitative data is a significant, and often misunderstood, part of the research process. One could take multiple methods or approaches to analyzing qualitative data. Determining which method to use might not be an easy choice. The researcher must decide which method is the most appropriate based on multiple factors: What is the research paradigm? What kinds of problems or questions drive the research? What kind of sampling is used? What is the place of theory in the research? We explore these questions and more in Chapter 13 in our discussion of qualitative data analysis, with a focus on grounded theory.

Grounded Theory

Grounded Theory Defined

Since its original publication, or "discovery," in 1967, grounded theory has emerged as one of the most commonly used methods for analyzing qualitative data. **Grounded theory** is a systematic process of theory generation that takes place through the analysis of qualitative data. This process includes both inductive and deductive logical reasoning. Glaser and Strauss (1967) coined the phrase grounded theory while conducting qualitative research on death and dying. Glaser and Strauss argued that only a theory developed from the data could adequately represent what was happening (Glaser & Strauss, 1967).

Much of the basis for grounded theory came out of **symbolic interactionism.** For symbolic interactionists, individual meaning is found in social interactions. Scholars study these individual meanings as ways to build and understand theory (look back to the chapter on the interpretive paradigm for more on symbolic interactionism). Communication is generated by interpreting various meanings and symbols in interaction. For grounded theorists, the interpretation and interaction between individuals is integral to theory creation and communication (Glaser, 1978; Glaser & Strauss, 1967). The relationship between grounded theory and symbolic interactionism in theory creation was summed up well by Stanley and Cheek (2003) when they explained how symbolic interaction shapes grounded theory as a method: "people sharing a common circumstance will also share some common meanings attached to that circumstance" (p. 144). In essence, the sharing of individual interpretations of some phenomenon, such as how people experience dying, leads to collective experiences, which leads to common understandings of phenomenon (theory).

Two Major Approaches to Grounded Theory

You can approach grounded theory in multiple ways. We cannot cover all of them in this text. We would like to focus on two approaches, the Glaserian approach, popularized by Glaser (1978, 1992, 1998), and Glaser and Strauss (1967), and the Straussian approach, popularized by Strauss and Corbin (1991, 1998). While the two approaches share similarities, philosophical differences provide distinction. The differences depend on the intended final product, the research question(s)/problems, the literature that is reviewed, the sampling, the data analysis process, and how the final developed theory is evaluated.

No matter which approach you take, each one shares four of the same elements: codes, concepts, categories, and themes. We will discuss how to find and analyze each of these four elements in the "Process of Grounded Theory" section of the chapter. **Codes** are identifying terms that permit key points in data to be gathered. For example, issues (theoretical or non-theoretical) will jump out at you while reading transcripts. Such issues are the basic level of grounded theory. **Concepts** are conglomerations of codes around similar content. You may notice as you read and analyze transcripts that participants are saying similar things. **Categories** are broad groups of concepts used to create theory. The bringing together of concepts into groups helps us make sense of the world. Finally, **theory** is a set of explanations about the social world. Often theories are developed using the grounded-theory process.

First, the intended final product differs depending on whether you use a Glaserian or a Straussian approach. Those who prefer the Glaserian approach see grounded theory as a method of analysis that produces conceptual hypotheses. The hypotheses are used to generate future research. The purpose of the analysis is to generate concepts and hypotheses from the analysis (Glaser, 1998; Glaser & Strauss, 1967). In the Straussian process, the final product is a verified theory that improves overall understanding of a phenomenon (Strauss & Corbin, 1991). The approach differs from the Glaserian by taking the concepts and hypotheses a step further into the development of a verifiable (testable) theory.

Second, the nature of the research questions or problems, and how and when they emerge, differentiate the Glaserian and Straussian approaches. In the Glaserian approach, the general problem area, or focus of the study, is identified before the study begins. The area is focused once the data are analyzed. In the Straussian approach, the general problem area (focus of study) is identified before the study begins through the use of literature, personal experiences, and various other means.

Third, the reviewed literature differs for the Glaserian and Straussian approaches. In the Straussian approach, the literature is reviewed before the study starts to aid in the creation of concepts or themes. During data analysis, more literature is reviewed and used as further data for the study (Strauss & Corbin, 1991). The Glaserian approach does not review the literature before the start of data collection. While the researcher will have an idea of their topic, an extensive theoretical review of literature is not conducted before the data are analyzed. Instead, the literature is integrated into the data analysis (Glaser, 1978; Glaser & Strauss, 1967).

Sampling or data collection is the fourth way in which the two approaches differ. The sample techniques start out fairly similarly. For the Glaserian approach, after preliminary sampling, subsequent sampling is guided by concepts or themes "discovered" in the data (Glaser & Strauss, 1967). One of the goals of the sampling is to find comparative cases (cases that differ from one another). For the Straussian approach, the sampling is guided by theory, analytic questions or concerns, and research hypotheses or questions (Strauss & Corbin, 1998).

The way(s) in which the data are analyzed is the fifth difference between the two approaches. The Glaserian approach has two phases (steps) to coding qualitative data: 1) **open/substantive coding** and 2) theoretical coding

(Glaser & Strauss, 1967). LaRossa (2005) defines open coding as breaking data apart to delineate concepts or categories to represent chunks of data (themes). In open coding, written data from the field or from transcripts are reviewed line by line. Everything is coded in the transcripts to get a better understanding of what is occurring. A researcher typically compares the codes that have already emerged to support identification of additional emergent codes. This is known as the **constant comparison** approach and is a great way for researchers to identify similarities and differences in the data.

The second phase is **theoretical coding.** The data are selectively coded or analyzed based on a theoretical lens. With both open and theoretical coding, the codes are developed from the transcripts and compared with other codes in the transcripts, eventually themes will emerge in the data. We will talk more about themes shortly. For example, if you are interested in cultural identity, you will focus on the data and look for transcripts that specifically address the development, management, and other components of identity. This selective sampling could mean you neglect to focus on other aspects of the data, but your focus is on a theoretical aspect (Glaser, 1978).

The Straussian approach also employs axial coding. **Axial coding** is the inductive and deductive process of relating or linking codes to one another and creating concepts (Charmaz, 2006). While Strauss and Corbin (1991) consider axial coding to be an important part of grounded theory, other grounded-theory scholars have argued that this type of coding is optional, particularly since comparative and relating of codes often occurs in open and theoretical coding already (Charmaz, 2006).

How the final developed theory is evaluated is the last way in which these two approaches differ. Glaserian uses fit, work, relevance, and modifiability to evaluate a theory developed from an analysis (Glaser, 1978; Glaser & Strauss, 1967). Straussian evaluation criteria are a bit more general. Criteria such as generalizability, reproducibility, and conceptual density of the categories are used to evaluate the developed theories (Strauss & Corbin, 1991, 1998).

> Detectives approach an investigation in different ways. While all detectives try to decipher clues to solve crimes, the manner in which they collect clues and analyze the clues varies quite a bit. Sherlock Holmes and his associate Dr Watson used the process of deduction to solve crimes. Inspector Gadget got lucky with solving crimes; thankfully he had Penny to secretly save the day and interpret the clues for him. While Inspector Clouseau tried to use deduction to solve crimes, only through a series of silly mishaps did a solution fall into his lap. Collectively, these classic detectives all solved crimes in different ways, but had the same intent, to solve crimes. Just like with grounded theory, no matter what approach one takes, the overall intent is fairly similar (with minor differences depending on the approach).

Process of Grounded Theory

To conduct a grounded-theory analysis (we will focus on the Straussian approach) involves seven main steps.

1) Review existing literature on a given theory or construct. Let's say you are interested in how people form or shape their cultural identity. You would review previously published studies by researchers like Collier (1998, 2005) and Collier and Thomas (1988) to gain an understanding and glimpse of how cultural identity is formed or shaped.

2) You need to collect qualitative data: interviews, ethnographic field notes, focus group comments, etc. We outlined various qualitative methods in Chapters 10–12.

3) Qualitative data are easier to analyze if in some tangible form, such as a transcript. Thus, many grounded theorists transcribe focus group and open-ended interviews. Ethnographic field notes may also serve as tangible data.

4) The open coding stage is next. You examine each line of your transcripts and look for similar content that focuses on "identity" issues. Using a comparative approach, label each line of a transcript that deals with "identity." These are the codes. Then go back through and comment on whenever you see similarities and differences between the codes. These are the concepts. This is the axial coding stage. You may notice that a few of the participants talk about how their identity is shaped by the media or how identity is formed when the participants are children.

The fifth and sixth stages often happen hand in hand. 5) The fifth stage is memoing. **Memos** are write-ups of ideas about theoretical relationships that emerge during coding (Glaser, 1978). As you begin to notice how cultural identity is shaped by media and family, you may develop ideas about the relationship between media, family, and cultural identity. These ideas, while interesting may not make a lot of sense. However, taken into consideration with other communication, constructs may lead to a strong theory of cultural identity development.

6) Sort the memos you have collected. In sorting you draw connections between the memos you have gathered and the broader discipline. Research in communication studies, for example, shows media has an effect on human development, as does the family. Thus, it makes intuitive sense that media and the family would affect cultural identity.

7) The final stage is the write-up. In this stage you clarify the theory you developed and describe how your data support your arguments.

Strengths and Weaknesses of Grounded Theory

Grounded theory provides qualitative researchers with a useful tool to analyze qualitative data. The method has disadvantages or weaknesses. Grounded theory method of analysis has two main weaknesses. First, since the method is a subjective form of analysis, reliability and validity are difficult to establish. Reliability and validity differ in qualitative versus quantitative methods. Since grounded theory relies on subjectivity, it does lack some of the reliability and validity present in other qualitative analytical tools, such as content analysis. Second, as with all qualitative methods, detecting and/or preventing research bias is difficult if not impossible. The nature of bias was discussed in Chapters 10–12.

Grounded theory has two advantages or strengths. First, grounded theory is a rigorous and systematic procedure for analyzing qualitative data. Rather than simply looking for ideas in a text, this analytical method details steps that one should follow to understand text(s). Second, grounded theory offers a way to describe and explore individual experiences. Unlike quantitative methods, which look for an objective reality, qualitative methods look for subjective and individual experiences. Grounded theory is a helpful tool to grasp such experiences.

Alternative Methods of Qualitative Data Analysis

While grounded theory is an effective way to analyze qualitative data, other approaches are available. In Chapter 14 we talk about content analysis. Often people assume that content analysis is only for quantitative purposes; this is not the case. You will see in Chapter 14 how we provide ways you could apply many of the same aspects of quantitative content analysis to qualitative data.

A thematic analysis is a straightforward way to analyze qualitative data, particularly data related to interpersonal/relational issues (and one with few steps). Owen (1984) outlined a three-step process one can take when analyzing transcripts of qualitative data: recurrence, repetition, and forcefulness. **Recurrence** is when the same message(s) is implicitly repeated by a person, or by multiple people in the transcripts.

> Let's say you go through a collection of transcripts looking for how people shape or form their cultural identity. You may see multiple people mention things like "self," "become me," or "personhood." While the terms are not the same, they imply a sense of being someone, a sense of identity. Many participants may discuss things like "television," "soap operas," *Cosby Show*, *Simpsons*, or *Family Guy*, which could imply the media's effect on cultural identity formation.

The second step in Owen's (1984) model is repetition. **Repetition** is when you look for explicit cases of key words, phrases, or key wording that are repeated in transcripts. With the recurrence step you have already found that thematic concepts like "self" appear a few times in the texts you are analyzing. When key phrases, words, etc. are repeated, the repetition shows the significance of such themes for the users.

> Thus, if your participants repeat "image of self" and then closely after that "media," you can infer a relationship between the two.

The third step is forcefulness. **Forcefulness** (or intensity) includes vocal inflection, volume, or pausing used to stress or minimize some statements in speech. In a written text, the use of underlining, italicizing, bolding, using ALL CAPS, using color, highlighting, or other ways to differentiate some font from another font stresses or minimizes some messages over others.

> A person in an interview may say something like, "I really think who I am comes from a lot of different places. I mean . . . I am [person points to themselves] who I am partially because of how I was brought up." In this case, the non-verbal act of pointing to themselves further emphasizes their sense of self-identity.

Grounded-Theory Exercise

Whenever Stephen discusses social penetration theory (Altman & Taylor, 1973; Taylor & Altman, 1987) with his Communication Theory class, they regularly do a variation of an exercise that involves analyzing "getting to know one another" exchanges. The exercise will help in your understanding of how to conduct grounded-theory method.

Question

We would like you to think back to the most recent time you sat down to "get to know another" person. Specifically, we would like you to recall the verbal or non-verbal behavior, actions, and/or statements that occurred during the exchange. What meaning(s) do you give to that behavior, action, and/or statements?

Activity

In the next class period, all of the examples are compiled on sheets of paper and handed out to each student. No names or identifying information are included. Students are given time to work in groups to conduct a coding of the responses. Students are instructed to conduct an open coding followed by an axial coding of the responses, keeping in mind the purpose of the exercise is to explore issues related to social penetration theory. The following is an example of responses. Try your hand at coding the responses.

Question Responses

1. I just went on this date with a guy and it was okay, I guess. We spent a lot of time at dinner talking about simple things, I guess. We talked about movies, music, and where we're both from. I'm from Finland and he is from Estonia. When we left dinner I knew some things about him at least.

2. Last week I went to dinner with a hot French girl. I went in to shake her hand and she went in to kiss my cheek; that surprised me. I was not ready for that greeting at all.

3. I remember an interview for an internship last week and when I went into the office I saw that the interviewer or the boss I think it was had really messy hair. I was not sure what to think of this. It was all over the place. He was not what I expected. (American student)

4. I met my girlfriend's father last night. I walked up to him and shook his hand. My girlfriend is Russian and so is her father. He had such a strong handshake I thought he was going to break my hand. I was warned that he was going to be firm with me because he wanted to show me he was in charge. Russians. (Finnish student)

5. I remember meeting my new teachers a few weeks ago and all of them looked me in the eyes. It was really strange for me. I think they wanted me to look them in the eyes too. I am not used to that. I am from Vietnam and we do not look the teacher in the eye as it is sign of disrespect but here in Finland we need to or they think we not listen or care.

What similarities or differences do you see between the statements regarding their initial interactions (getting to know another person)? What did you learn about how the individuals interact with others? Aside from analyzing the initial interaction, what else could you analyze from these short excerpts? What did you learn about doing grounded theory in this exercise? Could you use this kind of analytical approach in your own research?

We all need tools to complete our jobs. For detectives or inspectors, these tools used to be magnifying glasses and a keen sense of logic. Now detectives or inspectors have all sorts of high-tech gadgets at their disposal to solve crimes. In the days of Inspector Clouseau (1960s–1970s), solving a crime from DNA found on a single strand of hair was not yet possible; today this is a reality. Grounded theory, like the development of crime-solving tools, represents an advance in analyzing qualitative data. This method offers a variety of approaches for users, which makes this tool a useful way to analyze your qualitative data.

Summary

This chapter described various techniques you could use to analyze qualitative data. While we focused a great deal of the chapter on grounded theory, there are numerous other analytical techniques available. The key is to find one that fits your needs. The following chapter is a combination of qualitative and quantitative approaches. In Chapter 14 we explore content analysis.

Key Steps & Questions to Consider

1. Grounded theory is a systematic process of theory generation that takes place through the analysis of qualitative data. This process includes both inductive and deductive logical reasoning.
2. There are two approaches to grounded theory, the Glaserian approach, popularized by Glaser, and Glaser and Strauss, and the Straussian approach, popularized by Strauss and Corbin.
3. Codes are identifying terms that permit key points in data to be gathered.
4. Concepts are conglomerations of codes around similar content.
5. Categories are broad groups of concepts that are then used to create theory.
6. Theory is a set of explanations about the social world.
7. Open coding is breaking data apart to delineate concepts or categories to represent chunks of data (themes).
8. In theoretical coding, the data are selectively coded or analyzed based on a theoretical lens.
9. Axial coding is the inductive and deductive process of relating or linking codes to one another and creating concepts.
10. The grounded-theory method of analysis has two main weaknesses: reliability and validity are difficult to establish, and detecting and or preventing research bias is difficult if not impossible.
11. Grounded theory has two advantages or strengths: grounded theory is a rigorous and systematic procedure for analyzing qualitative data, and grounded theory offers a way to describe and explore individual experiences.
12. Owen's three-step thematic analysis (recurrence, repetition, and forcefulness) is a useful tool for analyzing qualitative data.

Activities

1. Grounded theory may be one of the most flexible methods in your communication studies arsenal. To see the breadth, you can conduct a grounded-theory analysis of research articles using grounded theory. Type "grounded theory articles" into Google, Bing, Yahoo, or your favorite search engine. Copy the titles for the first 50 scholarly articles you find. Use Owen's

three-step process to analyze the articles. Look for recurrence, repetition, and forcefulness in the titles. What themes emerge from the analysis?

2. Repeat the process from the first activity, but use the terms "grounded theory" and "communication studies" (leave the quotation marks around the search words this time around). What different themes emerge when your data set is narrowed?

 ## Discussion Questions

1. What are the variations between codes, concepts, and categories in grounded theory? When (or in what order) are each employed?

2. Debate the major differences between Glaserian and Straussian approaches to grounded theory. In your opinion, which is the stronger approach?

3. Think of your own interests in communication studies. How might the use of grounded-theory method be an approach for exploring your research interests? How is a grounded-theory approach going to change the results of your analysis?

Key Terms

Axial coding	Forcefulness	Repetition
Categories	Grounded theory	Symbolic interactionism
Codes	Memos	Theoretical coding
Concepts	Open/substantive coding	Theory
Constant comparison	Recurrence	

14 CONTENT ANALYSIS

What Will I Learn About Content Analysis?

In the photos you see U.S. President Barack Obama and Republican Challenger Mitt Romney during the 2012 presidential campaign. The two candidates raised almost 2.1 billion dollars for their respective campaigns (Ashkenas, Ericson, Parlapiano, & Willis, 2012; Federal Election Commission, 2013). The funds came from a variety of sources and were used for numerous things during the 2012 campaign. One of the issues discussed quite a bit during the election, and in the 2008 election, was the significance of Super PACs, or Super Political Action Committees and their potential impact on the election. Super PACs have no limitations on the amount of money they can donate to candidates. Such organizations spent millions of dollars in 2008 and 2012 trying to promote or defeat candidates in numerous elections. What could be interesting to look at is how do Super PACs' advertising differ from the advertising put out by the candidates? Super PACs are not managed by the political parties and are free to create their own messages. Could this freedom lead to a different kind of message production or agenda? Content analysis could be used to explore the question. In Chapter 14, you will learn how to conduct research in communication using content analysis.

Introduction to Content Analysis

Content Analysis Defined

Content analysis has various definitions. Berelson (1952) described content analysis as a research technique for objective, systematic, and quantitative descriptions of manifest and latent content of communication. Krippendorff (1980) considered content analysis to be a research tool for making replicable and valid inferences from data to their context. Cole (1988) stated that the method is a way to analyze written, verbal, or visual communicative messages. Berger (1991) stated that content analysis is "a research technique that is based on measuring the amount of something (violence, negative portrayals of women, or whatever) in a representative sampling of some mass-mediated popular form of art" (p. 25). Neuman (1997) defined content analysis as a method for gathering and analyzing the content of text. A "text" for Neuman is anything written, visual, or spoken. Each definition shares some common elements that we use to make our definition of content analysis. **Content analysis** is a research method that systematically describes, categorizes, and/or makes inferences about communication messages. Thus, the claims that one can make using content analysis vary extensively depending on whether you are using qualitative or quantitative analysis. In this chapter, we dissect each part of the definition.

History of Content Analysis

In the 18th century, Swedish scholars analyzed 90 hymns entitled the *Songs of Zion*. The hymns not from the state-sponsored Swedish church, were gaining in popularity among people, and many in the establishment declared the songs to be blasphemous. Scholars and clergy conducted a content analysis of religious symbolism in the *Songs of Zion* and the state sponsored songs and found no significant differences. Thus, the *Songs* were deemed acceptable for mass use (Dovring, 1954). This study revealed the utility of content analysis as a way of exploring communicative messages. In the 19th century, content analysis was used again to analyze hymns, advertisements, magazine and newspaper articles, and political speeches (Harwood & Garry, 2003). The method really took off during World War II when the U.S. government sponsored projects by Harold Laswell to study propaganda. The projects revealed the extent and influence of propaganda on public opinion (Laswell, et al., 1965). Laswell and his colleagues continued to develop methods of content analysis during and after World War II.

Concurrently, individuals interested in personality traits, inspired particularly by the work of Edward Sapir, began to use content analysis to study human behavior. Research such as Dollard and Mowrer's (1947) studies on discomfort and relief, and Raimy's (1948) research on positive–negative ambivalence, expanded our understanding of human psychology. Gerbner and his research team started to research the effects of a growing presence on American's lives—television (Gerbner, Holsti, Krippendorff, Paisley, & Stone, 1969). Since then, content analysis has been used to analyze media, advertising, interpersonal, organizational, rhetorical, and other kinds of communicative messages. Content analysis is one of the fastest growing methods in mass communication (Macnamara, 2005; Neuendorf, 2002).

Content analysis is currently employed to study a wide array of theoretical questions. Researchers have extensively used content analysis to study media processes and media effects. Some examples include those below:

1. Himelboim, McCreery and Smith (2013) used content analysis to explore political views and ideology on Twitter.
2. Cagle, Cox, Luoma, and Zaphiris (2011) used content analysis to describe how Muslims are depicted in American media.
3. Waters and Lo (2012) discussed how non-profit organizations use Facebook.
4. Eskjoer (2013) explained the influence of global media systems on shaping the discussion about global climate change.
5. Stephens (2012) categorized news stories and polling of news media before the U.S. invasion of Iraq.

Other studies have combined media (mass communication) research with other areas of communication studies:

1. Leonard and Toller (2012) explored the role that websites play in discussing suicide.
2. Rose, Mackey-Kallis, Shyles, Barry, Biagini, Hart, and Jack (2012) examined the performance of gender via self-created images on Facebook.
3. Garner, Kinsky, Duta, and Danker (2012) expanded organizational dissent into primetime television by looking at how individuals dissent on primetime television.

In content analyses of non-media-related communication, researchers have found out quite a bit about human behavior. For example, look to the information below:

1. Giles, Linz, Bonilla and Gomez (2012) found that minority groups are more likely to be stigmatized by police officers in police/driver interaction.
2. Bisel and Arterburn's content analysis (2012) identified five reasons why organizational members refrain from giving negative upward feedback: predicting harm to themselves, constructing the supervisor as responsible, questioning their own expertise, predicting the supervisor's deafness, and constructing the timing as inopportune.

The purpose of providing these varied references is to show the depth of what content analysis can do and, in fact, these examples are just the tip of the iceberg. Content analysis can be a useful methodological tool for a variety of research purposes. While the majority of content analyses are quantitative in nature, researchers increasingly conduct qualitative content analyses as well. The following sections of this chapter describe step by step how to conduct a content analysis.

Data in Content Analysis

The data for a content analysis all depend on what you want to study (as with any research method). Before collecting your data, you should have a clear objective, research question(s), or hypotheses. Once you have these, you can be more certain that your data and analysis are relevant for the research. Remember, content analysis systematically describes, categorizes, and/or makes inferences about communication messages. Based on the definition, the data for a content analysis can be almost anything. If you look back to Chapter 7 on research data, data are texts, observations, self-reports, and other reports of communication. Under this broad umbrella is a plethora of options. The key for a researcher is to make sure that you are choosing the right data and you have an appropriate sample from your population to address or answer your research objectives, questions, and/or hypotheses.

In Waters and Lo's (2012) study of non-profit organizations' use of Facebook, the data were 225 random Facebook pages. Since Waters and Lo were interested in how non-profits in different nations use Facebook, it was appropriate for them to use Facebook pages of non-profits in different nations as data. Their sample was random and the three nations (75 Facebook pages per nation) were chosen based on previously studied cultural differences between the nations. Therefore, their choice of content and sample was purposeful. Waters and Lo could have chosen any random number of

Facebook pages from any nation in the world, but the nations were chosen for a reason. In the Garner et al. (2012) study about dissent on primetime television, the authors sampled "two weeks of primetime programming, defined as 8:00 p.m. to 11:00 p.m., on CBS, ABC, NBC, FOX, and CW. We recorded three hours of programming on five channels for 14 days, giving a sample of 210 hours of television" (p. 614). Since the authors were studying organizational dissent on primetime television, the use of primetime television episodes as their data was appropriate. The networks listed were appropriate choices because they represent large segments of the American primetime viewing public. The choice of two weeks is appropriate as it gives the researchers sufficient time to effectively measure regular television programming, as opposed to only measuring one night.

A few key points about data need to be made at this time. First, the objective(s) of the study determine the data of the study. Second, when collecting data for a content analysis you need to be systematic in why you choose certain kinds of data. Each of the studies listed in this chapter justified their data: why the data, why the period of data collection, why the size, etc. . . . Third, when you write up your report, provide a detailed description of the sample including the size of the data, the topic area, the time period, and any other pertinent information you can think of to help other people duplicate your research.

Let's say we want to conduct a study comparing television advertising sponsored by the Romney and Obama campaigns and by PACs during the 2012 Presidential election. Our main kind of data is presidential television advertisements during the 2012 presidential campaign. Specifically, we need to somehow get a hold of all ads produced, aired, and paid for by the Obama and Romney campaigns, and by the various PACs. This may seem like a lot of work . . . and it is. However, this is your data collection. Unlike collecting surveys or interviews where we are interacting with humans, with this kind of content analysis our collection is archival. In other kinds of content analysis we may work with people. We will talk about those later. Once we have found all of the ads, via YouTube or other Internet search engines, we recommend saving them somewhere so we do not lose them!

Now that we have defined the type of data you can use in content analysis, the next section of Chapter 14 describes the process of categorizing data.

Content Analysis Categories

Content categories are areas, themes, groupings, classes, or types with explicit boundaries into which units of content (data) are coded for analysis. Content categories develop from the following question: what content categories produce the data needed to answer the objectives of the research? When conducting a content analysis, it is imperative to first conduct a thorough review of the literature to determine what categories other researchers have used in their content analyses of communication processes. Conducting a content analysis where you create categories based on previous research is called a **deductive content analysis.** For example, say you are interested in exploring the different political beliefs that presidential candidates express during elections. Numerous scholars have already developed categories for such an analysis, so looking to their work to develop categories for a content analysis is to your benefit (Benoit, 1999; Benoit & Glantz, 2012; Dover, 2006; Kaid & Ballotti, 1991; West, 1993).

If you choose to create your own categories, you are conducting an **inductive content analysis.** The categories we choose or develop in a content analysis need to be mutually exclusive. For example, if you are conducting a content analysis on the beliefs of presidential candidates as displayed in their advertising, you should focus your study on their advertisements and the different beliefs depicted in the ads. The different beliefs (your categories, in this case a thematic analysis) should not overlap, but be mutually exclusive. Categories that overlap make it more difficult to distinguish differences or infer anything about communication messages. We will talk more about this later in the chapter.

> Benoit (1999) in his functional theory argued that political campaign messages, like advertisements, are comparative messages. These kinds of messages have three functions: to acclaim or praise a candidate, to criticize or attack a component, or to respond to or defend a candidate after an attack. These functions are categories, themes, groupings, and ways to analyze political campaign messages. You could analyze the advertisements in the 2012 election using these three categories.

Now that we have discussed data and the basics of content categories, the next section of this chapter defines units of analysis and explains how units of analysis are counted.

Units of Analysis

We should consider two important issues when determining units of analysis. First, in every content analysis, the researcher must choose the scale of the content they are going to code. Second, researchers need to think about how they are going to count the units of analysis. The research objectives of a study determine the scale of the content being coded. In our study of presidential advertising, we have a lot of options for our units of analysis. Do we want to analyze individual words in the ads, whole sentences, symbols in the ads, themes in the ads, or ads as a whole? The **unit of analysis,** therefore, is the specific element you are analyzing in the data. Let's say with our study that we decide to code sentences in the ads to determine the functions of the ads. We can choose from two kinds of units of analysis: recording and context units.

The **recording unit of analysis** is the content you are analyzing, which can be identified and counted. In our presidential election study, individual sentences in every ad are the recording units. We can count sentences, and we can separate sentences into different categories. If we analyze an ad, we can separate the sentences into the different functions of a political ad as defined by Benoit (1999). If a sentence does not fit one of the categories, we can always create a miscellaneous category, but be careful of overlapping categories. Remember, we want the categories to be mutually exclusive.

The **context unit of analysis** is significant because when we conduct content analysis we must often consider the context surrounding the recording unit. A sentence in an advertisement sponsored by the Romney campaign may say "President Obama is a leader." However, the next sentence may say, "However, he is a failed leader." Therefore, looking at the context surrounding the initial recording unit is essential to make sure you do not code a sentence into the wrong category.

Once you have decided on your recording unit and taken care not to code them into incorrect categories (considering the context), an important question is how do you count your data? You can count data three ways in content analysis: frequency, space and time, and intensity or direction. Frequency refers to the number of times a unit is recorded in a message. Space is, for example, the amount of printed space devoted to a message in a newspaper ad, or how much of the front page of a newspaper is devoted to some idea. Counting in time, for example, could be how many minutes a person speaks about a subject in an interview, or how many minutes are devoted to covering an election on the nightly news. Intensity or direction is how favorable or unfavorable, for example, an issue is discussed in a news story. News editorials are inherently biased. A content analysis of news editorials could dissect the level of bias.

While quantitative and qualitative content analysts will often count data in similar ways, their coding schedule, pilot testing, and analysis will often differ. The following two sections of this chapter address these issues. The following section discusses how to prepare a coding schedule, how to pilot test a content analysis, and how to check for intercoder reliability.

In our study of campaign ads, we are focusing on the individual sentences in the ads. Thus, the sentences are the units of analysis. As previously mentioned, we need to look at the context in which the sentence is placed so we do not place a sentence in the wrong category. In this particular study, let's count the frequency of categories so we can state how *often* a particular category or function of a political campaign ad is used.

Coding Schedule, Pilot Testing, and Intercoder Reliability

Depending on how you approach the creation of categories for a content analysis (inductive or deductive), you may have pre-determined categories or coding could take place at the same time as category creation or development. If you want to conduct a content analysis you need to systematically code the data to find your recording units of analysis. A helpful way to code data is by creating a coding schedule or coding sheet. A **coding schedule** is a sheet where a researcher tracks, records and/or categorizes the communication they are coding. Figure 14.1 is an example of a simplified coding sheet we could use to analyze the presidential campaign ads in the 2012 presidential election.

Name of Coder: _____
Advertisement Number (provide each ad with a number to keep track of it): _____
Advertisement Sponsor: _____
Dates Advertisement Aired: _____

Sentence (unit of analysis)	Category
1.	_____ Acclaim/Praise _____ Criticize/Attack _____ Respond/Defend _____ Miscellaneous
2.	_____ Acclaim/Praise _____ Criticize/Attack _____ Respond/Defend _____ Miscellaneous
3.	_____ Acclaim/Praise _____ Criticize/Attack _____ Respond/Defend _____ Miscellaneous
4.	_____ Acclaim/Praise _____ Criticize/Attack _____ Respond/Defend _____ Miscellaneous
5.	_____ Acclaim/Praise _____ Criticize/Attack _____ Respond/Defend _____ Miscellaneous

Figure 14.1 Sample Coding Sheet for Presidential Campaign Commercials

With such a coding sheet, you could analyze individual sentences in presidential campaign advertisements and place each sentence into an individual category as proposed by Benoit (1999), and as identified in the previous section above. The categories describe the purpose of the sentences in the advertisements. We recommend first conducting a pilot study with a portion of your data. A **pilot study** is a trial run. Imagine you collect 120 ads from the 2012 presidential campaign and then conduct a preliminary content analysis on 10 percent of the ads (12). The purpose of the pilot study is to check the coding process and see what problems potentially emerge in the coding and the analysis. We will talk about this in a moment.

Next, consider how many people will be coding the data. If you have more than one coder, you need to think about how much agreement exists between the different coders in categorizing the data. **Intercoder reliability** is a statistical analysis of how similar/different coders are in coding content categories. Neuendorf (2002) stated that intercoder reliability is a "necessary criterion for valid and useful research when human coding is employed" (p. 142). Various statistical measures are available to evaluate intercoder reliability: percent agreement (a basic measure), Cohen's kappa (κ), Spearman's *rho*, Pearson's correlation (*r*), and Krippendorf's *alpha*. For more information on these measures see Neuendorf (2002) or Popping (1988). In most cases, your reliabilities should be above .75.

Now you have an understanding of why you should pilot test your content analysis, develop a coding schedule, and conduct an intercoder reliability analysis. The following section outlines how you can report your results.

Quantitative and Qualitative Analysis

You can approach your data analysis and write up your results for a content analysis in various ways. Depending on whether you are conducting a quantitative or a qualitative analysis, your approach to results reporting may differ. Computer programs such as SPSS have made quantitative analysis easier to conduct. In a quantitative analysis, the reporting of your coding could start at a very basic level where you report the percentage or number of times a particular category occurs in the sample. You can then take quantitative analysis a step further by comparing the categories using a chi-square to determine which category is the most frequently occurring. Beniot and Glantz (2012) conducted chi-squares in their analysis of 2008 general election presidential TV spots. In their analysis they found, among other things, that television ads contained more attacks (65 percent) than acclaims (34 percent), and stressed policy (58 percent) more than character (42 percent). We discuss how to conduct a chi-square in the inferential statistics chapter.

In qualitative content analyses, focusing on the narrative in a text or the signs or symbolism in a text are two ways you can present your data. In a narrative analysis, you focus your analysis on the conscious or intended meanings (**manifest meaning**) and the unconscious or unintended meanings (**latent**

meaning) in a text. Your focus on the storytelling aspects of a text can focus on many aspects of the data, all depending on the research objectives. If you focus on the signs or symbols in a text, you are conducting a semiotic analysis and focusing on the symbolism in the data. Then your reporting will focus more on the latent meanings of texts (Newbold, Boyd-Barrett, & Van Den Bulck, 2002).

Leonard and Toller (2012) used a comparative approach, similar to a narrative approach, to compare the different ways posters on MDS (MyDeathSpace. com) communicate about suicide. Leonard and Toller found individuals' posts revolved around six categories about suicide: "(a) sympathy of the deceased or their loved ones, (b) method of suicide, (c) judging the deceased and others, (d) explanations for suicide, (e) regret for death, and (f) loved one's response to posters" (p. 392). Each category tells a different story of how individuals who post on MDS cope with suicide. Leonard and Toller illustrated these categories by providing qualitative examples of each category (posts from the web), such as the following post, which helps illustrate "Judging the Deceased and Others": "Selfish these parents I've seen on MDS who kill themselves. No matter how bad it is, you have a responsibility to your kids" (Leonard & Toller, 2012, p. 394).

We could approach our study of 2012 presidential election campaign ads from either a qualitative or a quantitative approach. Our coding sheet is set up to conduct a quantitative analysis. If we sit down and watch 120 ads from each candidate for the 2012 election and code each of them ($N = 240$) based on the functional theory set forth by Benoit (1999), we could easily break down the frequencies of how often ads acclaimed/praised, criticized/attacked, responded/defended, or did something else for a candidate. We place each ad in one category. We then organize the results into a table like Figure 14.2 (a hypothetical table, not a real analysis of presidential ads):

Candidate	Acclaim/Praise	Criticize/Attack	Respond/Defend	Misc.
Obama (120)	65 (54.16%)	30 (25%)	25 (20.84%)	0
Romney (120)	45 (37.5%)	55 (45.83%)	20 (16.67%)	0
$n = 240$	110 (45.83%)	85 (35.42%)	45 (18.75%)	0

Figure 14.2 Frequency Distribution of the Function of Presidential Television Ads in the 2012 Election

Content analysis is a useful method. The method can help us analyze large bodies of data and address a plethora of research objectives. However, content analysis does have its limits. Content analysis does not address causality. While content analysis can point out changing trends or identify categories or themes, the method cannot answer why these categories or themes emerged or developed. Thus, you should be cautious not to over-estimate your results when conducting a content analysis. We will discuss issues of causality later in the book.

Summary

This chapter was a how-to guide to content analysis. Content analysis can be approached from the social scientific, interpretive, and critical/cultural paradigms. It is a multi-faceted method. Hopefully after reading the chapter, and the accompanying student paper, you feel comfortable enough to try your own content analysis. The next chapter, Chapter 15, is a how-to guide to surveys.

 ## Key Steps & Questions to Consider

1. Content analysis is a research method that can describe, categorize, and/or make inferences about communication messages.
2. Content analysis dates back to the 18th century with research on the *Songs of Zion*. Content analysis grew tremendously during World War II with the work of Laswell and his colleagues.
3. The type of data you use in content analysis is flexible and depends on your research objectives. Data can vary from texts to various kinds of analyses of human behavior.
4. The recording unit of analysis is the content you are analyzing, which can be identified and counted. For example, we can count sentences, and we can separate sentences into different categories.
5. The context unit of analysis is the context surrounding the recording unit. Context is significant because when we conduct a content analysis we must often consider the context surrounding the recording unit.
6. If you want to conduct a content analysis, you need to systematically code the data to find your recording units of analysis. A helpful way to code is by creating a coding schedule or coding sheet. A coding schedule tracks, records and/or categorizes the communication you are coding.
7. A pilot study is a trial run of your content analysis where you work out any potential kinks in your process and procedures.
8. Intercoder reliability is a statistical analysis of how similar or different coders are in coding content categories. You can use percent agreement (a basic measure), Cohen's kappa (κ), Spearman's *rho*, Pearson's correlation (*r*), or Krippendorf's *alpha* to test reliability. Your reliabilities should be above .75.
9. For quantitative analysis, the reporting could start at a very basic level where you report the percent or number of times a particular category occurs in the sample. Quantitative reporting can be taken a step further when you compare the categories using a chi-square analysis to see which categories occur the most.

10. In qualitative analyses, focusing on the narrative in a text or the signs or symbolism are two ways to present data. In a content analysis, you focus analysis on the conscious or intended meanings (manifest meaning) and the unconscious or unintended meanings (latent meaning) in a text.

11. Remember, a content analysis does not show causality.

 ## Activities

1. Divide the class into groups. Have each group watch the same episode (or multiple episodes) of a television sitcom (e.g., *How I Met Your Mother, Two and a Half Men, Family Guy, The Simpsons*). The assignment for each group is to code the humor in the episode(s) using a quantitative approach. Group 1 is tasked with finding and using pre-existing humor categories (a deductive content analysis). Group 2 will develop their own categories (an inductive content analysis). Group 3 will let the categories emerge from the data (grounded theory; refer to Chapter 13 for a refresher). Compare the results from the three groups. What differences are evident in the results? How did the different approaches influence the results?

2. Using the results from Activity 1, have each group run intercoder reliability on their results.

3. Run a variation of Activity 1 using a television soap opera. The focus is on images as text. What does a content analysis of images as presented in a daytime soap opera tell us about how Americans are portrayed?

 ## Discussion Questions

1. How can the context unit of analysis influence our understanding of the data in the content unit of analysis?

2. What role does the unit of analysis play in a content analysis? Why should a researcher be concerned with the unit of analysis?

3. How might a quantitative researcher and a qualitative researcher approach the same content analysis study differently? What aspects of content analysis may change between quantitative and qualitative?

4. Why is intercoder reliability relevant in a content analysis study? After all, all the coders are looking at the same data and using the same categories.

Key Terms

Coding schedule	Inductive content	Pilot study
Content analysis	analysis	Recording unit of
Content categories	Intercoder	analysis
Context unit of analysis	reliability	Unit of analysis
Deductive content	Latent meaning	
analysis	Manifest meaning	

Undergraduate Student Paper

Good Housekeeping and negative social comparison

Benjamin Smith

In our society, body image has become very important to most people to various extents. Women are constantly bombarded through the media with what the ideal figure is etc. . . ., which inevitably leads to many problems. I will use content analysis to analyze the magazine *Good Housekeeping*, which has an audience of 23,916,000, to see the breakdown of what they focus on in terms of body image for women, the target market of the magazine (Hearst Women's Network, Good Housekeeping Demographic Profile, n.d.). Obviously, there are different aspects to achieving a healthy body image, such as exercise, eating healthy, and the way you present yourself (appearance). I believe an analysis of the contents of *Good Housekeeping* will show that there is an uneven distribution in the various aspects in achieving a healthy body image, which is detrimental to the self-esteem and overall wellbeing of women in society.

Method

To conduct my analysis of *Good Housekeeping* I will be using content analysis. I have obtained the June 2011 issue of *Good Housekeeping* and picked three categories to look at as targets. The first category is food. This category is looking at any pages that target health foods, healthy options, and diet foods to target weight loss and healthy habits. The second category I am looking for is body appearance, which includes pages or articles that deal with the woman's appearance, such a slimming outfits and styles/make-up that are looking to make you appear younger, healthier, and thinner. The last category I am looking at is actual exercise for weight loss and healthy living.

Benjamin has an effective opening to his paper. He sets up the reason for his paper and why content analysis (body image), why the reason is relevant to society, and the primary source of his content (*Good Housekeeping*).

First, Benjamin may find one issue of a magazine is insufficient for his content analysis. The articles and ads in one issue may not represent the normal content of the magazine. A random selection of multiple issues spanning a year (or even multiple years) may provide stronger results.

Second, Benjamin can strengthen his analysis by explaining how he developed the three categories. Are the categories based on previous studies (a deductive content analysis)? He obviously did not use an inductive content analysis since categories are pre-determined. A scholar needs some foundation for the categories for the research to be solid.

Finally, he needs to identify his recording unit of analysis. Is he breaking down the magazine by sentences, paragraphs, articles, pages? What role do images play? How will he account for the contextual unit of analysis?

Remember, we are dealing with a lower-level undergraduate student paper. All the questions we are posing may be outside the scope of the class assignment. Make sure your level of detail is consistent with your professor's expectations.

My research question: is there an uneven distribution in body image factors in the media targeting women? I predict an uneven distribution in the three categories that are vital to achieve healthy living, weight loss, and an overall body image as described above. After sorting through the pages of *Good Housekeeping* and categorizing the pages that fit into one of the three categories, I will analyze them and look at the prevalence of each to see if there is an even distribution or if more emphasis is put on certain categories that will cause the women to be ineffective in their pursuit of the overall healthy body image, weight, and healthy lifestyle.

Theory

Social Comparison Theory

Social comparison theory deals with how individuals compare themselves with others in our society. As we experience and see others, we continuously compare ourselves with others, making either positive or negative comparisons based on how we feel about ourselves (Schwartz & Andsager, 2011). Generally, the media portrays body images that are nearly impossible to achieve, which undoubtedly leads to frustration and lower dissatisfaction among the individuals making the comparisons. The media no longer portrays just body images, but also ways to achieve a better body image. If there is a skewed coverage of how to achieve a better body image, by this I mean more emphasis put on one aspect instead of the many aspects needed, then there will not be success in achieving the desired outcome. This, as part of the social comparison theory, will lead to increased dissatisfaction among viewers of the media because there will be lower self-esteem as they make their comparisons. This will occur because the ways to achieve the ideal body image are supposedly given to you in the media, but you are still unable to achieve the outcome even when you are told directly how to.

This whole process can repeat itself, leading to women actually going the opposite way of what they are trying to achieve, which is a better body image. The media will therefore be causing more harm with regards to the social comparison theory then they would if they gave an even distribution of the categories needed to achieve a healthy body image and overall lifestyle.

Results

Good Housekeeping breaks down their publication into the categories they cover and the percentage of which they cover. Of the three categories I am looking at, their relating categories are Food & Nutrition, Health (Exercise/Wellbeing) and Beauty/Grooming (Hearst Women's Network, Good Housekeeping Editorial Coverage, n.d.). Food & Nutrition are said to account for 20.2 percent of their publication, Health for 7.5 percent and Beauty/Grooming for 6.2 percent (Hearst Women's Network, Good Housekeeping Editorial Coverage, n.d.). After looking through the June 2011 issue, I found 39 of the 202 pages were targeting health food/nutrition, 21 pages targeting Beauty, which deals with body image appearance, and one instance targeting exercise for healthy living/weight loss. Therefore, my percentages are the following, Food/Nutrition is 19.3 percent, Beauty/Grooming is 10.4 percent and Health is .5 percent. Food/Nutrition is close to what *Good Housekeeping* reports (20.2 percent reported compared with 19.3 percent found); Beauty/Grooming is fairly close to the reported value (6.2 percent reported compared with 10.4 percent found). The last finding is the health, which is reported at 7.5 percent and found at .5 percent. Although *Good Housekeeping* openly reports what the magazine breakdown is, and that the focus is not evenly distributed, the actual distribution is skewed a lot more than reported, which may have drastic impacts on women's self-esteem. *Good Housekeeping* magazine touts itself as being the most trusted source for advice about food, diet, beauty, health, family, and home (Hearst

Benjamin has integrated theory providing a strong foundation for the study. Social comparison theory is useful for understanding the content of his analysis. He can strengthen the section by providing evidence and source support for many of the claims he makes. For example, he states "The media no longer portrays just body images, but also ways to achieve a better body image," yet no documentation is provided to prove the statement.

Benjamin can strengthen his results section in a number of ways. First, he can move the data provided by the Hearst Women's Network from Results to the end of his Introduction section. A reader assumes any results in the Results section are from the current study, not from a previous study.

Second, a reader can get lost wading through all the categories and percentages. A table (or a series of tables) can better help a reader with such data. Refer back to Figure 14.2 and see how quickly you can identify key results. The write-up can then be focused on the highs and lows of the data.

Finally, Benjamin could move the comparison of his results with Hearst Women's Network's information and interpretation of the results to a new Comparison & Interpretation section or to the Conclusion section of his paper.

Women's Network, About Good Housekeeping Magazine, n.d.). The fact that there is not an even distribution in their coverage of these three categories can lead to more harm to the women they are serving, as all three categories are necessary to achieve the outcome these women are presented with in the magazines.

Conclusion

With the combination of media influences and various theories, such as the social comparison theory, it becomes clear that what articles and topics that are targeted towards women could potentially have a profound impact on their health and self-esteem. To have a healthy lifestyle and better body image, it is important to not only eat right, as 19.3 percent of *Good Housekeeping* covered, but there also needs to be an equal amount of exercise and even appearance that plays a key role in a healthy body image. When one of these is focused on more than others, it can lead to false perceptions of what needs to be done. If a woman believes eating healthy meals is all that is needed to have a more positive body image and slim down, then if the food alone does not accomplish that, then there is a higher likelihood that she will have more negative comparisons about herself. It is for this reason that media such as *Good Housekeeping,* who have a reputation as a trustworthy source for women, need to portray a fuller picture for the women they are targeting in order to actually improve their self-image, instead of possibly making problems worse.

References

Hearst Women's Network. (n.d.). About Good Housekeeping Magazine. *Good Housekeeping.*

Hearst Women's Network. (n.d.). Good Housekeeping Demographic Profile. *Good Housekeeping Media Kit.* Retrieved from: www.ghmediakit.com/r5/home.asp.

Hearst Women's Network. (n.d.). Good Housekeeping Editorial Coverage. *Good Housekeeping Media Kit*. Retrieved from: www.ghmediakit.com/r5/home.asp.

Schwartz, J., & Andsager, J. L. (2011). Four decades of images in gay male-targeted magazines. *Journalism & Mass Communication Quarterly, 88*(1), 76-78.

15 SURVEYS

What Will I Learn About Surveys in This Chapter?

Most of us have taken a customer service survey. These surveys are designed to measure our level of satisfaction with an organization and its services. You may have been asked how satisfied you were with service at a fast-food restaurant, a hotel, or with a recent purchase. These surveys used to be mailed to people's homes (some still are). Most surveys are now offered online. A second kind of survey you may have taken is a questionnaire in one of your classes where you had to answer different questions about communicative, sociological, or psychological processes or behaviors. Students regularly fill out these kinds of surveys on university campuses.

Surveys have a storied history in social scientific research, government, and economics. William the Conqueror had a census collected (1085–1086), which was called the *Domesday Book* (Hyman, 1991; Miller, 1983; Neuman, 2011). After this census, the gathering of population data became common government practice, which continues today. Researchers also began to collect survey data on how people lived: Henry Mayhew chronicled urban life in London from 1851 to 1864, and W. E. B. DuBois (1899) detailed urban conditions among African Americans in his text, *Philadelphia*

Negro. After James Cattell (1890) proposed the idea of empirically measuring mental and emotional processes, surveys became a regular part of social scientific research.

Why Use Surveys?

A **survey** is a social scientific research instrument in which respondents are asked questions about their own or other individuals' attitudes, behaviors, beliefs, perceptions, and/or values. While many of these categories overlap, major differences exist depending on how a researcher approaches a study. Figure 15.1 shows some basic examples of things you can focus on in a survey.

While surveys are useful for data collection, they are not always the most appropriate method. Surveys are most appropriate for use in the following situations: when you need new data and when people are best at providing the data about what you are studying.

First, use a survey to collect new data on some phenomenon. For example, you cannot use a survey if you are interested in studying the social identities of Confederate and Union soldiers during the U.S. Civil War. You are unable to collect surveys since the soldiers are long dead. Instead you will need to look through historical documents and read the accounts of soldiers, look through newspaper articles, and the like. The fact you can't access the population is important; we talked about this in Chapters 7 and 9. If you can't access the population, you can't collect the data. So ask yourself the following two key questions: 1) are you able to collect the data and 2) do you need to collect the data using a survey?

The second reason to use a survey is because people are best at providing the data about what you are studying. A fundamental purpose of a survey is to measure an individual's own perceptions of their attitudes, behaviors, beliefs, perceptions, and/or values. If you are interested in studying public opinion about a presidential decision, a survey may be appropriate. You could

1. Attitudes/Beliefs and Opinions—What type of job is the President doing? Do you believe that television news is fair and balanced?
2. Perceptions—To what extent does the media present things as they are in reality?
3. Values—To what extent do you care for your family, even when you have to sacrifice what you want?
4. Behaviors—How many hours a week do you watch television?
5. Numerous other aspects of human life can be explored using surveys, such as: demographic characteristics (sex, age, and religious identification), expectations (do you plan on going to college in the future?), and knowledge (who is the secretary of the U.S. Treasury?).

Figure 15.1 Examples of What You Can Ask About in a Survey

measure individuals' personal opinions on the decision and about the President. Public opinion polls are a standard survey form. Another standard survey form is a communication or psychological self-report, like the Personal Report of Communication Apprehension (McCroskey, 1982). Using this survey, a researcher can measure an individual's level of communication apprehension. When the respondent fills out the survey, they are reporting their personal perception of how much communication apprehension they have. If you think back to Chapter 7 (data), some researchers criticize self-reports because respondents tend to over- or under-estimate their attitudes, behaviors, beliefs, perceptions, and/or values (Fisher, 1993; Ganster, Hennessey, & Luthans, 1983; Oetzel, 1998). To solve for an over/under-estimation, researchers encourage the use of other-report surveys (Podsakoff & Organ, 1986; Spitzberg & Hecht, 1984). We will talk more about self- and other-report surveys later in this chapter. For now, just remember that self-report surveys give the subjects a chance to answer questions about themselves, which can provide in-depth information about phenomena.

> While video cameras and clerks in stores can tell a lot about how "satisfied" we may be about our shopping experiences at different shopping locales, we as shoppers are probably the most qualified to judge our overall satisfaction. This is why we are sometimes asked to fill out customer service questionnaires, or customer service surveys. The same can be said about opinion polls during elections. The news networks and companies like Gallup could rely on how many people are at various rallies and such, but instead use polls to tell the public who is leading in public opinion. Granted, these polls are not perfect, which we will talk more about.

How to Create a Survey

As discussed in Chapter 7 on data, Chapter 8 on evaluating research, and Chapter 9 on hypothesis and research questions, one of the purposes of research from a social scientific approach is to measure multiple variables and test hypotheses and research questions. This is facilitated using well-designed surveys. Creating a survey for distribution to participants involves three macrosteps. The steps are detailed in Figure 15.2.

Choose a Theoretical Framework and Develop Hypotheses or Research Questions

The first step in creating a survey is to choose your theoretical framework(s) that will guide the study. You must ask yourself, "What am I studying?" "What phenomena am I interested in testing or exploring with my survey?" You will have a hard time coming up with any kind of survey instrument if

> **Step 1. Theoretical**
> a. Choose a theoretical framework(s) that will guide the study.
> b. From your theoretical framework(s), develop hypotheses or research questions that the survey will help you test.
>
> **Step 2. Structural**
> a. Create new survey questions and response categories or use pre-existing survey instruments.
> b. Choose a type of survey (mail, online, paper, etc. . . .).
> c. Be sure the survey is clearly laid out with easy to follow instructions.
>
> **Step 3. Logistical**
> a. Decide on how you want to collect and store the data.
> b. Pilot test the survey instrument.

Figure 15.2 Steps in Survey Creation

you cannot answer these questions. Second, you should develop research questions(s) and/or hypothesis/hypotheses for your proposed study. Survey research is **deductive research**. This means you begin with a theory of interest and then propose hypotheses or research questions. Your hypotheses or research questions are statements of how variables are related to one another. Your survey is designed to measure the variables and, thus, test the hypotheses or research questions that help you arrive at conclusions about the theory. We discussed this process in Chapter 9, but a little refresher may help.

Let's say we are interested in testing whether Facebook users get the same gratifications they seek from using Facebook. An extensive body of literature exists on gratifications sought and obtained (boyd & Ellison, 2007; Chen, 2011; Herzog, 1940; Katz, Blumler, & Gurevitch, 1974; McQuail, 2005; Ruggiero, 2000). Research has shown, for example, that users of sites such as Facebook seek out friends and believe they get friends from these sites (Raacke & Bonds-Raacke, 2008). Hypotheses or research questions could be derived from previously written research to better understand Facebook and the gratifications sought and obtained. Once the hypotheses and/or research questions are generated, the next step is to either create an entirely new survey, or to use a pre-existing survey instrument.

Once you have decided on the focus of your study, you need to consider the following issues: 1) whether you want to create a new survey or use a pre-existing one, 2) the type of survey you want to use, and (3) making sure your survey is easy to use. A big decision you need to make, and one

Stephen has grappled with in the past, is whether you use pre-existing scales or if you create an entirely new scale to measure a particular phenomenon. Pros and cons occur when doing both. New researchers may find using a pre-existing measure helpful because you do not have to generate a lot of questions. Creating a new instrument to measure a phenomenon involves quite a bit of statistics since you must demonstrate that the instrument is both statistically valid and reliable. If you want to create your own survey, you may need to conduct multiple pilot tests and run the questions through numerous statistical tests (exploratory and confirmatory factor analyses, for example). Such analyses are well beyond the scope of this text. Therefore, we recommend you use pre-existing scales when possible,[1] although we recommend their use with caution. One of the things Stephen and Dan have seen is students choosing random measures and deciding to use them for their research. Your theoretical framework(s) must guide your measure selection. Choose a measure or measures that help you address your hypotheses or research questions. For example, imagine collecting 100 surveys on communication apprehension when the real purpose of your study is to explore self-disclosure.

Survey Questions and Response Categories

Let's say you want to create your own survey instrument or you have an assignment requiring you to generate survey questions. Consider the following when you design your survey: What kinds of questions and levels of questions should you include in a survey? How do you make sure the questions you include are valid and reliable? How can you avoid confusing questions? To what extent should you consider the perspective of the participants when writing the questions? Are you leaving anything out of the survey? These are just a few of the many issues you need to consider when designing and/or choosing your survey questions. Multiple checklists and various suggestions are available to help you create surveys (Babbie, 1990; Hocking, Stacks, & McDermott, 2003; Neuman, 2011; Wrench, Thomas-Maddox, Richmond, & McCroskey, 2008). Figure 15.3 has recommendations to help you create well-constructed surveys.

1. Try to use multiple levels of questions.
2. Be cautious of the language you use in the survey.
3. Avoid double-barreled questions.
4. Avoid leading questions.
5. Avoid double negatives.
6. Avoid overlapping or unbalanced response categories in questions.
7. Be sure the survey is well organized.

Figure 15.3 Elements of Well-Constructed Survey Questions

Multiple Levels of Questions

First, most surveys will include nominal-, ordinal-, and interval-level questions (think back to Chapter 7 on data). Some surveys will include ratio-level, and open-ended questions. Examples of nominal-level questions include demographic questions (e.g., sex, political affiliation, and religion). You should include such questions when they are important to your topic of study. If religion is not important to your subject, then you may not need to ask about it.

Ordinal-level questions are also often used in surveys. Such questions could, for example, ask people about their income level or educational level. If you decide to include these types of questions (and maybe nominal-level ones as well), you need to plan what kinds of statistical tests you will use to analyze the data. We will talk more about data analysis shortly.

Interval-level are the most common type of questions you will find on surveys. Interval-level are typically Likert and semantic differential/bipolar adjective-type questions. A great deal of social scientific research relies on interval-level questions to measure human behavior. Look back to Figure 7.2 ("Organizational Dissent Scale") for an example of Likert-type questions that are typical for a communication survey.

Another kind of question you can include on your survey is an open-ended question. While most survey questions limit a respondent's choices (answers), open-ended questions allow respondents to answer any way they want. Here's an example of an open-ended question: "Describe the feelings you have in the moments before you give a speech or presentation in front of a group of people." The question allows respondents to open up about their feelings with a variety of statements, words, drawings, or whatever they want. Open-ended questions can be helpful for researchers since they provide information you do not expect with Likert-type questions. You can analyze open-ended questions statistically using methods such as content analysis (which we talked about in Chapter 14).

A combination of various question types can make any survey "better." Different levels of measurement (nominal, ordinal, interval, ratio, and open-ended) allow researchers to analyze data using varied methods and approach a phenomenon from a variety of angles.

In a recent survey, Stephen and his research team included a variety of questions to investigate Finnish conflict styles and individualism/collectivism. Their survey included various demographic questions, such as: "What is your marital status?" with the response options Single, Married, Divorced, Widowed, Partnered. They included ordinal-level questions, such as: "How long have you worked for your current employer, if you are employed?" with the response options Less than a year, 1–2 years, 3–5 years, 6–10 years, 11–15 years, 16–20 years, more than 20 years. The survey included numerous interval-level (Likert-type) questions. An example of a Likert-type question is: "Based on this 5-point scale: (1 = strongly agree to 5 = strongly disagree), people in other cultures have a better lifestyle than you do in your culture." An example of an open-ended question is: "What is your religion? (Please write in your religion. If you do not have one, please write that down.)"

Survey Language

The language choices we make when writing survey questions can have a tremendous effect on how participants understand and answer questions. When writing survey questions or instructions, try to avoid jargon, slang, and abbreviations. **Jargon** is language specific to a particular group, profession, or trade. For example, communication, like all disciplines, has a lot of jargon. Let's say you are interested in how social media use differs between the United States and Nicaragua (Spencer, Croucher, & Hoelscher, 2012). You might want to explore "teledensity," or the number of media (Internet) connections per person, and its effects on media use. If you ask respondents about "teledensity," many will not understand the question.

You should also avoid **slang,** or nonstandard vocabulary made up of informal words. Unlike jargon, slang does not have to be associated with a particular group. Slang varies based on an individual's language. Seemingly simple words have taken on new meanings with the explosion of the Internet. "Friend" and "unfriend" take on entirely new meanings with Facebook users. When Stephen first moved to Finland he found many of the English words he used had different meanings to English-speaking Finns. He was in a meeting and said he went somewhere that was an armpit of a town. People did not understand him, because it is not common outside of the United States, Canada, and maybe the UK to call a place an armpit. The word "armpit" is slang for an undesirable place. So, be cautious of using slang in surveys, as it can confuse respondents.

Abbreviations can cause problems with survey collection. If we were to create a survey asking students their thoughts on the viability of a new committee in the NCA to measure the effectiveness of offering more GIFTS sessions at the national conference, would you understand what we are talking about? Chances are slim. The NCA is the National Communication Association (the largest association for communication researchers, teachers, practitioners, and students). GIFTS stands for Great Ideas for Teaching Speech. Every year the national conference has sessions (meeting times) where communication scholars share great ideas they have for teaching speech or communication.

Double-Barreled Questions

A **double-barreled question** contains two or more questions. For example, if you are conducting a dining services survey of your campus cafeteria you might ask: "Do you like the food and beverage options provided on campus?"

Respondents may want to answer both yes *and* no to the question because they may like the food options but not like the beverage options. For example, the school may be a "Pepsi campus" and a respondent is a Coca-Cola fan. The question is not meant to confuse the respondents, yet is asking two separate things. A better way to ask about food and beverage options is to ask two separate questions: "Do you like the food options on campus?" and "Do you like the beverage options on campus?"

Leading Questions

A second kind of question you should avoid in a survey is a leading question. A **leading question** directs respondents toward one answer over another. Avoid questions such as: "You agree with the President's recent decision to . . . don't you?" This wording tells them you assume the President made a good decision and the respondents should too. When conducting a survey, you want respondents to believe all of their responses are equally valid; leading questions do not portray a sense of respecting respondents' opinions.

Double Negatives

A third kind of question to avoid is the double negative. Basic grammar rules tell us this is a poor sentence: "I have never played no musical instruments." In fact, grammatically and logically the sentence means one has played musical instruments. We should avoid double negatives in survey questions. An example of a double negative survey question is: "Do you disagree that politicians should not be required to have term limits?" The question is confusing. A good rule is to just keep the questions simple: "Politicians should be required to have term limits (agree or disagree)."

Overlapping/Unbalanced Categories

When respondents answer questions on a survey, their options need to be mutually exclusive, exhaustive, and balanced. **Mutually exclusive categories** mean the response options do not overlap. Take for example a question about television viewing: "How many hours a day do you watch television?" with the response categories: 1–4, 4–8, 8–12, 12–16, 16–20, 20–24. The problem is the categories overlap. Here's a better way to list the categories: 1–4, 5–9, 10–13, 14–17, 18–21, 22–24. Now, the hours do not overlap and are mutually exclusive.

Exhaustive categories mean everyone has a category to choose. Earlier we showed you a nominal-level question that Stephen used to collect data in Finland: "What is your marital status?" and the options were (Single, Married, Divorced, Widowed, Partnered). Stephen's research team determined that the options were exhaustive. The team added "Partnered" to the survey since in Finland many individuals are legally and informally "Partnered." Everyone taking the survey should have had an option that suited them.

Balanced categories provide participants with a balance of opinion options. A typical Likert-type question may have responses ranging from "strongly agree" to "strongly disagree." The continuum provides balanced categories. The two polar opposites provide a balance of opinions. If you provide only "strongly agree" and "agree" you are providing leading categories for your respondents. Semantic differentials often have adjectives pairs such as honest/dishonest, cheap/expensive, kind/mean, etc.

Organization of the Survey

The organization of a survey is of key importance. The structure of a survey, particularly the order in which you put your questions is often based on research preference. However, you should follow some norms. When including interval- or ratio-level questions, here are a few things you should think about. First, try to put all of the questions with the same type of responses (answers) together. For example, put all of the questions that range from *strongly agree* to *strongly disagree* together, and all of the questions that range from *very unsatisfied* to *very satisfied* together. Clustering these kinds of questions together will generally make it easier for your respondents to answer questions with less confusion.

Second, most surveys tend to keep together the questions that focus on the same context. Many surveys will focus on multiple issues and each issue might include more than one measure. You will commonly see all measures that focus on one issue clustered together (pages 1–2 for example), and then the measures that focus on another issue clustered together (pages 3–4 for example). This can help your participants remain in the same mindset while they answer questions on each separate issue.

Third, you need to consider where you place nominal-level questions; should they be at the start or the end of the survey? This really is a personal preference of the researcher. We have both seen surveys with the demographic (nominal-level) questions at the end and at the beginning. The key is to keep the questions together, as you do not want to disrupt the rhythm of the respondents. Once respondents begin answering demographic or other nominal questions, it may seem odd to have more at a later stage. The same can be said about open-ended questions. Once respondents switch into an open-ended mindset, it can be difficult to get them back into a closed-ended mindset. Remember, the responses for open-ended questions can take up space on the survey. Thus, these kinds of questions are generally placed at the end of surveys.

Fourth, any sensitive questions should be placed at the end of the survey. Let's say you are doing a survey on jealousy and one of your variables you want to correlate is sexual promiscuity. You may want to start by asking about self-perceived jealousy using Likert-type items, then ask demographic questions, and finally ask about sexual activity or promiscuity. You do not want to ask about sexual activity or promiscuity first because the questions embarrass, anger, or lead respondents to start answering in either a socially desirable or dishonest way.

Types of Surveys

We would like to describe two types of surveys. Each type has advantages and disadvantages. The first kind is a paper-based survey. **Paper-based surveys** are just what they sound like—the survey is printed on paper and provided to participants. The survey is usually given to participants in one of four ways: face-to-face, take-home, in the mail, or over the telephone. With face-to-face surveys, the respondents fill out the survey with the researcher present. Many of you may have participated in research at your school where you take a paper survey for extra credit in a lab or classroom; this kind research is a paper-based, face-to-face survey. If you are allowed to take the paper-based survey home and turn it in later, then you have a take-home survey. Sometimes researchers will mail surveys to potential respondents. Mailing surveys to respondents can help broaden the reach of a study. Typically, the researcher will include a self-addressed stamped return envelope with the survey. The final delivery method for paper-based surveys is over the telephone. Researchers will call respondents and conduct surveys over the phone. Using this method, the researcher will ask the respondent the survey questions, and then record the answers on the survey.

Web-based is becoming a popular kind of survey. **Web-based surveys** are presented and collected entirely online. As people increasingly use the Internet, it is no surprise that researchers have turned to the Net as a way to collect data. Websites like SurveyMonkey are an easy way to distribute surveys. Once the surveys are online, invitations can be sent to people to fill out the surveys. A researcher can then export the collected data from SurveyMonkey (or similar programs) into a statistical software package and analyze the results. Figure 15.4 shows the advantages and disadvantages of paper- and web-based surveys. Based on these advantages and disadvantages, you can choose whether paper- or web-based is the most appropriate survey for you.

Survey Issue	Face-to-Face	Take Home	Mail	Web-Based
Cost	Highest	High	Medium	Cheapest
Delivery Speed	High	Medium	Slowest	Fastest
Possible Length of Survey	Longest	Same	Same	Shortest
Response Rate	Highest	High	Lowest	Medium
Ability to Ask:				
Probing Questions	Yes	No	No	No
Open-Ended Questions	Yes	Limited	Limited	Limited
Sensitive Questions	Limited	Limited	Yes	Yes
Ability to Use Visual Aids	Yes	Limited	Limited	Yes
Social Desirability Bias	Highest	High	Lowest	Medium
Interviewer Bias	Highest	High	None	None

Figure 15.4 Advantages and Disadvantages of Paper- and Web-Based Surveys

Clear Instructions

Have you ever tried putting together a complex piece of furniture, had a hard time programming electronics, or been confused by a school assignment? Clear instructions are a plus in all facets of life. We should also remember Murphy's Law: if something can go wrong, it probably will. Easy-to-follow instructions are important to facilitate the smooth completion of a survey. Easy-to-follow instructions = more participants completing the survey.

Stephen has been asked many clarifying questions by participants taking his surveys. Here's an example of survey instructions and questions participants have asked. "Please indicate in the space provided the degree to which each statement applies to you by marking whether you 1) strongly agree, 2) agree, 3) are undecided, 4) disagree, or 5) strongly disagree with each statement. There are no right or wrong answers." Participants have asked: Do I use numbers, or should I use roman numerals? Can I use pen or pencil? If I write in an answer, can I erase it before I turn in the survey? The key is to pre-empt as many questions as possible and to make your survey easy to follow.

> To prepare for such questions, Stephen and his team try to make sure participants know how to answer each set of questions. The consent document given to participants contains the following statement: "Please be sure to follow all instructions as closely as possible. Also, you may use pencil or pen to complete this survey. You may also change your answers for any question, as long as you do so before you turn in the survey." Stephen's team is sure that more things still need to be added to the statement; those additions will come in time.

Logistical Concerns

Once the survey is written, you need to think about two logistical concerns. First, you need to think about how you are going to collect and store the data, and second think about pilot testing the survey. The decision about collecting and storing the data is likely guided by the type of survey you are using. If you are web-based, the survey data will be collected and stored online. If you are paper-based, you need to think about how you will collect and where you will store the surveys. We will talk more about collection in a moment. How long you must store survey data depends on your college or university, and some Human Studies Review Boards require that you store data for 2–5 years.

Pilot testing is always a good idea. A pilot test allows you to check your survey instructions and questions with a representative sample population. Pilot testing is a way to test how well your survey will function among your real sample. We will not discuss here how many participants are needed for a pilot, since that is determined by how many questions you have. For now, just be aware that we strongly encourage you to pilot test any survey instrument.

How to Administer a Survey

The administration or data collection stage is when you are ready to go out into the field and collect your data. This can be a very exciting process. We identify three key things you must consider: 1) Who are the participants? 2) How are you collecting the data? and 3) Is your survey a one-shot or a longitudinal design? Whenever you design a new survey or use a pre-existing survey, a question that should guide you is: to what population do you intend to generalize? Once you have determined your intended population, you need to decide on your sample and how you will locate that sample (think back to Chapters 7–9). Wright (2012) was interested in emotional support and perceived stress among college students using Facebook. College students were the population for his study. His sample for the study was 283 university students recruited from communication courses at a Southwestern university in the United States.

For Wright, collecting his data was relatively easy since his sample was easily accessible: university students. University students are easy to find and are generally used to filling out surveys. He more than likely had his participants either fill out the surveys online or had the students fill out paper-based surveys (he did not state in the article how the surveys were completed). If your sample is harder to reach, finding the sample population and collecting the survey may not be easy. In Croucher et al. (2012), the researchers' population was average citizens in India ($n = 657$), Ireland ($n = 311$), Thailand ($n = 232$), and the United States ($n = 592$). The total sample ($n = 1,792$) was located via various social networks, religious organizations, and universities or colleges.

For Wright, his survey was what we call a one-shot survey, or a **cross-sectional** design. This means he collected the surveys at one point in time. The results of his survey revealed what the respondents felt about the phenomena at the given moment when they completed the surveys. While this tells us a lot about the respondents and their feelings, it does not tell us anything about how their feelings may change over time. If Wright or another researcher wanted to measure how perceptions, traits, or behaviors change over time they would need to conduct a **longitudinal design.** In this type of surveying, respondents are given the same questions over a period of time to track any changes in perception, traits, or behaviors. If changes occur, researchers attribute those changes to some variable within the study. We will talk more about longitudinal design in Chapter 18 on experimental design. All in all, how you administer a survey depends largely on the population to which you are generalizing.

How to Analyze Survey Data

The data analysis stage follows survey administration. Analyzing survey data is a four-part process: 1) check the surveys for errors, 2) enter the data, 3) double-check what you have entered, and 4) analyze the data. The first thing you should do after you get your data collected is go through it and see if you have any errors. Errors can be lots of things. You may have returned paper-based surveys with lots of unanswered questions. What you do depends on the number of unanswered questions. For example, you have 100 survey questions and two unanswered questions. Statistical solutions are available to "fix" the survey. Talk with your instructor about how you can replace missing values with means, and the ethics of such a decision. Another issue you may encounter is when a participant answers every question with the same value. Sometimes you will get people who do not really care about your research and simply circle the same answers for every question. In these cases you need to decide whether you keep or discard their survey data. Stephen often discards these surveys and puts a note in his final manuscript about how: "'X' many surveys were discarded because they were incomplete or improperly completed."

Second, you need to enter your data. Entering data can be time consuming, especially if you use paper-based surveys. You need to type every answer into some kind of computer program. If you use a web-based survey, a lot of time can be saved because you can export or import the data into a computer program for data analysis. Web-based programs like SurveyMonkey allow you to distribute a survey and then import the data into Excel or SPSS (Statistical Package for Social Sciences), one of the most used statistics programs. Other statistical software programs include SAS, XLSTAT, R, or MATLAB. Check with your instructor which statistical programs are available on your campus and which one the instructor prefers.

No matter what program you use to enter your data (particularly if you enter data by hand from paper-based surveys), you must make sure you double-check the numbers. As you go through your surveys you are likely to make mistakes. Over time, you will enter a lot of data. Recently Stephen's team hand-entered 1,200 surveys. Each survey had 115 questions for a total of 138,000 responses. The team was bound to enter a few wrong numbers (e.g., a 3 instead of a 2 for a question, a 4 instead of a 5). Go through and double-check your data! Now, before you get scared and think you have to check everything, a good rule is to double-check 20 percent of the data. If you find you make few errors in 20 percent, then the rest of your data should be acceptable. If you find the 20 percent you check is laced with errors, then check everything.

Finally, you need to analyze the data. Chapter 16 on descriptive statistics and Chapter 17 on inferential statistics outline ways in which you can analyze the quantitative survey questions. Chapter 14 on content analysis offers ways you can analyze open-ended survey questions. The type of analysis you use depends on the type of questions and variables you have on the survey (see Chapters 14, 16, and 17).

Advantages and Disadvantages of Surveys

Survey research has numerous advantages and some limitations. The seven main advantages to survey research are: 1) cost, 2) speed, 3) quantity of participants, 4) ability to distribute in a variety of places and methods, 5) ability to ask a lot of standardized questions, 6) standardization of questions can lead to more reliable results, and 7) surveys can lead to more generalizeable results. Surveys provide researchers with a relatively cheap and fast way to garner responses from a lot of participants in a variety of places using lots of means (Neuman, 2011). With surveys, unlike other methods, researchers are able to ask standardized questions. Standardized questions are the same for each participant, without deviation. Asking such questions provides reliable results, as a researcher can argue that each participant was asked the same *exact* questions. While many qualitative methods may have strict interview or focus group scripts, deviations from the script can occur, which makes it impossible to state *all* participants are asked the exact same questions. Standardization is one of the reasons that surveys lead to generalizable statistical findings.

Survey research has four main limitations: 1) surveys do not focus on context, 2) a survey is an inflexible instrument, 3) surveys generally need a large number of participants to be reliable, and 4) self-report surveys may trigger a social desirability bias. The first disadvantage of survey research is that surveys do not focus on context. Researchers who use surveys generally are not researching context. By nature, a method of research emphasizing standardization is not going to also focus on context. Thus, contextual cues and issues of subjective nature will be lost. Second, a survey is an inflexible instrument or document. Part of the standardization aspect of surveys is that, aside from open-ended questions, surveys do not leave room for free expression. Participants are asked to circle or mark how they feel about various things or issues. There is *very* little room for open expression of feelings, aside from the numbers provided on most surveys. Third, surveys, unlike qualitative research, need a large number of participants to be statistically reliable. This requirement can be difficult for many researchers, particularly those taking a class like yours where you have limited time and resources. Fourth, some participants may answer questions in ways to make themselves look better; this is considered the social desirability effect (Fisher, 1993). If a researcher is interested in how often people express jealousy, it can be difficult to get honest answers from some participants because jealousy is perceived as a negative behavior. People do not want to be seen negatively, so they are more likely to not answer questions honestly and instead portray themselves positively. Ultimately, the researcher must weigh the advantages and disadvantages of surveys, along with their needs when determining whether surveys are the right method for them.

Summary

This chapter was a how-to guide to surveys. Generally surveys are conducted by social scientific researchers, but can also be conducted by interpretive and critical/cultural researchers depending on the focus of the questions or survey. Hopefully after reading the chapter, you will feel comfortable enough to go out there and conduct your own survey. The next chapter, Chapter 16, is a how-to guide to descriptive statistics.

Key Steps & Questions to Consider

1. A survey is a social scientific research method in which respondents are asked questions about their own or other individuals' attitudes, behaviors, beliefs, perceptions, and/or values.

2. Surveys have a storied history or tradition. The first "surveys" date back to the 11th century.

3. Two reasons to use surveys are because you want or need to collect new data, and because the people you are surveying are best at providing or answering the questions you are asking.

4. Be sure that your survey is based on some theoretical framework.

5. Survey research is deductive research.

6. Avoid jargon and slang in survey questions.

7. Avoid double-barreled and leading questions in surveys, as well as double negatives.

8. Try to have mutually exclusive, exhaustive, and balanced response categories for survey answer options.

9. Try your best to have an organized survey. If the survey is not easy to follow, people will get confused and not do the survey, or do it incorrectly. The same is true for easy-to-understand instructions. Make the instructions as easy to understand as possible!

10. There are two main kinds of surveys: paper- or web-based. Paper-based surveys are on paper and given to participants. The survey is given to participants in one of four ways: face-to-face, take-home, in the mail, or over the telephone. Web-based surveys are presented and collected entirely online.

11. When you administer the survey, consider two things: 1) who are the participants, and 2) how are you collecting the data?

12. Analyzing survey data has four parts: 1) check the surveys for errors, 2) enter the data, 3) double check what you entered, and 4) analyze the data.

13. There are seven advantages to survey research: 1) cost, 2) speed, 3) quantity of participants, 4) ability to distribute in a variety of places and methods, 5) ability to ask a lot of standardized questions, 6) standardization of questions can lead to more reliable results, and 7) surveys can lead to more generalizeable results.

14. There are four limitations to survey research: 1) surveys do not focus on context, 2) a survey is an inflexible instrument, 3) surveys generally need a large number of participants to be reliable, and 4) there is a possible social desirability bias with self-report surveys.

 Activities

1. *Team task 1: find the flaws.* Your instructor will divide the class into teams and assign an online survey to each team. The *Washington Post* has a site of surveys (www.washingtonpost.com/politics/polling) useful for the task. Each team is tasked with finding as many flaws as possible in their assigned survey. The flaws must meet the standards established in this chapter.

2. *Team task 2: build a survey.* (Each team will need access to a computer.) Each team will develop a brief survey (20–25 questions) on a communication research question of their choice. The questions will be a variety of formats (e.g., Likert scale, yes/no, open-ended). Each team will be assigned a different online survey instrument (e.g., SurveyMonkey, KwikSurveys, Zoomerang, eSurveysPro, SurveyPlanet) and then build their survey. Teams will keep detailed notes on satisfaction or frustration levels in using the site to create their survey. Teams will share both their completed surveys and their detailed survey-construction notes.

 Discussion Questions

1. Think back on your personal experience with starting a survey but not completing the task. What about the survey made you quit? The length of the survey? The type of questions asked on the survey? The format of the survey? Share and compare your experience with others. Use the information to help guide construction of your own research surveys!
2. Think about your own communication research interests. Will a survey be an effective method for collecting data to answer your research questions? What limitations might you face? Share your thoughts with your classmates. Did they have similar or different limitations? Would those limitations also affect your study?

Key Terms

Balanced categories	Jargon	Pilot testing
Cross-sectional design	Leading question	Slang
Deductive research	Longitudinal design	Survey
Double-barreled question	Mutually exclusive categories	Web-based survey
Exhaustive categories	Paper-based survey	

Note

1 Instructors will sometimes encourage students to create their own scales and use them for assignments. Such assignments are perfectly acceptable as these assignments push students to develop questions and explore phenomena. However, such measures are not statistically valid and/or reliable unless rigorously tested. For more information on statistical tests like factor analyses and on how to statistically test the validity and reliability of surveys, see Agresti and Finlay, 2009; Field, 2009; Levine, Bresnahan, Park, Knight Lapinski, Lee, and Lee, 2003; Pedhazur, 1997; Podsakoff and Organ, 1986).

16 DESCRIPTIVE STATISTICS

What Will I Learn About Descriptive Statistics?

This is a picture of the Rockefeller Center Christmas Tree in New York City. Every year the tree is put up and lit in late November and remains up until early January. The lighting of the tree brings thousands of people (tourists and locals) to the Rockefeller Center and is aired live on national television (along with live celebrity performances). The tree may cost tens of thousands of dollars to bring to New York and to maintain, but its presence brings in countless more dollars to New York City. In fact, in 2004 it was estimated that the tree alone brought in an estimated 3.7 billion dollars of tourism a year to New York City with many tourists visiting specifically to see the tree at Christmastime (Cummings, 2004).

The sum $3.7 billion is a descriptive statistic and outlines the economic impact of one tourist attraction. The tree is a highly visible and successful symbol of Christmas and New York City. The amount of money the tree brings to the city shows the accomplishment. We used the tree as the opening example for a chapter on descriptive statistics to demonstrate how statistics are all around us, and not some scary thing only scientists and other kinds of researchers use. You could study the advertising and communicative effects of the tree in multiple ways: 1) from an advertising perspective, where you could look at whether or not the tree is a successful advertising device for the businesses in the Rockefeller Center and New York City, and 2) explore individual cultural perceptions of the tree. We explore in Chapter 16 such questions and other aspects of descriptive statistics. In this chapter you will learn about descriptive statistics. Before we move on you should have a definition of statistics and descriptive statistics. **Statistics** is a way of organizing, describing, and making inferences from data. Statistical methods are used in the natural, physical, and social sciences (communication). **Descriptive statistics** shows how sample data appear in numerical and visual terms. In this chapter, and in Chapters 7–8 and 15–18, we talk more about the language of statistical methods and how to apply these methods.

Representations of Data

We cannot recall how many students have asked us for tips on how to better understand quantitative research. We both admit quantitative methods, like other methods, may not be the easiest method to grasp, unless you think step by step. Stephen recommends that the first step when doing quantitative research is to find some way to look at your data in picture form. Representations of data can be very helpful in showing us what we have to work with, and what we don't. Various kinds of tables, charts, graphs, and other representations show data in a non-numeric form. The choice of form comes down to the type of data, or variables, with which we are working.

If you are working with nominal and/or ordinal data (which you can review in Chapter 7), pie and/or bar charts are the most appropriate choices to represent your data. A **pie chart** is a circle divided into proportional parts representing statistical data. Each part of the circle represents a specific category. You may have seen, for example, pie charts in newspapers or magazines with part of the circle representing "male" and part representing "female." Figure 16.1 is based on a sample of individuals who completed the Organizational Dissent Scale (Kassing, 1998) ($n = 1481$). The pie chart visually represents the difference in number between men and women in the sample. A quick glance at the pie chart reveals the sample has more males than females. The pie chart shows how visualization can be helpful when you begin your data analysis by showing what is going on with your data. However, pie charts are rarely used in research papers and articles since they do not offer sophisticated insight about data distribution.

A more advanced option is the bar chart. A **bar chart** displays the category (variable) on the horizontal axis of the chart and the numeric value of the variable on the vertical axis. Therefore, in the case of males and females in the same organizational dissent study, a bar chart would look like Figure 16.2.

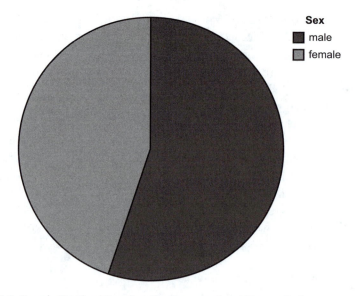

Figure 16.1 Sample Pie Chart Based on the Organizational Dissent Scale

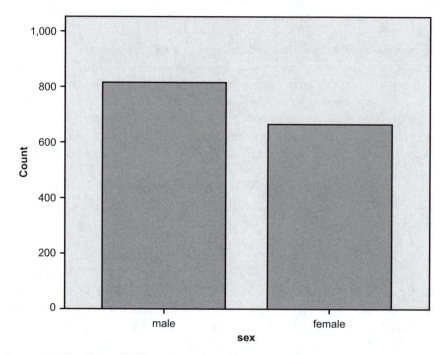

Figure 16.2 Bar Chart of Males and Females in the Same Organizational Dissent Study

In this case, the horizontal axis (*x*-axis or abscissa) defines the variables, while the vertical axis (*y*-axis or ordinate) lists the quantities of the variables. Bar charts can be taken a step further. With a bar chart you can compare multiple groups on various categories or variables. One of the variables of interest in organizational dissent research is how long an individual has worked

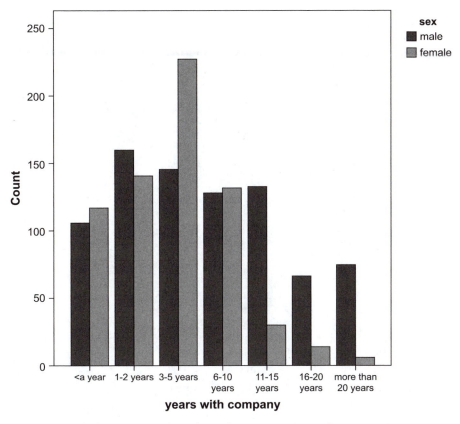

Figure 16.3 Bar Chart Showing the Relationship Between Sex and How Many Years an Individual Has Worked for a Company

for a company. With a bar chart you show the relationship between sex and how many years an individual has worked for a company (Figure 16.3). A quick glance at the table shows clear differences between males and females in the mean number of years they have worked with a company.

If you are working with interval and/or ratio data, a histogram is the most common visual representation for your data. You will, however, rarely see this graph or representation reported in research papers or journals. Just like with pie charts and bar charts, histograms are most often used to help researchers understand their data during preliminary analysis.

A **histogram** is similar to a bar chart. However, in this case continuous data are represented on the x-axis, unlike nominal or ordinal data with a bar chart. Another difference you will notice with a histogram is how the bars are generally connected on a histogram (unless there is a gap in values), while the bars are never connected on a bar chart. The example in Figure 16.4 is taken from a study in progress on communication apprehension (CA). You may remember hearing about CA from a public speaking class. CA is a person's fear or anxiety of real or anticipated communication with others (McCroskey, Simpson, & Richmond, 1982). The values in this table represent the mean CA scores of 336 individuals.

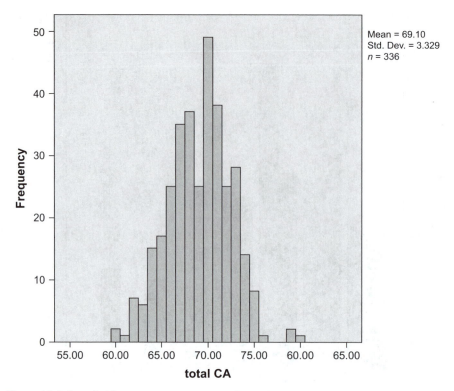

Figure 16.4 Sample Histogram

Statistical programs such as SPSS and SAS make the creation of visual representations fairly simple. Once you have data entered into one of the programs, a visual representation is just a few clicks away. However, just because we can create these representations does not mean we need to make them for everything. A key question to consider regarding visual representations is: do I need it? If you can describe the data easily with a visual, then make one; if not, then don't.

What kind of visual representation could you use to explain tourism to New York City during the holiday season? You could statistically track and display where individuals are from (nationality), how long they stay, average spending of tourists and businesses, predict future spending, and categorize the reasons why people come to New York . . . just to name a few. The key is that you can visually represent anything you want to measure statistically.

Measures of Central Tendency

Measures of central tendency are attempts to reduce data down to a single descriptive statistic that can quantify something into a typical or average measurement. Various measures of central tendency are available, and each differs in how they define typical or average.

The most basic measure of central tendency is the mode. The **mode** is the most frequently occurring measurement, number, item, score, etc. in the data. Consider the following (hypothetical) example about the home-nation of tourists who visit the tree in Rockefeller Center from a sample of 1,570 individuals.

Data 16.1

100 Canadians	75 Russians
300 Americans	65 Swedes
400 Chinese	150 Indians
110 Japanese	55 Brazilians
180 Germans	30 Italians
90 Mexicans	15 Ethiopians

What is the mode for tourists visiting the tree? The most frequently occurring nationality is Chinese ($n = 400$). This is a case of a unimodal sample (one mode). A sample with two modes is bimodal, and three modes are trimodal. A sample with four or more modes is not desirable because the sample is flat or platykurtic (we will talk more about this a little later in the chapter). Modes are rarely used in communication research. Modes by themselves are not really all that meaningful. However, there can be exceptions, which we will discuss shortly.

The **median** is the midpoint of a distribution with 50 percent of the scores above and 50 percent below the midpoint. Consider the following fictitious example of yearly salaries for an academic department.

Data 16.2

Faculty Member #1—$135,456
Faculty Member #2—$25,500
Faculty Member #3—$32,456
Faculty Member #4—$54,365
Faculty Member #5—$37,668

What is the median yearly income in this department? When you sort the data from highest to lowest:

$25,500 $32,456 $37,668 $54,365 $135,456

The middle score—$37,668—is the median. However, the procedure only works if you have an odd number of scores. If you have an even number, there is no middle score. Add a sixth person to the department (Faculty Member #6—$34,500). The sorted data now look like this:

$25,500 $32,456 $34,500 $37,668 $54,365 $135,456

Since the data have no one middle score, you need to calculate the sum of the two middle scores ($34,500 and $37,688) and divide by 2 ($34,500 + $37,688/2 = $36,094). The median can sometimes be a nice measure to get a rough estimate of the middle of a distribution, but it is not the average, or the most exact measurement of the center of a distribution. We discuss this more later in the chapter. You should not stress about calculating the median by hand; statistical computer programs do it for us! (But we should still know what the software is doing.)

The third kind of measure of central tendency is the **mean**, which is an average of the scores. The mean is the most commonly reported measure of central tendency. A mean is the sum of the data divided by the number of cases making up the sum. We're going to present you with a couple of equations. Don't get scared by the equations. Look for the "big picture" and all the pieces will fit together. Remember, we have computers to help with the calculations. The formula for the mean requires taking all the scores, adding them together, then dividing by the number of scores (Equation 16.1).

$$\overline{X} = \frac{\Sigma X}{n}$$

In this formula $\overline{X}$ is the mean, Σ is the symbol to add up the values of your variable (X), and then divide by the number of cases (n). Here is an example for you to try on the following set of numbers, which represent the number of vacation days people take to visit New York per year ($n = 30$).

Data 16.3

1, 2, 3, 3, 4, 4, 5, 5, 6, 6, 7, 8, 8, 9, 9, 10, 10, 11, 15, 15, 17, 18, 18, 19, 20, 22, 23, 25, 30, 30

$$\overline{X} = \frac{363}{30}$$

Therefore, $\overline{X} = 12.1$. In case you were wondering, the median (9 + 10/ 2) = 9.5, and the data distribution has *many* modes (3, 4, 5, 6, 8, 9, 10, 15, 18, and 30).

Now, we have these three measures of central tendency, mode, median, and mean. The question is: when do I use which one? Numerous schools of thought have an opinion on this matter; we offer three "rules" to follow.

When to Use Which Measure of Central Tendency

Rule 1: If your data are nominal you should use the mode to report the data. For example, if you are reporting data about the most common hair color on campus, the mode would be the most appropriate measure.

Rule 2: If you are reporting ordinal, interval and/or ratio data, you should use the mean as these types of variables lend themselves to having an average (mean). Most preferred media on a scale of 1 to 5 (ordinal), Likert or Likert-type scales (interval), and/or questions asking how many hours per day you watch television (ratio) all have means.

Rule 3: Keep in mind the mean can be sensitive to extreme scores. Therefore, when you have extreme scores and the data are skewed (we will talk more specifically about skew in a minute), you should use the median.

Go back to the earlier example (16.2) with the faculty data. The median is \$37,668, while the mean is \$57,089. The mean is quite a bit higher than the median (almost \$20,000 higher!). This difference is due in large part to the \$135,456 salary. So, remember, the mean is sensitive to extreme scores.

Variability

While you will typically find the mean reported in most research articles (or another measure of central tendency), another statistic often reported indicates how the data are dispersed or varied. You should know about three main kinds of variability: range, standard deviation, and variance. The simplest kind of variability is **range,** which you find by subtracting the lowest score from the highest score in a distribution ($r = h - l$).

Let's look at the set of scores in Data 16.3. The range is equal to (30 − 1), or 29. The range simply tells us the difference between the highest and the lowest numbers in a set of scores. The range does not tell us anything about the frequency of scores, as we could have multiple 30s in a distribution and few of anything else. The range only tells us the distance between scores on the x-axis.

A second kind of variability is the **variance** (s^2), which is a measure of how much distribution exists around a single point in a distribution, typically the mean. To calculate the variance, you need to first know the deviation (d) scores, which are found by subtracting every x score from the mean ($d = x - $ mean). Once you have the deviation scores, you can compute the formula for the variance, see below (Equation 16.2):

$$s^2 = \frac{\sum d^2}{n-1}$$

The variance from 16.3 is:

$$s^2 = \frac{4^2}{30-1} = \frac{16}{29} = .55$$

The variance is rarely reported in scholarly research, since it is difficult to subtract every score from the mean. However, squaring the values changes how the values were originally entered and measured. Thus, most researchers take the square root of the variance for a more parsimonious measure of variability; this is called the standard deviation.

The **standard deviation** (represented by the symbol sigma, σ), shows how much statistical variation exists from the mean, and is the square root of the variance. For the data in Data 16.3, the σ = .74. The standard deviation is the average distance between a score (measurement) and the mean. Larger standard deviations (ignoring the sign) represent more variability in the distribution, while smaller standard deviations represent less variability. So, in our number of vacation days example (16.3), the standard deviation is .74. This means the average difference between any person's number of vacation days and the mean is .74 days. The formula for the standard deviation is as follows (Equation 16.3):

$$\sigma^2 = \sqrt{\frac{\sum (X - Mean)^2}{n-1}}$$

The standard deviation is a standard unit of measurement that tells us how far scores "deviate" or differ from the mean. The standard deviation is helpful for research involving hypothesis testing and inferential statistics. For now, know that as you read communication journal articles you will find the two most often used descriptive statistics are the mean and the standard deviation. McEwan and Guerrero (2012) studied friendship maintenance behaviors among college students. They reported the means and standard deviations of various friendship maintenance behaviors, which helped illustrate the ways in which college students build and maintain friendship networks (p. 428). The reporting of such descriptive statistics is standard practice for researchers in communication and other scholarly disciplines.

As with the creation of visual representations, statistical programs such as SPSS and SAS can easily compute central tendency and variability. You don't have to compute the mean, standard deviation, and variance by hand, but it's good to know *how* the formulas work. Once you know how to use a statistical program, you enter the data, click a few buttons, and presto, you have your results.

If you are working at an advertising firm in New York City, the uses of central tendency and variability are endless. Firms regularly ask individuals about their shopping habits: how much they spend at specific stores, where they shop, why they shop at specific places, etc. . . . These kinds of questions represent various kinds of variables and surveys. The job of the researcher is to put the responses into a form others can understand. So, what is the average amount of money people spend during the holiday season (mean/SD), where do people shop (mode), and why do they shop at specific places (mode)?

Distribution Shapes

Now that you have an understanding of visual representations of data, central tendency, and variability, we can discuss how these elements can affect the shape of your data distribution. Visual representations such as a histogram can show the shape of a distribution. A distribution has four key characteristics: symmetry, skew, modality, and kurtosis.

Your data distribution can be **symmetrical** or **asymmetrical.** Imagine you have a histogram. Now draw a line down the center of it. If the left and the right side of the distribution are identical to each other (or fairly close to identical) then the distribution is **symmetrical.** If the two sides are not identical, then the distribution is **asymmetrical.** A symmetrical distribution will have an identical mean, median, and mode in a bell curve. A perfect bell curve is hard to come by, but Figure 16.5 shows a hypothetical distribution of how

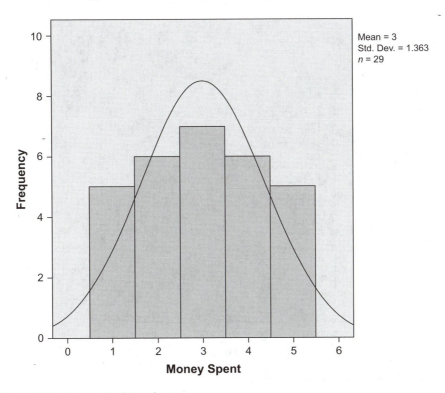

Figure 16.5 Symmetrical Distribution

many hundreds of dollars the average New Yorker spends on Christmas a year. You will notice the distribution is symmetrical and bell shaped. A symmetrical distribution (or one close to it) is what we call a normal distribution. Distributions that are close to symmetrical have specific aspects, which allow higher-level statistical testing than extremely asymmetrical distributions.

A asymmetrical distribution, however, indicates a high probability that the data are skewed one way or another. **Skewness** means the majority of scores are shifted either to the right or the left of a distribution's center. A good way to look at skew is to look at the "tail" of a distribution. People's income is a classic example of how a distribution can be skewed. Most people's income is skewed to the lower end of the pay scale, while some people make a lot of money. This is an example of **positive skew,** where the majority of the scores shift to the left of the distribution (lower end) and the tail of the distribution points out to the higher numbers. A distribution can also be negatively skewed. A **negative skew** is when the majority of the scores shift to the right of the distribution (higher end) and the tail of the distribution points to the lower numbers. An example is retirement age. Generally speaking, the older you get the closer you get to retirement, so more people retire when they are 65 or older, than when they are 50 or younger. Skewed distribution points to a random or constant error in the data (think back to Chapter 9). Figure 16.6 depicts a positively skewed, and Figure 16.7 shows a negatively skewed distribution. In Figure 16.6 you can see most of the data are on the left-hand side of the histogram, while in Figure 16.7 the data are on the right-hand side.

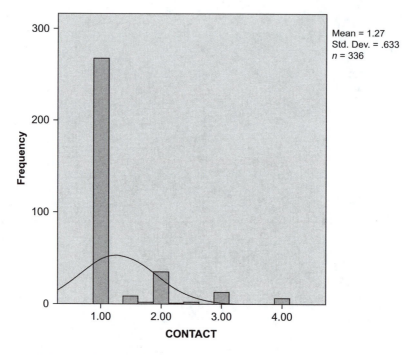

Figure 16.6 Positively Skewed Distribution

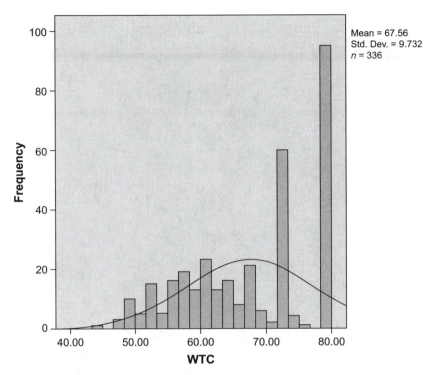

Figure 16.7 Negatively Skewed Distribution

Data that are extremely skewed can lead to misleading statistics, as skewed distributions can push up or pull down the mean. Consider salaries again. A company may say that its average (mean) salary is relatively good. Unfortunately, the mean may be pulled up by a select few very high-paid employees, which skew the mean. While it is important to know in which direction, if at all, your distribution is skewed, the modality of your distribution is also important. **Modality** refers to the number of peaks in your distribution. A distribution can be unimodal with one peak, or noticeable "hill" in the distribution. A distribution can also be bimodal (two peaks), or multimodal (multiple peaks). Imagine we were to ask 100 people about their communication apprehension (CA). Fifty of those people have never taken a speech class before and 50 of the people are on their college speech and debate team. Chances are we will have two very separate kinds of scores in this distribution; one group will likely have lower CA than the other group. The difference between the two groups will probably create a bimodal distribution like the one displayed in Figure 16.8. The distribution clearly shows two distinct groups of individuals.

The final way to describe your distribution is by analyzing its kurtosis. **Kurtosis** measures how peaked your distribution is. The more peaked the distribution, the more kurtosis it has; a distribution with high kurtosis is considered **leptokurtic** (leaping). This type of distribution does not have a

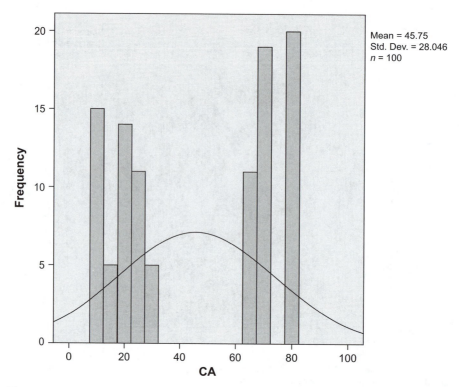

Figure 16.8 Bimodal Distribution

lot of variance and means most of the scores are similar. A leptokurtic result may occur because individuals in a culture may tend to answer questions similarly. On the other hand, a distribution with little kurtosis is considered **platykurtic** (plateau or flat). A platykurtic result generally means each score is happening with almost the same amount of frequency. Playtkurtic distributions typically have multiple modes, like the distribution in Data 16.3. The multiple modes could be attributed to a variety of factors: the instrument you are using could be unreliable or invalid (recall what we covered in Chapters 7 and 9), or you might have a constant or random error. Figure 16.9 depicts a leptokurtic distribution and 16.10 a platykurtic distribution. When you compare the two pictures you can see how the data are distributed differently. In 16.8 the data lump together in the middle, while in 16.9, the data do not cluster together.

The level of skewness and kurtosis is relatively easy to compute in your data since SPSS and SAS can compute the figures for you. Is there a threshold for skewness and kurtosis? No official cut-off criteria exist for determining when skewness or kurtosis is *too* large and your data are *too* asymmetrical, and thus non-normal. Some statisticians will get concerned about skewness and kurtosis at −1/1, while others will not be bothered at −7/7 (Burdenski, 2000; Curran, West, & Finch, 1996; Looney, 1995).

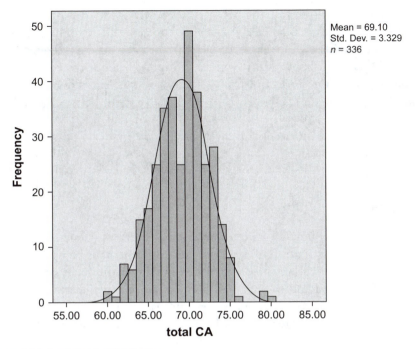

Mean = 69.10
Std. Dev. = 3.329
n = 336

Figure 16.9 Leptokurtic Distribution

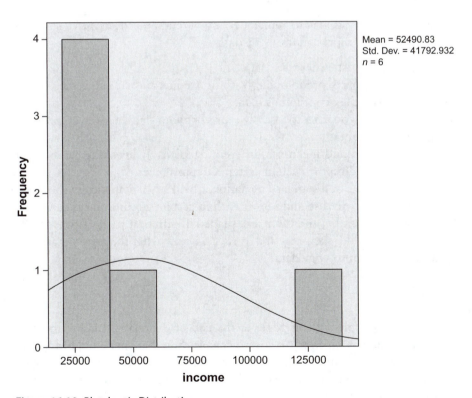

Mean = 52490.83
Std. Dev. = 41792.932
n = 6

Figure 16.10 Platykurtic Distribution

When analyzing tourism data about New York City, or any other city, be sure you consider who you are sampling (remember the discussion about sampling from Chapter 9). If you ask 50 tourists about their spending during a Christmas visit to New York City and one is a billionaire on a spending spree your data might be skewed. You will have to question what effect the billionaire has on your data. You may decide to use the median since the billionaire on the spending spree will affect your mean and skew those results.

Summary

This chapter was a how-to guide to descriptive statistics. Generally statistics are used by social scientific researchers, but can sometimes be used by interpretive and critical/cultural researchers depending on the focus of the study. Hopefully after reading the chapter, and the accompanying student paper, you will feel comfortable enough to try and use some descriptive statistics. The next chapter, Chapter 17, is a how-to guide to inferential statistics.

 ## Key Steps & Questions to Consider

Here are some key things to remember as you compute descriptive statistics or prepare visual representations of data.

1. Descriptive statistics describe data.
2. Pie and bar charts predominantly show frequencies of categories, while histograms display continuous data.
3. Ask yourself if you *need* to visually represent your data before you produce a visual representation.
4. Mode, median, and mean are different, statistically speaking. Remember why we use and report each in certain circumstances.
5. Range, variance, and standard deviation are different statistically speaking. Remember why we use and report each in certain circumstances as well.
6. Distributions can be, and often are, shaped in different ways. This is attributed to things like skewness and kurtosis. Know what these things are and what they mean to your data.

 ## Activities

1. Read the example student paper at the end of the chapter. Using the data from the student paper, try to construct a pie chart, bar chart, and histogram.
2. Using the data from the student paper, prepare tables of data in APA style.
3. Compare the charts from Activity 2 with the tables from Activity 3. Which set of data representation is appropriate for the data? Which set of data representation best informs the reader?

Discussion Questions

1. Why is it important to measure data at various levels of sophistication (nominal, ordinal, interval, and/or ratio)?
2. Read the example student paper at the end of the chapter. What kind of data was used in Michael's piece? Was it appropriate for his study? Why or why not?
3. What data could be collected that keep a research focus in communication studies?
4. What descriptive statistics are appropriate for the data you have collected?

Key Terms

Asymmetrical	Median	Standard deviation
Bar chart	Modality	Statistics
Descriptive statistics	Mode	Symmetrical
Histogram	Negative skew	Variance
Kurtosis	Pie chart	
Leptokurtic	Platykurtic	
Mean	Positive skew	
Measures of central tendency	Range	
	Skewness	

Undergraduate Student Paper

The opening to the paper may create a few confusions for the reader. First, the title mentions cinema, yet the introduction talks about social activities not cinema. Second, the title and introduction refer to gender, yet the research question uses the term female. Female identifies a person's sex, not one's gender. Ask your instructor to discuss the differences between sex and gender. The two terms are routinely conflated in survey research. Finally, a reader may be confused why female is in quotation marks in the research question. Stephen and Dan are not really sure why the student chose to place the word in quotation marks. Remember, your goal is clarity for your readers.

The student clearly identifies the sample population as non-random, but could provide more clarity by discussing if it is going to include all college students, or limiting to a specific group of college students (e.g., traditional, non-traditional, first year, seniors). The student could

Social and gender theory in the cinema

Michael J. Caiola

For my paper, I decided to study the relationship between social activities and gender roles. I found little research on this topic and thought it would be interesting to look more into this topic. This topic is vast so I decided to boil the question down into one concise problem: do *"female" students have a better and more interactive social life?*

Method

I used the survey method to collect data for this project. I decided to collect from just students in college as they seemed the most likely to be in social situations. With the vast amount of people at college and the college lifestyle, social inter-actions are plentiful. This limited my distribution to a non-random sample. I also did not want just my friends and people I associate with to give me my data so I decided to make an online survey.

Using this online survey and Facebook, I was able to limit my pool to just students at my college (on the college Facebook network). Using this network, I began to distribute this online survey to students and get the responses orga-nized in a spreadsheet form. In addition, the online form was anonymous and there was no way to obtain any information on the identity of the participant. This allowed the participant to keep his or her identity safe while answering the questions truthfully. This fact is important, as I did not want male students to embellish how masculine they are or for females to embellish how feminine they are.

The survey itself consisted of nine questions. Four questions were about movie choices, four were about social interactions, and one question asked what gender the participant associates. The gender question allows us to group the data into two sections: male and female. The movie questions rank the preference of the movie genres thriller and chick-flick on a Likert 10-point scale. First, we asked the participant to rank preferences of thrillers, then preference of chick-flicks and then which one was enjoyed the most. In addition, I asked an interval question to see how many movies the participant saw in the last year. I figured a low score on this question might not make them acceptable for this survey. We then asked four ratio questions about the participants' social life. The first asked the participant to estimate how many friends were at the college. The next two asked how many friends the participant normally talks to each week and how many did he or she actually talk to the previous week. Then we asked one more question, how many friends the participant talked to earlier today. This last question allowed us to decide if the data we were getting was accurate. If it was too large of a number, we felt the data were corrupt and omitted it from our research.

Theory

The theory I studied was actually a combination of two theories. The first theory was social theory. Social theory is a large theory that incorporates anything that has to do with or interprets social phenomena. Usually this is shown by networking charts or some sort of graph theory. We took a more liberal approach and combined it with Gender Role Theory. Gender Role Theory focuses on how different sexes represent themselves in the real world. According to the World Health Organization, "'sex' refers to the biological and physiological characteristics that define men and women. [While] 'Gender' refers to the socially constructed roles, behaviors, activities, and attributes that a given society considers appropriate for men and women" (WHO, 2011).

Using this, we decided to select one or two attributes that can distinguish someone as

also identify which online survey website was used. Not all online survey websites are created equal (as you hopefully discovered from the Team Task 2: Build a Survey activity).

Any confusion between wording in the title and the introduction starts to clear up as more details are provided about the organization of the survey. A paper title and introduction should, however, provide a reader with a strong understanding of the content of the paper. How could the student have rewritten the title and introduction to avoid any confusion?

The student repeats the sex/gender conflation. A gender question will not necessarily provide sufficient data for sorting into male and female.

The student does an excellent job of identifying the justification for the different types of questions (Likert, interval, ratio). Concluding with a check for data corruption is a strong choice.

The student provides a strong description here of the distinction between gender and sex. An

masculine or feminine or for lack of better words: male or female. To do this we chose two different movie genres: thrillers and chick-flicks. The thriller genre signifies a more masculine choice as it usually utilizes action, suspense, and male lead getting a pretty girl. The chick-flick genre signifies a more feminine choice as this genre usually involves attractive young men being the object of affection. In addition, chick-flicks usually allow an outlet for emotion. This could be done through crying, sadness, happiness, or even joy. This study does not cover individual actions but instead groups these emotions all under chick-flicks.

For the purposes of this study, we shall define a chick-flick to be any movie that fits the description above. That movie has a main demographic of women, allows for an outlet for emotion, features attractive men, or is a romantic movie. Keep in mind several movies overlap genres and themes but thrillers and chick-flicks seem to be on the opposite sides of the scale. Originally, we were going to use action movies, but there has been a trend in the last decade to make action movies have a steady romantic B-plot. Although these plots are not always well developed, we decided that with thriller we satisfy the same requirements with less hassle.

Data

After sifting through our data and picking out the participants that corrupted data or filled out the form incorrectly, this left us with 19 participants—11 males and nine females. The data can be seen in Table 1. Looking at the data we could see that, on average, men chose thrillers over chick-flicks, while females chose chick-flicks over thrillers. This is good and means we were correct with our first assumptions and that the questions are modeled correctly. To be more formal we ran a one-sample test (Table 2) on the entire sample—nothing jumped up as significant so we continued onto the main data.

---

overview of this distinction in the introduction may have helped clear points of confusion earlier in the paper.

The theory explanation is a little thin and could use more development to better see how the research question is being addressed by the theories.

The study could be strengthened by using established definitions for thriller and chick-flick (supported, of course, with source citations).

Review the section in chapter 15 on mutually exclusive categories. Is the student going to run into data collection issues when the movie genres may overlap?

The Table 1 raw data are normally not expected to be included in the write-up of a study. However, the instructor may have required inclusion as part of the assignment.

However, this does not tell us anything about the connection between male and female genre choices and social interactions. First, we did an ANOVA to see if we have correlation between thriller preferences, chick-flick preferences, and the comparison preference with total amount of friends (see Table 3). As the table shows, there is no significant correlation between them. If Sig. < .05 then we would have a significant correlation. Nevertheless, that does not mean we do not have a result; in fact using our data we can say there is definitely no correlation between gender roles and total amount of friends.

As mentioned above we want to know the role of gender on a greater and more interactive social life. If we take the total number of friends to satisfy how great a social life is, we still need to look into interactive social life. We looked at our data in an ANOVA again but this time over friends talked to during a normal week (see Figure 4). These data seem even more random, getting nowhere near .005. So once again, we can conclude, that gender roles have no correlation with the amount of friends one interacts with on a regular basis.

Although two null hypotheses were not the main intention of this paper, all is not lost. With a sample of only 19 people, we cannot really say if we fully represented the population. With more data, there is a chance that we could have a correlation. In fact, playing with some of our data we see that there seems to be a significant correlation between those who are more feminine and to the amount of people one talks to in a single day (see Figure 5). We believe that this is purely a coincidence although it is statically significant.

Our next step would be to collect more data and from a bigger population. Then we could recalculate these statistical tests and see if we have additional correlations and if our only significant correlation still holds. However, optimally we should shoot for more than 19 participants in a sample, so that we know our results hold some merit. In addition, we could look into the

The student ran a number of different statistical tests and produced some interesting results. However, normally the details about the planned statistical packages are explained and justified in the method section of the paper showing the study has been carefully planned.

emotions a movie evokes and add additional gender role questions.

In conclusion, we tried to find a correlation between gender roles and social interactions. We defined gender roles simply by movie choice and we defined social interaction with amount of people talked to. To improve upon this we could get more data and more detailed questioning. Our results we found this time showed no significant correlation but we believe there may be one with more data points.

Gender	Past Year	Thriller	Chick-Flicks	Be-tween	Esti-mate	Normally in a week	Pre-vious Week	Today
Male	10	8	6	3	40	30	30	10
Male	5	9	6	2	205	60	65	23
Male	5	10	10	3	30	15	10	8
Male	10	1	2	5	40	15	20	9
Male	10	8	4	2	80	40	30	10
Female	10	1	8	10	15	5	4	6
Female	10	7	10	5	50	15	20	8
Female	5	4	8	7	25	12	25	8
Male	5	8	3	2	30	5	7	3
Female	5	1	8	10	26	15	20	8
Female	5	6	5	5	8	7	6	3
Female	5	4	8	8	6	10	16	12
Female	5	6	6	5	0	5	7	3
Male	10	7	5	4	50	25	25	10
Male	10	6	6	5	100	40	50	20
Male	10	7	7	4	57	23	9	14
Female	10	7	4	4	40	20	15	15
Male	10	8	7	3	30	20	30	15
Male	10	8	2	2	15	5	20	1

ONE-SAMPLE TEST

	t	df	Sig. (2-tailed)	Mean Difference	95% Confidence Interval of the Difference	
					Lower	Upper
Thriller	9.835	18	.000	6.10526	4.8011	7.4094
Chick	11.141	18	.000	6.05263	4.9112	7.1940
Compared	8.182	18	.000	4.68421	3.4814	5.8871
Friends	4.214	18	.001	44.57895	22.3557	66.8022
NormalWeek	5.751	18	.000	19.31579	12.2594	26.3722
LastWeek	6.083	18	.000	21.52632	14.0917	28.9609
Today	7.396	18	.000	9.78947	7.0087	12.5703

ANOVA

		Sum of Squares	df	Mean Square	F	Sig.
Thriller	Between Groups	75.956	12	6.330	.680	.732
	Within Groups	55.833	6	9.306		
	Total	131.789	18			
Chick	Between Groups	37.781	12	3.148	.299	.964
	Within Groups	63.167	6	10.528		
	Total	100.947	18			
Compared	Between Groups	76.939	12	6.412	1.094	.483
	Within Groups	35.167	6	5.861		
	Total	112.105	18			

ANOVA

		Sum of Squares	df	Mean Square	F	Sig.
Thriller	Between Groups	35.789	10	3.579	.298	.961
	Within Groups	96.000	8	12.000		
	Total	131.789	18			
Chick	Between Groups	28.697	10	2.870	.318	.953
	Within Groups	72.250	8	9.031		
	Total	100.947	18			
Compared	Between Groups	37.605	10	3.761	.404	.910
	Within Groups	74.500	8	9.313		
	Total	112.105	18			

ANOVA

		Sum of Squares	df	Mean Square	F	Sig.
Thriller	Between Groups	82.956	10	8.296	1.359	.339
	Within Groups	48.833	8	6.104		
	Total	131.789	18			
Chick	Between Groups	85.781	10	8.578	4.525	.021
	Within Groups	15.167	8	1.896		
	Total	100.947	18			
Compared	Between Groups	76.855	10	7.686	1.744	.221
	Within Groups	35.250	8	4.406		
	Total	112.105	18			

Reference

World Health Organization. *WHO 2011*. Retrieved from: www.who.int/gender/whatisgender/en/index.html.

17 INFERENTIAL STATISTICS

Chapter Outline

- Foundations of Inferential Statistics
- Tests of Mean Differences (*t*-tests, ANOVAs, and Chi-square Tests)
- Tests of Relationship and Prediction (Correlation and Simple Regression)
- Key Steps & Questions to Consider
- Activities
- Discussion Questions
- Key Terms
- Undergraduate Inferential Regression Paper

What Will I Learn About Inferential Statistics in This Chapter?

In 2012, a man named Nate Silver shot to stardom with his website, "fivethirtyeight.com." What Nate Silver did was he combined numerous state and national polls into a regression equation to generate his own predictions about who would win various state and national elections. His predictions were often very different from those of the Associated Press, Gallup, and the Quinnipiac Poll. However, in the end, his predictions about who would win elections in state elections and particularly the presidential election were more accurate than all other polling agencies or groups. On election night he was interviewed by numerous news agencies and he said Obama would win more than 300 electoral votes. His prediction was right. The picture above shows that result.

When Silver was asked how he made his predictions, he explained that it was a complex regression equation, a type of inferential statistics. Silver was predicting with all of the evidence he had at his disposal that various candidates, such as Obama, would win or lose elections. Silver entered the political polling business, which is big money during elections, as news agencies and politicians clamor daily to know the status of various candidates. We used Nate Silver's work with fivethirtyeight.com as the opening example for a chapter on inferential statistics to demonstrate the importance of statistics. On election night in 2012, Silver's name was mentioned on every major news network, as his method for polling appeared to be the most accurate and scientific. If you are interested in communication research and its many facets, you can definitely use inferential statistics. If you are interested in studying politics from a communication perspective, you could study: the effects of advertising on perception of a candidate, differences between men and women in voting behavior, the relationship between religious identification and political affiliation, and you could analyze how media outlets cover political stories. In Chapter 17 we explore such questions and other aspects of inferential statistics. In Chapter 16 we defined statistics as a way of organizing, describing, and making inferences from data. **Inferential statistics** allow us to make conclusions (inferences) from a sample to a population. In this chapter we talk about how to conduct inferential statistics.

What is Inferential Statistics?

In Chapter 7 we talked about the Central Limit Theorem, and how when you collect a sample from a population you can make inferences or estimations about a population from your sample. Don't worry, we will talk more about this process throughout this chapter. It is this process of inference that is the key to inferential statistics. Through the process of inferential statistics, you are able to statistically test what you think you know about the population based on your sample. There are two main families of inferential statistics that you can use: tests of difference or tests of relationship/prediction. We will describe each of these in this chapter and explain how you can conduct various tests for each. The second section of the chapter is a description of one group of inferential statistics, tests of difference.

Tests of Difference

If you are interested in comparing differences between men and women on the amount of self-disclosure in an intimate relationship using a Likert scale, interval data, this would be a test of difference (a *t*-test). If you want to compare differences between freshmen, sophomores, juniors, and seniors at your school on communication apprehension (CA) interval data, this would be a test of difference (a one-way ANOVA). If you are interested in analyzing how FOX, CNN, and MSNBC covered the final presidential debate of 2012, this would be a test of difference (a chi-square test). Numerous differences exist between the statistics you would use to explore each of these proposed studies. Let's discuss the properties of each, how to do them, and how they differ.

T-test

A *t–test* is a multipurpose test that is used when you are comparing two group means. With this test your dependent variable must be continuous (interval- or ratio-level data) and the independent variable, which is called the grouping variable, is a nominal or ordinal variable. *T*-tests can be used in regression analyses but they are most often used and associated with testing differences between two group means. For example, you could use a *t*-test to explore: whether males or females have higher GPAs on your campus, whether Americans or Japanese express more fear of the film *The Exorcist* (we could measure fear by measuring heart rates during the film), whether winter temperatures are colder on average in January in Finland or Canada, and whether your understanding of research methods improved from the start of this class to the end of this class. *T*-tests can do all of this. There are two kinds of *t*-tests: independent samples *t*-test and dependent samples *t*-test. An **independent samples *t*-test** is used when you are comparing the means of two groups that are not matched or the same, like male and female GPA. A **dependent samples** or **paired samples t-test** is used when you are comparing the means of two groups that are matched in some way, such as when someone takes a test at the start of the semester and then the same test at the end of the semester, and you compare the results. There are some basic principles of the *t*-test that you should know.

Principles of a T-test

1. The dependent variable must be an interval- or ratio-level variable.
2. The independent variable must be a nominal- or ordinal-level variable.
3. The dependent variable should be normally distributed, meaning there should not be a high skewness or kurtosis.
4. The larger the sample, the less likely the difference between the two means analyzed is created by sampling error. We discussed sampling error quite a bit in Chapter 9.
5. The further apart the means, the less likely the difference was created by sampling error.
6. The more homogeneous the sample, the less likely the difference between the two means was created by sampling error.
7. *T*-tests evaluate the extent to which data distributions do not overlap. Overlap is smaller to the extent that the difference between means of two distributions is large and/or the standard deviations are small.

Dependent Samples T-test

The purpose of a dependent samples *t*-test is to compare the mean score at one point to the mean score at a second point. For example, Stephen used to give his students in Statistics 101 the final exam on the first day of class and then the same exam during the final exam period. He would then compare their scores from the first day to the last day of class to see how each student's scores differed. This pretest and posttest format is the essence of a dependent samples *t*-test. He was able to compare their individual results and the class average from the first test to the second test. His hope of course is that the class improved in their knowledge of statistics.

Conducting a dependent samples *t*-test is relatively easy in SPSS, one of the most used statistical software programs. Stephen collected data among Muslim immigrants in France in 2006 and again in 2012 regarding their tendency to approach and avoid arguments. The same individuals filled out Infante and Rancer's (1982) 20-item Argumentativeness Scale (a Likert scale). Stephen is interested in whether there has been a change in argumentativeness levels among immigrants as they have adapted to life in France. This calls for a dependent samples *t*-test, as the grouping variable is the same person with two different means, the test in 2006, and the test in 2012. To conduct this test, there are a few simple steps in SPSS.

Steps to Conducting a Dependent Samples T-test in SPSS

1. Go to "Analyze" and choose "Compare Means."
2. Within "Choose Means" select "Paired-Samples t-test."
3. Once you click on "Paired-Samples t-test" a new box will open. You will see the following buttons: "Options," "Bootstrap," "Reset," "Paste," "Cancel," and "OK."
4. At this point in your studies you do not need to be concerned with "Options" and "Bootstrap." "Reset" will reset everything you have done. "Paste" will allow you to paste things in. "Cancel" closes the box and "OK" runs the *t*-test.
5. Scroll down your list of variables to select the pair of variables you want.
6. You need to choose the first one and then hold down the *Ctrl* key on your keyboard and then select the second variable you want.
7. Then click on the arrow to transfer this pair over for analysis. You can conduct more than one analysis at a time; just repeat this process.

Then press the "OK" button and your analysis will be conducted.

In Stephen's data on Muslim immigrants he selected his two variables and pressed "OK." The following three outputs (Figures 17.1–17.3) show the

		Mean	n	Std. Deviation	Std. Error Mean
Pair 1	ApproachARG	29.4594	320	6.91041	.38630
	approach1	28.5961	320	7.17493	.40109

Figure 17.1 Output—Paired Samples Statistics

		n	Correlation	Sig.
Pair 1	Approach ARG & approach1	320	.879	.000

Figure 17.2 Output—Paired Samples Correlations

	Paired Differences							
			Std.	95% Confidence Interval of the Difference				Sig.
	Mean	Std. Deviation	Error Mean	Lower	Upper	t	df	(2-tailed)
Pair 1 Approach ARG– approach1	.86328	3.47481	.19425	.48111	1.24545	4.444	319	.000

Figure 17.3 Output—Paired Samples Test

results of the dependent samples t-tests for a Muslim immigrant's tendency to approach argumentativeness:

The first output (Figure 17.1) shows the means, standard deviations, and standard error of the mean of a Muslim's tendency to approach argumentativeness in 2006 (approachARG) and in 2012 (approach1). The second output (Figure 17.2) shows the correlation between the pre- and the posttest. In this case, the tendency to approach argumentativeness is highly correlated in 2006 and 2012 ($r = .879$, $p < .0001$). We will talk more about correlations in a few short pages. The third output (Figure 17.3) is the most important one as it shows if there is a significant difference between the two means. In this case, there is a significant difference in tendency to approach argumentativeness in 2006 and 2012. To report the results of this test, you should write it up like this:

> On average, Muslim immigrants' tendency to approach arguments after moving to France in 2006 ($M = 29.459$; $SD = 6.91$) significantly decreased by 2012 ($M = 28.596$; $SD = 7.174$), $t(319) = 4.444$, $p < .0001$, $r = .879$.

Let's break down what this statement is saying. First, "On average, Muslim immigrants' tendency to approach arguments after moving to France in 2006

(M = 29.459; SD = 6.91) significantly decreased by 2012 (M = 28.596; SD = 7.174)," is showing the reader the mean differences between 2006 and 2012. Second, "t (319) = 4.444, p < .0001, r = .879" represents the following: "t = 4.444" is your t value. Your t value is an arbitrary number, as it merely tells us the chance that two means are different from one another. We need more information to determine whether or not this t value is significant or not. That information follows below. "(319)" is the degrees of freedom in this study. **Degrees of freedom** or df is the number of independent values in any given calculation minus the number of estimated parameters.[1] What this basically means is the df is the number of values that can vary in a calculation. The df formula and the amount it varies is best represented by $n - 1$. In this case the df equals 320 (the sample size) minus 1 or 319. The alpha level significance for this t-test is "p < .0001". The p level tells you if the test is significant or not (remember, to be significant the p must be less than .05) and if you should reject the null or not. In this case there *is* a significant difference, so the two means are significantly different from one another and we should reject the null. Finally, "r = .879" is the correlation between the value at 2006 and 2012. We will talk more about this shortly.

Independent Samples *T*-test

Independent samples t-tests are used when you are comparing the means of two groups that are not matched/the same. For example, you could compare the amount of self-disclosure between men and women in an intimate relationship. Like a dependent samples t-test, conducting an independent samples t-test is relatively easy in SPSS. Stephen recently collected data among Finns about various communication behaviors, such as self-disclosure. These individuals completed the Revised Self-Disclosure Scale (Wheeless, 1978). His interest was in whether there were differences between men and women on the frequency of self-disclosure. This calls for an independent samples t-test, as the grouping variable is two different groups, men and women, with mean scores on frequency of self-disclosure. To conduct this test, there are a few simple steps in SPSS.

Steps to Conducting an Independent Samples T-test in SPSS

1. Go to "Analyze" and choose "Compare Means."
2. Within "Choose Means" select "Independent Samples t-test."
3. Once you click on "Independent-Samples t-test" a new box will open. You will see the following buttons: "Options," "Bootstrap," "Reset," "Paste," "Cancel," and "OK."
4. Just like with the dependent samples t-test, choose your dependent variable. In this case you only choose one and not two.

5. Highlight it and click the arrow to move it over to the "Test Variable(s)" box. In Stephen's analysis of self-disclosure frequency this variable is named "DisAmount." You then need to choose your grouping variable; this is your independent variable. Stephen wanted to compare males and females, "gender."
6. You need to tell the computer which gender groups to analyze (Define groups). Stephen coded males as 0 and females as 1 in his SPSS file.
7. As with the dependent samples *t*-test you can run one or multiple tests at once.
8. Press the "OK" button and your analysis will be conducted.

The following two outputs (Figures 17.4 and 17.5) show the results of the independent samples *t*-tests for male and female frequency to self-disclose in intimate relationships:

	Gender	n	Mean	Std. Deviation	Std. Error Mean
DisAmount	Male	993	3.0135	.71534	.02270
	Female	910	3.3105	.66973	.02220

Figure 17.4 Output—Group Statistics

		Levene's Test for Equality of Variances				
		F	Sig.	t	df	Sig. (2-tailed)
DisAmount	Equal variances assumed	2.996	.084	−9.329	1901	.000
	Equal variances not assumed			−9.355	1900.127	.000

Figure 17.5 Output—Abbreviated Version of the Independent Samples *T*-test from SPSS

Figure 17.4 shows a few things. It shows how many males and females are in the sample, the mean, standard deviation, and standard error of disclosure frequency for each sex. Figure 17.5 is an abbreviated version of the independent samples *t*-test from SPSS. The first thing you may notice in this output is that there are two *t* values and something called "Levene's Test for Equality." Levene's test is exploring whether the variances between the two groups are equal. If Levene's test is significant we can be assured that variances are significantly different and the assumption of homogeneity of variances has been violated. In this case you will report the values on the bottom, "Equal variances not assumed." In the case of this particular *t*-test, we can assume equal variances, so we will report the values on the top. This is how we can report these results:

> Females ($M = 3.31$; $SD = .669$) significantly self-disclose more than males ($M = 3.013$; $SD = .715$), $t(1901) = -9.329$, $p < .0001$.

T-tests are widely used in communication research. Ivanov, Parker, and Pfau (2012) used dependent samples *t*-tests to explore the effects of attitudinal attacks on attitude change. In their study, they found that some inoculation messages could generate resistance to persuasive messages, while other messages would not. Yun, Costantini, and Billingsley (2012) used independent samples *t*-tests to test the effects of taking a public speaking course on writing skills. They found that students who take a public speaking course have better writing structure and syntax.

> In the 2012 election commentators talked a lot about how women were more likely to have a favorable opinion of Obama, while men were more likely to have a favorable opinion of Mitt Romney. The commentators were more than likely getting this information from a *t*-test or a more advanced statistical test that was operating like a *t*-test. In essence what they were doing was asking likely voters how they felt about the candidates and their likelihood of voting for each candidate. This kind of information is important for candidates and their teams as it can help them know how to tailor their messages and campaigns.

One-Way Analysis of Variance (ANOVA)

A **one-way analysis of variance (ANOVA)** has many characteristics similar to a *t*-test. This test is a way to compare more than two groups (such as ethnicity, religious identification, level in school, etc. . . .) on an interval- or ratio-level variable. For example, you could use an ANOVA to examine: 1) how individuals based on their academic year at your school (e.g., freshman, sophomore, junior, and senior) differ on communication apprehension, 2) how years working for a company potentially affect an individual's willingness to dissent about organizational decisions, and 3) how people from different nations (more than two) differ on their tendency to approach arguments. Each of these questions can easily be addressed by ANOVA. There are some basic principles of an ANOVA that are similar to the *t*-test. In the case of an ANOVA, the result is the *F*-test.

Principles of a One-Way ANOVA

1. The dependent variable must be an interval- or ratio-level variable.
2. The independent variable must be a nominal- or ordinal-level variable.
3. The dependent variable should be normally distributed; there should not be high levels of skewness or kurtosis.
4. The larger the sample, the less likely the difference between the means is created by sampling error.
5. The further apart the means, the less likely the difference was created by sampling error.
6. The more homogeneous the sample, the less likely the difference between the means was created by sampling error.
7. ANOVAs evaluate the extent to which multiple distributions do not overlap. Overlap is smaller to the extent that the difference between means of multiple distributions are large and/or the *SD*s are small.

While calculating the *F* in an ANOVA is a complex process, we thankfully have programs like SPSS to help. Conducting an ANOVA is an easy process. For this example, we are going to use data Stephen collected on communication apprehension (CA) in: the United States, India, the United Kingdom, Germany, Spain, and France. There are a few simple steps in SPSS.

Steps to Conducting a One-Way ANOVA in SPSS

1. Go to "Analyze" and choose "Compare Means."
2. Within "Choose Means" select "One-Way ANOVA."
3. Once you click on "One-Way ANOVA" a new box will open. You will see the following buttons: "Contrasts," "Post Hoc," "Options," "Bootstrap," "OK," "Paste," "Reset," "Cancel," and "Help."
4. Choose your dependent variable(s), the one(s) you want to analyze. Highlight it and click the arrow to move it over to the "Dependent List" box. You can analyze multiple variables if you want, but let's focus on one for now. In Stephen's analysis of CA, he named his CA variable totalCA. So, you click on totalCA and then click the arrow to move it over to the "Dependent List."
5. As we are interested in how people from different nations differ in totalCA, our factor (independent variable) is nation. So, click on nation and move it to "Factor."

6. Click on "Options" and then click the "Descriptive" and the "Means plot" boxes. The Descriptive box will provide you with descriptive statistics, and means plot will visually show you your data. Then press "Continue."
7. Click "Post Hoc," choose "Tukey," "Scheffé," and "Games-Howell," click "Continue," and then "OK." The ANOVA will then run. See Figures 17.6–17.9 below.

| | | | | | 95% Confidence Interval for Mean | | | |
| | | | | | | | | |
totalCA	N	Mean	Std. Deviation	Std. Error	Lower Bound	Upper Bound	Mini- mum	Maxi- mum
United States	505	70.4040	3.18404	.14169	70.1256	70.6823	58.00	83.00
India	410	71.5098	4.49843	.22216	71.0730	71.9465	60.00	85.00
United Kingdom	336	69.0952	3.32918	.18162	68.7380	69.4525	60.00	80.00
Germany	271	67.8561	8.91802	.54173	66.7895	68.9226	56.00	88.00
Spain	217	70.3410	3.09178	.20988	69.9273	70.7547	62.00	81.00
France	179	69.7598	6.96567	.52064	68.7324	70.7872	56.00	84.00
Total	1918	69.9838	5.20054	.11875	69.7509	70.2167	56.00	88.00

Figure 17.6 Output—Descriptives

totalCA	Sum of Squares	df	Mean Square	F	Sig.
Between Groups	2572.671	5	514.534	19.966	.000
Within Groups	49273.828	1912	25.771		
Total	51846.499	1917			

Figure 17.7 Output—ANOVA

In the first output above (Figure 17.6), you have the means, standard deviations, errors, and sample sizes for each nation. Figure 17.7 is the ANOVA output. In this output you have the F value (19.966), numerator df (5), denominator df (1912), SSb (514.534), SSW (25.771), and significance level p (.0001).

Figure 17.8 is a line plot of the data. While these outputs tell us a lot, what is missing is a direct comparison between each nation. Are Germans significantly less apprehensive than others? The data would lead us to think that, but we can't be sure. This is where the *post-hoc* comparisons come in.

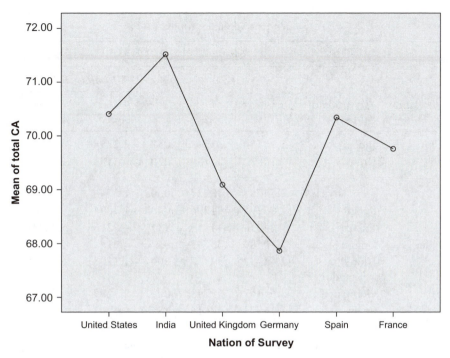

Figure 17.8 Line Plot of Output Data

Post-hoc comparisons are follow-up tests that determine whether all groups or certain pairs of group means are significantly different from one another. There are numerous *post-hocs* you can choose. The most commonly used ones are Tukey's and the Scheffé test. **Tukey's** should be used when you have an equal number of participants or items in your independent categories or groups. The **Scheffé test** can be used when you have an unequal number of participants or items in your independent categories or groups. This test is also a more conservative test, which means the criteria for statistical significance is stricter than Tukey's. Both the Tukey's and the Scheffé test assume equal variances. If equal variances are not assumed, a good test to run is the Games-Howell test. This *post-hoc* operates much like the other *post-hocs*, but it does not assume equal variances. In the case of this particular ANOVA, if you look at Figure 17.6, you will see each nation has a different number of participants. Also, equal variances in this case are assumed. So Scheffé's test is appropriate.

If you look to Figure 17.9 ("Multiple Comparisons") it shows direct mean comparisons between each nation on CA. You can see that the United States scored 1.308* more than the United Kingdom on CA. The (*) means this is a statistically significant difference ($p < .05$) between the two nations. These comparisons are helpful in better understanding specific differences between groups. To write up these ANOVA results, we could do it like this:

A one-way ANOVA was conducted using nation as the independent variable and CA as the dependent variable. A significant difference was found: $F(5, 1912) = 19.966$, $p < .0001$, $\eta^2 = .05$. A Scheffé *post-hoc*

		Dependent Variable: totalCA				
		Scheffe				
					95% Confidence Interval	
(I) Nation of Survey	(J) Nation of Survey	Mean Difference (I–J)	Std. Error	Sig.	Lower Bound	Upper Bound
United States	India	−1.10580	.33747	.057	−2.2298	.0182
	United Kingdom	1.30872*	.35739	.020	.1183	2.4991
	Germany	2.54787*	.38227	.000	1.2746	3.8211
	Spain	.06295	.41206	1.000	−1.3095	1.4354
	France	.64418	.44159	.831	−.8266	2.1150
India	United States	1.10580	.33747	.057	−.0182	2.2298
	United Kingdom	2.41452*	.37357	.000	1.1703	3.6588
	Germany	3.65367*	.39743	.000	2.3299	4.9774
	Spain	1.16874	.42616	.185	−.2507	2.5882
	France	1.74998*	.45478	.011	.2352	3.2647
United Kingdom	United States	−1.30872*	.35739	.020	−2.4991	−.1183
	India	−2.41452*	.37357	.000	−3.6588	−1.1703
	Germany	1.23915	.41448	.112	−.1414	2.6197
	Spain	−1.24578	.44211	.160	−2.7183	.2268
	France	−.66454	.46976	.849	−2.2292	.9001
Germany	United States	−2.54787*	.38227	.000	−3.8211	−1.2746
	India	−3.65367*	.39743	.000	−4.9774	−2.3299
	United Kingdom	−1.23915	.41448	.112	−2.6197	.1414
	Spain	−2.48493*	.46244	.000	−4.0252	−.9446
	France	−1.90369*	.48894	.010	−3.5322	−.2751
Spain	United States	−.06295	.41206	1.000	−1.4354	1.3095
	India	−1.16874	.42616	.185	−2.5882	.2507
	United Kingdom	1.24578	.44211	.160	−.2268	2.7183
	Germany	2.48493*	.46244	.000	.9446	4.0252
	France	.58124	.51257	.936	−1.1260	2.2885
France	United States	−.64418	.44159	.831	−2.1150	.8266
	India	−1.74998*	.45478	.011	−3.2647	−.2352
	United Kingdom	.66454	.46976	.849	−.9001	2.2292
	Germany	1.90369*	.48894	.010	.2751	3.5322
	Spain	−.58124	.51257	.936	−2.2885	1.1260

*. The mean difference is significant at the 0.05 level.

Figure 17.9 Output—Multiple Comparisons

comparison was conducted, which indicated numerous differences between the nations in CA levels (Here you could create a table of your own like the multiple comparison output in SPSS).

There are a few important points to this write-up. First, "$F(5, 1912)$" is showing the reader the different degrees of freedom in the study, 5 is the numerator df and 1912 is the denominator df. Further, "19.966" is the F value for the ANOVA, which we know is significant because of the p value, "$p < .0001$." The final element is "$\eta^2 = .05$." This is partial eta squared for the ANOVA. Partial eta squared represents the effect size for the difference in the ANOVA test. A partial eta squared can range from 0 to 1. A small partial eta squared means there is no difference, while a large one means there is difference between the groups. A small effect size ranges from .01 to .05, a medium effect size ranges from .06 to .13, while a large effect size ranges at .14 and above. All in all, the ANOVA is a helpful method to use to explore differences between more than two groups on a continuous variable.

In the 2012 election, commentators also talked a lot about racial divides in the election. Both candidates were interested in who particular ethnic or racial groups would vote for in the election. The polls leading up to the Presidential election showed Caucasians (Whites) slightly favored Romney, while all other groups favored Obama by significant margins. After the election, these predictions held. Romney won roughly 59 percent of the Caucasian vote. Obama won 93 percent of the African American, 71 percent of the Hispanic, 73 percent of the Asian, and 58 percent of the Other vote. Knowing such differences can help both parties target their messages for the next elections.

Chi-square

The third test of difference is not like the ANOVA or t-tests. ANOVAs and t-tests assume the population you are generalizing to and the samples you are working with are normally distributed. These types of tests (and correlation and regression) are called **parametric** tests. A **non-parametric** test is used when: you are not able to make assumptions about how data in the population are distributed, your sample may not represent the population, and the data you are working with are categorical (ordinal or nominal). A **chi-square** is a non-parametric test in which you compare the observed frequencies of a variable against the expected frequencies to see if there is a statistical difference between the two. A basic principle underlying the chi-square is that a sample will break down into equal groups. For example, if you have 250 dogs and divide them into five breeds statistically you should expect to have 50 of each breed. However, it rarely happens that a sample will break down into equal groups as expected. What we observe can be rather different than what is statistically expected. There are some required elements of a chi-square you must have.

Principles of a Chi-square

1. All of the variables under analysis must be nominal variables.
2. Larger samples are more representative of the population.

Let's return to the 2012 election. In the election, pollsters would regularly ask men and women (nominal variable) whom they were going to vote for (a nominal variable). This is a classic question that could be analyzed using a chi-square. If a pollster sampled 100 people and asked them if they were going to vote for Romney or Obama, statistically each candidate should get 50 votes. This does not happen very often though. This is where chi-square can help us. To conduct this particular chi-square using SPSS is easy.

Steps to Conducting a Chi-square in SPSS

1. Go to "Analyze," choose "Descriptive Statistics," and then choose "Crosstabs."
2. Once there you will find a box with: "Exact," "Statistics," "Cells," "Format," "Bootstrap," "Row(s)," "Column(s)," "Layer 1 of 1," "OK," "Paste," "Reset," "Cancel," and "Help."
3. If we are interested in how the sexes differ in their preference for a political candidate, our two variables are sex and presidential preference. In a simple chi-square we are comparing how groups (rows) compare on a particular variable (column). In this case, you will click on sex and move it over to row(s) and move prespreference (what we named presidential preference) over to column(s).
4. You need to tell SPSS to run a chi-square. Click on "Statistics" and click the box for "Chi-square" and then click "Continue."
5. Click "Cells" and make sure "Observed" and "Expected" are clicked, and press "Continue." Then press "OK."
6. You should get something like this, the outputs in Figures 17.10–17.12:

	Cases					
	Valid		Missing		Total	
	n	Percent	n	Percent	n	Percent
sex * prespreference	100	100.0%	0	0.0%	100	100.0%

Figure 17.10 Case Processing Summary

			Prespreference		
			Obama	Romney	Total
Sex	Male	Count	20	30	50
		Expected Count	26.5	23.5	50.0
	Female	Count	33	17	50
		Expected Count	26.5	23.5	50.0
Total		Count	53	47	100
		Expected Count	53.0	47.0	100.0

Figure 17.11 Output—Sex Prespreference Crosstabulation

	Value	df	Asymp. Sig. (2-sided)	Exact Sig. (2-sided)	Exact Sig. (1-sided)
Pearson Chi-Square	6.784[a]	1	.009		
Continuity Correction[b]	5.781	1	.016		
Likelihood Ratio	6.865	1	.009		
Fisher's Exact Test				.016	.008
Linear-by-Linear Association	6.717	1	.010		
N of Valid Cases	100				

a. 0 cells (0,0%) have expected count less than 5. The minimum expected count is 23,50.
b. Computed only for a 2 × 2 table

Figure 17.12 Output—Chi-square Tests

We can see many things when we look at these outputs. First, Figure 17.10 shows us that all 100 cases (people) answered the question. Figure 17.11 shows how many of each sex preferred each candidate. You can see more men preferred Romney, while more women preferred Obama. The Count is what is observed in the data, while the Expected Count is what is statistically expected for each sex and their presidential preference, when the null hypothesis is true. Figure 17.12 is the result of the chi-square test. The Chi-square result is: $\chi^2 = 6.784$, $p = .009$, which is indeed very significant. This means there is a significant difference between what was expected and observed. You would write up the results of this test as such:

> There was a significant association between a voter's sex and their preference for president, χ^2 (1) $= 6.784$, $p = .009$. Based on these results, men more prefer Mitt Romney, while women more prefer Barack Obama.

Chi-squares are regularly used in communication research and in business, advertising and marketing especially. Steimel (2012) used chi-square to explore memorable messages that volunteers receive from the organizations they serve and how these messages relate to the volunteer experience. In advertising and marketing, one way in which chi-square is prominent is in taste-testing. We have all heard that two out of three people prefer one beverage over another. This is a simple chi-square analysis; think about it. One of the activities at the end of this chapter is for you to conduct a taste test using chi-square.

> In the 2012 election Americans often heard news reports about how men were more likely to vote for Romney over Obama. A simple chi-square analysis could produce such a result.

Tests of Relationship and Prediction

While statistics are helpful at comparing data, there are tests that can also help us understand relationships between variables and predict how variables will affect other variables.

Correlation

When Stephen was nine years old he wanted to play tennis with his friends. His mom got him a tennis racquet and he went out to play. He was horrible at it, as he had never played before. He came home and put the racquet away. His mom said the more you practice at it the better you will be. He kept practicing and today he is not a bad player; Roger Federer has nothing to worry about though. Stephen's tennis ability and the amount he practices can be related in three ways: 1) positively related, which means the more he practiced the better he got; 2) negatively related, which means the more he practiced the worse he got; or, 3) not related at all, meaning that as he practiced his playing abilities would remain the same. These three relationships are the fundamental principles of a correlation. A **correlation,** aside from being a statistical term, is a statistical measure of the degree to which two or more variables (interval or ratio) in a sample are related to one another. The statistical term for correlation is Pearson product-moment correlation coefficient, which is represented by (r). Correlations range from −1.00 to +1.00. A 0.00 correlation represents no relationship between the variables. A correlation (r) of .00 to .25 is a weak correlation, .26 to .50 is a moderate correlation, while .51 and above is a strong correlation. Correlation of −.55 and +.55 have the same magnitude, just different directions, as one is positive, and the other is negative. We will talk in a moment about direction of correlations.

There are four types of correlations (relationships) you can have: positive, negative, curvilinear, and no relationship. In the following paragraphs we will provide examples of each, focusing on just two variables for each relationship. Please keep in mind that with correlations you can correlate multiple variables with one another at a time; however, for simplicity we are focusing on just two variables at a time.

A positive correlation is when both variables move in the same direction. As one variable increases in value, the other increases (+/+), and as one variable decreases in value, the other decreases in value (–/–). Here is an example of a positive correlation ($r = .107$, $p < .001$).

Figure 17.13 shows that the more someone is willing to express articulated dissent in an organization, the more they are also willing to express displaced dissent regarding an organization (Kassing, 1998).

In Figure 17.14, you can see a negative correlation. A negative relationship means as one variable increases in value, the other decreases (+/–), and as one variable decreases in value, the other increases in value (–/+). In this correlation, the more someone is willing to approach an argument, the less willing they are to avoid an argument ($r = -.35$, $p < .001$).

A curvilinear relationship is positive or negative when it begins, but then switches directions. Take for example the example of severity of an illness and medication dosage. The more medication you take, generally the better you will feel (+/+). However, eventually you can take too much medication and your body may start to reject the medication and you could get sick from the medication (+/–). Figure 17.15 is an example of this kind of relationship.

The final kind of relationship is one where there is no relationship. Sometimes variables simply are not related to each other. Argumentativeness, for example, is more than likely not related to how much a person likes country music. This relationship should more than likely be non-existent, so we are not even going to try to create a figure for it.

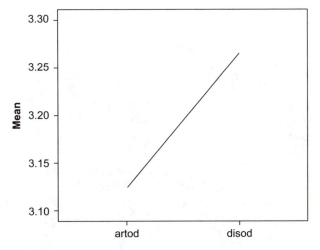

Figure 17.13 Positive Correlation

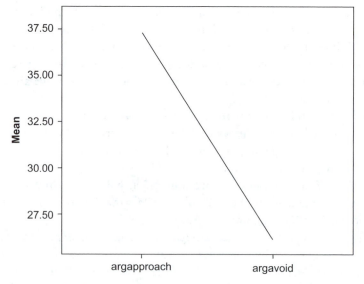

Figure 17.14 Negative Correlation

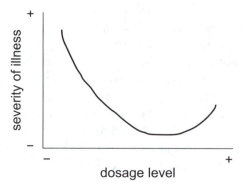

Figure 17.15 Curvilinear Relationship

Principles of Correlations

1. The variables you are correlating must be interval- or ratio-level variables.
2. They work for a large sample, as larger samples are more representative of the population.
3. Try to have fairly similar sample sizes for each of your variables. If one variable has 200 responses and the other has 50, this can lead to sampling error issues.
4. A correlation does not mean one variable causes another variable to change. Correlations do not equal causality! We will talk more about cause and effect in the experiments chapter.

Correlations can be one- or two-tailed. If you have a directional hypothesis or research question, you have an idea of the relationship between the variables, so you should explore that particular relationship (one-tailed). If your hypothesis or research question is non-directional, you have less certainty of the relationship, thus a two-tailed correlation is used to explore the relationship.

Conducting the correlation is actually one of the easiest tests in SPSS, compared to the other statistical tests. We are going to look at some data on organizational dissent, an individual's willingness to voice opposition or contrary opinions in an organization (Kassing, 1998). Stephen collected data on dissent in the United States among 592 organizational members in the Northeast and Midwest United States. There are three kinds of organizational dissent, two of which that happen in the organization: articulated and latent dissent. Articulated dissent is when you dissent to those individuals above you in the hierarchy, like a boss. Latent dissent is when you voice dissent to your peers. To see how these two kinds of dissent are correlated is a simple process.

Steps to Conducting a Correlation in SPSS

1. Go to "Analyze" and choose "Correlate," and then choose "Bivariate."
2. You will see the following buttons: "Options," "Bootstrap," "Pearson," "Kendall's tau-b," "Spearman," "Two-tailed," "One-tailed," "Flag significant correlations," "OK," "Paste," "Reset," "Cancel," and "Help." For now you do not need to worry about many of these options.[2]
3. To run the correlation, highlight each variable you want and move them over to "Variables" list (you can double click on them if you want). In this case we want: artod and latod.
4. Click on "Options" and choose "Means and standard deviations," and then click "OK."
5. Click "OK" on the main "Correlation" screen and you will get your outputs (Figures 17.16 and 17.17):

	Mean	Std. Deviation	n
artod	3.1682	.62904	584
latod	2.9210	.73044	582

Figure 17.16 Output—Descriptive Statistics

		artod	*latod*
artod	Pearson Correlation	1	.117*
	Sig. (one-tailed)		.002
	n	584	582
latod	Pearson Correlation	.117*	1
	Sig. (two-tailed)	.002	
	n	582	582

*Correlation is significant at the 0.01 level (one-tailed).

Figure 17.17 Output—Correlations

Figure 17.16 shows you the means, standard deviations, and number of individuals who completed each of your variables. You can see the means and standard deviations for articulated dissent (artod) ($M = 3.168$; $SD = .629$) and for latent dissent (latod) ($M = 2.921$; $SD = .730$). Figure 17.17 is the correlation output. This output shows that articulated and latent dissent are positively correlated ($r = .117$). Next to the correlation you will notice *. If you look at the bottom of the output you will see a note that says "*. Correlation is significant at the 0.01 level (one-tailed)." We ran a one-tailed because we had an idea of the direction of the correlation, and thus we should run a one-tailed correlation. When we do not know the direction of the correlation, we should run a two-tailed correlation. We can therefore interpret this correlation as such:

> There was a significant positive correlation between articulated and latent dissent ($r = .117$, $p < .001$).

Bakker and de Vresse (2011) in an analysis of 16- to 24-year-olds found a variety of Internet uses are positively related to numerous kinds of political participation. For example, online social networks and online forum use are positively related to political participation. In the 2012 presidential election both candidates extensively used social networks and social media to reach out to potential voters. In 2008, the Obama campaign was much more successful in the use of online media than the McCain camp, which could partially explain the Obama victory.

Regression

The second relational statistic is one that takes correlation, or the study of relationships, a step further and tests how a variable(s) predicts another variable. **Regression** is predicting a dependent variable from one or multiple independent variables. Regression analysis is all around us. If any of you have tried to buy a car and gone into negotiations, you have probably heard about your credit score. This term that puts fear into the hearts of some Americans is basically a regressions score. What it tells creditors is how likely you are to pay back debt. The score is based on various indicators, such as your previous debt, payment history, number of bills/debts, demographics, etc. . . . Creditors, like a car dealer or mortgage company, will look at this score to make a risk analysis about you and the goods they are trying to get you to buy.

If you are doing a regression, you are basically trying to plot out a line of best fit, or to fit a model that best predicts the dependent variable with your independent variable(s). The equation for this line of best fit (the regression equation) is: $Y = a + bX + \varepsilon$. Y is the dependent variable, what you are trying to predict. Alpha or a is the value of Y when the value of X equals 0. Beta or b is the slope of the regression line, which is how much Y changes for each unit change in X. X is the value of the independent variable, what is predicting Y. ε is the amount of error; for simplicity we assume ε is 0 in regression analyses.

Let's take an example of how to predict argumentativeness related to levels of religiousness. Y equals the level of argumentativeness. The alpha (a) equals an individual's average level of argumentativeness, let's say 25. The beta (b) is the impact on Y for each increase in an individual's level of religiousness; let's say +5 on Infante and Rancer's (1982) argumentativeness scale. X is an individual's level of religiousness. For every three levels of religiousness ($X = 3$), $Y = 25 + (5)(3) = 25 + 15 =$ an argumentativeness level of 40. Other variables may also predict argumentativeness (ε), but this regression only predicts the effect of religiousness on argumentativeness.

As with a correlation, it is helpful with regression to visually represent data. You can do this with a scatterplot. Figure 17.18 shows examples of

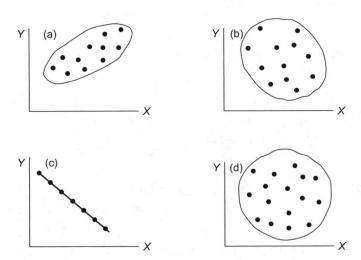

Figure 17.18 Examples of Scatterplots

scatterplots, which show one variable (X) predicting Y. In (a) you can see a positive correlation, which can also represent X having a strong positive effect on Y. In (b) you can see a slightly negative correlation, meaning X has a slight negative effect on Y. In (c), there is a perfect negative correlation, so X predicts Y perfectly. In (d) there is no real relationship between X and Y, which means X does not predict Y.

Principles of Simple Linear Regression

1. The dependent variable (what you are predicting) needs to be an interval or ratio variable.
2. The independent variables will normally be interval or ratio variables. In more advanced kinds of regression you can have independent variables that are nominal or ordinal. We will not spend time on this right now as using these kinds of variables can get rather complicated.
3. The sample you collect to conduct a regression should be as representative as possible of the population.
4. The variables should be normally distributed; there should not be high levels of skew or kurtosis.
5. Strive for as large a sample as possible to best represent the population.

Running a regression analysis, like many statistical tests, is not a complex procedure if you know your dependent and independent variable.

Steps to Conducting a Simple Linear Regression in SPSS

1. Go to "Analyze," then choose "Regression," then choose "Linear."
2. Once in the "Linear" regression box, you will see the following commands: "Statistics," "Plots," "Save," "Options," "Bootstrap," "Previous," "Next," "Enter," "Reset," "Paste," "Cancel," and "OK."
3. Choose your "Dependent variable" and "Independent variable(s)." The analysis for this example is some data looking at how much religiosity (religious devotion) predicts trust in a medical practitioner in India. The dependent variable is Trust. The independent variable is Religiosity. With this data file, highlight the dependent variable, and move it over to "Dependent:". Click on the independent variable you want and move it over to "Independent(s):".

For a basic linear regression you do not need to click on anything else. If you want to do more advanced regressions you can use other buttons, but that is something called Multiple Regression. So, at this point press "OK." You will get the following four outputs (Figures 17.19–17.22):

Model	Variables Entered	Variables Removed	Method
1	RELIGIOSITY[b]	.	Enter

a. Dependent variable: trust.
b. All requested variables entered.

Figure 17.19 Output—Variables Entered/Removed[a]

Model	R	R Square	Adjusted R Square	Std. Error of the Estimate
1	.667[a]	.445	.444	1.62658

a. Predictors: (Constant), RELIGIOSITY.

Figure 17.20 Output—Model Summary

Model		Sum of Squares	df	Mean Square	F	Sig.
1	Regression	652.130	1	652.130	246.482	.000[b]
	Residual	812.245	307	2.646		
	Total	1464.375	308			

a. Dependent variable: trust.
b. Predictors: (Constant), RELIGIOSITY.

Figure 17.21 Output—ANOVA[a]

Model		Unstandardized Coefficients		Standardized Coefficients		
		B	Std. Error	Beta	t	Sig.
1	(Constant)	1.685	.246		6.857	.000
	RELIGIOSITY	.780	.050	.667	15.700	.000

a. Dependent variable: trust.

Figure 17.22 Output—Coefficients[a]

Figure 17.19 shows the variables entered into the regression. "Variables Entered" shows the independent variable and beneath that, the dependent variable is listed. Figure 17.20 shows the relationships, predictive nature of the two variables, and the standard error. You will first see the correlation between the two variables (.667). If you square the correlation, you get the coefficient of determination, the R^2. The R^2 explains how much one variable predicts the other variable. In this case, the R^2 is .445. This means, religiosity predicts 44.5 percent of an individual's trust in their medical practitioner in India. The Output also contains the R^2_{adj}, which is the adjusted R^2. This is the R^2 adjusted or modified as it takes into consideration the number of independent variables and the sample size. The smaller your sample size, and the more independent variables you have, the more likely your R^2_{adj} will drop significantly from the R^2. The R^2_{adj} is a more conservative, and in many ways, a more realistic value of the total prediction in the regression. Figure 17.21 is an ANOVA table; it should look similar to the one from a few pages earlier. You can see the F-value, the alpha (p) and the df. The F and p tells you that the regression is significant, $F = 246.482$, $p < .0001$. Figure 17.22 shows the beta (b or slope) value and how significant the beta is. Most researchers will report the standardized coefficient, in this case .667, $p < .0001$. This can be interpreted as such: religiosity increases an individual's trust in their medical practitioner ($b = .667$). This is how you can write up these regression results:

> Religiosity was a significant predictor of an individual's trust in their medical practitioner $F(1, 307) = 246.482$, $R^2_{adj} = .444$. Religiosity significantly increased trust in medical practitioners ($b = .667$).

Regression is one of the most used statistical methods in communication research. Yanovitzky, Stewart, and Lederman (2006), for example, found alcohol use by peers was a strong predictor of students' personal alcohol use. Hollander (2010) found that Americans who perceived President Obama as a Muslim in September 2008 were most likely to see him as a Muslim in November 2008 during the election. The point of these two random articles is to show the diversity of regression in communication research.

The primary method behind Nate Silver's predictions was regression. In 2012, he combined various independent variables to make predictions about who would win various elections. Through a systematic selection of independent variables, Silver was able to make the most accurate predictions of any analyst examining the 2012 campaigns. After his predictions came true, just about all of them, Silver gained almost rock star status, which partially shows the power of statistics.

Summary

This chapter was a how-to guide to inferential statistics. Generally, statistics are used by social scientific researchers, but can sometimes be used by interpretive and critical/cultural researchers depending on the focus of the study. Hopefully after reading this chapter, and the accompanying student paper, you feel comfortable enough to try and conduct inferential statistics. The next chapter, Chapter 18, is a how-to guide to experiments.

Key Steps & Questions to Consider

1. Inferential statistics make inferences or help us make conclusions about data.
2. There are two main kinds of inferential statistics, tests of difference and tests of relationship or prediction.
3. There are two kinds of *t*-tests, the dependent and the independent *t*-test. Both help us better understand mean differences between two groups. The result of a *t*-test is a *t*-value.
4. A one-way analysis of variance (ANOVA) is a way to explore mean differences between more than two groups. With an ANOVA you conduct an *F*-test.
5. To understand differences between groups when conducting an ANOVA you need to perform *post-hoc* analyses, such as Scheffé or Tukey's.
6. The chi-square test is a test where you compare the observed frequencies of a variable against the expected frequencies to see if there is a statistical difference between the two. This is a non-parametric test.
7. A correlation is a statistical measure of the degree to which two or more variables (interval or ratio) in a sample are related to one another. Correlations range from –1.0 to +1.0.
8. A regression is predicting a dependent variable from one or multiple independent variables.

Activities

1. Spend one week collecting examples of inferential statistics you see in your everyday life. Keep an eye on the shows you watch, the papers and books you read, the statements people make. Remember, sayings like "9 out of 10 dentists recommend . . ." are statistical statements! Notice how often inferential statistics permeate our lives.
2. Try tracking down the study that provided one or more of the inferential statistics you collected from Activity 1. Review the statistical tests used in the study. Were the appropriate statistical tests used in the study?
3. Make a chart of the different statistical tests, which identifies when each is appropriate to use. Consider the data type (e.g., interval, ratio level), type of variable, form of distribution, etc.
4. *Special Challenge:* see if you can find a research study, which supports the "9 out of 10 dentists recommend/prefer/agree" statement!

5. Work through the following chi-square example. You are interested in the soda preference of students on your campus. You ask 90 students to take a taste test. Fifty people prefer Diet Coke, 17 prefer Coke Zero, and 23 prefer Coca-Cola. What should be the expected frequencies? What are the observed frequencies? Is there a statistical difference? In the online companion we go through how to enter this data and the answer.

 Discussion Questions

1. Review the provided student paper by Jessica Sturtevant. Sturtevant identified a number of reasons her study did not provide statistically significant results. Discuss how your class could replicate the study with modifications to generate different results and insights.

Key Terms

Analysis of Variance (ANOVA)	Independent samples *t*-test	Scheffé test
Chi-square	Inferential statistics	*T*-test
Correlation	Non-parametric	Tukey's
Degrees of freedom	Parametric	
Dependent samples *t*-test	*Post-hoc* comparisons	
	Regression	

Notes

1 Unless you are reporting a table or statistical equation using an ANOVA, you probably will not need many of these numbers. However, it is good to know where to find them in case you need them. The degrees of freedom for the denominator are the degrees of freedom for the within group $(N - k)$. The degrees of freedom for the numerator are the degrees of freedom for the between group $(k - 1)$. The variation due to the interaction between the samples is SS between groups. The variation due to differences within individual samples is SS within groups.

2 There are three options we want to explain. Spearman and Kendall's tau-b are kinds of correlations you can run when you have non-parametric data. When your data are not normally distributed or you are working with ordinal data, these tests can be run instead of Pearson, which is the one used for parametric data. Two-tailed versus one-tailed is the other issue we want to clarify at this point. When you have a directional hypothesis, choose a one-tailed test; when your hypothesis is non-directional, choose a two-tailed. The difference is that a two-tailed is used when you cannot predict the nature of correlation.

Undergraduate Student Paper

Students' use of online media and attitude toward intellectual property

Jessica Sturtevant

Abstract

As the use of online media has become more popular, issues such as online copyright and illegal download-ing have become more prevalent. College students, as avid users of online media, are a key population in these developments. This study surveyed college stu-dents about their use of online media and their attitudes towards intellectual property issues and looked for patterns among the results. Although no statistically significant connections emerged, by exam-ining both the actual media use and the abstract opinions of students, this study shows the importance of this issue and of future research in the area.

Introduction

The use of online media, including listening to music and watching videos online, has become com-mon, especially among young adults. As the use of and the market for media online has spread, so have issues concerning copyright. The increasing availability of music and video online has affected how consumers acquire media and how they view it. This study focused on college students, a group at the forefront of media use and innovation. Participants were questioned about their use of online media and their attitudes towards issues of online copyright. The results were analyzed for patterns and correlations.

The first factor the researcher looked at was gender and its effects on media use. Gender has been linked to use of the Internet in previous studies, for example Su-Yen Chen and Yang-Chih Fu's (2008) study of Internet use and academic achievement among Taiwanese adolescents. Chen and Fu found males used the Internet more frequently

> The study shows an important reason for conducting research. Even when the results do not prove a hypothesis or research question, the study is still worthwhile. Such studies show us what is *not* connected or relevant.

than females, and males and females used the Internet for different purposes: males were more likely to play online games, and females were more likely to search for information or socialize online (Chen & Fu, 2008). This study and others like it prompted the first research question:

> *RQ1:* Does the gender of a student affect the amount of online media use?

The goal of this study was to see if there are connections between the use of online media and attitudes toward issues of online copyright. These issues include the idea of intellectual property—what rights does an artist have to a work, and how should those rights be protected online? Studies such as Friedman (1996), Jones (2000), and Oberholzer-Gee and Strumpf (2007, 2009) discussed these issues in a general sense and try to offer solutions, but little research has been done that looks specifically at the relationship between media use and attitudes of copyright and intellectual property. To look at this relationship the study asked:

> *RQ2:* Are students who use more online media more likely to support having media generally available online?

> *RQ3:* Are students who use more online media more likely to support lenient punishments compared with those who use less online media?

Method

Students' use of online media and opinions about online copyright issues were measured using a two-part questionnaire. The first section used a Likert scale ranging from "never" to "often (almost every day)" to measure frequency of online media use in seven categories, including listening to music online, downloading and buying music online, watching TV shows and movies online, and watching clips

The student has a nice lead into the research questions. The reader is guided to the RQs.

on YouTube. Students were also asked about use of Netflix, iTunes or other subscription services. The scores were averaged together to get a comprehensive score of each participant's media use.

The second section of the questionnaire addressed students' opinions about online copyright. Participants were asked if they believed media should be generally available online, what compensation artists should receive, how they felt about punishments for illegal downloading, and how informed they felt themselves and the public to be about these issues.

The questionnaire was administered to 47 second-year students at Marist College. Participants were between the ages of 18 and 20; 17 were male and 30 were female. The researcher went door to door in one section of the dorms to get a sample of Marist students. All surveys were completed anonymously to encourage honesty and detailed responses.

The data for this study were analyzed using three separate tests, one for each research questions. For research question one, an independent samples *t*-test was conducted comparing participant gender and media use. For research questions two and three, a Spearman correlation analysis was used to compare participant media use and opinion of whether media should be generally available or not, and participant media use opinion about punishments (Wrench, Thomas-Maddox, Richmond, & McCroskey, 2008).

Results and Discussion

The gender of the participant did not have a significant effect on the amount of online media use, $t(22.863) = -.20$, $p = ns$. Both men ($M = 3.4534$, $SD = .68292$) and women ($M = 3.4877$, $SD = .35718$) had very similar rates of media use. This is contrary to what Chen and Fu (2008) discussed; however, this may be due to the smaller sample and different age group (college students compared with adolescents) and to the fact that Chen and Fu looked at all different uses of the Internet and the current study focused only on media use. The use of a comprehensive score for media use may have made the

The first section used a Likert scale but we're in the dark about the second section. Description of the method section should be thorough so the reader can gather a comprehensive overview of data collection. The questions in the second section look solid, but what format was used to gather the data—as you have and will continue to discover in your understanding of methods—can be critical in research design.

Refer to the chapter on data and ask yourself the following questions: Do 18–20-year-olds represent all college students? Is a door-to-door sampling from one section of a dorm representative of college students? The student could address the questions by tightening up the research questions (e.g., "Are 18–20-year-old college students. . .") or should address limitations at the end of the paper.

Review the data standards for using an independent samples *t*-test and a Spearman correlation analysis. Remember, you have an unbalanced data comparison with 17 males and 30 females. Do the data fit with the selected tests?

The sample size is fairly small for statistical analysis. Be sure and check with your teacher or advisor about their expectations for sample size. The sample size for this study was appropriate for the parameters set by her professor.

Normally, all the statistical results are provided in their own section of the paper. Then limitations, interpretations, and alternate interpretations are provided in a separate section of the paper. Shifting to limitations and explanations in the middle of providing results may lead to confusion.

results slightly less accurate than comparing the use of each type of media between participants.

The prediction that students who use more online media would be more likely to support having media available online was not verified by the results, *r* (45) = -.01, *p* = *ns*. Most of the students supported having media accessible, regardless of how often they personally used online media (39 students responded media should be available; four said it should not be available; and four said it should be available with conditions). However, all of the students reported using online media on a regular basis, so this study only compared whether the frequency of online media use was a factor, not whether people who use online media differ in their opinions from those who do not use it at all.

Finally, participant media use was not significantly related to opinion about punishments for illegal downloading or file sharing, *r* (45) = -.05, *p* = *ns*. However, it seems logical that those who use more online media (and may use it illegally) would be more likely to support fewer or more lenient punishments than those who use less media, and this result, though not statistically significant, was closer to being significant than either of the others, so it is possible that with a larger sample there may be a correlation.

Conclusion

Though this study did not make any significant connections between students' use of online media and attitudes towards issues of copyright and intellectual property, it did begin to examine an important and multi-faceted issue. All the students in the study reported using online media, with most students using some form almost every day and many using all seven types described. All the students surveyed expressed some opinion about copyright issues, with most in favor of media being generally available online but many proposing solutions to meet the needs of the artists as well as the needs of the consumers. There are connections and patterns among these results, though they may not be statistically significant.

Further research is needed to look at the relationship between media use and attitudes toward intellectual property in more depth, examining larger samples and audiences other than college students to see if these results hold true, or if the trends change in a larger sample.

References

Chen, S., & Fu, Y. (2009). Internet use and academic achievement: Gender differences in early adolescence. *Adolescence, 44*(176), 797-812.

Friedman, A.J. (1996). Summary: Five solutions to intellectual property issues in a digital age. *Leonardo, 29*(4), 321-322.

Jones, S. (2000). Music and the internet. *Popular Music, 19*(2), 217-230.

Oberholzer-Gee, F., & Strumpf, K. (2007). The effect of file sharing on record sales: An empirical analysis. *Journal of Political Economy, 115*(1), 1-42.

Oberholzer-Gee, F., & Strumpf, K. (2009). File sharing and copyright. In J. Lerner & S. Stern (Eds.). *Innovation policy and the economy 2009: Volume 10.* Cambridge, MA: MIT Press.

Wrench, J.S., Thomas-Maddox, C., Richmond, V.P., & McCroskey, J.C. (2008). *Quantitative research methods for communication.* New York, NY: Oxford University Press.

18 EXPERIMENTAL DESIGN

What Will I Learn About Experiments and Experimental Design?

When we think about experiments, we typically imagine people in labs wearing white coats and tinkering with flammable liquids and chemicals. We all have images of such experiments. We have seen them in movies and television, and maybe even conducted a few experiments in a physics or chemistry class. The purpose of such experiments is to test the effects of one or more variables on another variable (when you mix chemical X with chemical Y, what happens?). While such experiments typify the "average" science experiment, they are not the only kinds of experiment on the block.

Conducting an experiment is a process. To perform an experiment, you should consider various questions. 1) What variables are under investigation? 2) What data are being collected and analyzed? 3) Where is the source of your data? 4) How is the experiment being conducted? 5) How will the experimental data be analyzed? We explore these questions and others in Chapter 18 on experimental research.

What is Experimental Design in Communication Research?

Experiment

The focus of this chapter is on experimental design. An **experiment** is a methodological design process to show how one or more variables that have been manipulated by a researcher influence another variable. A researcher should attempt to control any other variables that might affect the relationship between the variables. The purpose of an experiment is to identify any causal relationships between the variables. We know there is a lot to digest in this definition. Don't worry, we are going to break down all the elements in this chapter.

Causality

An experiment is a process where a researcher investigates a possible cause-and-effect relationship between variables. A **causal argument** is not an easy thing to make. In order to make a causal argument you must meet the following three criteria. First, there must be a manipulation of an independent variable before a change happens in the dependent variable. Second, changes in the dependent and the independent variables must be correlated (happen together). When the independent variable changes, the dependent variable should change soon afterward. Third, any change in the dependent variable should be explainable only by the independent variable, and not by any other **intervening variable** or alternate factor or explanation.

Let's consider the following example: when an anesthesiologist gives a patient anesthesia for a surgery (independent variable), the intended effect is for the patient to go to sleep for the surgery (dependent variable). The amount of anesthesia given depends on a lot of factors: the patient, the type of surgery, etc. Before and during the procedure, the anesthesiologist is careful to monitor the level of anesthesia to make sure the patient has the right amount for the desired duration of unconsciousness. We trust anesthesia will knocks us out and the effect is not caused by some other intervening variable. Through numerous trials and experiments, researchers have proven the reliability and "safeness" of anesthesia.

When conducting experiments to make causal claims, researchers follow a careful step-by-step process. We will outline this process in Figure 18.1 and then describe in more depth each aspect of the process.

1. Preparation
   a. State the research problem and the hypotheses or research questions.
   b. Decide if experimental methods are appropriate.
2. Variable and Method Selection/Definition
   a. Define the independent and dependent variables.
   b. Identify any potential intervening variables.
   c. Choose the appropriate measures, surveys, etc. to use in the experiment.
3. Experiment Design
   a. Experimental control.
   b. Comparison groups, random assignment, pretest and posttests.
   c. Types of designs.
4. Evaluate the Experiment
   a. Internal validity.
   b. External validity
5. Analyze the Data (Use the most appropriate statistic. See Chapter 17 for a variety of statistical options.)

Figure 18.1 Basic Steps of Experimental Research

Experiment Preparation

Before conducting an experiment, you must consider two main questions. First, what is the broad research problem (issue)? Second, what hypotheses or research questions are you interested in studying? In Chapters 3–9 we discussed various issues related to how you formulate and generate hypotheses or research questions. Before you begin an experiment you need to know what you want to study.

Second, ask if an experiment is necessary. After you have done some preliminary research and determined the general topic(s) of interest, you must ask a very important question: is an experiment necessary? Remember, an experiment helps us determine causality. Causality means one or more variables cause or lead to a change in another variable. In many research studies you want to show causality, while in other studies you are not interested in showing causality.

Flip back a few pages to Chapter 17 on inferential statistics. In that chapter we referenced various studies. One study that did use an experimental design was by Yanovitzky, Stewart, and Lederman (2006). The authors were interested in sampling college students for their perceptions about alcohol use based on distant versus proximate peers in predicting college students' drinking behavior. The study used a cross-sectional design. In Yun, Costantini, and Billingsley's (2012) study on the effects of taking a public speaking class on writing abilities, the researchers used a longitudinal experimental design.

The researchers were interested in the effects of taking a university public speaking course on a student's writing abilities. Thus, testing the students' writing abilities was essential at the start of the course (a pretest) and then at the end of the course (a posttest).

Think about any medicine you have taken in your life . . . aspirin, ibuprofen, a prescription from a physician. All of these medications have gone through what we call a clinical trial. To test the safety, governments require drug developers to strictly test medications. The first step is for the developers of the medications to state what the medications will do (their intended purpose). The second step is a clinical trial (and experiment). We will outline the next steps later in this chapter.

Variable and Method Selection/Definition

You need to define your independent and dependent variables in many studies. With experiments in particular, you may also need to identify intervening variables. You must also choose appropriate measures to explore those variables.

You need to define your variables of interest. With experiments you are exploring the effects of one or more independent variables on a dependent variable. You may need to consider any potential intervening variables that may affect the causal relationship between the independent and the dependent variables. In Yun et al.'s (2012) study of the effects of taking a public speaking class on writing abilities, the following five hypotheses were posed (p. 287):

H1: Individuals exposed to a public speaking class will have greater gains in their writing skills of *writing context* than those not exposed to a public speaking class.

H2: Individuals exposed to a public speaking class will have greater gains in their writing skills of *content development* than those not exposed to a public speaking class.

H3: Individuals exposed to a public speaking class will have greater gains in their writing skills of *writing structure* than those not exposed to a public speaking class.

H4: Individuals exposed to a public speaking class will have greater gains in their writing skills in *use of sources and evidence* than those not exposed to a public speaking class.

H5: Individuals exposed to a public speaking class will have greater gains in their writing skills in *control of syntax* than those not exposed to a public speaking class.

In each hypothesis, exposure or not to a public speaking class is the independent variable. The dependent variable in each hypothesis has been italicized; the dependent variable for each hypothesis focuses on an aspect of writing ability. You will find that in well-written experimental studies the researchers take care to clearly identify and explain their variables in the "Method" section of the article.

Yun et al. (2012) did not identify any potential intervening variables in the Method section or in the Review of Literature. However, as only two of their hypotheses were supported (we will talk more about data analysis shortly), the researchers offered a potential intervening variable in the Discussion section. The researchers noted that the outcomes of public speaking and writing classes were different, and thus future studies should take into consideration the different outcomes. Therefore, if they conducted another experiment on the same topic, the researchers may alter their materials to consider the pedagogical differences between public speaking and writing courses.

Think back to Chapter 15 on surveys and Chapter 7 on data. One of the issues discussed in both chapters was the different methods available for collecting data using a survey. You have many tools at your disposal if you want to conduct an experiment: self-report or other-report surveys, observations, and other codeable forms of data. Many researchers collect self-reports or other-reports from participants at various points in time (longitudinal data). Some prefer to observe human behavior. Yun *et al.* (2012) had students write a 3–5 page paper at the start and the end of the semester (about 12 weeks apart). The papers were on a variety of topics. The papers were then graded based on a standardized writing rubric by trained coders. You have many experimental measures available in a study. The key is to choose the most appropriate ones for your study. The choice will be based on your literature review of what other researchers have done and on your knowledge of the subject.

When conducting a clinical trial to determine the effectiveness and safety of a new medication, researchers have to ask themselves a few questions related to variables. What independent, dependent, and intervening variables could affect our understanding of how the medication affects the human body? Let's say researchers are testing a new headache pill. The researchers assert: patients exposed to "Headache Pill X" will have less headache pain than patients exposed to other headache pills. The independent variable is "Headache Pill X" exposure and the dependent variable is the level of headache pain. When doing the trials, the researchers must determine if any intervening variables could affect their causal argument that "Headache Pill X" reduces headache pain. We will talk more about how researchers do this shortly. Finally, the researchers have lots of ways to measure the pain relief of the pill. They could use self-reports from volunteers who take the pills, they could observe the volunteers, or they could take measurements of blood pressure or other vitals of the patients to estimate pain. Medical researchers think about all these things.

Types of Experiments (Design)

Experimental Control

So, you've decided to conduct an experiment. You've defined your variables, and chosen the appropriate measures for the experiment. The next step is to choose the design of your experiment. You can conduct an experiment in myriad ways. The purpose of an experiment is to establish a causal relationship between variables. To do this, the independent variable must be manipulated in some way. Experimental design is the key because causality cannot be established without **experimental control.** Experimental control is evaluating the manipulation of the independent variable for effectiveness and to ensure you have controlled for (removed the effects of) alternative variables. You can take multiple steps to check for effective manipulation of the independent variable(s). The options are called **manipulation checks.** These steps, often statistical procedures, check (test) if the participants perceived the independent variable(s) the way a researcher intended. In Ivanov, Parker, and Pfau's (2012) examination of inoculation, the researchers conducted t-tests as manipulation checks of their inoculation messages (the independent variables).

To achieve experimental control, three things are essential (Rashotte, 2007): comparison groups, random assignment of participants to independent variable conditions, and pretest-posttest testing.

Comparison and Control Groups

When conducting an experiment, some of the participants need to be exposed to (given) the independent variable and some should not be exposed. The group exposed to the manipulated levels of the independent variable(s) are called the **comparison group.** In the Yun et al. (2012) study on the relationship between taking a public speaking class and writing ability, the comparison group was participants in the public speaking class. The participants completed the writing assignment at the start of the semester and then at the end of the semester so the researchers could see if the public speaking class had any effect on their writing abilities. The researchers then compared the scores of the comparison group to a separate group called the control group. A **control**

group is not exposed to the independent variable(s). In the case of Yun et al., the control group was students enrolled in a history class. The researchers excluded history students who had already taken a public speaking class. The control group completed the same writing assignments as the comparison group. Comparing the control and the comparison groups allowed Yun et al. to argue the effects of the public speaking class on writing ability.

In both of the Yun et al. (2012) groups, the participants knew they were being measured for some kind of experiment. In some experiments the participants do not know if they have been exposed to the independent variable(s). A **placebo** is when an individual thinks they have received a treatment, but have not. Often in medical studies, researchers will give volunteers sugar pills. The pills, which have no effects on the body, are given to help differentiate the true effects of medications. People often believe a medication is working when in fact they are getting the placebo (and thus the phrase "placebo effect"). Placebo groups are sometimes used in social scientific and in communication research.

Random Assignment

Remember, one of the goals in an experiment is to compare the results of the control and the comparison groups on some measures (generally pre- and posttests, which we will discuss in a bit). To facilitate the most reliable and valid comparison, and to ensure your groups are equivalent, you should randomly assign participants. This is called **random assignment.** If your groups are not equivalent, you could have selection bias or other characteristics present in one group that are not present in another group. Think back to the discussion of random sampling from Chapters 7 and 9. While random assignment is slightly different, many of the same principles apply. You want to be confident your groups represent your population as closely as possible. The best way to do this is by randomly assigning.

Pre- and Posttests

Researchers often use pretests and posttests. A **pretest** is a measure (test) of the dependent variable before the manipulated independent variable. A **posttest** is the same exact measure (test) of the dependent variable after the delivery of the manipulated independent variable. The purpose of giving a pre- and posttest is to determine if a change has occurred in the participant from the time of the pretest to the time of the posttest. If the participants in the comparison group have been exposed to the manipulated independent variable, the researchers can attribute the change in participant behavior to the independent variable, causality (as long as a few other conditions are met of course, which we talked about earlier). In the Yun et al. (2012) study, the researchers had all the students in the comparison and the control groups write a 3–5 page paper at the start of the class (pretest) and at the end of the class (posttest). The researchers then analyzed the papers based on a writing rubric. They then compared the results for students in the history class (control group) and the public speaking class (comparison group) to see if there were improvements in student writing skills.

To show causality, researchers need to control the manipulation of the independent variable(s). Utilizing comparison and control groups, random assignment, and pre- and posttests, along with manipulation of the independent variable(s), helps researchers make causal claims. When studies are conducted with all of these elements, the studies are true experimental designs. If one or more of these elements are absent from the design the study is considered a pre-experimental or quasi-experimental design. We discuss these types of designs next.

Pre-Experimental Designs

Pre-experimental designs lack one of the three elements we listed above: comparison and control groups, random assignment of participants to groups, and/or pretests and posttests. We will outline two examples of pre-experimental design: the one-shot case study and the one-group pretest-posttest design.

One-Shot Case Study

The **one-shot case study** is a design where some manipulation of the independent variable occurs, and after the manipulation the measurement of the dependent variable is taken. For example, imagine you want to measure the effectiveness of a political campaign on voting behavior. After the election, you give a survey to a group of voters and you ask them about their perceptions of the candidate. Your research tries to argue, based on the results of the survey, that the campaign had an effect on the voters' political opinions. However, without a measure of the voters' opinions before the campaign, a researcher cannot show causality.

One-Group Pretest-Posttest

The **one-group pretest-posttest** design adds the element of a pretest to the one-shot case study. In this type of design, the researcher administers a pretest of the dependent variable, the independent variable is manipulated, and then the dependent variable is measured again (posttest). Take the study on the effectiveness of a political campaign on voting behavior. With a one-group pretest-posttest design you would measure individuals' opinions about the political candidate before the start of the campaign (pretest), the campaign happens (the independent variable), and then you measure the opinions about the political candidate after the campaign (posttest). Finally, you compare the results of the pretest and the posttest for changes in political opinion, and attribute these changes to the manipulated independent variable. This type of design is a more sophisticated design than the one-shot case study

One-Shot Case Study		X	O
One-Shot Pretest Posttest	O	X	O

Figure 18.2 Pre-Experimental Designs

Notes: O = measurement of dependent variable; X = independent variable manipulation.
Source: Campbell & Stanley (1963).

design because it has the pretest component, which provides for a point of comparison. This is what happened in the Yun et al. (2012) study on the effects of taking a public speaking class on writing skills. See Figure 18.2 for a visual depiction of the pre-experimental designs.

While a pre-experimental design provides for statistical reliability and validity, it is difficult to absolutely state the independent variable caused a change in the dependent variable. Quasi-experimental designs take pre-experimental designs a step further in sophistication. We will outline two designs: the time-series design and the nonequivalent control group design.

Quasi-Experimental Designs

Time-Series Design

The **time-series design** measures the dependent variable at various points of time before and after the manipulation of the independent variable. The purpose of measuring the dependent variable at various points in time is to assess degrees of change in the dependent variable over time. This kind of design is needed or useful when you are interested in measuring the development or change in the dependent variable. Let's return to the impact of a political campaign on voters' opinions about a candidate. It would be advantageous to measure the voters' opinions at various stages before a major debate (let's say once a week before the debate) and then the debate takes place. After the debate, measure the opinions again (this time every three weeks). This type of measurement design may reveal changes in opinions toward the candidate before and after the debate. While this kind of design is more sophisticated than the pre-experimental designs, it is still subject to problems. The design lacks random assignment and a control group, and thus the researcher should not claim causality.

Nonequivalent Control Group Design

A **nonequivalent control group** design has two groups—a control and a comparison group. Both groups are given a pretest and a posttest. However, only the comparison group is exposed to the independent variable. In the Yun et al. (2012) study on the effects of taking a public speaking class on writing skills, the researchers used this kind of design. Both groups were

Time-Series Designs	O_1	O_2	O_3	X	O_4	O_5	O_6
Nonequivalent Control Group					O_1	X	O_2
					O_3		O_4

Figure 18.3 Quasi-Experimental Designs

Notes: O = measurement of dependent variable; X = independent variable manipulation.
Source: Campbell & Stanley (1963).

given a pretest and posttest (the writing assignment graded by independent coders). The comparison group was exposed to the independent variable (the public speaking class). The control group (the history class) was not exposed to the independent variable. This design, like the time-series design, is more sophisticated than pre-experimental designs. However, the approach lacks random assignment, which limits its ability to prove causality. See Figure 18.3 for a visual depiction of the quasi-experimental designs.

The quasi-experimental designs provide more evidence for causality than the pre-experimental designs. However, neither the pre- nor the quasi-experimental designs incorporate random assignments. The lack of random assignment threatens the reliability of the experiments and limits the causal argument. True experiments, on the other hand, incorporate all the necessary elements for the best cause-and-effect argument. We will outline three designs: the pretest-posttest control group design, the posttest-only control group design, and the Solomon four-group design.

True-Experimental Designs

Pretest-Posttest Control Group Design

The **pretest-posttest control group** design uses pretests and posttests, comparison and control groups, and random assignment to assess the effects of an independent variable(s) on a dependent variable. The design is identical to the nonequivalent control group, except that it includes random assignment of study participants into either comparison or control groups. Pieterse, van Dulmen, Beemer, Ausems, and Bensing (2006) used this design to assess communication messages during cancer genetic counseling. The study involved offering counselors feedback on counseling. However, not all the counselors (participants) received feedback during the study. Those who did not receive feedback were the control group. The purpose of giving some counselor feedback or training was to assess the effectiveness of the communication messages. A weakness of this experimental design is that, even though participants are randomly assigned to groups, the researchers may not know enough information about the participants to determine if differences in the group affected the outcomes.

The assignment of participants to groups, even random assignment, may lead to limited statistical power.

Posttest-Only Control Group Design

The **posttest-only control group** design includes random assignment, posttests, comparison and control groups, and random assignment. Beckie (1989) used this design in an analysis of the impact of an educative telephone program on levels of knowledge and anxiety of patients undergoing coronary artery bypass surgery after hospital discharge. With a posttest-only control group design, patients were randomly assigned to either an experimental or a control group. A significant difference between the state anxiety level of the experimental and the control group was evident. While this type of design does use random assignment, without a pretest it is impossible to measure a change in behavior due to the manipulation of the independent variable.

Solomon Four-Group Design

The **Solomon four-group design** contains two extra control groups, comparison groups, random assignments, two pretests, and four posttests. The Solomon is the most sophisticated design possible in experimental designs. The Solomon eliminates many of the validity threats we will discuss in the next section of this chapter. The combination of comparison and control groups permits researchers to ensure rival variables have not affected the final results. Kvalem, Sundet, Rivo, Eilertsen, and Bakketeig (1996) studied adolescent condom use and employed this kind of design. They evaluated the effectiveness of a school sex education program in Norway. The results showed an interaction between the pretest and the intervention (independent variable) affected condom use (dependent variable). The Solomon's main limitation is the amount of time and effort required compared with other designs. See Figure 18.4 for a visual depiction of the true-experimental designs.

Pretest-Posttest Control	R	O_1	X	O_2
Group Design	R	O_3		O_4
Posttest-Only Control	R		X	O_1
Group Design	R			O_2
Solomon Four-Group	R		X	O_2
Design	R	O_1		O_4
	R	O_3	X	O_5
	R			O_6

Figure 18.4 True-Experimental Designs

Notes: O = measurement of dependent variable; X = independent variable manipulation; R = random assignment.

Source: Campbell & Stanley (1963).

When conducting medical experiments you will find a variety of different experimental designs used. One of the keys for showing a drug "works" is to have control and comparison groups. It is essential for pharmaceutical companies to be able to say that the drug functioned this way in one group and this way in another group. If the company, and the doctors doing the trials, can show medically that the comparison groups had benefits from the drug that were not present in the control groups . . . they can show some causality.

Evaluating Experiments

Since experiments are concerned with showing causality, researchers are particularly concerned with being sure that experiments have high validity and reliability. Reliability and validity are critical to accurately state that an independent variable(s) causes any change in a dependent variable. Look back to Chapter 8 and the discussion of reliability and validity. Reliability is the notion that instruments should perform the same way over time. Validity is the extent to which a test measures what it's supposed to measure. The same threats to reliability that are present in other kinds of social scientific inquiry are present in experiments: 1) errors in data entry, 2) instrument confusion, and 3) random human differences.

Numerous threats to validity are unique to experiments. In order for a measure to have validity in an experimental design, you must be sure that the measures are not biased because you are trying to show causality. To show causality you must rule out rival or intervening variables that interfere with demonstrating the causal relationship. You should be aware of two kinds of bias that can affect an experiment's ability to show causality (Cook & Campbell, 1979): time progression effects and reactivity effects.

Time Progression Effects

Experiments, unlike one-shot studies, take place over a period of time. The period of time can be short or long. As the study is taking place, time itself is a variable that must be considered. **Time progression effects** are the factors that act like separate independent variables as causes or effects because an experiment does take place during a period of time. We will identify six time progression effects: history, instrumentation, maturation, mortality, statistical regression, and testing.

History refers to an event(s) that happens during the experiment that is outside of the study, but may affect the outcome of the study. One way to try to counter for the history effect is to have a control-and-comparison group exposed to all the same elements or events. If an outside event happens and if differences exist between the groups, you can assess those differences as caused by the independent variable(s) and not the outside events. Take the Yun et al. (2012) study on the relationship between taking a public speaking class and writing ability. Two of their five hypotheses were confirmed. It is possible that outside events in the students' lives may have influenced the experiment: taking another course may have affected writing ability or some students in the control group may have joined a writing club or something.

Instrumentation is when the instrument (measure) is changed during the course of the experiment. Let's say you give the pretest and then notice some things in the instrument you want to change. So, you change some of the questions and then give the posttest with the revised instrument. Can you adequately compare the results of the pretest and the posttest since you changed the instrument? The change brings into question issues of validity and reliability. If you notice something you MUST change, we recommend you change it and then test the group two more times. Let the first test serve as a pilot "dry run," and not your pretest.

Maturation is a naturally occurring process in experiments. Participants develop mentally, physically, emotionally, etc. The developmental process itself thus serves as an independent variable when trying to argue that some trait, behavior, or process causes a change in another trait, behavior, or process. For example, let's say you want to argue that an individual's religiosity (religious devotion) causes them to use certain kinds of media. You may find religiosity is an evolving part of our lives. Thus, it would be very, very hard to show it causes media usage. If you want to show that exposure to violent media causes children to be violent you would need to consider how children's minds and emotions develop rapidly. Therefore, some children will learn to understand the differences between fact and fiction faster than others. You will need to consider the developmental process in your study.

Mortality is the simple fact that some participants will start an experiment but not finish. For a variety of reasons people drop out of experiments. Stephen started an experiment on cultural adaptation in 2006 in France. He had 529 Muslim immigrants complete a survey. In 2012, 398 of those 529 original participants completed the follow-up survey. He was unable to find some of the original participants: they moved, did not respond to phone calls or emails, did not want to participate, and a couple had died in those six years. Participants have the right to drop out of an experiment. In 2018 when Stephen returns to collect more data, he knows he will lose some participants, but hopes not too many.

Statistical regression is when your sample includes participants who represent the extremes of the dependent variable. Let's say you have a measure ranging from 0 to 100. If a person scores a 0 on the pretest, where can they go on the posttest except for up? One could argue that in the Yun et al. (2012) study individuals who were extremely poor at writing at the start of the semester would only get better, no matter what class they were taking in college (public speaking, history, or English). Thus, statistical regression acts like another independent variable to consider.

The **testing** effect is more likely to happen when participants complete a pretest and a posttest. What happens is that participants become sensitized to the answers or procedure. As the participants have already taken the pretest, they know—or think they know—the "right answers." Therefore, the participants can often get a higher or more appropriate score the second or subsequent time around because they already had practice taking the measure. Think about any time you have had the chance to retake an exam, particularly the *same* exam. Since you took the exam once before, you should have done better on it the second time around because you had a "trial run."

Reactivity Effects

When people participate in an experiment they respond to many elements of the experiment's conditions. People are asked to do all sorts of things they would not do in their normal everyday lives. **Reactivity effects** are a set of threats to an experiment's validity that center on the participant's responses to the design of an experiment. We will discuss six reactivity effects: compensation behavior, demand knowledge, experiment apprehension, researcher attributes, selection, and treatment diffusion.

Compensation behavior becomes a threat to validity when the control group finds the comparison group is being treated differently than they are. If the control group finds out the comparison group is getting paid more for the study, the control group may become angry and underperform, or the group may perform better to try to get the same kind of payment. Either way, this knowledge alters their natural experimental behavior. You can control by taking steps to make sure members of each group do not communicate with one another and/or share information about the study with each other.

Demand knowledge is a threat to a study because you may not want participants to know the goals of the study. If participants think they know the goals of a study, they may provide answers they think the researchers want or they may provide opposite answers to play with the research team. When trying to show causality, we do not want this kind of bias in a study. What we want is for the participants to answer questions as honestly as possible. However, when participants are aware of the goals of a study, or think they are, the answers are not going to be as honest. Research has demonstrated that when individuals know they are being watched in the workplace, their productivity goes up. This is known as the Hawthorne Effect.

Some people are also apprehensive about being in experiments. Experiment apprehension is when participants are nervous or excited about participating in an experiment. Along with being nervous or excited, some questions in experiments can be very personal. Many people will alter their answers to appear more favorable to the experimenters. This process of altering answers to look more favorable is called the social desirability bias; we talked about it in Chapter 15 on surveys. Building trust with participants is key to help them feel comfortable in giving honest answers.

Sometimes the researchers have personal characteristics that can affect the data collection process; this is the threat of **researcher attributes.** For example, if conducting research among female rape victims then having female members on the research team would be advantageous. Survivors of sexual assault are generally more comfortable sharing personal or intimate details about such violence with individuals of the same sex.

The **selection** threat happens when a researcher is unable to randomly assign participants into comparison or control groups. Yun et al. (2012) were not able to randomly place students into a public speaking or a history class. The researchers were "stuck" with the students they had that semester in the different classes. Thus, as the authors pointed out, any potential differences between the students could be attributed to a selection bias.

Treatment diffusion, also known as contamination, happens when participants in the treatment group tell people in the control group about the treatment. The discussion of the treatment contaminates the control group. For example, the 1996 Kvalem et al. study on condom use in Norway had four groups: two control and two comparison. Two groups received the treatment (the training) and were then measured on their condom use. Discussions between the comparison group and the control group may have biased the study since the control group represented people not receiving condom use education.

Looking at the laundry list of validity threats to experiments, we can understand why it can take so long for new drugs to be tested. The Food and Drug Administration (FDA) is rigorous when it comes to verifying the safety of medicines. Whenever a medicine is put on the market we can be certain it will work for us about 99.9 percent of the time. We say 99.9 percent because there is always an element of error we talked about in earlier chapters. Error is present in experiments because of all of the threats to validity. We have all heard of medicines like Yaz or Vioxx being recalled because of consumer health threats. Some danger is almost always involved in medicines, and clinical trials often reveal some of these threats. However, the threats to experiments help us recognize the need for rigorous experimental design. In medical research and science, a failure to set up a valid and reliable design could lead to death. In communication and the social sciences such a failure could lead to poor results, misreporting, and even unethical reporting.

Summary

This chapter was a how-to guide to experiments. The focus of experiments is on showing causality. Experiments are a very social scientific way of doing research. Hopefully after reading the chapter you have a better understanding of experiments. While experiments are a tall order, maybe you feel comfortable enough to try one out after reading this chapter and the ones before it. The next chapter, Chapter 19, is a how-to guide to rhetorical criticism.

 ## Key Steps & Questions to Consider

1. An experiment is a methodological process to test the effects of one or more variables that have been manipulated by a researcher on another variable.

2. You must meet three criteria to make a causal argument: manipulation of the independent variable before a change happens in the dependent variable, the changes in the dependent and the independent variables must happen together, and any change in the dependent variable should only be explainable by the independent variable, not by an intervening variable.

3. Before conducting an experiment, formulate the broad research problem and the hypotheses or research questions. Then ask yourself if an experiment is necessary.

4. Many tools are available if you want to conduct an experiment: self-report or other-report surveys, observations, and other codeable forms of data.

5. Experimental control is evaluating the manipulation of the independent variable for effectiveness and to ensure you have controlled for alternative variables.

6. Three things are needed for experimental control: comparison groups, random assignment of participants to independent variable conditions, and pretest-posttest.

7. The group of participants who are exposed to the manipulated levels of the independent variable(s) is called the comparison group.

8. A control group is not exposed to the independent variable(s).

9. A placebo is when an individual thinks they have received a treatment but have not.

10. A pretest is a measure (test) of the dependent variable before the manipulated independent variable. A posttest is the same exact measure (test) of the dependent variable given after the delivery of the manipulated independent variable.

11. A one-shot case study is a design where manipulation of the independent variable occurs, and after the manipulation the measurement of the dependent variable is taken.

12. A one-group pretest-posttest design is when the researcher administers a pretest of the dependent variable, the independent variable is manipulated, and then the dependent variable is measured again (posttest).

13. A time-series design measures the dependent variable at various points of time before and after the manipulation of the independent variable.

14. A nonequivalent control group design has a control and a comparison group. Both groups are given a pretest and a posttest. Only the comparison group is exposed to the independent variable.

15. A pretest-posttest control group design uses pretests and posttests, comparison and control groups, and random assignment to assess the effects of an independent variable(s) on a dependent variable.

16. A posttest-only control group design includes random assignment, posttests, comparison and control groups, and random assignment.

17. A Solomon four-group design contains two extra control groups, comparison groups, random assignments, two pretests, and four posttests. In experimental design, the Solomon is the most sophisticated design available.

18. Time progression effects are factors that act like separate independent variables as causes or effects because an experiment does take place over a period of time. The six time progression effects are: history, instrumentation, maturation, mortality, statistical regression, and testing.

19. Reactivity effects are a set of threats to an experiment's validity that center on a participant's responses to the design of an experiment. The six reactivity effects are: compensation behavior, demand knowledge, experiment apprehension, researcher attributes, selection, and treatment diffusion.

 ## Activity

1. Major challenge! Develop a chart for easy reference of all the different experimental design options available to a communication researcher.

 ## Discussion Questions

Pick one of the articles mentioned in the chapter. Look up the article in your library (your instructor or a reference librarian can help you find it). Your instructor may decide to divide up the class into groups with each group assigned a different article.

1. Consider how your article could be adapted to meet at least three different experimental designs.
2. Identify the specific strengths and weaknesses for your study in each of your three chosen experimental designs.
3. Which experimental design is the best option and why?

Key Terms

Causal argument
Comparison group
Compensation behavior
Control group
Experiment
Experimental control
History
Instrumentation
Intervening variable
Manipulation checks
Maturation
Mortality

Nonequivalent control group
One-group pretest-posttest
One-shot case study
Placebo
Posttest
Posttest-only control group
Pre-experimental designs
Pretest
Pretest-posttest control group

Random assignment
Reactivity effects
Researcher attributes
Selection
Solomon four-group design
Statistical regression
Testing
Time progression effects
Time-series design
Treatment diffusion

19   RHETORICAL CRITICISM

Chapter Outline

- Overview of Rhetoric and Rhetorical Criticism
- Rhetoric Defined
- Rhetorical Criticism Defined
- Theoretical Approach Selection in Rhetorical Criticism
- Conducting a Rhetorical Criticism
- Key Steps & Questions to Consider
- Activities
- Discussion Questions
- Key Terms
- Undergraduate Rhetorical Criticism Paper

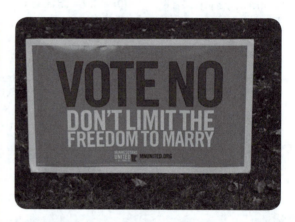

What Will I Learn About Rhetorical Criticism?

This is a pair of photos showing yard signs supporting opposite sides of a political issue in Minnesota. The issue of gay marriage has varied across the United States with different states taking a variety of positions. Some states support gay marriage, others offer a compromise called civil unions (or civil partnerships), and some have laws barring gay marriage. The state of Minnesota had already passed a law in 1997 prohibiting marriage between persons of the same sex, and voiding any contractual rights if married in a different state (Minnesota Statutes, 2007). However, members of the legislature believed the law could be overturned by the state courts and wanted to strengthen the ban by embedding the prohibition in the state's constitution.

Organizations sprang up to support and oppose amending the state's constitution. The competing organizations hosted fundraisers, selected spokepersons, created (and updated) websites, produced and distributed paraphernalia (yard signs, buttons, stickers), and engaged across the range of social media (e.g., YouTube and Facebook). And individuals sustained the causes by "sharing" messages through social media, hosting house parties, writing letters to editors, and other actions of support. The yard signs are just the "tip of the iceberg." The political process continues on many fronts. Consider that every two years the United States has elections for state and national political positions. We see political ads, new stories on TV and in newspapers, brochures, fliers, and . . . yard signs. We watch candidates give stump speeches, challenge each other in debates, and march in local community parades. All of these speeches, ads, stories, documents, and debates are examples of rhetoric and are opportunities for communication scholars to engage in rhetorical criticism. In Chapter 19, you will learn how to conduct a rhetorical criticism as a form of communication scholarship.

Introduction to Rhetoric and Rhetorical Criticism

Rhetoric and rhetorical criticism are the oldest forms of scholarship in the communication discipline, dating back to the ancient Greeks who were focused on determining what constituted an effective speech. The study and practice of rhetoric became so important for the ancient Romans it was listed as part of a core classical education. A Roman citizen studied rhetoric, grammar, and logic (by the Medieval period, the three disciplines together were called the **trivium**) (Salisbury, 1180/2009). The study of rhetoric has continued, in one form or another, for thousands of years since.

Rhetorical criticism is different in two ways from most other forms of communication scholarship. First, rhetoric and rhetorical criticism are major areas of study in the discipline. Unlike other forms of research methods, rhetoric and rhetorical criticism stand alone within communication studies. Some communication scholars focus their entire careers on the study of rhetoric and rhetorical criticism, and entire organizations are dedicated solely to the study of rhetoric (e.g., Rhetoric Society of America, International Society for the History of Rhetoric, Canadian Society for the Study of Rhetoric). In fact, one organization, the **Kenneth Burke Society,** focuses on the writings of just one scholar. Second, rhetorical criticism is more subjective than other communication research methods. A criticism is, at its core, an argument about how a symbol can be understood using a particular theory as a filter. The criticism or argument provides a new way to understand the world around us, and maybe better ways to engage with others around us.

The study of rhetoric and rhetorical criticism can be a daunting task. Rhetoric and rhetorical criticism have a close relationship with many of our sister disciplines including philosophy, English (particularly composition, poetics, and literary theory and criticism), sociology, religion, anthropology, and psychology. The inter-disciplinary connections make rhetoric and rhetorical criticism a robust field of study. However, the breadth and depth also make rhetoric and rhetorical criticism a complicated and complex area of study. For example, the *Encyclopedia of Rhetoric and Composition* is devoted to listing, defining, and explaining the specialized language and concepts. We remember when we first started studying rhetorical theory. The terminology and the range of theoretical concepts was intimidating and can quickly overwhelm a young scholar. We are not, obviously, going to cover every aspect of rhetoric and rhetorical criticism in one chapter. We will provide a good starting framework. Take your time as you begin to explore rhetoric and rhetorical criticism. Learn which theories "speak" to you and then take the time to explore those theories in more detail. You may decide if rhetoric and rhetorical criticism is your niche in the discipline!

Defining Rhetoric

Before we look closer at rhetorical criticism as a research method, we need to spend some time with the word "rhetoric." As we talked about earlier, rhetoric is an ancient concept dating back to the ancient Greeks in the 5th century bce.

The modern word "rhetoric" has several negative associations: from the politician who is "all rhetoric and no action," to a speech "full of rhetoric" but lacking substance, to rhetoric as deceptive practice. However, to a communication scholar, rhetoric and rhetorical criticism are powerful parts of our discipline. Scholars have long viewed rhetoric as the art of persuasion. For example, in the 4th century bce Aristotle defined rhetoric as "the faculty of observing in any given case the available means of persuasion" (Aristotle, 4th Century bce/1991). Modern scholars have defined rhetoric in a similar fashion. Cathcart (1991) argues that "rhetoric . . . refers to a communicator's intentional use of language and other symbols to influence or persuade selected receivers to act, believe, or feel the way the communicator desires" (p. 2). Kuypers (2005) defines rhetoric as "the strategic use of communication, oral or written, to achieve specifiable goals" (p. 5). Foss (2004) takes the process one step further noting rhetoric has the power to shape how we perceive reality. Foss says, "reality is not fixed but changes according to the symbols we use to talk about it. What we count as real or as knowledge . . . depends on how we choose to label and talk about things" (p. 6). Rhetoric is an important part of our discipline with the power to change our beliefs, attitudes, and actions, and even alter how we understand the world around us. The criticism of rhetoric plays an important role for understanding how people may be influenced by **symbols**. A rhetorical critic, therefore, seeks to recognize how people understand and respond to symbols, and how the use of symbols can shape our perceptions of reality.

Defining Rhetorical Criticism

Rhetorical criticism as part of modern education started in the early 1900s and focused on speakers and their speeches. The most common research was the "Great Man" criticism (e.g., an important person giving an important speech on an important occasion). We admit sexism was involved in "Great Man" criticism, but at this point in history, men gave most of what were considered significant speeches. However, as we all know, the times have changed and powerful women giving momentous speeches are now part of our society.

The scope of what contemporary rhetorical scholars critique has expanded considerably since the 1900s. We've moved well beyond just looking at speeches (though criticism of a speech is still central to rhetorical criticism). The communication to be critiqued is now called an **artifact.** An artifact is an identifiable moment of communication from a specific time, place, and person(s). As Foss (2004) notes, an artifact is any tangible evidence a communication act occurred.

Possible artifacts include:

1. A compelling speech.
2. A fascinating sermon.
3. An effective essay.
4. A thought-provoking interview.
5. An interesting narrative or story.
6. An engaging television show (or a group of similar television shows).
7. A stimulating public demonstration.
8. An inspiring song lyric (or set of lyrics).
9. A curious political campaign.
10. An eye-grabbing roadway billboard.
11. Any other artifact from a communication moment, which surrounds us every day!

Consider our opening situation with the gay marriage yard signs. We have a broad variety of artifacts from which we can choose for a rhetorical criticism. We could stick with just the yard signs, but the limited text may not provide enough communication for a beginning rhetorical scholar. So, let's consider what other related artifacts we can choose. We could critique the websites or the Facebook presence of either/both campaigns; we could critique a collection of editorials or letters to editors about gay marriage from major newspapers. We could critique a speech (or multiple speeches) from one (or more) politicians. We could critique statements from popular figures in society (e.g., athletes, actors, and musicians).

As we move closer to the actual process for conducting a rhetorical criticism, we must distinguish between being a **popular critic** versus being a **rhetorical critic**. Pierce (2003) argues that popular critics evaluate based on personal preference or taste. A popular critic seeks to influence the general public's perception. For example, movie reviews, ESPN commentaries, and ratemyprofessors.com are sources of popular criticism. A rhetorical critic, however, evaluates based on rhetorical theories and principles. According to Pierce, a rhetorical critic must be prepared to defend their analysis and criticism, defend the standards or methods used to conduct their criticism, and defend their effectiveness of the criticism.

Part of your task as a rhetorical critic is selecting an artifact for analysis. Hart and Daughton (2005) and Foss (2004) provide a good process for selecting an artifact for a beginning scholar. Foss recommends starting the process by listing what you like or dislike. Yes, you can critique something you find annoying. In fact, some scholars prefer to select an artifact they dislike. Prepping and writing a rhetorical criticism is a time-consuming task. If you start off with something you like, you may be tired of the subject by the time you are finished with the criticism. Picking something you dislike, on the other hand, has no similar downside. Foss also suggests you may decide to select something you find confusing and want to better understand, or something that grabs your interest. However, Hart and Daughton (2005) caution that you must have a solid argument for why you selected a specific artifact. Not all artifacts are created equal and we must avoid "criticism-by-whim" (Hart & Daughton, p. 32). Your argument for selecting an artifact may focus on the historical importance, the societal influence, or the political prominence of the artifact.

> Our Minnesota gay marriage artifacts have the advantage of drawing on the historical (potential to amend a state constitution), the societal (gay marriage has broad social implications), and the political (politicians have taken sides on the issue).

Selecting an Approach for a Rhetorical Criticism

Once you have selected your artifact, you need to select a rhetorical theory to frame your criticism. A rhetorical theory is used to filter the symbols in the artifact so we can see new insights about the artifact. The theory is really a set of standards used for evaluating the artifact. Selecting a theory is important since the theory will guide the direction of the criticism. Don't worry about selecting the best theory. No particular theory is "best" for analyzing an artifact. A lot depends on what about the artifact you find interesting. What questions do you have about the artifact? Your interest and questions should help determine the approach appropriate for your analysis.

We do not have the space in one chapter to provide details of all the possible approaches available for a rhetorical criticism. Dozens of books and entire undergraduate and graduate classes are devoted to exploring rhetorical theories. You may decide that rhetoric and rhetorical criticism is your "thing" and end up reading the books and taking many of the courses! Instead, we provide a framework for three of the most common methods used in rhetorical criticism. When you pick your specific rhetorical theory, you may need to do some additional readings on the method to expand your understanding to perform the criticism.

Neo-Aristotelian Criticism

The first rhetorical approach we will "unpack" comes from our classical Greek roots. An understanding of **neo-Aristotelian** criticism (also known as classical or traditional criticism) is based on the classics of ancient Greece and Rome, primarily the writings of Aristotle and Cicero. You may decide to use a neo-Aristotelian approach if your artifact is a speech. Neo-Aristotelian has limited use for other types of artifacts.

Neo-Aristotelian focuses on the **five canons of rhetoric** and is primarily used for critiquing speeches. The Greeks developed the concepts embedded in the five canons and the Romans codified the five canons as part of rhetorical education. Cicero is recognized as the first person to formally list the canons in his work *De Inventione*. The five canons are invention, organization, style, delivery, and memory (though memory gets little attention in contemporary neo-Aristotelian criticism and is sometimes humorously referred to as the "forgotten" canon).

Most neo-Aristotelian criticism focuses on the canon of invention. Invention in rhetoric is different than our popular understanding of creating something new (e.g., building a better mousetrap). **Invention** in rhetoric is the discovery of ideas and arguments for use in a persuasive appeal. Invention critiques how a speaker uses logos, ethos, and pathos to persuade an audience toward a speaker's goal. Aristotle's *Rhetoric* is the foundation for logos, ethos, and pathos as **artistic proofs** used in persuasion. **Inartistic proofs** are factual such as laws, statistics, oaths, and contracts. Inartistic proofs can be used to build an argument, but artistic proofs are more adaptable to the persuasive goal of the speaker.

Logos critiques the speaker's reasoning, arguments, and use of evidence. **Ethos** evaluates the speaker's credibility and character, especially as related to the topic, occasion, and audience for the speech. Ethos is rather distinctive since the standards for critiquing pathos are more in the hands of the audience than speaker. **Pathos** explores the speaker's attempts to emotionally connect with the audience. Weak pathos may induce sympathy with the speech; strong pathos will arouse empathy. For example, the speaker may tell a moving story and hope the audience will bond with the characters or situation in the story.

Reinard (2010) provides an effective neo-Aristotelian checklist based on the work of Lewis and Tabor (1966).

Neo-Aristotelian Checklist

1. Ethos:
   Is the speaker intelligent?
   Does the speaker reveal good character?
   Is the speaker a person of good will?
   Is the speaker telling the whole truth?
   Is the speaker credible?
   Does the speaker's reputation enhance the speech?
2. Pathos:
   Does the speaker establish identification with the audience?
   What types of appeal are used?
   Are appeals specific and concrete?
   Does the speaker stimulate attention and interest?
3. Logos:
   Does the speaker proceed from assumption and hypotheses that are fair and reasonable?
   Is the speaker's analysis of the subject complete and clear?
   What types of argument are used?
   Does the speaker's reasoning meet appropriate tests of validity?
   Are the supporting materials sufficient?
   Are data sufficiently documented?
   Does the speaker substitute emotional appeals for evidence and argument?

The marriage amendment issue has plenty of supporters on both sides of the issue. A neo-Aristotelian criticism focusing on one or more political candidates who have taken a stance on the issue is a good approach. We could easily collect statements from the candidate web pages, statements provided to newspapers, statements made during political debates, and statements from candidates' standard stump speech (and every politician has a standard stump speech!). The Internet is a blessing to rhetorical critics who can rather easily collect all these sorts of artifacts with a series of web searches. Once we have the package of information, we can decide if we want to focus on just one speech or a composite drawn from the variety of artifact sources at our disposal. Remember, we will need to have a good argument as to why we decided to limit or expand the scope of what we include as our artifact. Then we can use the Reinard (2010) checklist to work our way through the neo-Aristotelian criteria and see what criticism emerges.

Metaphor Criticism

The second rhetorical approach we will explore is metaphor criticism. A **metaphor** is used when the qualities of one concept are used to characterize the nature of a person, thing, or idea. A critic needs to be careful of confusing a simile with a metaphor. A simile is easily identified by the use of "like" and "as". An example may be helpful.

> Metaphor = My friend is a tiger on the dance floor stalking its prey.

> Simile = My friend moved across the dance floor *like* a tiger stalking its prey.

While we do not encourage the use of *Wikipedia* for scholarly work, the site does provide an effective list of fairly common metaphors (http://en.wikipedia.org/wiki/List_of_English_language_metaphors). A few minutes reviewing the list may prove helpful for identifying metaphors in an artifact.

A critic using the metaphor approach analyzes artifact(s) by identifying metaphor(s) used by the artifact. The critic then evaluates the metaphor(s) to better explain how the communication may persuade our beliefs, values, and actions. The key in metaphor criticism is to determine what qualities are highlighted or repressed by the metaphor, and what those qualities say about the artifact. Consider our earlier example about the tiger-friend. The animal metaphor brings to mind many qualities about a tiger—a tiger is a large, powerful, and strong carnivore and predator that attacks and feeds on other animals. A quick critique of our tiger-friend on the dance floor does not paint a pretty picture. Consider how the critique may change if the artifact is "my friend is a tiger on the football field stalking its prey." What may have been an unflattering image of a dancer turns into a compelling picture of an athlete.

Let's consider an approach for how we might conduct a metaphor criticism. The marriage amendment has produced a bounty of posts on social media sites—from Facebook, to Twitter, to tumblr, and other sites—we could gather together the posts, from one or multiple sites, and analyze what metaphors are in play. Metaphor criticism is a good opportunity for visual analysis. A search of web images for "vote no Minnesota" and "vote yes Minnesota" produces thousands (actually hundreds of thousands!) of hits. Identifying, analyzing, and drawing out the implications for the dominant metaphors in each position might be a fascinating study.

Fantasy Theme Analysis

The third popular rhetorical approach we explore is fantasy theme analysis (also known as **symbolic convergence theory**). **Fantasy theme analysis** is part of a larger group of theories defined by Brock, Scott, and Chesebro (1990) as dramaturgy. If you choose to continue your studies in rhetorical criticism, you will explore narrative analysis and Burkeian dramatism, the other areas of dramaturgy.

The fantasy theme approach to rhetorical criticism was developed by Dr Ernest Bormann at the University of Minnesota. Fantasy theme analysis is an effective method if your interest is how communication (evident in your selected artifact) can shape perceptions of reality. Fantasy theme analysis works from the concept that a group can develop a shared viewpoint called a "rhetorical vision" (Bormann, 1972, p. 398).

A rhetorical vision occurs when a series of fantasy themes merges to form a fairly cohesive viewpoint. The rhetorical vision provides the participants with shared expectations, which are revealed in their shared vocabulary. A critic can work to build a shared vocabulary by identifying the heroes, villains, victims, storylines, scenes, repeated stories, insider humor, and other commonalities within the group's communication. While a fantasy theme analysis can develop from a single artifact, the approach works well when you have a set of artifacts all from the same group. The rhetorical vision emerges when similar patterns emerge across the various artifacts.

> Finally, what artifacts might we consider if we were interested in a fantasy theme analysis of the marriage amendment question? Let's return to social media. Facebook has become a dominant method for gathering together people who share opinions on social issues. Both Minnesota campaigns have Facebook pages to support their cause. The pages have posts from supporters and detractors. Sometimes the posts are simple statements of support (e.g., "I'm voting no!" or "I support the 'Vote Yes' campaign."). However, a number of the posts are personal stories about how a yes/no vote will impact their personal lives, families, and communities. The stories are a perfect opportunity for a fantasy theme analysis. We can use the stories for identifying the heroes, villains, victims, and other components that form a fantasy theme.

Other Approaches in Rhetorical Criticism

A variety of other approaches are available to rhetorical critics. Just a few are social movement criticism, genre criticism, cluster criticism, feminist criticism, Marxist criticism, cultural criticism, ideological criticism, and postmodern criticism. Now we can see how a scholar can spend an entire career studying rhetoric and rhetorical criticism!

One final note on rhetorical criticism. Boundaries between the various rhetorical approaches are subjective and concepts may cross over between the approaches. While one criticism may use a Marxist theory and another uses a feminist theory this does not mean the criticisms are in conflict. The various approaches each provide their own insights into the artifact(s). Indeed, a rhetorical critic may employ more than one approach in a variety of combinations.

Organizing a Rhetorical Criticism

Writing up a rhetorical criticism can take many forms. However, a basic criticism does follow some general guidelines. Following the structure we outline below will help a beginning critic ensure all the bases are covered (see how we slipped a sports metaphor into the explanation!).

Rhetorical Criticism Outline

1. Your description of the communication/artifact/symbols to be critiqued. Your description may include a justification for the artifact you've selected. What makes the artifact worthy of your (and your readers') time and attention?
2. Your description of the situation where the communication occurred—what social, historical, economic, political, and other circumstances are relevant to the artifact?
3. Your explanation of the rhetorical approach, which will guide your criticism. You may need to include a justification for the rhetorical approach you selected. Be thorough and detailed in explaining the rhetorical approach. Your explanation sets the standards for implementing your criticism.
4. You may choose to include a section discussing other studies, which have used the same rhetorical approach.
5. Your critique of the artifact using the selected rhetorical approach. Include specific examples from the artifact to illustrate how the criticism applies.
6. Your discussion of the implications of the criticism—so what can we learn from your criticism? The implications are critical. Zachry (2009) argues that rhetorical criticism must be more than just identifying and labeling the parts in an artifact. The criticism needs to provide an interpretation of what the identified/label parts mean.

Do not worry if you have the "correct" interpretation in your criticism. Artifacts can have many meanings, and different critics may see different meanings. Your obligation is to present strong arguments, which support your critical insights. The strength of an argument is critical in rhetorical criticism. Since we do not have objective standards of analysis in rhetorical criticism, your arguments and how well you support your arguments are key.

Summary

This chapter was a how-to guide to rhetorical criticism. Rhetorical criticism is a more critical/cultural method, but it can also lean toward the interpretive or social scientific depending on the researcher's approach. It is a multi-faceted method. Hopefully after reading the chapter, and the accompanying student paper, you will feel comfortable enough to try your own rhetorical criticism. The next chapter, Chapter 20, is a how-to guide to critical/cultural methods.

Key Steps & Questions to Consider

1. There are numerous definitions of rhetoric.
2. Rhetorical criticism is conducting an analysis of a rhetorical "act."
3. What is the difference between being a popular critic and a rhetorical critic?
4. The communication critics' "critique" is called an artifact.
5. No particular theory is "best" for analyzing an artifact.
6. Neo-Aristotelian focuses on the five canons of rhetoric and is primarily used for critiquing speeches.
7. Logos critiques the speaker's reasoning, arguments, and use of evidence.
8. Ethos evaluates the speaker's credibility and character, especially as related to the topic, occasion, and audience for the speech.
9. Pathos explores the speaker's attempts to emotionally connect with the audience.
10. A critic using the metaphor approach analyzes artifact(s) by identifying metaphor(s) used by the artifact.
11. Fantasy theme analysis is an effective method if your interest is how communication (evident in your selected artifact) can shape perceptions of reality.

Activities

1. *Selecting artifacts.* Review the list of possible artifacts provided in the chapter and think about all the forms of communication you are inundated by each day. Take just one day and make your own list of possible artifacts for rhetorical criticism. Pay attention to the music you listen to, the TV shows you watch, the news you read, and the billboards, signs, posters, fliers you see around you. Bring your list of artifacts to class and see who can make the strongest argument for why an artifact is worthy of criticism.
2. *Selecting a rhetorical approach.* Using one of your artifacts from Activity 1 (or the gay marriage artifacts), discuss how each of the three approaches we reviewed in the chapter may provide diverse critical insights.
3. *A rhetoric dictionary.* Starting with the list of terms in Key Questions, develop (individually or as a class) your own dictionary of terms in rhetoric. Continue to build on the dictionary as your study of rhetoric and rhetorical criticism progresses.

Discussion Questions

1. What other artifacts could we collect and critique as part of the Minnesota marriage amendment?
2. How does Activity 2 illustrate how each approach illuminates different persuasive strategies? Remember, no one rhetorical approach is best nor is any critique the "correct answer." Each approach provides different viewpoints of the artifact(s).

Key Terms

Artifact	Kenneth Burke Society	Rhetorical critic
Artistic proofs	Logos	Rhetorical criticism
Ethos	Metaphor	Symbols
Fantasy theme analysis	Neo-Aristotelian	Symbolic convergence
Five canons of rhetoric	Pathos	theory
Inartistic proofs	Popular critic	Trivium
Invention	Rhetoric	

Undergraduate Student Paper

Secondhand smoke and the five canons of rhetoric

Steven Arning

Smoking cigarettes has been determined through scientific research to be harmful to a person's health. Smoking has since been determined as being the number one cause of preventable death in the United States. Organizations now provide information about smoking and help in people's efforts to quit smoking. One television advertisement put on the air by the American Cancer Society, and which concerns the risks associated with secondhand smoke, will be discussed. Rhetorical criticism will be provided on the advertisement using the "five canons" rhetorical criticism method. The advertisement's invention, organization, style, delivery, and memory will be analyzed. The use of pathos in this advertisement is the most relevant aspect and its effectiveness will also be explored.

A brief summary of the advertisement is a crucial part in understanding the criticism on the ad. The TV spot opens with a white screen and the words, "smoking sections in restaurants . . . " in the center of the screen. There is a sound of people talking in the background; the sound is much like that of a restaurant. The screen then shows a man's face, probably in his early 30s, and he says with sarcasm, "A smoking section in a restaurant?" He then says, "that's like a peeing section in a pool." The ad then flashes to images of cigarettes burning on the edge of a dinner plate, and a man exhaling cigarette smoke. A fact is then displayed on the screen, "a half hour exposure to 2nd hand smoke dramatically increases a person's short term risk of a heart attack." The American Cancer Society's logo is displayed on the screen. The man then says "Hey it's your air."

The first aspect of the advertisement to be discussed is the invention of the commercial, or the

The student has a nice introduction. He leads us into the paper with a crisp attention getter, significance about the issue, and sets up the rhetorical approach—the five canons with a specific focus on pathos.

The student's description of the artifact is solid. His description provides both the text and effective visual descriptions so a reader can "see" what occurs in the TV ad. He can strengthen the section by explaining how the ad is significant and worthy of criticism. He might argue significance by listing the amount of money spent airing the ad, or responses from supporters, critics, and the general audience to the ad.

speaker's lines of arguments or ideas. The speaker makes a metaphor to describe a similar situation to a smoking section in a restaurant. The situation described in the metaphor is simple and one with which everyone, no matter what audience, is familiar. His message is simple, displaying the facts: "a half hour exposure to 2nd hand smoke dramatically increases a person's short term risk of a heart attack." And let people think about it for themselves. The message uses pathos extremely effectively and will be discussed in further detail later in this criticism. His use of inartistic proofs, such as facts, lies mainly in the one line about exposure to secondhand smoke, and the credibility lies in the organization that is backing the advertisement, the American Cancer Society. It is an organization that is largely recognizable and credible.

The organization of the advertisement was very effective. A metaphor was used to catch the attention of the audience, which for this particular commercial is just about anyone who goes to restaurants occasionally. They caught the audience's attention and then provided facts to back up the metaphor, a very effective order. The images of the burning cigarettes and the person exhaling smoke give the viewer time to take in the metaphor and begin to understand it before they are told the facts to support the claim. The commercial would not be as effective had it been in the opposite order. The audience may not have "tuned in" as early on had they not had that "attention grabbing" metaphor at the start of the commercial.

The style of the advertisement is definitely an aspect that adds to the feeling of the ad—fear of the facts. The whole ad is in black and white and there is no music, and the crackling sound of the burning cigarettes is amplified. It appears to be very serious from the start and it's clearly not going to provide "happy" news. There is simply a feeling of fear: the information you are hearing is going to scare you. The ad is blunt, and

The student reintroduced us to his chosen rhetorical approach. Notice how he plans to weave metaphor in with his use of the neo-Aristotelian criticism. Steven could use more description and explanation of both the neo-Aristotelian approach and metaphor to enhance his criticism. The section gets a little confusing since it starts with a focus on invention, but then shifts more to metaphor. He may have considered moving the sentences about the organization's credibility to the previous section when he describes the artifact. The credibility can help support significance for critiquing the ad.

The student's critique of the ad's organization relies extensively on metaphor. As he was developing his criticism he may have decided that metaphor may have been a stronger approach than using the five canons of rhetoric.

simply puts out the facts. There are little distractions throughout the 30 seconds of video. The words are clearly displayed on blank backgrounds, which forces people to read the facts with nothing else to look at.

The delivery of the information is very effective in its "down to earth" style. The speaker in the advertisement speaks in a simple, everyday way that could never be seen as hard to understand. He uses no sophisticated words and speaks of metaphors anyone could relate to. He speaks in a sarcastic tone, as though the things he is saying are common sense. It gives off the feeling that he is casually telling you something he has realized, as most people find out new facts, hearing them by word of mouth from another friend or affiliation. The speaker also has a smirk of sorts on his face when he discusses the metaphor, again implying that having a smoking section in a restaurant is a ridiculous idea that should never have been implemented, and has been the wrong way of doing things for years. The fact that the typed words on the screen have ". . ." at the end of each line is also an effective way to keep the viewer anxious to hear what's coming next. They are again "tuned in" to hear the next line.

The memory for the advertisement is probably the most difficult part to understand. The speaker appears to have a basic knowledge of what second-hand smoke can do to a person. He knows slightly more than the average person because he is trying to explain a fact to people that not many know. There was obviously research performed by the American Cancer Society in order to provide true and accurate facts. The ad will stand out in viewers' minds in the future because of the new information they have learned, first, that even sitting in a restaurant can be harmful to a person's health and, second, the overall feel of the commercial will hopefully stand out in the audiences' minds. The overall feel of the advertisement ushers in the final topic, the use of pathos in the ad.

The use of pathos in this advertisement is the most dominant aspect of the advertisement. Pathos can be defined as "the quality or power, especially in literature or speech, of arousing feelings of pity, sorrow, etc." In this particular advertisement the feeling that is portrayed is one of fear, and anxiousness. Viewers are realizing that they have possibly been in danger the last time they were in a restaurant and they will potentially be placed back in that same danger the next time they go out to a restaurant or event. The fear is that they are helpless in a restaurant where they are slowly inhaling smoke with every breath. The way the ad is designed adds to the fear. The black and white look to the ad and the manner by which the speaker presents the information create a feeling that this is a serious deal, and not a joke. The image of the person exhaling the smoke is frightening because it portrays the idea that a person sitting in the non-smoking section of the restaurant is inhaling and is possibly unaware.

This is a very effective and educational advertisement for the American Cancer Society. The arguments are clearly displayed with the use of a metaphor as well as clearly stated facts to support the overall argument. The imagery is simple, yet effective, in providing fear-invoking scenes. Most Americans have a simple understanding of what smoking does to a person's body: if you smoke, you are slowly killing yourself. This commercial adds onto that general knowledge by describing a situation the average viewer has most likely been subjected to and describes the dangers associated with that situation.

Reference

American Cancer Society. (2011, May 10). *YouTube—Broadcast Yourself.* Retrieved from: www.youtube.com/watch?v= zJ0PUB2bhCU>.

The student identifies a central purpose for the American Cancer Society advertisement. The ad is more than informative. The ad is designed to influence viewers' attitudes about secondhand smoke, and maybe compel viewers to action. The student may find a tighter application for the critique by focusing on pathos and metaphor instead of all five canons. Finally, the student should have provided a source citation for the quotation defining pathos.

20 THE PROCESS OF CRITIQUE

James P. Dimock

Chapter Outline

- What is Critique?
- Marxism vs. Postmodernism
- Key Steps & Questions to Consider
- Activities
- Discussion Questions
- Key Terms
- Undergraduate Student Paper

What Will I Learn About Critical Theory in This Chapter?

In 1843, Marx (1978) observed that in his German homeland "everything is being forcibly repressed" (p. 12) and so it was necessary to engage in "a ruthless criticism of everything existing, ruthless in two senses: The criticism must not be afraid of its own conclusions, nor of conflict with the powers that be" (p. 13). The concept of "ruthless criticism" that defines critical theory and critical research is called **critique** (sometimes spelled "*Kritik*" to acknowledge the German origins and to separate critical theory research from other forms of criticism such as literary criticism or rhetorical criticism). In this chapter you will learn how to engage in critique from both a Marxist and a postmodern perspective.

What is a Critique?

Criticism must begin with something to criticize. This focus of our criticism, often called an **artifact** or a **text,** is something we are interested in evaluating. The "text" is the communication act or event we wish to study. Because we are communication scholars, we are interested in **symbolic** objects (the use of symbols to influence the way people understand and interact with the world).

A text may be narrowly defined (a single speech or communication situation) or broadly defined (the discourse of a given period or epoch). Typically, for a text to be an object of critique, it must have some boundaries—something that separates the text from the **context** (the objects that surround the text and are not part of it).

The process of identifying a text begins with a **description** of the text. If the text is well-known, the description may not be detailed. An unfamiliar text, however, requires the critic to depict the text in enough detail that readers can understand and appreciate it. The description is then typically followed by a **justification** for the criticism. The critic must explain why this particular text is suitable or appropriate for criticism. The importance and relevance of some texts are immediately obvious but other, lesser known or seemingly insignificant texts will require the critic to explain why this criticism should be undertaken.

Jim, Dan, and Kirstin published a critique of the movie *Brokeback Mountain* in 2013. The movie was fairly well known, received critical acclaim, was nominated for eight and won three Academy Awards (won for Best Director, Best Original Score, and Best Adapted Screenplay). They did not have to spend a lot of time describing the movie. However, just winning a stack of awards does not mean a movie (the text) is suitable for criticism. Jim, Dan, and Kirstin argued that the film had the capacity to influence perceptions of same-sex partners and same-sex marriage (an issue that has seen monumental shifting of opinions in recent years). Once the text has been described and the decision to critique it has been justified, we are ready to begin the actual critique.

In our everyday language we often think of criticism as being some kind of negative judgment about us or our work, but not all criticism is negative. Say, for example, I think Ridley Scott's film *Alien* is better than the sequel, *Aliens* directed by James Cameron. I am engaging in a basic form of criticism by comparing and contrasting two similar texts. My criticism of the films is **impressionistic** since it reflects my impressions or feelings about the two films—I like *Alien* better than *Aliens*. While I like both movies, the original appealed to me in ways the sequel did not. You may disagree because the first film lacked the fast-paced action sequences of Cameron's follow-up. Because we are both reporting our impressions about the films, your feelings are just as valid as my feelings. When we engage in impressionistic criticism, we are really saying much more about ourselves than we are about the object of our criticism. I may like the more cerebral horror sci-fi while you like action-packed shoot 'em ups. But in order to engage in critique at a scholarly level, we need to move beyond talking about our own, personal feelings. Our criticism must become **reflexive** and be based on some criteria or standard of criticism.

What the critic does next depends on how he or she identifies. A critic who associates with Marxist theories is more than likely engaging in **extrinsic** criticism, while postmodern critics engage in **intrinsic** criticism. Extrinsic criticism considers texts and artifacts in relation to some **normative** standard. The normative standards are most often trans-historical and trans-cultural principles by which a communication practice can be judged. So a Marxist critique, which holds that contemporary industrial practice is wrong because it steals the workers' *labor* and thereby *alienating* the working class, is applying standards that should exist in all times, in all places, and for all persons regardless of the historical or cultural context. All workers own their labor and to alienate them from their labor is, by definition, oppression.

Postmodern critics, skeptical of metanarratives upon which these norms are based, are much more likely to engage in intrinsic criticism. Every text, every system of discourse, has a logic and organization of its own. Intrinsic criticism confines the focus on the text itself. Recall that Hegel and Marx both maintained that within an object lies its negation, the internal contradiction that threatens the integrity of the text. By identifying these contradictions, dilemmas, and paradoxes, the postmodern critic destabilizes meanings and invites new interpretations of the text.

Marxism vs. Postmodernism: A Matter of Perspective

As we saw in Chapter 5 on the critical paradigm, Marxism and postmodernism share a commitment to ethical and political ends. Their differing perspectives lead them to approach research in different ways and to undertake research for different reasons. Marx did not believe genuine reform could come from academics and intellectuals. Only the proletariat, the workers themselves, could truly change the conditions of their lives and throw off oppression. In *The Communist Manifesto*, Marx and Engels (1964) wrote:

> The socialistic bourgeois want all the advantages of modern social conditions without the struggles and dangers necessarily resulting therefrom. They desire the existing state of society minus its revolutionary and disintegrating elements. They wish for a bourgeoisie without a proletariat. The bourgeoisie naturally conceives the world in which it is supreme to be the best. (p. 107)

Intellectuals and academics are members of the petite bourgeoisie and thus their interests, according to Marxists, will always be those of the bourgeoisie. Their aim is not to restructure the society so there is no longer class, and thus no longer class conflict, but to provide the working class with the material benefits of the modern, industrial world while maintaining themselves as a privileged elite.

A strictly Marxist approach to communication research, then, would emphasize **praxis,** or the practical application of theory to the material conditions around us. Because Marxism is a materialistic, historical, and scientific theory, Marxist researchers can avail themselves of any of the social scientific methodologies you have read about in this book. It is not the methods of research that matter as much as the motivation for the research and the ends to which research is used. If research works to strengthen working-class and proletarian unity, it is Marxist.

Other theorists see a more active role for academic and communication scholars. Chomsky (1987), one of the most outspoken critics of the capitalist system, argued that intellectuals do not have special privileges but responsibilities:

> Intellectuals are in a position to expose the lies of governments, to analyze actions according to their causes and motives and often hidden intentions. In the Western world at least they have the power that comes from political liberty, from access to information and freedom of expression. For a privileged minority, Western democracy provide leisure, the facilities, and the training to seek the truth lying hidden behind the veil of distortion and misrepresentation, ideology, and class interest through which the events of current history are presented to us.
>
> (p. 60)

Cloud (1994) argued along the same lines that the task of a cultural critique is "to unmask the shared illusions of a society as ideas promulgated by and serving the interests of the ruling class, or those who control the production and distribution of material goods" (p. 145). Ideology is a false consciousness, a screen that separates us from the reality of the human condition. The better we can see and understand the relations of production and understand the workings of power, the more able we are to resist them. Thus the role of the critic is not to lead the fight for change but to participate in it using his or her understanding of communication to support the struggle for change.

Like Marxist critics, postmodernists are concerned with power and praxis. Their concern differs from Marxists. The postmodernist critic has no specific vision of what society without oppression may look like or if one is even possible. Marxism attempts to construct a basis upon which a socialist society can be built. Postmodernism, on the other hand, is **deconstructionist** and seeks to deconstruct the systems and forms of oppression (Foucault, 2006).

In his work on "critical rhetoric," McKerrow (1989) offers one of the best explanations of what a critical theorist does. The critic has two tasks. The first is the critique of domination, or "demystifying the conditions of domination," and the critique of freedom or "a self-reflexive critique that turns back on itself even as it promotes a realignment in the forces of power that construct social relations" (McKerrow, 1989, p. 91). Critical communication scholars look at the practices of domination from a variety of perspectives while at the same time turning criticism back on itself, continually inviting more criticism rather than declaring the final judgment has been passed on a subject.

Summary

This final chapter in the textbook introduced you to how to conduct a critical-cultural critique. As you can see from the chapter, you can approach a critical/cultural critique in numerous ways. The key is to pick one that is a good fit for your research point of view or theoretical stance. We hope that after reading the chapter you will feel a little more prepared to carry out this type of study. On a final note, think back to the introduction and the story of Sir Edmund Hillary and remember "even the fearful can achieve." You have finished the textbook , which is one phase of your research methods journey. We wish you all the best in your future research and scholarly endeavors. Stephen and Dan look forward to seeing your work presented at conferences and published in the journals.

 ## Key Steps & Questions to Consider

1. Identify the artifact or text to be criticized.
2. Describe the text or artifact so the readers can get a full understanding of it.
3. Justify why the text is worthy of criticism.
4. Explain the purpose and what you hope to accomplish through the critique.
5. Determine if you are engaging in extrinsic criticism or an intrinsic criticism.

 ## Activities

1. Let's return to our activity from Chapter 5 on the critical paradigm. Pull out the activity notes from your backpack/notebook/computer/tablet from the Chapter 5 activity. The notes may help streamline this activity.
2. Divide everyone into groups. Each group is given a different issue. The issues are slavery, prohibition, women's suffrage, same-sex marriage, and child sex abuse by priests. Each group will prepare a brief presentation using the process of critique described in this chapter.

 ## Discussion Questions

1. What similarities and differences do you see between rhetorical criticism (Chapter 19) and the critical process (Chapter 20)?

2. How will your research claims about truth and reality be different between an experimental study and a critical/cultural study?
3. Think about what is happening in current politics, sports, or the arts. What events may be relevant for critique?

Key Terms

Artifact	Extrinsic	Praxis
Context	Impressionistic	Reflexive
Critique	Intrinsic	Symbolic
Deconstructionist	Justification	Text
Description	Normative	

Undergraduate Student Paper

The ethics of Pimpthisbum.com

Suzanne Lumberg White

"When Sean Dolan saw signs being carried by homeless people," he didn't see an economic crisis. According to Sabo (2009), "[H]e saw an opportunity" (para. 1). Sean and his father, Kevin, had approached a homeless man named Tim Edwards with a proposition. Exchange his usual "will work for food" sign with one reading "Pimpthisbum.com." For his efforts, the Dolans would then pay him $100 a day.

So a website dedicated to helping the homeless was born. Visitors to the website can buy him anything from a cheeseburger to laser hair removal to a college education. Edwards joked to CBS (2009) that he is "the world's first online bum" (para. 10). But, as *Cullers* (2009) has pointed out, "some homeless advocates are upset over the word 'pimp' and are alleging that Tim is being exploited" (para. 1). The Dolans' website has gotten the attention they wanted. Attention for their advertising firm. They have made the front pages of newspapers all over the world and appeared on nearly every single major news network. The Dolans have achieved their ultimate goal of proving that they can sell anything. So if Pimpthisbum.com is able to raise money to help the homeless, isn't a little bit of exploitation okay? While some have argued that Pimpthisbum raises our awareness of the homeless and puts a needed face on the issue, I argue, based on the critical ethical theory of German philosopher Jürgen Habermas, that the Dolans have engaged in unethical communication.

Habermas's philosophy of ethical communication is, to quote Burleson and Kline (1979), "formidable," "obscure," "dense and technical" but Habermas is also one of the most important social philosophers of the 20th century and one of the most important of the critical theorists. Because his work concerns both communication and ethics, his framework is appropriate to use in critiquing Pimpthisbum.com.

In the first two paragraphs, Suzanne does two things. First, she gives her readers a description of the text she has selected for criticism. Her description provides readers with enough information about the text to be able to understand what is going on without getting bogged down in unnecessary details. Second, Suzanne justifies the text as an object of criticism. On one hand, the website is trying to do something about the problem of homelessness but Suzanne questions the ethics of this sort of appeal.

For Habermas, communication is unethical when it undermines what he called the lifeworld and, according to Foss, Foss, and Trapp (2001), the lifeworld entails communicative action. Habermas asserted that when communicative action is blocked, unethical impersonal systems take over. Marmura (2008) points out that while all complex societies require some level of systems, "social inequality and ultimately . . . social pathology originate" when those systems become "unmoored from the interests and values of the communities" (p. 4). In order to prevent the colonization of the lifeworld by systems, we need to engage in communicative rationality that requires the use of constatives, regulatives, and avowals.

First, ethical communicative action requires the use of regulatives. Regulative utterances negotiate the relationship between the people. So when I ask you if you're ready for me to speak, it says something about what I think of the relationship between us. These regulatives result in mutual understanding. Unethical communication systematizes the relationship, defining it through noncommunicative means like power differences and structures.

Second, ethical communication must involve avowals. Avowals are speech acts relative to our feelings, affections, and intentions. Foss, Foss, and Trapp (2001) explain that avowals don't refer to the world around us or to our relationships with others but reflect our internal states, and the validity of an avowal is determined by "the sincerity of the stated intentions" (p. 259). Unethical communication, then, involves the use of dishonest or insincere avowals.

Finally Habermas (1979) claimed that in order to present an ethical message, the author must present constatives. Habermas says in *Communication and the Evolution of Society* that constatives "imply an unmistakeable validity claim, a truth claim" (as cited in Foss, Foss, & Trapp, 2001, p. 257). For instance, this round has five people. These statements that can be validated protect the world from manipulative systems. Unethical communication occurs when regulatives are inappropriate, when avowals are insincere, and constatives are not valid.

Now that we understand Habermas's criteria for ethical action we can now apply those criteria to Pimpthisbum.com.

First, unethical messages, involve inappropriate regulatives, or a distorted understanding of relationships. It is important to bear in mind the purposes of the relationship between Edwards and the Dolans. It is about raising the profile of the Dolans' marketing firm. By making Tim popular, they say, "we can make anything popular." And Pimpthisbum is riddled with links to major media outlets that have covered the story. But what this does is to commodify Edwards, to turn him into an object to be marketed and sold for the Dolans' profit. Thus the relationship between them is inappropriate and Pimpthisbum is unethical according to this criterion.

Second, a rhetor must use sincere avowals. In public statements, Sean and Kevin Dolan and Ascendgence Tactical Online Marketing repeatedly depict Pimpthisbum as a way to help the homeless. For example, Edwards has said, "The whole idea of this project is to get people off the street" (as cited in CBS, 2009, p. 10). But we already know that isn't true. The whole idea is to raise the public profile of the Dolans and their advertising firm, Ascendgence. More importantly, it undermines our ability to treat Edwards's avowals as valid. Edwards is being paid by the Dolans. We simply cannot assume that he is any more sincere than a $100 a day buys. If we can't accept Tim's avowals at face value, then we have to conclude that Pimpthisbum is unethical according to yet another of Habermas's criteria.

Finally, in order to present an ethical message, the author must first present constatives—or asserted truth. In Habermas's theory of ethics, constatives are the ultimate check on systemic colonization of the lifeworld because they can be verified. We can hold statements up to reality and see if they line up. Mamura points out that unchecked "bureaucratic standards of rationality or the profit orientation of commercial enterprise" make the "ability to question, or even recognize the rules which govern [our] actions [become] greatly diminished." By putting an altruistic mask on an entirely commercial motive, the Dolans violate the third and final of Habermas's criteria.

Now that we have examined how Pimpthisbum.com fails to fulfill Habermas's model, we must return to our research question: So if Pimpthisbum.com is able to bring attention to the problem and raise money to help the homeless, isn't a little bit of exploitation okay? And to answer this question we will look to two implications, first because Edwards's voice is constrained by commercial interests and second because Edwards actually obscures the face of the homeless.

First, Edwards's ability to function as voice for the homeless is distorted by commercial interests. Habermas's Edwards is repeatedly described as funny, upbeat, educated, and does not blame others for being homeless. This explanation of homelessness is great . . . if you are ultimately not interested in dealing with the problem of homelessness. A report available at the website for the National Coalition for the Homeless (2009) demonstrates a clear link between rising homelessness and the foreclosure crisis. Certainly, some people are homeless because they made bad choices . . . many are victims of mental illness, domestic violence, lack of affordable housing and other factors beyond their control. If the faces of tragic circumstances don't sell products, this helpful exploitation will not even presented.

Finally, positioning Edwards as 'the face' of homelessness obscures important dimensions of the problem. The Dolans have made a "homeless man the symbol of all homelessness" (Daily Write). But Edwards isn't a poster-child for homelessness the way Rosa Parks came to symbolize segregation or Matthew Shepard became a face for victims of hate crimes. The difference is rather clear: 'the symbol of homelessness' in America should look like

Suzanne applies the extrinsic standards in her evaluation putting her scholarship at the Marxist end of the critical spectrum. Second, she uses actual statistics about homelessness in the United States to point out the conflict between the image of homelessness created by the Dolans and the reality of homelessness. The Dolans' discourse contributes to a false consciousness that Suzanne's critique attempts to correct.

the homelessness in America. According to Pimp-thisbum's (n.d.) website, they say "but we human-ized homelessness by focusing on a particular individual" (para. 4). This particular homeless individual, however, looks and sounds a lot more like the demographic the Dolans are interested in than the typical homeless person. According to the National Coalition for the Homeless (2007), 51 percent of the homeless population are, like Tim Edwards, male. But the homeless are far less likely to be white, like Edwards. The fastest growing segment of the homeless population is families with children. Edwards, an educated and articulate white man, is not the face of homelessness and doesn't give the homeless a voice. Instead his image obscures the voices of millions of people. It isn't just that the Dolans are capitalists. It is that they let their interest in system of profit obscure important issues and questions about an important problem that is getting worse.

In the conclusion we get a clear indication of praxis, that Suzanne's motives are not just to critique Pimpthisbum. com but to confront the problem of homelessness.

Although the Dolans seemed to make a difference, their help has proven to be unethical, and poten-tially harmful to our future. The goal of my paper is to not just engage in a criticism of communi-cation but to be a critical communicator just as Habermas engaged in communicative action. Buying someone a virtual cheeseburger does not ethically confront the issue of the homeless. To put it simply, it is not about pimping but rather caring and communicating . . . and that is something we can all do.

References

Burleson, B. R., & Kline, S. L. (1979). Habermas' theory of communication: A critical explication. *The Quarterly Journal of Speech, 65,* 412–428.

CBS. (2009, March 9). Is it right to pimp this bum? Retrieved from: cbsnews.com.

Cullers, R. (2009, March 27). Pimp this bum: Salvation or exploitation. *Adweek*. Retrieved from: www.adweek.com/adfreak/pimp-bum-salvation-or-exploitation-14427.

Foss, S. K., Foss, K. A., & Trapp, R. (2001) *Readings in contemporary rhetoric.* Long Grove, IL: Waveland Press.

Habermas, J. (1979). *Communication and the evolution of society* (T. McCarthy, Trans.). Boston, MA: Beacon Press.

Marmura, S. (2008). Surveillance, mass culture and the subject: A systems/lifeworld approach. *Democratic Communiqué, 22*(2), 1–18.

National Coalition for the Homeless. (2007). Who is homeless? Retrieved from: www.nationalhomeless.org/publications/facts/Whois.pdf.

National Coalition for the Homeless. (2009). *Foreclosure to homelessness 2009: The forgotten victims of the subprime crisis.* Retrieved from: www.nationalhomeless.org/advocacy/ForeclosuretoHomelessness0609.pdf.

Pimp This Bum. (n.d.). About the PTB project. Retrieved from: pimpthisbum.com.

Sabo, T. (2009, March 26). PimpThisBum.com employs irony on homeless man's behalf. Retrieved from: CNN.com.

REFERENCES

Agresti, A., & Finlay, B. (2009). *Statistical methods for the social sciences* (4th ed.). Upper Saddle River, NJ: Prentice Hall.

Ajzen, I. (1985). From intentions to actions: A theory of planned behavior. In J. Kuhland & J. Beckman (Eds.). *Action-control: From cognitions to behavior* (pp. 11–39). Heidelberg, Germany: Springer.

Althusser, L. (1989). Ideology and ideological state apparatuses (B. Brewster, Trans.). In D. Latimer (Ed.). *Contemporary critical theory* (pp. 60–102). San Diego, CA: Harcourt Brace Jovanovich.

Altman, I., & Taylor, D. A. (1973). *Social penetration: The development of interpersonal relationships.* New York, NY: Holt, Rinehart & Winston.

Alvesson, M., & Skoldberg, K. (2000). *Reflexive methodology: New vistas for qualitative research.* London, UK: Sage.

Ang, I. (1990). Culture and communication: Towards an ethnographic critique of media and consumption in the transnational media system. *European Journal of Communication, 5,* 239–260.

Angrosino, M. V. (1992). Metaphors of stigma: How deinstitutionalized mentally retarded adults see themselves. *Journal of Contemporary Ethnography, 21,* 171–199.

Angrosino, M. V. (1997). The ethnography of mental retardation: An applied perspective. *Journal of Contemporary Ethnography, 26,* 98–109.

Angrosino, M. V. (1998). *Opportunity house: Ethnographic stories of mental retardation.* Walnut Creek, CA: AltaMira.

Aristotle. (1991). *On rhetoric: A theory of civic discourse* (2nd ed.) (G. A. Kennedy, Trans.). New York, NY: Oxford University Press.

Arnett, E. C., Harden Fritz, J. M., & Bell, L. M. (2009). *Communication ethics literacy.* Los Angeles, CA: Sage.

Ashkenas, J., Ericson, M., Parlapiano, A., & Willis, D. (2012). The 2012 money race: Compare the candidates. *NYTimes.com.* Retrieved from: http://elections.nytimes.com/2012/campaign-finance.

Audi, R. (Ed.). (1999). *Cambridge dictionary of philosophy* (2nd ed.). New York, NY: Cambridge University Press.

Babbie, E. (1990). *The practice of social research* (5th ed.). Belmont, CA: Wadsworth.

Babbie, E. (2002). *The basics of social research* (2nd ed.). London, UK: Wadsworth.

Bakker, T. P., & de. Vresse., C. H. (2011). Good news for the future? Young people, Internet use, and political participation. *Communication Research, 38,* 451–470.

Basso, K. (1970). "To give up on words": Silence in western Apache culture. *Southwestern Journal of Anthropology, 26,* 213–230.

Baynard, P., & Flanagan, C. (2005). *Ethical issues and guidelines in psychology.* London, UK: Routledge.

Beckie, T. (1989). A supportive-educative telephone program: Impact on knowledge and anxiety after coronary artery bypass graft surgery. *Heart Lung, 18*(1), 46–55.

Benoit, W. L. (1999). *Seeing spots: A functional analysis of Presidential advertisements, 1952–1996.* Westport, CT: Praeger.

Benoit, W. L., & Glantz, M. (2012). A functional analysis of 2008 general election presidential TV spots. *Speaker & Gavel, 49,* 1–19.

Berelson, B. (1952). *Content analysis in communication research.* New York, NY: The Free Press.

Berg, B. L. (1998). *Qualitative research methods for the social sciences* (3rd ed.). Boston, MA: Allyn & Bacon.

Berg, B. L. (2009). *Qualitative research methods for the social sciences* (7th ed.). Boston, MA: Allyn & Bacon.

Berger, A. (1991). *Media research techniques.* Newbury Park, CA: Sage.

Berlin, I. (1963). *Karl Marx: His life and environment.* New York, NY: Time, Inc.

Bernard, R. H. (1999). *Social research methods: Qualitative and quantitative approaches.* Thousand Oaks, CA: Sage.

Bisel, R. S., & Arterburn, E. N. (2012). Making sense of organizational members' silence: A sensemaking-resource model. *Communication Research Reports, 29,* 217–226.

Blumer, H. (1969). *Symbolic interactionism: Perspective and method.* Englewood Cliffs, NJ: Prentice Hall.

Bormann, E. G. (1972). Fantasy and rhetorical vision: The rhetorical criticism of social reality. *Quarterly Journal of Speech, 58,* 396–407.

Bourner, T. (1996). The research process: Four steps to success. In T. Greenfield (Ed.). *Research methods: Guidance for postgraduates* (pp. 7–11). London, UK: Arnold.

boyd, d. m., & Ellison, N. B. (2007). Social network sites: Definition, history, and scholarship. *Journal of Computer-Mediated Communication, 13,* 210–230. doi:10.1111/j.1083-;6101.2007.00393.x.

Briggs, C. L. (1986). *Learning how to ask: A sociolinguistic appraisal of the role of the interview in social science research.* Cambridge, MA: Cambridge University Press.

Brock, B. L., Scott, R. L., & Chesebro, J. W. (1990). *Methods of rhetorical criticism: A twentieth-century perspective* (3rd ed.). Detroit, MI: Wayne State University Press.

Bruner, J. (1993). The autobiographical process. In R. Folkenfilk (Ed.). *The culture of autobiography: Constructions of self representations* (pp. 38–56). Stanford, CA: Stanford University Press.

Burdenski, T. (2000). Evaluating univariate, bivariate, and multivariate normality using graphical and statistical procedures. *Multiple Linear Regression Viewpoints, 26*(2), 15–28.

Cagle, A., Cox, L., Luoma, K., & Zaphiris, A. (2011). Content analysis of the portrayal of Muslims in American media. *Human Communication, 14,* 1–16.

Cahnman, W. J., Maier, J. B., Tarr, Z., & Marcus, J. T. (Eds.). (1995). *Weber and Toennies: Comparative sociology in historical perspective.* Piscataway, NJ: Transaction Publishers.

ai, D. A., Wilson, S. R., & Drake, L. E. (2000). Culture in the context of intercultural negotiation: Individualism-collectivism and paths to integrative agreements. *Human Communication Research, 26,* 591–617.

Cameron, D. (2001). *Working with spoken discourse.* London, UK: Sage.

Campbell, D. T., & Stanley, J. C. (1963). *Experimental and quasi-experimental designs for research.* Chicago, IL: Rand McNally.

Carbaugh, D. (1988). *Talking American: Cultural discourses on Donahue.* Norwood, NJ: Ablex.

Carbaugh, D. (1995). "Are Americans really superficial?": Notes on Finnish and American cultures in linguistic action. In L. Salo-Lee (Ed.). *Kieli & kulttuuri oppimisessa ja opettamisessa* [Language & culture in learning and teaching] (pp. 53–60). Jyväskylä, Finland: University of Jyväskylä.

Carbaugh, D. (2005). *Cultures in conversation.* Mahwah, NJ: Lawrence Erlbaum Associates.

Carey, M. A. (1994). The group effect in focus groups: Planning, implementing and interpreting focus group research. In J. Morse (Ed.). *Critical issues in qualitative research methods* (pp. 225–241). Thousand Oaks, CA: Sage.

Cartwright, D., & Zander, A. (1968). *Group dynamics: Research and theory.* New York, NY: Harper & Row.

Cathcart, R. S. (1991). *Post-communication: Rhetorical analysis and evaluation.* Indianapolis, IN: Bobbs-Merrill.

Cattell, J. M. (1890). Mental tests and measurements. *Mind, 15,* 373–381.

Chang, C. (2012). Ambivalent attitudes in a communication process: An integrated model. *Human Communication Research, 38,* 332–359.

Charmaz, K. (2006). *Constructing grounded theory: A practical guide through qualitative analysis.* Thousand Oaks, CA: Sage.

Chen, G. M. (2011). Tweet this: A uses and gratifications perspective on how active Twitter use gratifies a need to connect with others. *Computers in Human Behavior, 27,* 755–762. doi:10.1016/j.chb.2010.10.023.

Chomsky, N. (1987). The responsibility of intellectuals. In J. Peck (Ed.). *The Chomsky reader* (pp. 59–82). New York, NY: Pantheon Press.

Christians, C. G. (2000). Ethics and politics in qualitative research. In N. K. Denzin & Y. S. Lincoln (Eds.). *Handbook of qualitative research* (2nd ed. pp. 133–155). Thousand Oaks, CA: Sage.

Cicero (1949). *Cicero: On invention. The best kind of orator. Topics* (H. M. Hubbell, Trans.). Cambridge, MA: Loeb Classical Library, Harvard University Press.

Cloud, D. (1994). The materiality of discourse as oxymoron: A challenge to critical rhetoric. *Western Journal of Communication, 58,* 141–163.

Cole, F. L. (1988). Content analysis: Concepts, methods and applications. *Nurse Researcher, 4,* 5–16.

Collier, M. J. (1998). Researching cultural identity: Reconciling interpretive and post-colonial perspectives. In D. V. Tanno & A. Gonzales (Eds.). *International and intercultural annual: Vol. 21. Communication and identity across cultures* (pp. 121–147). Thousand Oaks, CA: Sage.

Collier, M. J. (2005). Theorizing cultural identifications: Critical updates and continuing evolution. In W. B. Gudykunst (Ed.). *Theorizing about intercultural communication* (pp. 235–256). Thousand Oaks, CA: Sage.

Collier, M. J., & Thomas, M. (1988). Cultural identity. In Y. Y. Kim & W. B. Gudykunst (Eds.). *Theories in intercultural communication* (pp. 99–120). Newbury Park, CA: Sage.

Condit, C. M. (1990). The birth of understanding: Chaste science and the harlots of the arts. *Communication Monographs, 57,* 323–327.

Conquergood, D. (1991). Rethinking ethnography: Towards a critical cultural politics. *Communication Monographs, 58,* 179–194.

Conquergood, S. (1992). Ethnography, rhetoric, and performance. *Quarterly Journal of Speech, 78,* 80–97. doi:10.1080/00335639209383982.

Cook, T. D., & Campbell, D. T. (1979*). Quasi-experimentation: Design and analysis issues for field settings.* Chicago, IL: Rand McNally.

Couser, G. T. (1997). *Recovering bodies: Illness, disability, and life writing.* Madison, WI: University of Wisconsin Press.

Craig, E., & Wright, K. B. (2012). Computer-mediated relational development and maintenance on Facebook. *Communication Research Reports, 29,* 119–129.

Craig, T., & Tracy, K. (1995). Grounded practical theory: The case of intellectual discussion. *Communication Theory, 5,* 248–272.

Creswell, J. W. (1998). *Qualitative inquiry and research design: Choosing among five traditions.* Thousand Oaks, CA: Sage.

Creswell, J. W. (2009). *Research design: Qualitative, quantitative, and mixed methods approaches* (3rd ed.). Thousand Oaks, CA: Sage.

Croucher, S. M. (2003). A threatened dragon: An analysis of the perceptions of Chinese shopkeepers in Montréal's *Quartier Chinois* toward *La Loi* 101, a linguistic law mandating the supremacy of the French language in Québec. Unpublished thesis. Mankato, MN.

Croucher, S. M. (2005). Cultural adaptation and the situation of French immigrants: A case study analysis of French immigration and cultural adaptation. *International Journal of Communication, 15,* 147–164.

Croucher, S. M. (2006). The impact of external pressures on an ethnic community: The case of Montréal's Quartier Chinois and Muslim-French immigrants. *Journal of Intercultural Communication Research, 35,* 235–251.

Croucher, S. M. (2008). *Looking beyond the hijab.* Cresskill, NJ: Hampton Press.

Croucher, S. M. (2008a). French-Muslims and the hijab: An analysis of identity and the Islamic veil in France. *Journal of Intercultural Communication Research, 37,* 199–213. doi: 10.1080/17475750903135408.

Croucher, S. M. (2008b). What does it mean to be Québécois for the Chinese community in Montréal? An analysis of Montréal's *Quartier Chinois* and shopkeepers' sense of self. *Chinese Journal of Communication, 1,* 213–223.

Croucher, S. M. (2009). A mixed methods analysis of French-Muslims' perceptions of *La Loi* 2004–228. *Journal of International and Intercultural Communication, 2,* 1–15.

Croucher, S. M. (2009a). How limiting linguistic freedoms influences the cultural adaptation process: An analysis of the French-Muslim population. *Communication Quarterly, 57,* 302–318. doi: 10.1080/01463370903109929.

Croucher, S. M. (2011). Muslim and Christian conflict styles in Western Europe. *International Journal of Conflict Management, 22,* 60–74.

Croucher, S. M., & Cronn-Mills, D. (2011). *Religious misperceptions: The case of Muslims and Christians in France and Britain.* New York, NY: Hampton Press.

Croucher, S. M., Homsey, D., Guarino, L., Bohlin, B., Trumpetto, J., Izzo, A., Huy, A., & Sykes, T. (2012). Jealousy in four nations: A cross-cultural analysis. *Communication Research Reports, 29,* 353–360.

Croucher, S. M., Kassing, J. W., & Diers-Lawson, A. (2013). Accuracy, coherence and discrepancy in self and other reports: Moving toward an interactive perspective of organizational dissent. *Management Communication Quarterly, 27*(3), 425–442.

Croucher, S. M., Oommen, D., & Steele, E. L. (2009). An examination of media usage among French-Muslims. *Journal of Intercultural Communication Research, 38,* 41–57. doi: 10.1080/17475750903478113.

Cummings, B. (2004, November 28). A tree worthy of Rockefeller Center. *NYTimes. com.* Retrieved from: www.nytimes.com/2004/11/28/nyregion/28homefront.html.

Cupach, W. R., & Imahori, T. (1993). Identity management theory. In R. L. Wiseman & J. Koester (Eds.). *Intercultural communication competence* (pp. 112–131). Newbury Park, CA: Sage.

Curran, P. J., West, S. G., & Finch, J. F. (1996). The robustness of test statistics to nonnormality and specification error in confirmatory factor analysis. *Psychological Methods, 1*(1), 16–29.

D'Amato, P. (2012). The use and abuse of Gramsci's prison notebooks [Audio File]. Retrieved from: wearemany.org.

Denzin, N. K. (1989). *Interpretive biography.* Newbury Park, CA: Sage.

Denzin, N. K., & Lincoln, Y. S. (2003). Introduction: The discipline and practice of qualitative research. In *Collecting and interpreting qualitative methods* (2nd ed., pp. 1–46). Thousand Oaks, CA: Sage.

Dimock, J. P., Cronn-Mills, D., & Cronn-Mills, K. (2013). Climbing *Brokeback Mountain:* A wilderness-civilization dialectic reading. *Relevant Rhetoric: A Journal of Rhetorical Studies, 4,* 1–21. Retrieved from: http://relevantrhetoric.com/wp-content/uploads/BrokebackMountain.pdf.

Dollard, J., & Mowrer, O. H. (1947). A method of measuring tension in written documents. *Journal of Abnormal and Social Psychology, 42,* 3–32.

Dover, E. D. (2006). *Images, issues, and attacks: Television advertising by incumbents and challengers in presidential elections.* Lanham, MD: Lexington Rowman & Littlefield.

Dovring, K. (1954). Quantitative semantics in 18th century Sweden. *Public Opinion Quarterly, 18,* 389–394.

Dubin, R. (1978). *Theory building* (Rev. ed.). New York, NY: The Free Press.

DuBois, W. E. B. (1899). *The Philadelphia Negro.* New York, NY: Benjamin Bloom.

Durkheim, E. (1938). *Rules of the sociological method* (S. Solovay & J. Mueller, Trans.). G. Catilin (Ed.). Chicago, IL: University of Chicago Press.

Durkheim, E. (1955/1962). *Division of labor.* In A. P. Hare, E. F. Borgatta, & R. F. Bales (Eds.). *Small groups: Studies in social interaction* (pp. 5–9). New York, NY: Alfred A. Knopf, Inc. [Original work published 1947.]

Eagleton, T. (2003). *After theory.* New York, NY: Penguin Books.

Edelsward, L. M. (1991). *Sauna as symbol: Society and culture in Finland.* New York, NY: Peter Lang.

Eguchi, S., & Starosta, W. (2012). Negotiating the model minority image: Performative aspects of college-educated Asian American professional men. *Qualitative Research Reports in Communication, 13,* 88–97.

Ellis, C. (2004). *The ethnographic I: A methodological novel about autoethnography.* Walnut Creek, CA: AltaMira Press.

Ellis, C., & Bochner, A. P. (2000). Autoethnography, personal narrative, reflexivity. In N. K. Denzin & Y. S. Lincoln (Eds.). *Handbook of qualitative research* (2nd ed., pp. 733–768). Thousand Oaks, CA: Sage.

Engstrom, C. L. (2012). "Yes . . . , but I was drunk": Alcohol references and the (re)production of masculinity on a college campus. *Communication Quarterly, 60,* 403–423.

Eskjoer, M. (2013). The regional dimension: How regional media systems condition global climate-change communication. *Journal of International and Intercultural Communication, 6,* 61–80.

Federal Election Commission. (2012). Presidential campaign finance. Retrieved from: www.fec.gov/disclosurep/pnational.do.

Field, A. (2009). *Discovering statistics using SPSS* (3rd ed.). Thousand Oaks, CA: Sage.

Fisher, R. J. (1993). Social desirability bias and the validity of indirect questioning. *Journal of Consumer Research, 20,* 303–315.

Fitch, K. L. (1994). Criteria for evidence in qualitative research. *Western Journal of Communication, 58,* 32–38.

Foss, S. K. (2004). *Rhetorical criticism: Exploration and practice* (3rd ed.). Long Grove, IL: Waveland Press.

Foucault, M. (1972). *The archaeology of knowledge & the discourse on language.* New York, NY: Pantheon Books.

Foucault, M. (2006). Truth and power. In *The Chomsky-Foucault debate on human nature* (pp. 140–171). New York, NY: The New Press.

Fox, R. (2010). Re-membering daddy: Autoethnographic reflections of my father and Alzheimer's disease. *Text and Performance Quarterly, 30,* 3–20.

Frentz, T. S., & Rushing, J. H. (2002). "Mother isn't quite herself today:" Myth and spectacle in The Matrix. *Critical Studies in Media Communication, 19,* 64–86.

Gadamer, H-G. (2003). *Truth and method* (2nd revised ed.). New York, NY: Continuum.

Ganster, D. C., Hennessey, H. W., & Luthans, F. (1983). Social desirability response effects: Three alternative models. *Academy of Management Journal, 26,* 321–331.

Garner, J. T., Kinsky, E. S., Duta, A. C., & Danker, J. (2012). Deviating from the script: A content analysis of organizational dissent as portrayed on primetime television. *Communication Quarterly, 60,* 608–624.

Gasper, P. (2010). Marxism and the dialectic [Audio File]. Retrieved from: wearemany. org.

Geertz, C. (1973). *The interpretation of cultures.* New York, NY: Basic Books.

Gerbner, G., Holsti, O. R., Krippendorff, K., Paisley, W. J., & Stone, P. J. (1969). *Analysis of communication content: Developments in scientific theories and computer techniques.* New York: John Wiley.

Giles, H., Bourhis, R. Y., & Taylor, D. M. (1977). Towards a theory of language in ethnic group relations. In H. Giles (Ed.). *Language, ethnicity and intergroup relations* (pp. 307–343). London, UK: Academic Press.

Giles, H., Linz, D., Bonilla, D., & Gomez, M. L. (2012). Police stops and interactions with Latino and White (Non-Latino) drivers: Extensive policing and communication accommodation. *Communication Monographs, 79,* 407–427.

Gill, A. (1994). *Rhetoric and human understanding.* Prospect Heights, IL: Waveland Press.

Glaser, B. G. (1978). *Theoretical sensitivity: Advances in the methodology of grounded theory.* Mill Valley, CA: Sociology Press.

Glaser, B. G. (1992). *Emergence vs. forcing: Basics of grounded theory analysis.* Mill Valley, CA: Sociology Press.

Glaser, B. G. (1998). *Doing grounded theory: Issues and discussions.* Mill Valley, CA: Sociology Press.

Glaser, B. G., & Strauss, A. L. (1967). *Discovery of grounded theory: Strategies for qualitative research.* Chicago, IL: Aldine.

Goffman, E. (1959). *The presentation of self in everyday life.* Garden City, NJ: Anchor Books.

Goffman, E. (1961). *Encounters: Two studies in the sociology of interaction.* Indianapolis, IN: Bobbs-Merrill.

Goodall, B. H. L. (2006). *A need to know: The clandestine history of a CIA family.* Walnut Creek, CA: Left Coast Press.

Hall, E. T. (1989). *Beyond culture.* New York, NY: Anchor Books.

Hamming, J. (2008). The feminine "nature" of masculine desire in the age of cinematic techno-transcendence. *Journal of Popular Film & Television, 35*(4), 146–153.

Hart, R. P., & Daughton, S. (2005). *Modern rhetorical criticism* (3rd ed.). Boston, MA: Pearson.

Harwood, T. G., & Garry, T. (2003). An overview of content analysis. *The Marketing Review, 3,* 479–498.

Herzog, H. (1940). Professor quiz: A gratification study. In P. F. Lazarfel (Ed.). *Radio and the printed page* (pp. 64–93). New York, NY: Duell, Sloan & Pearce.

Himelboim, I., McCreery, S., & Smith, M. (2013). Birds of a feather tweet together: Integrating network and content analyses to examine cross-ideology exposure on Twitter. *Journal of Computer-Mediated Communication, 18,* 40–60.

Hocking, J. E., Stacks, D. W., & McDermott, S. T. (2003). *Communication research* (3rd ed.). Boston, MA: Allyn & Bacon.

Hollander, B. A. (2010). Persistence in the perception of Barack Obama as a Muslim in the 2008 Presidential Campaign. *Journal of Media & Religion, 9,* 55–66.

Holman Jones, S. (2005). Autoethnography: Making the personal political. In N. K. Denzin & Y. S. Lincoln (Eds.). *Handbook of qualitative research* (pp. 763–791). Thousand Oaks, CA: Sage.

Husserl, E. (1970). *The crisis of European sciences and transcendental phenomenology: An introduction to phenomenological philosophy.* Evanston, IL: Northwestern University Press.

Hyman, H. H. (1991). *Taking society's measure: A personal history of survey research.* New York, NY: Russell Sage.

Hymes, D. (1962). Models of the interaction of language and social life. In J. J. Gumperz & D. Hymes (Eds.). *Directions in sociolinguistics* (pp. 35–71). New York, NY: Holt, Rinehart & Winston.

Hymes, D. (1962a). The ethnography of speaking. In T. Galdwin and W. Sturtevant (Eds.). *Anthropology and human behavior* (pp. 13–53). Washington, DC: Anthropological Society of Washington.

Hymes, D. (1964). Introduction: Toward ethnographies of communication. *American Anthropologist, 66*(1), 1–34.

Hymes, D. (1974). *Foundations in sociolinguistics: An ethnographic approach*. Philadelphia, PA: University of Pennsylvania Press.

Infante, D. A., & Rancer, A. S. (1982). A conceptualization and measure of argumentativeness. *Journal of Personality Assessment, 46*(1), 72–80.

Ingram, D., & Simon-Ingram, J. (1992). Introduction. In D. Ingram & J. Simon-Ingram (Eds.). *Critical theory: The essential readings* (pp. xix–xxxix). New York, NY: Paragon House.

Ivanov, B., Parker, K. A., & Pfau, M. (2012). The interaction effect of attitude base and multiple attacks on the effectiveness of inoculation. *Communication Research Reports, 29*, 1–11.

Ivory, J. D., & Kalyanaraman, S. (2009). Video games make people violent—Well, maybe not *that* game: Effects of content and person abstraction on perceptions of violent video games' effects and support of censorship. *Communication Reports, 22*, 1–12.

Kaid, L. L., & Ballotti, J. (1991). *Television advertising in presidential primaries and caucuses*. Atlanta, GA: Speech Communication Association.

Kampmeier, R. H. (1972). The Tuskegee study of untreated syphilis. *South Medical Journal, 65*, 1247–1251.

Kassing, J. W. (1998). Development and validation of the Organizational Dissent Scale. *Management Communication Quarterly, 12*, 183–229.

Kassing, J. W. (2000). Investigating the relationship between superior-subordinate relationship quality and employee dissent. *Communication Research Reports, 17*, 58–70.

Katriel, T. (1990). "Griping" as a verbal ritual in some Israel discourse. In D. Carbaugh (Ed.). *Cultural communication and intercultural contact* (pp. 99–114). Hillsdale, NJ: Lawrence Erlbaum Associates.

Katriel, T., & Philipsen, G. (1981). "What we need is communication": "Communication" as a cultural category in some American speech. *Communication Monographs, 48*, 302–317.

Katz, E., Blumler, J. G., & Gurevitch, M. (1974). Uses and gratifications research. *The Public Opinion Quarterly, 37*, 509–523.

Kim, Y. Y. (2001). *Becoming intercultural: An integrative theory of communication and cross-cultural adaptation*. Thousand Oaks, CA: Sage.

Klimmt, C., Schmid, H., Nosper, A., Hartmann, T., & Vorderer, P. (2006). How players manage moral concerns to make video game violence enjoyable. *Communications: The European Journal of Communication Research, 31*, 309–328.

Kluever Romo, L., & Donovan-Kicken, E. (2012). "Actually, I don't eat meat": A multiple-goals perspective of communication about vegetarianism. *Communication Studies, 63*, 405–420.

Kramer, E. M. (2003). Gaiatsu and the cultural judo. In E. M. Kramer (Ed.). *The emerging monoculture* (pp. 1–32). Westport, CT: Praeger.

Krippendorff, K. (1980). *Content analysis: An introduction to its methodology*. London: Sage.

Kvale, S. (1996). *InterViews: An introduction to qualitative research interviewing*. Thousand Oaks, CA: Sage.

Kvalem, I. L., Sundet, J. M., Rivo, K. I., Eilertsen, D. E., & Bakketeig, L. S. (1996). The effects of sex education on adolescents' use of condoms: Applying the Solomon Four-Group Design. *Health Education & Behavior, 23*, 34–47.

Kuypers, J. A. (2005). *The art of rhetorical criticism*. Boston, MA: Pearson.

Lachlan, K. A., & Maloney, E. K. (2008). Game player characteristics and interactive content: Exploring the role of personality and telepresence in video game violence. *Communication Quarterly, 56,* 284–302.

LaRossa, R. (2005). Grounded theory methods and qualitative family research. *Journal of Family and Marriage, 67,* 837–857.

Laswell, H. D., Leites, N., Fadner, R., Goldsen, J. M., Grey, A., Janis, I. L., Kaplan, A., Mintz, A., Pool, A. D., Yakobson, S., & Kaplan, D. (1965). *Language of politics: Studies in quantitative semantics.* Cambridge, MA: MIT Press.

Lehtonen, J., & Sajavaara, K. (1985). The silent Finn. In D. Tannen & M. Saville-Troike (Eds.). *Perspectives on silence* (pp. 193–201). Norwood, NJ: Ablex.

Leitner, G. (1983). Indian English: A critique of the ethnography of speaking. *International Journal of the Sociology of Language, 44,* 153–167.

Lengel, L. (2004). Performing in/outside Islam: Music and gendered cultural politics in the Middle East and North Africa. *Text and Performance Quarterly, 24,* 212–232.

Leonard, L. G., & Toller, P. (2012). Speaking ill of the dead: Anonymity and communication about suicide on MyDeathSpace.com. *Communication Studies, 63,* 387–404.

Leonard, S. P. (2013). Phenomenology of speech in a cold place: The Polar Eskimo language as "lived experience." *International Journal of Language Studies, 7,* 151–174.

Leppänen, J. (2013). The unspoken pressure of tradition: Representations of East Asian classical musicians in Western classical music. Unpublished master's thesis, University of Jyväskylä: Jyväskylä, Finland.

Levine, T. R., Bresnahan, M. J., Park, H. S., Knight Lapinski, M., Lee, T. S., & Lee, D. W. (2003). The (in)validity of self-construal scales revisited. *Human Communication Research, 29,* 291–308.

Lewis, W. E., & Tabor, R. R. (1966). *Guidelines: Rhetorical criticism.* Norwalk, CA: Cerritos College.

Lindlof, T. R. (1995). *Qualitative communication research methods.* Thousand Oaks, CA: Sage.

Lindlof, T. R., & Taylor, B. C. (2002). *Qualitative communication research methods* (2nd ed.). Thousand Oaks, CA: Sage.

List of English language metaphors. (2012, September 11). In *Wikipedia: The free encyclopedia.* Retrieved from: http://en.wikipedia.org/wiki/List_of_English_language_metaphors.

Littlejohn, S. W. (1999). *Theories of human communication* (6th ed.). Belmont, CA: Wadsworth.

Lofland, J., & Lofland, L. H. (1995). *Analyzing social settings* (3rd ed.). Belmont, CA: Wadsworth.

Looney, S. W. (1995). How to use tests for univarite normality to assess multivariate normality. *American Statistician, 49*(1), 64–70.

Lyotard, J. F. (1993). *The postmodern condition: A report on knowledge* (G. Bennington & B. Massumi, Trans.). Minneapolis, MN: University of Minnesota Press.

MacLean, T. L. (2008). Framing and organizational misconduct: A symbolic interactionist study. *Journal of Business Ethics, 78,* 3–16.

Macnamara, J. (2005). Media content analysis: Its uses, benefits and best practice methodology. *Asia Pacific Public Relations Journal, 6,* 1–34.

Maiorani, A. (2007). "Reloading" movies into commercial reality: A multimodal analysis of the Matrix trilogy's promotional posters. *Semiotica, 166,* 45–67.

Malinowski, B. (1922). *Argonauts of the western Pacific.* London: Routledge.

Marx, K. (1978). Capital, volume one. In R. C. Tucker (Ed.). *The Marx–Engels reader* (2nd ed.) (pp. 294–438). New York, NY: Norton.

Marx, K., & Engels, F. (1964). *The communist manifesto.* New York, NY: Washington Square Books.

Marx, K., & Engels, F. (1978). The German ideology. In R. C. Tucker (Ed.). *The Marx–Engels reader* (2nd ed.) (pp. 146–200). New York, NY: Norton.

Mason, E. J., & Bramble, W. J. (1989). *Understanding and conducting research: Applications in education and the behavioral sciences.* Boston, MA: McGraw Hill.

McCroskey, J. C. (1970). Measures of communication-bound anxiety. *Speech Monographs, 37*(4), 269–277.

McCroskey, J. C. (1982). *An introduction to rhetorical communication* (4th ed.). Englewood Cliffs, NJ: Prentice Hall.

McCroskey, J. C., Simpson, T. J., & Richmond, V. P. (1982). Biological sex and communication apprehension. *Communication Quarterly, 30,* 129–133.

McEwan, B., & Guerrero, L. K. (2012). Maintenance behavior and relationship quality as predictors of perceived availability of resources in newly formed college friendship networks. *Communication Studies, 63,* 421–440.

McGuire, W. J. (1964). Inducing resistance to persuasion. Some contemporary approaches. In L. Berkowitz (Ed.). *Advances in experimental social psychology* (Vol. 1, pp. 191–220). New York, NY: Academic.

McKemmish, S., Burstein, F., Manaszewicz, R., Fisher, J., & Evans, J. (2012). Inclusive research design. *Information, Communication & Society, 15,* 1106–1135.

McKerrow, R. (1989). Critical rhetoric: Theory and praxis. *Communication Monographs, 56,* 91–111.

McMahon, J., McAlaney, J., & Edgar, F. (2007). Binge drinking behavior, attitudes, and beliefs in a UK community sample: An analysis by gender, age, and deprivation. *Drugs, Education: Prevention and Policy, 14,* 289–303.

McQuail, D. (2005). McQuail's mass communication theory (5th ed.). Thousand Oaks, CA: Sage.

Mead, G. H. (1934). *Mind, self, and society.* Chicago, IL: University of Chicago Press.

Merrigan, G., & Huston, C. L. (2009). *Communication research methods.* New York, NY: Oxford University Press.

Miles, M. B., & Huberman, A. M. (1994). *Qualitative data analysis: An expanded sourcebook* (2nd ed.). Thousand Oaks, CA: Sage.

Milford, M. (2010). Neo-Christ: Jesus, the Matrix, and secondary allegory as a rhetorical form. *Southern Communication Journal, 75,* 17–34.

Mill, J. S. (1957). *Utilitarianism.* Indianapolis, IN: Bobbs-Merrill. [Original work published 1861.]

Miller, W. L. (1983). *The survey method in the social and political sciences: Achievements, failures, and prospects.* London, UK: Frances Pinter.

Minnesota Statutes. (2007). Chapter 517. Domestic relations. *Minnesota Legislature— Office of the Revisor of Statutes.* Retrieved from: www.revisor.leg.state.mn.us/bin/getpub.php?pubtype=STAT_CHAP&year=2007&section=517#stat.517.03.0.

Morgan, D. L. (1988). *Focus groups as qualitative research.* Newbury Park, CA: Sage.

Morrison, D. E. (1998). *The search for a method: Focus groups and the development of mass communication research.* Luton, Bedfordshire, UK: University of Luton Press.

Morse, J. M. (1998). Designing funded qualitative research. In N. Denzin & Y. Lincoln (Eds.). *Strategies of qualitative inquiry* (pp. 56–85). Thousand Oaks, CA: Sage.

Mulford, R. D. (1967). Experimentation on human beings. *Stanford Law Review, 20,* 99–117.

Nan, X., & Zhao, X. (2012). When does self-affirmation reduce negative responses to antismoking messages? *Communication Studies, 63,* 482–497.

Neuendorf, K. A. (2002). *The content analysis guidebook.* Thousand Oaks, CA: Sage.

Neuman, W. (1997). *Social research methods: Qualitative and quantitative approaches.* Needham Heights, MA: Allyn & Bacon.

Neuman, W. L. (2011). *Social research methods: Qualitative and quantitative approaches* (7th ed.). Boston, MA: Allyn & Bacon.

Newbold, C., Boyd-Barrett, O., & Van Den Bulck, H. (2002). *The media book.* London, UK: Arnold (Hodder Headline).

Nicotera, A. M. (1996). An assessment of the argumentativeness scale for social desirability bias. *Communication Reports, 9,* 23–25.

Noth, W. (1995). *Handbook of semiotics.* Bloomington, IN: Indiana University Press.

Oetzel, J. G. (1998). The effects of self-construals and ethnicity on self-reported conflict styles. *Communication Reports, 11,* 133–144.

Ojha, A. K., & Holmes, T. L. (2010). Don't tease me, I'm working: Examining humor in a Midwestern organization using ethnography of communication. *The Qualitative Report, 15,* 279–300.

Olson, L. N. (2004). The role of voice in the (Re)construction of a battered woman's identity: An autoethnography of one woman's experiences of abuse. *Women's Studies in Communication, 27,* 1–33.

Owen, W. F. (1984). Interpretive themes in relational communication. *Quarterly Journal of Speech, 70,* 274–287.

Palmgreen, P., Stephenson, M. T., Everett, M. W., Baseheart, J. R., & Francies, R. (2002). Perceived message sensation value (PMSV) and the dimensions and validation of a PMSV scale. *Health Communication, 14,* 403–428.

Patton, M. Q. (1990). *Qualitative evaluation and research methods.* London: Sage.

Patton, O. (2004). In the guise of civility: The complications of maintenance of inferential forms of sexism and racism in higher education. *Women's Studies in Communication, 27,* 60–87.

Pedhazur, E. J. (1997). *Multiple regression in behavioral research: Explanation and prediction* (3rd ed.). South Melbourne, Australia: Wadsworth.

Peterson, J. C., Anthony, M. G., & Thomas, R. J. (2012). "This right here is all about living": Communicating the "common sense" about home stability through CBPR and photovoice. *Journal of Applied Communication Research, 40,* 247–270.

Petty, R. E., & Cacioppo, J. T. (1983). Central and peripheral routes to persuasion: Application to advertising. In L. Percy & A. Woodside (Eds.). *Advertising and consumer psychology* (pp. 3–23). Lexington, MA: Heath.

Pfau, M. (1992). The potential of inoculation in promoting resistance to the effectiveness of comparative advertising messages. *Communication Quarterly, 40,* 26–44.

Pfau, M., & Burgoon, M. (1988). Inoculation in political campaign communication. *Human Communication Research, 15,* 91–111.

Pfau, M., Kenski, H. C., Nitz, M., & Sorenson, J. (1990). Efficacy of inoculation strategies in promotion resistance to political attack messages: Application to direct mail. *Communication Monographs, 57,* 25–43.

Philipsen, G. (1975). Speaking "like a man" in Teamsterville: Culture patterns of role enactment in an urban neighborhood. *Quarterly Journal of Speech, 61,* 13–22.

Philipsen, G. (1976). Places for speaking in Teamsterville. *Quarterly Journal of Speech, 62,* 15–25.

Philipsen, G. (1989). An ethnographic approach to communication studies. In B. Dervin, L. Grossberg, B. J. O'Keefe, & E. Wartella (Eds.). *Rethinking communication 2: Paradigm exemplars* (pp. 258–267). Newbury Park, CA: Sage.

Philipsen, G. (1992). *Speaking culturally: Explorations in social communication.* Albany, NY: State University of New York Press.

Philipsen, G. (1997). A theory of speech codes. In G. Philipsen & T. Albrecht (Eds.). *Handbook of international and intercultural communication* (pp. 51–67). Thousand Oaks, CA: Sage.

Phillips, D. C. (1987). *Philosophy, science and social inquiry: Contemporary methodological controversies in social science and related applied fields of research.* New York, NY: Pergamon.

Pierce, D. L. (2003). *Rhetorical criticism and theory in practice.* Boston, MA: McGraw Hill.

Pieterse, A. H., van Dulmen, A. M., Beemer, F. A., Ausems, M. G. E. M., & Bensing, J. M. (2006). Tailoring communication in cancer genetic counseling through individual video-supported feedback: A controlled pretest-posttest design. *Patient Education and Counseling, 60,* 326–335.

Podsakoff, P. M., & Organ, D. W. (1986). Self-reports in organizational research: Problems and prospects. *Journal of Management, 12,* 531–544.

Pojman, L. P. (2005). *How should we live? An introduction to ethics.* Belmont, CA: Wadsworth.

Popper, K. R. (1968). *The logic of scientific inquiry.* New York, NY: Harper & Row.

Popping, R. (1988). On agreement indices for nominal data. In W. E. Saris & I. N. Gallhofer (Eds.). *Sociometric research: Volume 1, data collection and scaling* (pp. 90–105). New York: St Martin's.

Pratt, S., & Weider, L. D. (1993). The case of saying a few words and talking for another among the Osage people: "Public speaking" as an object of ethnography. *Research on Language & Social Interaction, 26,* 353–408.

Raacke, J., & Bonds-Raacke, J. (2008). MySpace and Facebook: Applying the uses and gratifications theory to exploring friend-networking sites. *CyberPsychology & Behavior, 11,* 169–174.

Ragin, C. C. (1994). *Constructing social research.* Thousand Oaks, CA: Pine Forge Press.

Raimy, V. C. (1948). Self reference in counseling interviews. *Journal of Consulting Psychology, 12,* 153–163.

Rashotte, L. S. (2007). Developing your experiment. In M. Webster & J. Sell (Eds.). *Laboratory experiments in the social sciences* (pp. 225–242). Burlington, MA: Elsevier.

Reinard, J. C. (2010, June 15). *Traditional criticism checklist of starting questions.* Retrieved from: http://commfaculty.fullerton.edu/jreinard/bookweb/traditio.htm.

Rose, J., Mackey-Kallis, S., Shyles, L., Barry, K., Biagini, D., Hart, C., & Jack, L. (2012). Face it: The impact of gender on social media images. *Communication Quarterly, 60,* 588–607.

Ruggiero, T. E. (2000). Uses and gratifications theory in the 21st century. *Mass Communication & Society, 3,* 3–37.

Salisbury, J. (2009). *The Metalogicon: A twelfth-century defense of the verbal and logical arts of the trivium* (D. McGarry, Trans.). Philadelphia, PA: Paul Dry Books. [Original work published 1180.]

Sallinen-Kuparinen, A., Asikainen, S., Gerlander, M., Kukkola, A., & Sihto, M. (1987). A cross-cultural comparison of instructional communication: Evaluation of an American, a Russian, a German, and a Finnish teacher's communicator style. In A. Sallinen-Kuparinen (Ed.). *Perspectives on instructional communication.* Jyväskylä, Finland: University of Jyväskylä.

Sanders, M. L., & Anderson, S. (2010). The dilemma of grades: Reconciling disappointing grades with feelings of personal success. *Qualitative Research Reports in Communication, 11,* 51–56.

Schaubhut, N. A. (2007). Technical brief for the Thomas Kilmann Conflict Mode Instrument: Description of the updated normative sample and implications for use. *TKI Technical Brief.* Mountainview, CA: CPP.

Schilling, L. S., Dixon, J. K., Knafl, K. A., Grey, M., Ives, B., & Lynn, M. R. (2007). Determining content validity of a self-report instrument for adolescents using a heterogeneous expert panel. *Nursing Research, 56,* 361–366.

Schullery, N. M. (1998). The optimum level of argumentativeness for employed women. *Journal of Business Communication, 35,* 346–367.

Sherif, C. W., Sherif, M., & Nebergall, R. E. (1965). *Attitude and attitude change.* Philadelphia, PA: Saunders.

Sherzer, J. (1983). *Kuna ways of speaking: An ethnographic perspective.* Austin, TX: The University of Texas Press.

Shyles, L., & Hocking, J. E. (1990). The Army's "Be all you can be campaign." *Armed Forces and Society, 16*(3), 369–383.

Siira, K., Rogan, R. G., & Hall, J. A. (2004). "A spoken word is an arrow shot": A comparison of Finnish and U.S. conflict management and face maintenance. *Journal of Intercultural Communication Research, 33,* 89–107.

Smith, F. L. M., Coffelt, T. A., Rives, A. P., & Sollitto, M. (2012). The voice of victims: Positive response to a natural disaster crisis. *Qualitative Research Reports in Communication, 13,* 53–62.

Spencer, A. T. (2011). Through the linguistic looking glass: An examination of a newspaper as negotiator of hybrid cultural and linguistic spaces. *Speaker & Gavel, 48,* 31–45.

Spencer, A. T., Croucher, S. M., & Hoelscher, C. S. (2012). Uses and gratifications meets the Internet: A cross-cultural comparison of U.S. and Nicaraguan new media usage. *Human Communication, 15,* 228–239.

Spitzberg, B., & Hecht, M. (1984). A competent model of relational competence. *Human Communication Research, 10,* 575–599.

Spradley, J. P. (1979). *Participant observation.* New York, NY: Holt, Rinehart & Winston.

Spradley, J. P., & McCurdy, D. W. (1972). *The cultural experience: Ethnography in complex society.* Prospect Heights, IL: Waveland Press.

Spry, T. (2001). Performing autoethnography: An embodied methodological praxis. *Qualitative inquiry, 7*(6), 706–732.

Stanley, M., & Cheek, J. (2003). Grounded theory: exploiting the potential for occupational therapy. *British Journal of Occupational Therapy, 66,* 143–150.

Steimel, S. (2012). Connecting with volunteers: Memorable messages and volunteer identification. *Communication Research Reports, 30,* 12–21.

Stephens, N. (2012). Tyranny of the perceived majority: Polling in the U.S. news media before the invasion of Iraq. *Critical Studies in Media Communication, 29,* 220–237.

Stewart, D. W., Shamdasani, P. M., & Rook, D. W. (2006). *Focus groups: Theory and practice* (2nd ed.). Thousand Oaks, CA: Sage.

Stolley, K. S. (2005). *The basics of sociology.* Westport, CT: Greenwood Publishing Group.

Strauss, A., & Corbin, J. (1991). *Basics of qualitative research: Grounded theory procedure and techniques.* Newbury Park, CA: Sage.

Strauss, A., & Corbin, J. (1998). Grounded theory methodology: An overview. In N. K. Denzin & Y. Lincoln (Eds.). *Strategies of qualitative inquiry* (pp. 158–183). Newbury Park, CA: Sage.

Szabo, E. A., & Pfau, M. (2002). Nuances in inoculation: Theory and application. In J. P. Dillard & M. Pfau (Eds.). *The persuasion handbook: Developments in theory and practice* (pp. 233–258). Thousand Oaks, CA: Sage.

Taylor, D. A., & Altman, I. (1987). Communication in interpersonal relationships: Social penetration theory. In M. E. Roloff & G. R. Miller (Eds.). *Interpersonal processes: New directions in communication research* (pp. 257–277). Newbury Park, CA: Sage.

Ting-Toomey, S. (1993). Communicative resourcefulness: An identity negotiation theory. In R. L. Wiseman & J. Koester (Eds.). *Intercultural communication competence* (pp. 72–111). Newbury Park, CA: Sage.

Ting-Toomey, S. (1999). *Communication across cultures.* New York: Guilford.

Toyosaki, S. (2004). Ethnography of cross-cultural communication: Japanese international students' accounts of US-American culture and communication. *Journal of Intercultural Communication Research, 33,* 159–175.

Tracy, S. J. (2010). Qualitative quality: Eight "big-tent" criteria for excellent qualitative research. *Qualitative Inquiry, 16,* 837–851.

Waisanen, D. J. (2013). Hermeneutic range in church-state deliberation: Cross meanings in the Los Angeles County Seal controversy. *Western Journal of Communication, 77,* 361–381.

Warren, C. A. B., & Karner, T. X. (2005). *Discovering qualitative methods: Field research, interviews and analysis.* Los Angeles, CA: Roxbury Publishing Company.

Waters, R. D., & Lo, K. D. (2012). Exploring the impact of culture in the social media sphere: A content analysis of nonprofit organizations' use of Facebook. *Journal of Intercultural Communication Research, 41,* 297–319.

Weber, M. (n.d.). Politics as a vocation. Retrieved from: www.sscnet.ucla.edu/.

Weber, M. (1991). The nature of social action. In Runciman, W. G. (Ed.). *Weber selections in translation* (pp. 7–32). Cambridge, MA: Cambridge University Press.

West, D. M. (1993). *Air wars: Television advertising in election campaigns, 1952–1992.* Washington, DC: Congressional Quarterly.

Wheeless, L. R. (1978). A follow-up study of the relationships among trust, disclosure, and interpersonal solidarity. *Human Communication Research, 4,* 143–157.

Williams, K. D. (2011). The effects of homophily, identification, and violent video games on players. *Mass Communication and Society, 14,* 3–24.

Wrench, J. S., Thomas-Maddox, C., Richmond, V. P., & McCroskey, J. C. (2008). *Quantitative research methods for communication: A hands-on approach.* New York, NY: Oxford University Press.

Wright, K. B. (2012). Emotional support and perceived stress among college students using Facebook.com: An exploration of the relationship between source perceptions and emotional support. *Communication Research Reports, 29,* 175–184.

Yanovitzky, I., Stewart, L. P., & Lederman, L. C. (2006). Social distance, perceived drinking by peers and alcohol use by college students. *Health Communication, 19,* 1–10.

Yun, K. A., Costantini, C., & Billingsley, S. (2012). The effect of taking a public speaking class on one's writing abilities. *Communication Research Reports, 29,* 285–291.

Zachry, M. (2009). Rhetorical analysis. In F. Bargiela-Chiappini (Ed.). *The handbook of business discourse* (pp. 68–79). Edinburgh, Scotland: Edinburgh University Press.

Zarrinabadi, N. (2012). Self-perceived communication competence in Iranian culture. *Communication Research Reports, 29,* 292–298.

Zenk, H. (1988). Chinook jargon in the speech economy of Grand Ronde Reservation, Oregon: An ethnography-of-speaking approach to an historical case of creolization in process. *International Journal of the Sociology of Language, 71,* 107–124.

INDEX

Page numbers in *italics* denotes a figure/table